THE DEVELOPMENT OF AGGRESSION IN EARLY CHILDHOOD

Revised Edition

THE DEVELOPMENT OF AGGRESSION IN EARLY CHILDHOOD

Revised Edition

Henri Parens

JASON ARONSON
Lanham • Boulder • New York • Toronto • Plymouth, UK

Published in the United States of America
by Jason Aronson
An imprint of Rowman & Littlefield Publishers, Inc.

A wholly owned subsidary of
The Rowman & Littlefield Publishing Group, Inc.
4501 Forbes Boulevard, Suite 200, Lanham, Maryland 20706
www.rowmanlittlefield.com

Estover Road
Plymouth PL6 7PY   1006539642
United Kingdom

British Library Cataloguing in Publication Information Available

Library of Congress Cataloging-in-Publication Data

Parens, Henri, 1928–
    The development of aggression in early childhood / Henri Parens.
—Rev. ed.
      p. ; cm.
    Includes bibliographical references.
    ISBN-13: 978-0-7657-0510-5 (pbk. : alk. paper)
    ISBN-10: 0-7657-0510-9 (pbk. : alk. paper)
    1. Aggressiveness. 2. Aggressiveness in infants. 3. Child
analysis. I. Title.
    BF175.5.A36P37 2008
    155.4'18232—dc22   2007029733

Printed in the United States of America

The paper used in this publication meets the minimum requirements of
American National Standard for Information Sciences—Permanence of Paper
for Printed Library Materials, ANSI/NISO Z39.48-1992.

to Rachel,
Erik, Karl, and Josh

CONTENTS

PREFACE

The study reported in this book was carried out from 1970 through the time of the book's conceptualizations and eventual publication in 1979. This decade was the third in an era of dramatic expansion of psychoanalytic theory. It was also at the dawn of significant challenges to existing theory. Both the expansions and the challenges were engendered by three major concerns. The first was voiced in the concerted call by Ernst Kris, as well as Heinz Hartmann in 1950 and then Anna Freud in 1958, that we test our major reconstruction-derived hypotheses regarding psychic functioning and development during the first two or so years of life by means of longitudinal direct child observations. First the work of Rene Spitz, which in the 1950s yielded his theory of "the structuring of the libidinal object," soon thereafter followed by the work of John Bowlby, which established the now prolific domain of attachment theory, then in the 1960s the work of Margaret Mahler, which integrated separation-individuation theory into the fabric of ego psychology, are three remarkably rich examples of the earliest yield of depth-psychological, longitudinal, direct observational study.

The second major concern that generated the theory expansion of the 1960s and 1970s was the continuing ferment among clinical theorists that certain analytic concepts could not be satisfactorily tested and conceptualized, for example, the concept *psychic energy*. Bear in mind that this had been the rationale for the rejection in the 1940s by American psychoanalysis of the death instinct basis of aggression theory. Hand in hand with this, several new models of the mind were developed, such as the information theory-based model elegantly conceptualized by Rosenblatt and Thickstun, in an attempt to provide psychoanalysis with models that could better explain what could not satisfactorily be accounted for by ego psychology.

The third major concern was the view held by some that existing clinical theories did not to date satisfactorily address the nature and the potential capabilities of the psychoanalytic process, a concern that eventuated in the widening scope of psychoanalysis. Along this line of concern, one set of clinicians found that ego psychology did not satisfactorily explain newly conceptualized clinical entities and syndromes, such as narcissistic personality disorders. This eventually led in the 1970s to the elaboration by Heinz Kohut of self psychology, a major psychoanalytic theory that he believed could satisfactorily replace ego psychology due to the latter's inherent limitations as a paradigm to account for critical aspects of human psychic experience and functioning.

The ferment was occurring during the 1970s and would, in the 1980s, become evident in an acceleration in the production of new models offered by a number of very creative analysts to further expand, add to, or replace, depending on individual proclivities and convictions, the expanding corpus of psychoanalytic theories.

This elaboration of models has occurred equally with regard to the psychoanalytic theory of aggression as it has for other component analytic theories. During the 1950s and 1960s much ferment was generated by a large number of analysts finding Freud's second theory of aggression not only flawed by its death instinct basis, but also misguiding in its proposition that aggression in the service of adaptation is a secondary formation, that is, requiring neutralization of what is in origin a self-destructive inner force to serve adaptation. Many clinicians, Americans especially, found much evidence in their patients of aggression that they believed to be inherently nondestructive. A new model was called for. With this, the 1949 model proposed by Hartmann, Kris, and Loewenstein, which was a revision but continuation of Freud's second theory of aggression, was also called into question. The principal change in theory called for was to account for aggression that is inherently nonhostile and nondestructive. The most detailed and fullest conceptualization of a new psychoanalytic theory of aggression then was that developed by Anthony Storr in 1968-1972. His achievement was applauded by no less than ethologist Konrad Lorenz, himself a student of aggression in animals other than Homo sapiens.

Most notable for the evolving psychoanalytic theory of aggression was the decade of the 1970s. Independently from past theorizing and from each other's work, as best as I can ascertain, the work of three theorists, Rochlin, Kohut, and Parens (this book) is extensive and, in critical areas, strikingly consonant. In 1973, Gregory Rochlin proposed an aggression theory based on the central assumption that it is in the face of a threat to one's narcissism that aggression is activated to defend the integrity of the self. Totally independently in 1977, Heinz Kohut eventually pulled together his ideas regarding aggression in the context of self psychology theory, and held that aggression is inherently adaptive and nondestructive (in my own words) and that it is in reaction to narcissistic injury that rage and hate are generated in humans.

I came to the study of aggression on a completely different road. As I detailed in this book, it was the findings from depth-psychological, longitudinal, direct observational research, gathered by my colleagues and me, that led to the hypotheses and the reconceptualizations of the psychoanalytic theory I detailed especially in Chapter 3. Freud has been by far my foremost teacher. Rene Spitz and Margaret Mahler are among my ideals and foremost models for depth-psychological observational research. Albert Einstein's writings emboldened me to make the leaps I found necessary from observational findings to the generation of hypotheses. Aside from Freud's second theory of aggression and the 1949 model of Hartmann, Kris, and Loewenstein, the latter being the one I held to prior to our starting the work reported in this book, my review of the literature was done after we had conceptualized and extensively written up our data-generated hypotheses (Chapters 1 and 5-9) and our proposed epigenesis of aggression (Chapters 10-16). It was gratifying to discover, after our concepts were developed, that a number of clinicians had suggested revisions of theory that corresponded with what we found observationally and put into ideas. It was exhilarating to discover Storr's well developed conceptualizations. It was long after this book had been published that I found a way of reconciling the differences between my conceptualizations and those of Rochlin and Kohut. In a review of my book, Morton Shane and Estelle Shane in 1982 suggested what I found to be a crucial point of consensus in my work on aggression, that of Kohut, of Rochlin, and, as I already knew, of Storr. In essence, we all stand in agreement that what generates hostility (hostile destructiveness, I say) in humans are experiences of "excessive unpleasure," be it narcissistic injury, extreme deprivation, helplessness of the ego, physical pain, or frustration. As I wrote then in Chapter 17 of this book, the implications of this single hypothesis for our understanding, clinical work, and for prevention are enormous.

It is furthermore rewarding to find that the major hypotheses generated by our observational findings hold in 1995 as they did in 1979. What holds foremost is the key hypothesis that "excessive unpleasure is what activates the inborn mechanism in humans that generates hostile destructiveness in them." It is not an inborn given. This hypothesis holds in all the models of aggression we have to date, except for those still extant that are based on Freud's death instinct-based aggression theory. The latter is to date, of course, still used worldwide by adherents of Melanie Klein's theory. We have, however, learned that some Kleinian theorists (including James Grotstein and James Gooch, for instance) have revised Klein's theory of aggression in a manner that renders it compatible with our view that excessive unpleasure is what causes the accumulation of hate and rage in humans. In addition, we find that even the 1983 aggression model of Stechler and Halton (a systems theory model) and the 1989 ethologically influenced model of inborn reactivity systems proposed by Joseph Lichtenberg are compatible with the hypothesis that aggression is constituted of several basic trends, which in this book I have identified as nondestructive aggression, hostile destructiveness, and nonaffective destructiveness, for reasons detailed in Chapter 3. This preface is not the place for me to elaborate further on how the theoretical model proposed in this book holds well in 1995 as one of the foremost models of aggression even beyond psychoanalysis. If allowances can be made for differences in conceptualizations that, for our interventional and prevention purposes, I believe to be unimportant, even the models proposed by academic psychology (which splits aggression into two separate entities, namely, assertiveness [nondestructive aggression in our theory] and aggression [hostile destructiveness in our theory]), by Dollard and colleagues' 1939 frustration-aggression theory, and in recent years by Otto Kernberg are all compatible with the theory proposed in this book, what I am now calling the "multi-trends theory of aggression."

Of continuing value too, I believe, in this writing first published in 1979 are the detailed narratives of the children's behaviors, specifically categorized to illustrate the data extensively enough, and document therewith the hypotheses to which they gave rise. We wanted to amply illustrate (and were grateful to the publisher for giving us the space to do so). These narrative data can be used for purposes beyond ours. Indeed, some of the uses to which others have put them are quite rewarding; others, not too surprisingly, are not.

Were I to write this book today, I would only change some terms, such as "discharge," and put less emphasis on aggressive "impulse" in my language. I really consider this type of change to be of minor importance. I was particularly made aware of the need to specify that my use of the word "discharge" means simply that, the expression or putting into action of aggression, by the assumption held by some readers that my use of "discharge" in the book pertained to Freud's "drive discharge" theory. It does not. I would ask today's reader to bear with the language of an ego psychology psychoanalyst writing in the late 1970s and to translate the words into the reader's preferred language; I only ask that the concepts be retained.

In my biased view of this work, it seems to hold today perhaps even better than in 1979. I say this because the theorizing contained in it gives us a clear understanding of what generates hostility and hate in humans and provides what I am convinced is a highly promising avenue for the *prevention* of internal and interpersonal violence and child abuse, among the most enormous problems we face in the 1990s.

Henri Parens
Philadelphia, 1995

ACKNOWLEDGMENTS

Deep gratitude is expressed first to the subjects, the children and their mothers, of our Early Child Development Project of The Children's Unit, Eastern Pennsylvania Psychiatric Institute and The Medical College of Pennsylvania. Their cooperation, the mothers' deep interest in and enhanced learning about their children, have been a source of pleasure to us and added motivation to our psychic developmental investigations.

Everyone is aware that a program like ours requires the energies and commitment of a number of people. The dedication, collaboration, and reliability of the members of our staff are deeply appreciated; personal gratitude is expressed to each: Peter G. Bennett, M.D., Andrina Duff, M.S.W., Estelle Harris, R.N., Rogelio C. Hernit, M.D., Betty Ives, B.A., Laurie Kotloff, B.A., Mrs. Barbara Millner, Leafy Pollock, M.S.W., and Elizabeth Scattergood, M.A. Much appreciated are Frannie Kane's excellent secretarial services to our project and her repeated typings of this manuscript. We are especially indebted to our audio-visual section (EPPI) for putting film and video data collecting facilities at our disposal. In this, appreciation is expressed to Jacques Van Vlack, in memoriam, for his artistry and large interest in our film-making; also, to Alma Lloyd for her continuing support of our child-mother and child development research, to John Adamson, Ph.D., for the use of The Children's Unit video equipment, and to Ed Benintende who recently joined us and has already extended himself generously.

Such a program, of course, could not exist without the encouragement, support and recognition of our efforts by certain key people. Without the ever-present support and expressed appreciation of Robert C. Prall, M.D., and his protection against fund cut-backs, we might not exist. Without the help of Selma Kramer, M.D., Chief of Child Psychiatry and Leo Madow, M.D., Chairman of the Department of Psychiatry at The Medical College of Pennsylvania, the past, present and future of our program would be in jeopardy. Their commendations have made us feel a vital part of the department. Much appreciation too is expressed to Bernard Borislow, Ph.D., Director of Research and Training at The Eastern Pennsylvania Psychiatric Institute, for his sympathetic support of our program and his efforts to bail us out in times of trouble.

Gratitude is a small word to express what I feel toward Margaret S. Mahler, M.D., not only for the extention of my understanding which accrues from her work, but especially here, for her reading large parts of my manuscript and for her helpful comments and encouragement.

My indebtedness to Rachel Parens for her contributions to this work is enormous. By critically editing the manuscript at several points in its evolution, she has contributed to its character and readability. By her interest in this work, and her patience with my preoccupations, arising from its vicissitudes, she greatly facilitated the production of this book.

Appreciation, too, to Jason Aronson, M.D., for his enthusiastic support and encouragement and to John Woodside for energetic and helpful editing.

INTRODUCTION TO
THE REVISED EDITION

Since this book was first published, further exploration of the evolution of the psychoanalytic theory of aggression compels me to revise my thinking about aggression from what it was at the time that I originally wrote about it. Because what I find most vital and useful in the original work still holds—in terms of the data contents and, especially, the basic concepts about aggression yielded by these data—I have elected to keep the original contents unchanged. Rather than rewrite the text, I prefer to simply amend it by means of this introduction.

I want to present this introduction in two parts: "Part I: The Reformulation of Theory—An Update" and "Part II: Implications for the Clinical Situation of Reformulation of the Theory of Aggression."

PART I: THE REFORMULATION
OF THEORY—AN UPDATE

With regard to the evolution of the psychoanalytic theory of aggression, the limited survey of it that I have made over time has led me to consider this evolution in terms of the models that I have found cogent for psychoanalysis. I admit that some theories peripheral to psychoanalysis have not drawn my interest and are not represented here.

As I report in this book, Freud's theory evolved into two drive theories. The first held that the sexual instincts' aim is the preservation of the species and the ego, or the self-preservative instincts' aim is the preservation of the individual. Here, aggression was not preeminent. The second theory consisted, on one hand, of the life instincts that subsumed the sexual and self-preservative instincts and, on the other, of the death instinct and that it is represented in the psyche by self-destructiveness. A number of problems, though, were created by this second drive theory. We would assume that mastery is in the service of self-preservation, but in 1930 Freud repeated that while somehow linked to the self-preservative instincts, mastery and assertiveness derive from the destructive drive. In this book, I reason that it is theoretically untenable to assume that assertiveness and mastery would, in origin, be anything other than an inherent and inborn part of self-preservative instincts. The wisdom of nature, I say, would not leave such adaptive abilities to be acquired solely or in origin by means of psychic defensive operations, that is, as secondary formations.

Freud's 1930 proposition of a death instinct–derived aggressive drive was much disputed, "even in analytic circles" (119). Hartmann (1939), Bibring (1941), Fenichel (1945), and Waelder (1956) were among those who argued that psychoanalytic data cannot test the hypothesis of a death instinct and that, therefore, this hypothesis cannot be addressed by psychoanalysis.

From this point, we have come a long way; though, of course, not all theorists of aggression have taken the same route, nor have they ended up in the same place. A number of models relevant to psychoanalytic thought have been proposed, most coming from psychoanalytic reconstructive findings and conceptualizations, some coming from psychoanalytically informed direct child observation, and some from theoretical orientations outside of psychoanalysis. Here I present an annotated list of clinically relevant models among those currently available to us.

THEORIES OF AGGRESSION

The literature on aggression is vast in each field that addresses this omnipresent, life-governing, and difficult-to-conceptualize subject. This is so for the literature on aggression in psychiatry and psychoanalysis (see chapter 2 for a partial review of prior work pertinent to the psychoanalytic theory of aggression; see also, the work of Patterson, starting with Patterson, Littman, and Bricker 1967; Hamberg and

Trudeau 1981). It is equally so for the literature in psychology (especially, Dollard et al. 1939; Bandura and Walters 1959, 1963; De Wit and Hartup 1974; see the substantial essay review by Feshbach 1970). Then there is the literature in genetics (Ginsberg 1982), physiology (Moyer 1968) and neurophysiology (Reis 1973, 1974), ethology (Lorenz 1963; Tinbergen 1968; Goodall 1979), sociology (starting with McCord, McCord, and Zola 1959), and more.

Here I limit myself to what I believe to be the most psychoanalytically clinically relevant models. I include several psychoanalytic models and two psychological ones, the Dollard et al. learning theory frustration-aggression model and the affect theory of Tomkins. My readings of a number of the aforementioned works lead me to the impression that these add confirmation to the cardinal hypothesis that I put forward in this book.

DEATH INSTINCT–BASED MODELS

As I note in the opening paragraphs of this introduction, Freud's second instinctual drive theory, with no elaboration or revision since its proposition in 1920, holds that aggression is the representative in our minds of a death instinct. This model is widely used today (especially in Europe and South America) by clinicians who base their work on that of M. Klein (1939). It was embraced by Winnicott (1947), who in the 1950s spoke of aggression as a vital force of growth. It is at times forgotten that Freud (1920) believed the death instinct–based aggression to be inherently self-destructive, not simply destructive. According to this model, to protect the self against self-destruction, aggression has to be inhibited, externalized, or neutralized.

The model proposed by Hartmann, Kris, and Loewenstein (1949) is a variant of Freud's second drive theory. That is, it holds to the major hypothesis that aggression is inherently destructive but with the renunciation of its death instinct basis. In their classical paper, Hartmann et al. simply, almost inconspicuously, dropped *self* from Freud's assumption that the drive is self-destructive. This model is continued today by Brenner (1982). One of the great problems of this model is that by removing the death instinct basis, it proposes a drive with no explanatory underpinnings. Unlike the academic psychology concept, where aggression is descriptive of behavior that is hostile and destructive, in the Hartmann et al. model, the inference is that aggression as a drive is inherently destructive—period. It is well known that Hartmann attempted to account for non-destructive aggressive trends, as did Freud, who postulated the ego function of neutralization; but, highly problematic, the attempt was made by proposing that there is noninstinctual energy available to the ego, a problem that I discuss in chapter 2.

EXPERIENCE-DEPENDENT MODELS

From 1949 on, out of clinical experience, a number of analysts progressively saw the need for a major modification of aggressive drive theory. Their texts suggest that in working independently over four decades, these clinician-theorists insisted that aggression consists of inherently nondestructive and destructive trends. I report that Rank (1949), Winnicott (1950), Waelder (1956), Lantos (1958), Greenacre (1960, 1971), Storr (1968, 1972), Spitz (1969), Solnit (1970, 1972), Rangell (1972), and a number of others have doubted that all human aggression arises from an inherently destructive drive. These clinician-theorists proposed that there also is an inherently nondestructive trend in aggression. Our own longitudinal child observational research (see chapter 4 of this book) led to our developing a set of hypotheses, first reported in 1973 (Parens 1973) and more extensively in this book, strongly supportive of this type of theory revision. In the following paragraphs, I detail why I now propose to call this the *multitrends theory of aggression.*

I should note here that the classical academic psychology model that separates assertiveness from aggression (hostility) is relevant to the multitrends model. Setting aside the question of psychoanalytic theorizing (i.e., depth psychological explanatory theorizing), as compared to classical psychological theorizing (i.e., observable behavioral theorizing), the academic psychology model that distinguishes and separates assertiveness from aggression seems to be the basis for the model proposed by Stechler and Halton (1983), who for long had been in dialogue with psychoanalytic aggression theorists.[1] Stechler and Halton based and developed their systems theory model from their longitudinal direct child observation research, a method conceptualized along the same lines as that used by Mahler and coworkers

(1975), especially, McDevitt (1983), Galenson and Roiphe (1981), Settlage et al., and my coworkers and myself. In the context of Stechler and Halton's model (1983), the academic psychology concepts of assertiveness and aggression—which in our model are labeled *nondestructive aggression* and *hostile destructiveness*, respectively— address the same psychodynamics as those of the two parenthetically noted trends of the multitrends theory.

The historically first experience-dependent model, Dollard's frustration-aggression theory (Dollard et al. 1939), seems to have also been the first to challenge the death instinct-based theory of aggression following Freud's 1920 formulation and re-affirmation in 1930.[2] Much researched and criticized, the frustration-aggression theory still holds sway and is pertinent to the theory that we have developed. Rather than review the criticisms leveled at this model, I wish to direct my interest here to two points: first, that although intensification of frustration is indeed going to generate and activate aggression (hostile destructiveness), it is not the only experience that will do so, a point noted by others and one that I comment on in a moment; second, that the theorizing did not sufficiently account for the fact that defense against its outward expression often leads to no manifest evidence of destructiveness following on excessive frustration. With this, documenting evidence of the frustration-aggression hypothesis is at times unconvincing. I think that, in and of itself, this hypothesis is convincing, but it is insufficient to explain the generation and activation of all human hostile destructiveness (aggression, in Dollard's model). Let me say here—and I discuss this further—that the frustration-aggression hypothesis can be subsumed with little difficulty into the multitrends theory.

Rochlin (1973) and Kohut (1977) each developed a clinically derived model of aggression based on the central assumption that narcissistic injury activates hostile destructiveness in humans. There are differences in their theorizing and in their models. These, however, are of little consequence to this presentation. My point is this: Given the pervasive knowledge of the frustration-aggression hypothesis that all aggression theorists had at the time, Rochlin's and Kohut's separately arrived-at consensus is striking, namely, in that the vicissitudes of narcissism and not just those of frustration are what determines the generation of what I call *hostile destructiveness*.

As I detail elsewhere (Parens 1989b), Rochlin (1973) views aggression as being activated by any threat to one's narcissism, as if activated in defense of it. He said, "To restore our self-esteem, assert our value, . . . the defensive functions of aggression are invoked. The aggression generated by the need for restitution may be enormous, but it is not, fortunately, always destructive; it may well be turned into creativity" (1). The last phrase is of interest; but Rochlin does not speak of ways by which such transformation of aggression into creativity is achieved, nor does he speak of any form of nondestructive aggression.

By contrast, Kohut's evolving views on aggression led to his proposing—along lines somewhat in agreement with the model I have proposed, a point brought to my attention by Shane and Shane (1982)—that aggression may be inherently nondestructive, that is, assertive, goal directed, in the service of mastery. Kohut (1977) held "that man's destructiveness as a psychological phenomenon is *secondary*; that it arises originally as the result of the failure of the self-object environment to meet the child's need for optimal . . . empathic responses" (116; my emphasis). Thus, in Kohut's model, nondestructive aggression is the earliest and most basic form that aggression takes as a drive, and human destructiveness is generated secondarily in reaction to narcissistically painful experience. As I discussed in 1989 (Parens 1989b, 104), Gunther (1980), who elaborated on Kohut's theory of aggression, developed an attractive explanation for how nondestructive aggression converts into rage by virtue of a "*primitivization* of the [aggression] response" (188–89). I, too, had come to a somewhat similar assumption, namely, that nondestructive aggression or nonaffective destructiveness (or both) is converted into hostile destructiveness by means of the influence on aggression of the affective experience created by excessive unpleasure, a process I describe in this book (chapter 3). This point especially bears on the Kernberg model, which I further discuss later in this introduction. For now, suffice to say that, like the Dollard frustration-aggression hypothesis, the Rochlin-Kohut hypothesis that narcissistic threat or injury leads to aggression or destructiveness can be plausibly subsumed into the multitrends model.

The model that proposes that threat (Rochlin) or injury (Kohut) to narcissism is what activates or generates aggression—specifically, hostile destructiveness—is consonant with the model proposed by Gilligan (1997), who intensively studied death row inmates. His findings led him to propose that humiliation and shame, especially, that arising at the hands of abusive caregivers, are the key generators of violence in humans. In this, Gilligan comes close to Kohut's central assumption of narcissistic injury. Gilligan proposes that violence is in the service of effecting justice for crimes committed by others, real or imagined, against the self. In this, he proposes, as does Rochlin, that this form of aggression is in the service of protecting the ego. Gilligan (personal communication, 1998) intentionally and perhaps wisely does not explore how his ideas about violence would fit within the troublesome question of an overarching theory of aggression.

SYSTEMS THEORY MODELS

Another attractive model of aggression, proposed by Lichtenberg (1989), is based on the assumption of inborn reactivity systems that serve adaptation. Lichtenberg's model seems to be ethologically derived. We could say that the Stechler and Halton model (1983) is also such a model, given its systems theory basis, but it is conceptualized along the lines of the academic psychology model, which, as I said before, separates assertiveness and aggression.

AFFECT THEORY-BASED MODELS OF AGGRESSION

Here, I want to take note of two models that I catalogue among those based on affect theory, that of Sylvan Tomkins and that of Otto Kernberg. I am not certain that Kernberg would agree with my designation of his as an affect-based model. It seems to be both affect based and an instinctual drive theory. I have no trouble with this. One could also link it to the academic psychology model that separates aggression and assertiveness. I say this because Kernberg focuses on what I call *hostile destructiveness*, and he does not address the issue of aggression, which is not destructive. But in my comments on affect theory–based models, I say why I categorize it here. But I want to speak to Kernberg's model first.

Over a number of years, Kernberg (1982, 1991) has proposed that early-life affective self-object experiences are the building blocks for what becomes organized into an aggressive drive. The specific affective component that serves as building block for the aggressive drive is the experience of rage. This hypothesis has served Kernberg well, and there is a cardinal feature of it with which my child observational and clinical findings are much in accord, namely, that experience is a central determiner of the hostile destructive trend in aggression. Furthermore, I agree with Kernberg that the cumulative experiences of rage, reactive to the excessively unpleasurable handling at the hands of one's libidinal objects, over time influence the quality of hostile destructiveness in traumatized humans. They do so by organizing a large load of hate that pervasively determines the quality of one's intrapsychic conflicts, object relations, and coping mechanisms. It seems paradoxical to me that although Kernberg makes this key assumption—and has done so since 1966, when he described the powerful model of internalization of experience occurring in the context of self-object affect—he has at times diminished the power of experience in organizing hostile destructiveness. I hear this in his assertion that we cannot influence or prevent the generation of excessive hostile destructive loading in humans (Kernberg 1994). Kernberg (1975) is right that severely troubled humans (borderline-character disordered) may have a biogenetically facilitated tendency to experience rage and envy. While I, too, believe such genetically determined tendencies occur in all of us, I ascribe more pathogenicity to the experience of trauma in these individuals than he seems to, from which I assert that in fact we can influence or prevent excessive hostile destructive loading in humans (see Parens 1994).

But here I want to point to three significant problems that I find in Kernberg's model of aggression. First, if one attempts to find correlates of human aggression within the wider domain of animal aggression, the experiential building block based on rage cannot account for the nature of prey aggression, which is pervasive in nature to a far greater degree than is the rage of *Homo sapiens*, however troubling the latter is. Furthermore, as a number of aggression theorists have asserted, prey aggression—which is in the service of self-preservation—is not produced by the affect rage but by the biological inherently self-preservative instinct activated by bodily needs. Also, if Kernberg's model explains aggression as a drive to address what is identified as aggression in the academic psychology model, it should be pointed out that the latter model addresses aggressive behaviors that are far removed from rage, such as anger, competitiveness, and so on.

The second problem in Kernberg's model is that longitudinal infant observation of a normal population—as was the case in our longitudinal study (reported in this book)—revealed much evidence of aggressive behaviors from the early months of life on that gave no evidence at all of arising from rage experiencing. The findings that I reported here in 1979 just do not support the assumption that rage is the factor that forges aggression as a drive. I assume that, no doubt, the rage experience is one of the negatively valenced affective experiences that contribute to the forging of the hostile destructive trend of the aggressive drive. Also, in my direct observational and clinical experience, I have not been led by children's behaviors to believe that hate is only built up of rage experiences; for instance, envy of another is very capable of producing hate. That the structuring of hate requires intense and/or repeated experiences of excessive unpleasure (pain), yes. But these need not invariably be linked with or lead to rage. Although we may be tempted to infer inhibited or otherwise defended-against rage, which may at times be the case, we have found that young children often express hate toward libidinal objects without observable evidence of rage. It is true that we cannot always assume that no antecedent rage experience—of days, months, or even years ago—underlies the hostile destructiveness manifest in a child's current object-related behavior.

But more to the point here is this, the third problem, and I find it with Tomkins's elegant theory as well: Although rage is no doubt one of the affective experiences that influence the quality of aggression as drive, it is not of itself a generator or activator of hostile destructive aggression, as are narcissistic threat or injury, frustration, and, as I have emphasized, the lowest common denominator among all of them, the experience of excessive unpleasure. (Note also that the death instinct–based aggression theory asserts that the death instinct is the cause of the manifestation of aggression in humans.) As I see it, like other painful affective states, including intense anxiety, fear, depression, envy, shame, and so forth, the factor in rage that does generate hostile destructiveness is that the rage experience is commonly, though not invariably, felt to be excessively unpleasurable. In this, as my colleagues and I said in 1987, rage, like other intensively painful affects, can generate or activate hostile destructiveness by its being an excessively unpleasurable experience. I further pursue these points later in this introduction.

A Comment on Tomkins's Model of Aggression

We have an aggression theory based on and explained by means of the affect theory developed by Tomkins (1962, 1991). I want to take a bit more time here to consider this model.

Tomkins, a foremost personality theorist, left us an elegant, complex model of the nature and place of affects in his long-term project on a theory of personality. As is common in comparing models, differences in Tomkins's theoretical frames and concept and term definitions make for some difficulty in any effort at a close comparison of his model and the multitrends model that I have developed since the 1970s.

Essentially, Tomkins (1962) has developed an aggression model conceptualized by means of his model of affect theory. He proposes that affects are innate responses to varying experiencing. I doubt anyone would argue this view of affects. Tomkins argues that, contrary to what Freud proposed, affects are not "subordinated to the drives" (6), nor are they by-products of the drives. Here we run into our first theory comparison problem, in that, as I detail in a moment, Tomkins defined drives quite differently than did Freud. In 1962, as in 1991, Tomkins asserted that while both drives and affects are motivational systems, "the primary motivational system is the affective system, and [that] the *biological drives* have motivational impact only when amplified by the affective system" (6; my emphasis).

I have long been troubled by the tendency among us to priority-rank all kinds of things where such rank-ordering is not necessary for and may even be detrimental to explanation (Parens 1991a). Yes, we must search for more adequately explanatory models, but such rank-ordering efforts at times miscarry. Here it is in terms of drives and affects; elsewhere, it is in terms of one theoretical model of psychic functioning being better than another or outmoding the other. For example, Freud himself tried to replace the topographic model with the structural model only to find that he actually needed both to explain psychic phenomena. We need not accept the importance rank-order given the two motivational systems being examined here, neither the one advanced by Freud nor the one advanced by Tomkins. Both instinctual drives, for those of us who find merit in the concept, and affects have long been recognized by psychoanalysts and other behavioral scientists to be critical co-determiners of emotional experience and behavioral motivation. For instance, Freud's second theory of anxiety (1926) is in essence a powerful affect motivational system, not an instinctual drive system. It activates the erection of psychic defense mechanisms; it is a cornerstone of psychic adaptation and personality formation; and it is a cornerstone of psychoanalytic theory. Freud's 1915 observation that the drives are plastic points to the influence of emotional-affective experience on their qualitative and quantitative organization.

That aside, I find Tomkins's model much deserving of our regard. However, substantial obstacles exist on the way to comparison with other psychoanalytic models.[3] First, Tomkins does not postulate an aggressive drive. His definition of aggression is much more limited than that of the other theories. Anger, which is much akin in conceptualization and definition to what I call *hostile destructiveness*, is considered by Tomkins to be a primary affect. He uses the word *aggression* to mean actual behavior—behavior that is determined by intensification of the affect anger.

A second problem for comparison is that for Tomkins (1962) the drives are strictly "biological drives" (28), which I see as being essentially physiologically driven. These include the need for air, the hunger drive, the sex drive, and the pain drive. In this, Tomkins's concept of drive is much simpler and easily understandable. But it differs significantly from Freud's 1915 definition of instinctual drive. As is well known, Freud (1905) had earlier rejected the conceptualization of hunger and such physiological motivational systems as representing what he, admittedly vaguely, conceptualized as instinctual drives. Freud subsumed the physiologic systems under the term *self-preservative drive* or *ego instincts*, with *instincts* here being used somewhat loosely (at least it is so in the English translation). Freud struggled, as we still do now, to conceptualize specific, inherently cohesive, powerfully motivating forces within us, the origins of which are in the borderland between the soma and the psyche. I understand this to mean that such a motivational system arises from a position that has interwoven roots in the somatic (including the biogenetic and constitutional) and the psychic (including the mental and emotional). This view of the concept of instinctual drive holds that experience plays on our biogenetic constitutional dispositions to forge these powerful, centrally organized motivational forces within us as instinctual drives. This concept does not lend itself easily to definition; it is powerful, but it is neither clean nor simple.

A major attractiveness of Tomkins's model, however, is the clarity that comes with the simplicity and definability of his concepts and terms. I agree that the affect system, as he conceptualizes it and as it is placed in his model, is a system defining of a key parameter of experience. A specific experience, later I refer to it as x, triggers an affective response that in turn defines and informs us of the nature and quality of this experience. It also makes much sense that affects amplify, that is, increase or decrease or even inhibit (interfere with), the biophysiological drives of hunger and sex, as well as the need for air and one's reactivity to pain. As all good theorists do, Tomkins runs into difficulty, specifically, I think, when he enters the neurophysiologic domain of his affect theory. I seriously doubt Tomkins's neurophysiological explanation of density of neural firing as sufficiently determining of affect differentiation or specification. He may prove to be right; but at the present time, in our knowledge, I cannot accept this model as being sufficiently explanatory.

But more important, I am not convinced as Krause (1995) is, and as Basch asserted in 1976, that an "affect system that is much more specific than that of opposing love and hate, or libido and aggression" (933) is most important for clinical practice. Although I do not doubt that there are affects important to life that do not fall under the heading of love or hate, I do doubt that the primary affects per se are as crucial to the clinical situation and to psychic and interpersonal life as are love and hate. As I said in 1991,

Emde . . . underscored that "positive emotions play an important adaptive role" (1989, p. 48). He proposed that "there is an affective core to self experience, [which provides] . . . a sense of continuity during times of developmental change" (p. 44). I [emphasized then] . . . that although hostility and its related affects contribute importantly to ego development and adaptation, when hostility affects are excessive, on the other hand, they play an important role in mal-adaptation and, like positive emotions, contribute to the affective core of self experience which has continuity during development. (Parens 1991b, 76)

I agree with Krause (1995) that "love and hate . . . [cannot] be considered as primary affects but as representations of the hedonic or unhedonic quality of" (933) emotional experience. But for the clinical situation and psychic life, they are central factors.

It seems to me that Tomkins's primary affects—interest, enjoyment, surprise, and even fear—are not dominant affects pertinent to the clinical situation; distress, contempt, and disgust may be so, in specific cases, but not in general. Of his primary affect series, shame and anger (as Tomkins defines it; i.e., akin to my concept of hostile destructiveness) are, I believe, of dominant clinical concern. But note that this primary affect series does not accommodate for feelings of love, nor of guilt, nor of anxiety (although fear, as Tomkins at times uses it, can be understood as anxiety). Nor does Tomkins's series account for the depressive series of affective experience, from sadness to depression, primitive aspects of which appear observably even within the first six months of life, well before shame appears. To be sure, sadness-depression, guilt, love, and hate need not be construed as primary affects—although I do think this must be the case for sadness-depression. Although we have much to gain by understanding Tomkins's concept of primary affects, as a clinician, I do not agree with Krause or Basch that this knowledge can better open our eyes to our patients' clinical conditions than a continued recognition of the enormous importance of love and hate, of conflicts due to ambivalence, to their psychic experiencing, transferences, and lives.

But here are my principal concerns about Tomkins's affect theory model of aggression. First, I find that this model of aggression has the virtue but also the limitation of speaking of what is visible, that is, affective behavior. In this, it explains at the same "safe" level as the academic psychology model that separates assertiveness (nondestructive aggression) from aggression (hostile destructiveness). This is the level that Kris (1950) and Hartmann (1950) believed analysts could add to by looking for the inferences of depth-psychological functioning that such behavioral observation could allow. This is what Anna Freud (1965) meant by the *sign-function of behavior* on which child analysts so rely in their clinical analytic work.

Second, I think that although Tomkins is right that affects can and do strongly influence the experience and expression of drive derivatives, affect theories of aggression in essence speak to the reactive component of the aggression experience. That is, they inform us about the feeling quality of experience once aggression is generated or activated. Our emotional reactive patterns and characteristics have been well studied and reported on extensively. When x happens, humans across cultures experience or react with z, be it with disgust, joy, or rage and (in the case of young children, eventually) hate. One large factor that distinguishes these theories from the other categories of drive theories annotated earlier is that theories of aggression based on affects do not address what may cause the generation or activation of rage and eventually hate. That is, they do not address the x, the generative factor, of the aggression experience. Analysts have, of course, opened themselves to argument and criticism by their need or, perhaps, ambition to explain aspects of human experience that are not directly visible. Only inference can reach at this level of experience, and with inference there always must be a degree of uncertainty.

Here I find myself in the same place that I have been before. In 1970 I ascribed Harlow's monkeys' attachment behavior to the inherent nature of what, in humans, many analysts speak of as our inborn libido[4] and that, perhaps, something akin to it was operative in monkeys as well (see Parens and Saul 1971). Harlow asked me in a letter, I thought good-naturedly but tongue-in-cheek, "But please tell me Dr. Parens, what is libido?" (see acknowledgments in Parens and Saul 1971). I assumed his question to be rhetorical; perhaps, I lacked the ability or the temerity to answer it. It is a good question, but I do not have an equally good answer. I am dealing with the same question here: What is aggression? I am not satisfied with a definition of aggression that only speaks to its reactive characteristics and patterns. This may come from the fact that my direct observational studies of aggression from birth on gave us opportunity—no, compelled us—to focus on what was causing the aggressive behaviors that we saw. Since then, a more driving factor compels me to focus on the cause of hostile destructiveness. It is that the multitrends model opens to view, perhaps more clearly than the others, the fact that the generation of excesses in hostile destructive behavior in humans can be influenced by preventive interventions. About this, we analysts have much to say, as evidenced in this book and elsewhere (Parens 1984; Parens, Giacomo, McLeer 1982; Parens et al. 1987; Parens et al. 1997).

Summing up for now, I want to say again that I have not included a number of psychology models of aggression, nor physiological models, nor animal behavior models. Even with the limitations of my models selection, a major problem arises in that they do not all define aggression uniformly. Some define aggression as meaning only destructiveness, what I speak of as hostile destructiveness. The classical model developed by academic psychology does this, so do a handful of analysts, such as Kernberg, Gedo, Lichtenberg, Stechler, and Halton. Some theories—for example, Kernberg's—do not account at all for nondestructive aggression. Others—for example, the academic psychology model—speak of it as a separate entity, as assertiveness. However, a long list of analysts consider aggression to be inherently constituted of destructive and nondestructive trends. The major English dictionaries do so as well. The analysts who have made this assumption include Waelder, Spitz, Winnicott, Greenacre, Storr, Solnit, Marcovitz, Joseph, Rangell, Rochlin, Kohut, Parens, and quite a number of others (see chapter 3).

I want to note here that Freud (1920) recognized the need to account for aggression that was not destructive. With his second drive theory, he proposed that all aggression arises from the death instinct, an assumption that would make the aggressive drive inherently self-destructive only. Because he needed to account for aggression that was not destructive, he proposed that the ego intervenes in neutralizing aggression so that it is diverted from its assumed inherent aim and harnessed into service for adaptation. In solving the problem this way, Freud wrote in one of the great weaknesses of his second theory of aggression in bringing with it the assumption that aggression in the service of adaptation is a secondary formation.

I must add one major vote in favor of a model of aggression that assumes aggression to be constituted of nondestructive and destructive trends from among especially well-qualified nonanalysts. Konrad Lorenz paid great tribute to Anthony Storr, when he wrote in his foreword to Storr's book (1968) that he, Lorenz, wished that he himself had thought of the conceptualization of aggression that Storr proposed in his 1968–1972 work. This is important given that Lorenz had proposed that aggression (animal fighting; i.e., nonspecified destructiveness) can be spontaneous, the implications of which include that it is inborn. According to Tinbergen (1968), Hinde challenged this assumption, asserting that fighting in the animal world is determined by the situation, not by an inner need to fight. This was reviewed by Tinbergen, who in fact thought that Lorenz and Hinde were less in disagreement than their words suggested. That is, he showed that both Lorenz and Hinde assumed that internal factors (however spontaneous) and external (situational) factors operate to trigger animal fighting. Certainly, Tinbergen read Lorenz rightly since Storr's hypotheses, which Lorenz praised so highly, do assume the operation of both internal and external factors in the eliciting of destructive aggression. It is important to note, though, that while Storr (and Paul Schilder) recognized that unpleasure experience plays a part in the appearance of what I call hostile destructiveness, he did not ascribe the generation of hostile destructiveness specifically to experiences of excessive unpleasure. This hypothesis I proposed later (i.e., this book). But by his clear delineation of two major trends in aggression, up to 1979, Storr's model was the furthest advanced toward a conceptualization of the multitrends theory of aggression, which I then proposed, although I did not call it the *multitrends theory* in the 1979 edition of this book.

Even with the limitations of the models that I selected, the cluster of aggression theories that I present is a somewhat confusing array of models. From my clinical work and continuing direct observations, as well as in my efforts to evaluate the merits of more currently proposed models, like those of Kernberg, Lichtenberg, Stechler, and Halton, I have increasingly come to find support for the model on which I report in this book (see also, Parens 1984). Here I want to briefly review the model that evolved from our direct observational research, and I wish to look more closely at some crucial details of the hypotheses that constitute what I now call the *multitrends theory of aggression*.

MULTITRENDS THEORY OF AGGRESSION

I report in this book, as I did in 1973, that the stimulus for our studies of aggression came from an unexpected compelling finding that challenged the classical view that aggression is inherently only destructive. We started looking at infants' behaviors afresh, to see what of aggression we would find.

From behavioral manifestations of aggression in children observed by us from birth on, we drew a number of hypotheses (detailed in chapter 3). Here is a condensed statement of these. First, categorizing the data led me to hypothesize that although we aggregated most of the aggressive behaviors we found into four categories,[5] in the leap from empirical data to formulation, I proposed that there are only three trends (or *currents*, as Freud said of the libido) in the aggressive drive. Although it is not essential to the model's heuristic value or explanatory capability, I continue to find that aggression, subsuming these three trends, is best understood as an instinctual drive.

The first trend is nondestructive aggression. Evidence of nondestructive aggression manifest from the first months of life on is especially what led us to doubt Freud's second theory of aggression, which holds that aggression derives from the death instinct. Other infant observers—Winnicott (1950), Spitz (1965, 1969), Solnit (1972), and Mahler (1981)—have come to similar conclusions. McDevitt's discussion (1983) of his observations of aggression also point in this direction. This trend fuels assertiveness, the overcoming of obstacles to one's goals, mastery of self and the environment, all nondestructive activities that require inner drivenness and vigor.

The second trend is nonaffective destructiveness. Observation led to the hypothesis that there is aggression that is inherently destructive without being hostile, as we find in behaviors that derive phylogenetically from prey aggression. This is destruction of animate structure for the sake of self-preservation. It is not driven by hostility. Of course, sucking and chewing occur from near birth and are essential for survival.

The third trend is hostile destructiveness. The rage reaction of infancy is the most primitive form of hostile destructiveness and is observable from neonatal life on. I assume that the wish to inflict pain or to destroy an object does not exist from birth on, only hostile destructiveness as a basic trend in aggression that emerges prior to the development of the infant's ego capacity to perceive it cognitively, direct it, or modify it. This is also before the child becomes capable of experiencing anger and hostility, which do not occur before the second half of the first year of life, nor of hate, which, I agree with McDevitt (1983), does not present until about eighteen months (Parens 1991b). The following hypotheses arose from these conceptualizations: First, given that a specific experiential condition is required for its activation, we propose that hostile destructiveness is not inborn and does not arise spontaneously. Second, it is the psychophysiologic mechanism for the generation of hostile destructiveness that is inborn. The condition required for its activation is quite specific: it is the experience of excessive unpleasure. Therefore, I assert that, third, experiences of excessive unpleasure are what activate the mechanism that generates hostile destructiveness in humans.

A SPECIFIC APPLICATION OF TOMKINS'S HYPOTHESIS THAT AFFECTS EMPOWER DRIVES

Here I think Tomkins's assertion (1962) is of interest that "the primary motivational system is the affective system, and [that] the *biological drives* have motivational impact only when amplified by the affective system" (6; my italics). Of course, he is speaking of the biological drives (e.g., hunger, sex, respiration), not the instinctual drives, and he does not include aggression among the drives, as many among us still do. But his insistence on affects' giving the drives motivational power may have some application with regard to aggression. First though, I want to remind us that Freud (1915) proposed that the instinctual drives are plastic, that they are affected by experience. Pertinent in this, too, is that, already in 1905, Freud held that the libido changes over time, an assumption that must follow from his conceptualizing psychosexual development, namely, that the libido undergoes differentiation from the oral to the anal to the genital phases and so on. In this, experience plays its part as well. But Tomkins specified that affects modify the drives, and we may apply this to that trend in aggression that I have labeled *hostile destructiveness*.

In chapter 3, where I speak of the aim of hostile destructiveness, I point to the irritability of the protoplasm as the biological model and correlate for what in psychological life gives rise to the hostile destructive trend in our aggression. I parallel the irritability of the protoplasm in somatic experience with unpleasure in psychic experience. Following on what I learned many years ago, I say that the irritability of the protoplasm is a biological reaction to the presence within the cell of a noxious agent, an agent that will harm it, if not outright destroy it. This irritability reaction accomplishes the aim, speaking perhaps teleologically, of ridding the cell of this noxious agent. I think it not outrageous to wonder if even within the cell a phenomenon akin to pain may be experienced (though, cells, of course, do not have pain nerve fibers in them). Can one playfully say that the microscopic brain of the protoplasm tells it, "You better get rid of this nasty thing if you want to stick around"? Be that as it may, it is inherent in irritability's psychic equivalent unpleasure that we experience it as being psychically dysphoric. But that is affect. Here, I think that we can apply what Tomkins proposed.

As I say in chapter 3 (and had already proposed in 1973), the inherent aim of aggression is to push us to explore, assert ourselves upon, control, assimilate, and master our own selves and our environment. Kohut, by the way, quite independently came to the same assumption (see Kohut 1977, 116). In chapter 3, I propose that the aim of nonaffective destructiveness (e.g., prey aggression in ethology) is to search and hunt down, assert oneself upon, catch (usually against resistance), bring under control, and finally tear down animal structure to make alimentary assimilation and survival possible. These differ importantly from the trend hostile destructiveness. These trends in aggression are present at birth.

The aim of hostile destructiveness directly follows from and is responsive to the experience of unpleasure. Its basic aim is to make sure that we can rid ourselves of anything that we fear will cause us harm. Inherently, it too is basically called on to serve survival, but it is of a different order than that of the other two trends. It is the affective experience of unpleasure that colors and creates out of our aggression, whose aim it is to help us master ourselves and our environment a trend that leads to all the havoc we know. I propose to go even further than does Tomkins. He says that affect amplifies and empowers motivation of the drive. I say that unpleasure colors, pervades leads to a conversion, a forging of nonhostile aggression into hostile destructiveness. In short, pushing Tomkins's hypothesis, I say that the affect unpleasure creates and generates hostile destructiveness.

I have now come to terms with the problem created by my 1979 hypothesis that hostile destructiveness is not an inborn component of the aggressive drive. I continue to hold that, unlike the other trends in aggression, the hostile destructive trend requires experience for its activation. It is then, by psychoanalytic definition, a secondary formation. Because of the life-protecting, underlying biological mechanism that generates it, hostile destructiveness is readily generated from birth on. But we are not born hostile and hating. We become so by virtue of the experiences we have. I have come to terms with my disagreement with death instinct theorists and proponents. It is affective experience that generates hostile destructiveness in us.

**FURTHER THOUGHTS ON THE MULTITRENDS
THEORY OF AGGRESSION**

I want to emphasize the specificity of the hypothesis, stated in short-hand fashion, that excessive unpleasure generates hostile destructive-ness (EU → HD). I want to especially underline that the EU → HD hypothesis is not equivalent to the frustration-aggression hypothesis. Excessive unpleasure is the lowest common denominator of all the factors (or sources) that generate or activate HD in humans. The con-cept of excessive unpleasure is not the same as the concept of frustra-tion of Dollard et al. nor that of narcissistic injury of Rochlin or Kohut. I insist on this because, on occasion, the hypothesis EU → HD has been equated with Dollard's frustration → aggression hypothesis. This is unacceptable because it disavows the critical ways in which the EU → HD hypothesis is at once more specific and more encompassing than the frustration-aggression hypothesis. It is more specific in that it discerns the experiential generating/activating factor to a higher level of discrimination (i.e., to a lower common denominator), and it is more encompassing because it allows for the inclusion of other ag-gression-generating/aggression-activating experiential factors, such as narcissistic injury or threat. Furthermore, the EU → HD hypothesis is embedded in the psychoanalytic knowledge that not all HD that is generated will become manifest in behavior at the time of its experien-tial activation; that is, it may be defended against and not be manifest in current behavior, a factor not emphasized by Dollard et al. Further-more, the EU → HD hypothesis defines the trend in aggression quite specifically, being embedded in a model that makes a point of discrim-inating better just what aggression we are talking about, a point I ad-dress in a moment. I believe, however, that the EU → HD hypothesis can subsume Dollard et al.'s 1939 frustration-aggression hypothesis, Rochlin's postulate that narcissistic injury elicits aggression in defense of the self, and Kohut's proposition (elaborated by Gunther 1980) that injury to the self is what activates rage and destructiveness. Frustration, narcissistic injury, as well as all types of physical and other emotional injury, have the same lowest common denominator: the experience of excessive unpleasure. Although Storr, Kohut, and Gunther did not specify the term, it is readily inferable in their writings. Kernberg has written that rage-building blocks lead to the development of the aggressive drive. From his writings since 1966, we may assume that the building blocks to which he refers are self-object rage experiences. However, Kernberg does not say what activates rage. At times in his writings, I can infer that it is experience; at other times, I cannot. This key hypothesis is also inferable in the models of Lichtenberg (1989) and Stechler and Halton (1983).

Of much relevance to us, recent neurobiological findings are convincingly showing how biogenetic endowment and experience co-determine many if not all aspects of character and, specifically here, aggression (Kandel et al. 1991; Post 1992; Brown 1992; Parens 1993a). On the side of experience, three equally influential factors psychically organize aggression in each of us: first, the vicissitudes of the genetically preprogrammed phasic tasks of development spelled out in the various developmental theories that we have (see Parens 1991a); second, parental and nonparental caregiving and actual life events, including traumatic and beneficent events; and, third, subjective experience and fantasy formation.

The multitrends model gives us a further large advantage. It calls for greater specificity when we speak of aggression. The word *aggression* does not mean the same thing in all instances in which it is used. At one time, one author or clinician may mean hostility; at another, destructiveness, which itself can be constructive or not. At still another time, one may mean anger, rage, or hate; at another, emphatic self-assertiveness, which is none of the above, as is the case with nonhostile competitiveness. And so forth. All are varying manifestations of aggression. In the multitrends model, the term *aggression* is defined at a more generic level of conceptualization. It is an umbrella concept, as Marcovitz suggested (1973).

I do not foresee that the multitrends model will be adopted by all analysts as being representative of our collective clinical experience. It is not necessary that we all agree on such a point of theory. What is necessary, though, is that we recognize the consensus held by all aggression theorists except those that directly derive their model from Freud's second drive theory. It is, as stated in my own words, that excessive unpleasure activates the inborn mechanism that generates hostile destructiveness. That is, experience is a critical co-determiner of how hostile destructive an individual becomes.

My colleagues and I have applied this model of aggression in our prevention work, and I have used it to address a number of issues to which it is relevant, such as development, affects, violence, and prejudice (Parens 1989a, 1991a, 1992, 1993c, 1999). My colleagues E. Scattergood, W. Singletary, and A. Duff and I have developed strategies for parents' coping with their children's aggression (see Parens et al. 1987). It is also a key working model in our *Parenting for Emotional Growth: A Curriculum for Students in Grades K thru 12* (1997).

SHOULD WE CONTINUE TO CONSIDER AGGRESSION TO BE AN INSTINCTUAL DRIVE?

When I wrote this book, most analysts accepted that aggression in our thoughts, feelings, and behaviors is the product of and the representative in us of an instinctual drive. Psychoanalysis has long been burdened by its many critics who reject the assumption of instinctual drives. Many analysts today think that we have not succeeded in addressing well enough the challenges to the concept of instinctual drives and that to maintain that aggression is an instinctual drive is no longer tenable. True, our critics have not been satisfied with our answers, and I doubt that we can explain it any better now than before. In addition, the concept is embedded in the controversy that has for some time surrounded psychoanalytic metapsychology, and it revives the complementing problems of our being unable to explain what is psychic energy. From this also follows the difficulty of explaining, other than metaphorically, what is a psychic impulse and that behavioral discharges of aggression cannot be equated with neuronal (electrochemical) impulse discharge, and we therefore should not speak of aggressive impulse discharges. For these and other reasons, there is much movement away from considering aggression an instinctual drive.

But the problem we are left with is that we have nothing satisfactory with which to replace it. Affect theorists have tried to develop aggression models. The most elegant of these, I find, as I noted earlier, is Tomkins's. But I find his model wanting because it does not tell us what generates the hostile destructive trend in aggression. Affect theory will not address what activates the motivational affective system that underlies aggression. I repeat here that, in this, what I say of affect models of aggression does not apply to Kernberg's model. He has held that aggression is an instinctual drive. He proposes that the drive becomes organized and that its building blocks are constituted of affect self-object experiences. It is the core affect rage in these experiences that organize into the aggressive drive. In this, Kernberg's theory is a drive theory.

Affect theory does not encompass what the concept instinctual drive does. Stern (1985, see 156–61) runs into a similar problem as I do when he finds the need to postulate vitality affects. That is, affects, enormously critical as they are to psychic experience and to our understanding of human motivation and behavior, do not explain all the motivational or emotional experiences we have. Stern quite rightly added the concept of vitality affects to denote affective experiencing as "a continuous process" (156) and not simply as a reaction to events. In a similar vein, the instinctual drives, as Freud (1915) defined them, are experientially continuous and not simply momentarily activated states of psychic being.

While it is well conceptualized, I find that Lichtenberg's model (1989) of five pre-wired motivational systems do not treat the problem of motivation better than the concept of instinctual drive. Conceptualizing human motivational experience and behavior, as Lichtenberg does, does not seem to me to explain, as well as do drives, the continuous state and continuous process aspect of motivation embedded in the concept of the drives. Although it waxes and wanes, a drive maintains a baseline constant state, whether it is libido or aggression. This includes the fact that each drive evolves into characteristic tendencies in each human being. For instance, where by virtue of much traumatization an individual's aggression has evolved to contain a large hostile destructive trend, that trend pervades the individual's motivations, thoughts, feelings, and behaviors. It acquires stability and is a constant in the individual's state of being.

In addition, the vegetative nature of the instinctual drive concept is so clearly biologically cogent. It cannot be surprising that, as a result, affective states co-determine the various trends in the drives, be it in the libido—affectional and sensual, as Freud defined them (Parens and Saul 1971)—and in aggression—nondestructive, nonaffective destructiveness, and hostile destructiveness (a thesis in this book).

I want to close this section by saying that I no longer consider it imperative that we consider aggression to be an instinctual drive or that we all agree on whatever overarching model may be conceptualized. Given the strong likelihood that we will not come to agreement on the best model of aggression, there are some issues about aggression that are imperative for psychoanalysis. They are imperative not only for the science of psychoanalysis, that is, description, documentation, explication, and theory formation, but also for explanation and guidance in our conduct of analytic and analysis-derived forms of treatment. These are factors that are directly relevant for the clinical situation. Such are, for instance, the normal-pathological aspect of aggression, the adaptive-maladaptive aspect of aggression, the trend-determining aspect of aggression, the generation (i.e., production) - accumulation-reduction aspect of aggression, the defensive operations adaptation requires and hostility and hate elicit, and more. But for me, among all these, none is more critical than the hypothesis that the findings reported in this book led me to propose: that excessive unpleasure is what activates that inborn survival-dependent mechanism that generates hostile destructiveness in us, abbreviated in the concept EU → HD. Just as irritability of the protoplasm activates within the protoplasm the mechanism that leads to the cell's efforts to rid itself of the noxious agent, so too excessive unpleasure activates in us the mechanism that serves our need to rid ourselves of that which causes us too much pain. The hostile destructive trend is forged out of aggression inherently constituted of the primary aggression trends that serve survival, nondestructive aggression, and nonaffective destructiveness (see chapter 3). This seems to be the consensus among all but the death instinct–based models of aggression.

PART II: IMPLICATIONS OF THIS REFORMULATION OF THE THEORY OF AGGRESSION FOR THE CLINICAL SITUATION

The frames of reference that we use to understand our patients guide us in our treatment of them. If we no longer assume that rage and hate, as well as the healthy aggression that we use in assertiveness and in the persistent pursuit of our wishes, arise from an inborn death instinct, how do we view our patients' material? If instead we assume that healthy nondestructive aggression is inborn, whereas hostility, hate, and rage arise in reaction to experiences of excessive unpleasure (pain), this unavoidably throws a very different light on the emergence of these aggression trends in internal conflict, in character formation, and in the transference. For instance, if excesssive unpleasure is what generates or activates hostile destructiveness, the emergence of hate and rage in the transference must be linked to pain, whether it is instigated by transference experiencing that owes its current emergence to past experiences of excessive unpleasure or by here-and-now ill-conceived interventions by the therapist. I believe that to best analyze genetically engendered hate transference, here-and-now transference interpretations would gain in veracity for the patient when conjointly attached to interpretations of analytically discovered genetic traumas or developmental strains. Transference experiencing that is felt by the patient to be irrational and unbearable may be better analyzed when the raison d'etre of the hate experienced is made emotionally cogent to the patient. I put forward a technical strategy probably used by many of us that facilitates the process of working through of ego-dystonic wishes and highly tenacious self-directed sadistic tendencies in the patient.

Understanding that hostile destructiveness is generated and develops in humans gives a different meaning to its emergence in the transference than when we assume it to come from untamed inborn dispositions. In my experience, clinicians tend to assume, as do mothers with their angry infants, that "something is wrong" (i.e., something is causing the infant much distress). Ted Jacobs (1991), for example, speaking of a "highly intelligent, verbally nimble, flamboyant, and professionally successful" Mr. V, soon recognized that under a surface of charm, Mr. V was menacing, as if a "raging fire burned within him" and he was bent on revenge against those who roused his rage. In time, Jacobs traced some of this rage to specific traumatic events.

[I] sought opportunities to bring to the fore not only the anger that smoldered beneath his surface charm but, *more specifically, the feelings of hurt that fed it.* When I spoke in sessions, my voice was calm, its tone soothing as I tried to convey my understanding of the trauma that Mr. V had experienced. Such an approach to someone who was responding to life with the rage of a wounded animal was, perhaps, not inappropriate. (35; italics added)

I draw attention to the manifest tentativeness and judicious caution in Jacob's words as he tells us that he did exactly what I think he should have done. I elaborate on this shortly. In considering what factors may have generated excessive hostile destructiveness in our patients and what contribution this may have made to their psychopathology, I put forward several generalizations.

First, psychoanalytic observational and clinical work with children amply reveals that the demands on human beings of the normal tasks of development are sufficient to generate much hostility in the child and so contribute centrally to the development of neurosis. We know from a century of clinical work that, as Freud (1913b, 1926) wrote, the core oedipal conflict is 'a conflict due to ambivalence', that it is due to the balance of love-and-hate feelings that the child experiences. Furthermore, we know that the anxiety this 'conflict due to ambivalence' induces is intense, is variably defended against but especially so by repression, and that it continues to influence the psyche from the repressed unconscious. But we now know that the oedipal conflict is but one piece of what happens to children. The normal child experiences a series of intrapsychic conflicts. There is the autonomy and anal conflicts (Parens 1989); the rapprochement crisis (Mahler, Pine, and Bergman 1975; McDevitt and Mahler 1989); again, the central conflict of the Oedipus complex; and then the second, powerful reexperiencing of both oedipal and separation-individuation conflicts during adolescence. In addition to all these, there are the ever-present average-expectable demands of the external world on the developing child. Each of these generates greater or lesser degrees of hostility and therewith ambivalence that, by definition, sets up cumulative intrapsychic conflict, demands attention, and challenges each of us throughout development. All of these are potential cumulative generators and/or mitigators of hostile destructiveness in the individual.

Second, given our assumption that experience is the powerful co-determiner along with biogenetic endowment of the generation of hostile destructiveness in humans (Parens 1993b), we have found in the observational research reported in this book and in clinical work that unpleasure experience is rendered more stressful—that is, it seems intensified and coped with less well—when primary ego apparatuses (primary adaptive functional capabilities) are impaired at birth and/or develop poorly (Greenspan 1992). I have analyzed a young boy with such a condition manifest from birth on who, among experiencing other intense sources of anxiety and conflict, became notably overly afraid of his own hostility toward his much loved parents. The benefits of our analytic work were readily discernible in his improved coping with feelings, wishes (aggressive and sexual), and overall adaptation. Improvement was already in evidence during his analysis and so continued long thereafter because of the stabilization of analysis-facilitated functioning and adaptation (see case illustration later in the introduction).

Third, we are all aware of how traumatizing events and conditions bring with them heightened levels of excessive unpleasure, which then generate higher levels of hostile destructiveness. In fact, like many colleagues, I am convinced that in patients who have been traumatized,[6] as is often the case with many neurotics and, especially so, with borderline patients, the analysis of their rage and hate, manifest in their transference, is essential for their deriving sufficient benefit from psychoanalytic treatment. A number of analysts have given much thought on how such difficult analysis with neurotics and borderline patients is best achieved. We know that intense hostility and hate in children press the ego into using defenses against their direct expression, which stabilize into troubled structure and character formations with troublesome consequences to adaptation and object relations. These defenses and their consequent structuralization resist resolution in analytic treatment. For instance, displacement, projection, projective identification, and splitting of psychic representations are defenses especially instigated by experiencing high levels of hostile-destructiveness toward self and libidinal objects. We know, as many analysts have proposed, that defenses of this order are especially encountered in severe neurotic, narcissistic, and borderline adaptations. Such pathologic adaptations cannot be modified unless the intense hostile destructive component of the ambivalence that gave rise to them is mitigated, an assumption especially emphasized by Settlage (1993, 18). We have long debated in psychoanalysis how far the psychoanalytic process can be carried out with severely disordered children and adults. Many psychoanalysts have demonstrated its feasibility with selected narcissistic and borderline patients, although measures beyond the analysis of transference and reconstruction are often required to make analysis possible. In many other instances, analysts attempt to approach an analytic experience by using psychoanalytic psychotherapy.

We all know how the power of hate and rage in the transference can make the task of analyzing difficult and can even make our efforts fail. We also all know that to be analyzed, this hate toward us must be felt by us (Winnicott 1947; Little 1966; Bird 1972; Eptsein 1977; Grotstein 1982; Kernberg 1984; Nason 1985; Carpy 1989; Gabbard 1991). We all understand the specification that it is not that we hate but that as our patients' transference objects, we must be able to let ourselves feel our patients' hate toward us. This means that we must be able to nonmasochistically tolerate it, to contain it in ourselves, to self-analyze our unavoidable realistic and countertransference reactions, and, when necessary, we need to avail ourselves of extra-analytic measures as limit setting, which is invariably needed with troubled children and adolescents. All these I think we must do so that the defenses that our patients implement to deal with their hate can be analyzed, its transference dynamics gradually interpreted, and the experiential sources of the hate progressively brought to awareness and gradually worked through in the analytic setting.

I should say here that I disagree with those who hold that intense hostile destructiveness (whether manifest simply as intense hostility, hate, or rage) expressed in the transference should not be directly addressed. I do not like it, but, in line with Winnicott (1947) and Kohut (1972), I welcome the patients' verbal and affective expressions of hate and even rage when they feel these toward me. It makes sense to me that to lessen the intensity and influence of hostile destructiveness in patients' psyches, I must analyze these affective drive derivatives. When a patient experiences such feelings toward me, they belong in that patient's transference to me, and this is the best avenue available to approach analyzing, mitigating, and significantly reducing that hate. But I do not agree with those colleagues who, for their own reasons, propose that these intense affective expressions should not be directly addressed. For instance, welcoming the expression of hate in the transference, Winnicott (1947) believed that it should be accepted and tolerated because it serves the patient in allowing individuation from the object. To achieve the individuation effect of hate, Winnicott believed that it should not be interpreted. But I am not convinced that hate is an effective facilitator of individuation. Yes, we know only too well, for instance, the 'normal neurotic' (a concept Selma Kramer often used in her teaching) adolescent's need to depreciate and devalue his or her idealized loved parents to facilitate age-adequate individuation from them. But this devaluation is not due to hate. It is due to the need to individuate and separate in the context of adequate object constancy, in the service of shifting one's central emotional investment in objects from the parents of childhood to the peer group from whence a mate will later be chosen (Parens and Saul 1971). This is a vastly different use and qualitative trend of aggression than what I am considering here. I do not believe that giving up on the object in painful disappointment, rage, and bitterness or destroying the hated object forges individuation and object constancy. It may foster separateness based on hate, but this is a separateness of painful loneliness. It often leads the patient to serious pathological adaptations, such as alcoholism and drug dependency (alternatives for objects) and antisocial structure formations (based on giving up valuing objects), and when this destruction of and by the object occurs early in life, in persons so biologically disposed, it may lead to schizoid adaptations. No, I do not believe that intense hate fosters separation-individuation toward adequate object constancy. In her brilliant conceptualization of separation-individuation, Mahler and her collaborators who have studied this developmental process (e.g., McDevitt 1975, 1996; McDevitt and Settlage 1971; Mahler 1968), as well as colleagues who have followed her (including myself, see Parens 1971; see also, Kramer and Akhtar 1988; Blum 1981, 1996; Settlage 1993; Settlage and McDevitt 1971; Akhtar 1996; Akhtar and Parens 1991; Akhtar, Kramer, and Parens 1996), emphasized that hate in the child-object relationship is a disrupter of the attainment of libidinal object constancy (Mahler, Pine, and Bergman 1975).

We all know too well by now that hate in the transference should be addressed openly and directly. Kernberg, too, has long believed that hate needs to be addressed directly, as does Gabbard (1991). But I do not find Kernberg's confrontational approach (1992) congenial, and I have doubts about its usefulness in the hands of many clinicians, however successfully used by Kernberg himself. I should say that I truly believe his approach to be effective in his hands; I have seen this work in the hands of Salvador Minuchin, who used a strikingly confrontational approach with quite some success in family therapy. Also, Kernberg does not seem to give as large a role to reconstruction as I believe is useful and even needed, a point I address in a moment. This may well be due to his conviction that experience is not as uniquely a determiner of the generation of hostile destructiveness as I believe it to be. Kernberg (1975) may be right that rage and envy may be biogenetically heightened in those who develop a borderline personality. I agree that humans inherited such dispositions, as there are biogenetic dispositions that determine "choice" of defenses and character traits. But direct observation and clinical work lead me to believe that experience in most instances can more than adequately explain why so many humans develop such high levels of hostile destructiveness.

Parenthetically, I have wondered if an overly weighted conviction that a biogenetic facilitation of the development of excessive hate in some humans may be the factor that has led Kernberg (1995) to believe that we cannot prevent the generation of excessive hostility in humans. In this, I am in vigorous disagreement with Kernberg (aside from my thoughts in this book, see Parens 1984, 1993c, 1994). I have found Kernberg's lesser emphasis (1992) on the value of reconstruction and his pessimistic position on the prevention of excessive hostility in humans puzzling. This is especially so since our theorizing on psychic development was much enhanced by his hypothesis that the structuring and forging of the drives is effected by experiential building blocks constituted of self-object affect (Kernberg 1966, 1982, 1992). If the drives are forged by affective experience, why could we not influence preventatively, say by facilitating by educational means parents' rearing their children in growth-promoting ways (1997)?

My own interventional inclination tends to be more in line with that of Buie and Adler (1973), who are among those who find Kernberg's confrontational approach problematic. However, I do not agree with Buie and Adler (1982) that abandonment and ego defect are generally the principal generative sources of hostile destructiveness in substantially troubled patients. These may well be the most operative factors in some patients, but too many other intrapsychic and experiential factors operate in others that lead to equally troubled personality formation and adaptation. In other words, as key factor in the experiential determination of the quality and quantity of hostile destructiveness accumulated and stabilized in our patients, the lowest common denominator, experiences of excessive unpleasure, can accomodate equally well all the specified generating factors identified by Buie and Adler, Rochlin (1973), and Kohut (1977), as well as others, including especially Dollard et al. (1939).

THE NEED FOR CONJOINT INTERPRETATION AND RECONSTRUCTION

I have found that interpretation of transference alone is not tolerable to the patient where the hostile destructiveness is high. I find that interpretation of transference hate can be tolerated better when the genesis of the hate is conjointly reconstructed. In such cases, reconstruction is essential—for patient and analyst. Yes, we must subject ourselves to and tolerate as transference objects our patient's hate in order to analyze the transference that it produces in the here and now (Gill 1982). But the patient can better analyze such transference hate when reconstruction of the experiential genesis of the hate and rage is conjointly interpreted at points in the analysis of the transference experience, that is, when this reconstruction can inform the child's or adult's experience of hate by giving meaning to it, to its likely reason for being. Giving meaning to what the patient commonly experiences as irrational hate (transference) by linking it to its reconstructed sources of excessive hurt and trauma will facilitate the ego's growing ability to neutralize, metabolize, and therewith reduce the hostile destructiveness experienced in the here and now. When the hate is intense, the overburdened ego cannot reliably perceive, on its own, why the child or adult hates, because high levels of hate weaken the ego's cognitive functional abilities.

To further complicate matters, high levels of hate affect the patient in paradoxical ways. It may, on one hand, give the self a sense of justified indignation, power, and omnipotence;[7] on the other, it may threaten ego disorganization and destruction of the object and the self and thereby lead to intolerable anxiety. The ego's reaction of anxiety and the self-protective defenses that it then uses to tolerate this anxiety often rob the ego of its ability to perceive the actual sources of excessive unpleasure that is instigating the hate experienced at a given moment in the transference. Projection, splitting, displacement, and so forth, all distort and contribute to the ego's blindness to the instigators of hate. Gradual analysis of these defenses is essential to uncover for and with the patient's ego the dynamics and genesis of the hate, and it brings with it opportunity to diminish its intensity by its interpretation and progressive working through in the transference.

I want to emphasize that I am speaking of analyzing neurotic and borderline hate and that what I am saying should not be construed to mean that a distinctive change in technique should be made by the analytic clinician. We aim for an evenly hovering attention, aware of and allowing ourselves to be buffeted by the patients' experiences in their relationships with us. As supervisees and beginners in observational research have made me especially aware, we do our listening, feeling, and looking with theoretical models that help us organize what we hear, feel, and see. Beginner observers in an open field will say that they do not know what to look for and listen for; they will ask for ways of orienting their attention. We do this as well in clinical psychoanalysis (see Cooper 1989). We listen with frames of reference in our minds to help us organize the data that we hear, feel, and see. We use psychosexual theory, structural theory, self-psychology theory, separation-individuation theory, and so on. It is to this orienting aspect of our stance that I address myself, to heighten awareness of evolving developments in the theory of aggression, so that we can better understand, conceptualize, and analyze our patients' hate and rage.

CASE ILLUSTRATIONS

What are some implications of these revisions of aggression theory for understanding the patient's dynamics and transference and for interpretation? Let me consider briefly a child whom I analyzed, as well as another child, whose analysis was presented over one year by a colleague[8] in a continuous case that I co-chaired a number of years ago with Selma Kramer, and let me also tell you about a young man whom I analyzed. Despite the weakness inherent in using data from a continuous case, I am using it for several reasons: first, because it came from a more painfully troubled child than I have ever analyzed and, second, because his hate was an enormous challenge for the analytic treatment, especially when considering that, being exceptionally intelligent and verbal, he was better able than many a child to put his experiencing into words.

IN THE ANALYSIS OF A MODERATELY EGO-IMPAIRED CHILD

I recommended psychoanalysis for Glen when he was nearly four years old because of intense anxiety, pleading, crying, and at times rage brought about by separation from his mother; an oppressive tantrum-threatening need to control virtually everything that his parents did, whether in the course of his care or not; and much repetition of whatever he did, be it in getting dressed, in eating, in separating, or in play. Glen's history of feeding and sleep difficulty, as well as his difficulty in being soothed and calmed from birth on, suggested a degree of neonatal minimal brain dysfunction with difficulty in organizing physiologic, reactive, and adaptive experiencing. This biologic disorder notwithstanding, at three and a half years, he appeared very intelligent, highly sensitive, and deeply, affectionately related to his parents. We found, however, that when intensely anxious, he withdrew from object interaction and evidenced echolalia.

I understood Glen's anxiety to rapidly become intense and then be increasingly disorganizing. During analysis, we reconstructed that he had been experiencing separation more traumatically than many children do, for at least two interacting reasons (and he still did so during the analysis; more on this later). First, in large part because of his minimal brain dysfunction, his adaptive abilities (ego) were not as innately or age adequately organized when the developmental tasks of separation-individuation (including attachment, of course) were in progress. Second, the intense hostility generated in him by painful everyday disappointments and by his excessively painful anxiety states circularly further intensified his anxiety and burdened his ego. In this, I have become clinically convinced that when the child's developing ambivalence toward love objects is heavily and negatively weighted by hostile destructive feelings—but not too heavily and negatively weighted so as to devalue attachment—that child will experience separation anxiety intensely.

In addition, when I saw Glen at three and a half years, owing to the age-adequate emergence of his Oedipus complex and castration complex, the anxiety that these piled on top of his already burdened

adaptive abilities led to the need for self-protective defenses that created a condition of too pathologic regression, with too controlling and
restrictive defenses and development-interfering symptom formation.
It was especially due to his heightened vulnerability to disorganizing
anxiety (i.e., his ego vulnerability) that I recommended analysis.

I should say here that like many other analysts, I have come to view
psychoanalysis as the treatment of choice for bringing about structural
change, even structural development (i.e., the optimization of adaptive
abilities), and not just as the preferred treatment for the resolution of
neurotic (intrapsychic) conflict. That is, my aim was to try to optimize
Glen's growing adaptive abilities, hoping to help him deal more optimally with painful experiencing, to effect a lessening of the harshness
of separation anxiety, castration anxiety, and ambivalence-derived
anxiety. This I hoped to do by gradually bringing intrapsychic conflicts to awareness and helping him in their age-appropriate manage-
ment and partial age-adequate resolution.

I believed that here was a young child in whom anxiety, by its tendency to rapid intensification, could too readily become disorganizing
and in whom intense anxiety was being experienced quite painfully
and, of itself then, probably generating hostile destructiveness. Elsewhere, several colleagues and I advanced the view that intensely painful affects can, in and of themselves, generate hostile destructiveness
(see Parens et al. 1987). We based this view on the hypothesis that
excessive unpleasure activates the mechanism that generates hostile
destructiveness in humans. I postulated that the analytic process (as
understood by Loewald 1960; Cooper 1988; Settlage 1993) would
make anxiety, hostility, and hate more manageable. For Glen, these
would then interfere less with his potential psychic and overall emotional development by being less disorganizing and by eliciting lesser
pathogenic-restrictive defenses than he was currently using. I want to
reiterate here that these negatively valenced affective experiences
were, I believe, genetic determinants of excessive unpleasure that generated much overburdening hostility and hate in this loving and lov-
able, moderately ego-impaired child.

Through the frequent use of four specific puppets (which represented the four members of his family), I learned that Glen held the
puppet that represented his beloved mother responsible for the pain
that he experienced when she left him to go to work for a few hours

during the week. Also, he repeatedly tried to push my father puppet out of the scene so that his puppet could "hump" (his word for what looked like sexual mounting) with the mother puppet, and he wanted to take father's things because he told me they were bigger and better than his. The hostility that he experienced during enactment of this material came from fairly intense castration and ambivalence-activated anxiety.

During the latter half of his analysis when outside the analytic setting, he was much more comfortable, coping better and improved behaviorally, with much analytic work organized around the theme that he had "bugs" in his stomach, his chest, his eyes, his ears, and so on, and that I, the doctor, had to perform operations to rid his body of these. I came to understand it as his wish that I would rid him of what he conceptualized metaphorically as an infectious source of his ego impairment and his hostile destructiveness. I did not get the impression that sexual enactments caused much anxiety in him, although they were enacted with a smile and excitement. It was in the conflict of rivalry with his father and the ambivalence that this engendered that troubled feelings became evident. The substantial ego growth that we saw made us optimistic that he could achieve age-adequate ego functioning.

I experienced Glen's hostility to be generated by several sources: by the narcissistic injury of feeling small when he wanted to be big; by being unable to have things his way and control what others did; by the obligatory disappointment of his pressing oedipal claims; and by being frightened of his father. Here, too, owing to his need for the auxiliary ego (the positive function of the loved object), separation anxiety generated much hostility.

In addition, I saw that he became acutely anxious when angry feelings emerged toward me. On a number of occasions, when he was angry with me, I noted and interpreted his withdrawing uncharacteristically from interaction with me, as if to prevent something terrible from happening. On one such occasion, in the course of angry puppet play, he abruptly stopped. He just sat in my chair by the couch, quiet, with little body movement, gaze avoiding, sober faced. I interpreted within the frame of the play that "it feels very, very bad to not be able to have what you want, and that makes you very angry with me because I won't let you hump with my wife." In regard to the switching from the play frame to the transference, I added, "But it makes you very sad and afraid when you are so angry with me, just like with Daddy." He listened quietly. Much work was done toward making him (his ego) better tolerant of the rage that he was experiencing by means of puppet enactments and interpretations of what was making the puppets angry with each other and what was making him angry with me, what his wishes and painful disappointments were with me and at home, and the dread that his anger toward me (and his daddy and mom) instigated.

Glen made excellent progress in his nearly three years of analysis. There was full resolution of his regressive defenses and symptoms and a marked reduction of obsessive-compulsive defenses. When Glen was six and a half years old, his reaction at termination of analysis further substantiated the traumatizing and hostility-generating effect that separation anxiety had had on him—given this ego-impaired child's heightened need for the anxiliary ego's complementing support. Glen had been making meaningful efforts in terminating analysis. He elaborated several themes on separating from me, including how to survive without my needing to operate on him to remove the bugs from his stomach, his chest, and so forth, on how he would be able to take care of those bugs on his own and with the help of his truly and sufficiently available parents. The next-to-last session took me by surprise. It consisted of an entire session of intense anxiety and episodic rage states with pleading and commanding toward me and his mother to reset the date for termination (for the first time in a long time, he had moved the session in progress from the consultation office into the waiting room, an event that occurred infrequently early in the course of his analysis, so determined was he in trying to coerce us, dealing with the two of us at once, to reset the date for termination). In spite of my concern, I believed that I should hold to our date, and I interpreted his being angry with me for leaving him now when he felt afraid that he could not feel strong and safe without me. I was concerned that the last session might be a painful continuation of this intense anxiety and rage, and I wondered if I had misjudged his ego growth and the work done. I was deeply touched when Glen came into the consultation room for the last session self-contained and sad but smiling softly and, of his own initiative and preplanning, when he took a series of photographs of the office, of me, of the highly cathected puppets, even of himself, in this transference setting. And he took all of his drawer's contents with him.

Let me briefly say that in analyzing his reaction to his rage, not only did I deal with his fear that he would not be able to contain his destructive feelings and actions, but I especially sought to help him understand what was causing his rage. We talked many times about his being angry with me when I interpreted (in the course of the puppet play) that he feared that Daddy would hurt him if he humped with Mom and that he felt very mad when he couldn't do what he wanted; when he couldn't control himself, me, and his parents; when he couldn't fix things himself; and when he believed that he was not big and strong as he wished.

IN THE ANALYSIS OF A BORDERLINE CHILD

The analyst who treated Michael first saw him when he was nearly five years old, a severe oppositional and out-of-control child. According to his analyst, "he refused to accept limits at home and in preschool, controlled his parents, taunted, grabbed and choked other children and his mother, and seemed to take pride and pleasure in doing what was unacceptable. There were many more complaints. Some of the genetic factors considered to facilitate the generation of hostility included troubled primary autonomous ego apparatuses; much irritability; and difficulty with comforting, feeding, and sleeping. We know that he wore a leg brace at three months, although we do not know for how long. His mother returned to work when he was three months old, and he was then mostly attended to by an ambivalently caring woman and man to whom he became attached and from whom he was separated at the age of three years, in consequence of which he suffered a moderate anaclitic depression. Especially contributory to the child's problems is that Michael's mother and father had great difficulty parenting Michael in growth-promoting ways (1997). They could not help him cope constructively with his narcissistic demands and rage nor with his feelings of loss, and they reacted to him with intense ambivalence. We know that Michael had eye surgical procedures, one at two years and the second at three years, and that the latter of these was a disaster. In addition to these genetic factors—and again, I believe, critical—is that Michael lived in an environment that, by virtue of his parents' serious difficulties in parenting, did not protect, help organize, nor contain Michael's painful experiencing in growth-promoting ways.

As we would expect, Michael made his analyst the object of his sadism. Near the end of the third year of analysis, the analyst was able to learn that Michael experienced him as (a) the object who would at one moment threaten to destroy Michael by insisting that Michael not externalize his "inner chaos" (Michael's words)—that is, that Michael contain his hostile destructive behavior in the office—and, at other moments, as (b) the object that Michael tortured to see evidence of his threatening inner chaos being externalized onto his transference object. Hitting his analyst, provoking him and even biting him, and wetting his furniture with urine seemed to make Michael feel powerful. When he yielded this power by complying with the transference object's urging self-control, Michael verbalized that he felt inner chaos and "empty inside." (Gabbard 1991 reports on an adult with similar verbalized experiencing.) These severe distortions needed to be understood by the analyst and the child, and they needed to be worked through via interpretation in the context of empathic and sympathetic containment.

This, of course, is not easily done. One reason involves the following (and I have found this in child and adult patients): A malignant condition had become organized in Michael that subjectively protected him against all imagined dangers; that hate and rage are experienced by the self as empowering and psyche organizing (a view shared by Pao 1965; Little 1966; Epstein 1977; and Gabbard 1991). In a child such as this one, libidinal yearnings make him feel vulnerable, in part because he cannot trust that the object will gratify emotional needs and protect him from hurt. Libido is not experienced by such a child (or adult) as filling the self with driving and organizing power, the power that Michael needed to protect against feeling his inner chaos. Unfortunately, rage can give a sense of inner power and purpose, whereas tantrums, as my collaborators and I have defined them, do not (Parens et al. 1987). Of course, we find in analytic treatment that the ego and the sense of self are threatened by the rage and hate attached to the self and object representations and are therefore often then externalized onto the external object (transference). Indeed, Michael protected his vulnerable sense of self by externalizing and attaching to the object the rage-whipped inner chaos that he experienced. Hurting and torturing the hated object then gives an immense feeling of relief, power, and pleasure to an otherwise vulnerable, self-hating, tortured child.

In his interpretations, the analyst was well aware of and sought on a number of occasions to help Michael explore his experiencing the analyst as threatening, to analyze Michael's projections, and to get to the sources of his sadism by reconstructing those earlier experiences in his life pertinent to the current analytic material that the analyst believed had contributed immensely to the generation of Michael's oppressive hostility and hate. Over the course of the one year of his analysis that we in the continuous case seminar were privileged to hear about, we gradually found this disturbed child to progressively reconstruct some of his traumatic experiencing and slowly improve mastery over sadistic attacks on his analyst and himself. When he externalized his inner choas, it progressively became less harsh, less frequent, and of shorter duration. Follow-up report on Michael indicated continued growth in his constructive adaptive functioning with continuing reduction in intensity and with better mediation of his hostile destructiveness, along with optimizing use of his nondestructive aggression.

IN THE ANALYSIS OF AN ADULT

From the analysis of a severely neurotic twenty-five-year-old man whose pathology included narcissistic and borderline features, I focus on a segment of our analyzing a large need that he had to suffer to allay intense feelings of guilt that arose out of his wish to outdo and destroy me. Several years of transference experiencing had now progressed to the emergence of a tenacious conviction that I would not allow him to have sexual feelings or a penis. This was now associated with expressed intense castration fears side by side with the dread that he would lose control and destroy me. These intense hate feelings, largely now oedipal triadic in character, were now tolerable to the ego because they were mitigated by progressively stabilizing transference feelings of trust and love. Once unable to tolerate ambivalence and having intermittently used splitting to protect himself and me, he was now able to tolerate his ambivalence, a most salutary psychic gain from our analytic work.

I came to understand that the severity of this young man's Oedipus and castration complexes, especially negatively biased by intense stabilized hostility, were largely due to preoedipal traumatization of the type produced by the child's efforts to cope amid conflict with and rage toward his narcissistic and overly controlling mother and his too passive, nonprotecting, notably insensitive and feeling-undiscerning (unempathic) father. In addition, analysis revealed that the revival of his Oedipus complex during early adolescence was compounded by the traumatic loss of his older, highly erotized sister and thus led to the overwhelming of his ego.

In the microscopy of analyzing his frequently evident need to suffer, I noted that a specific rage reaction would occur. When he would become enraged with me, his emergent tolerance for ambivalence caused him to visibly, verbally evidence acute guilt. As he dreaded being overtaken by guilt when enraged with me, he frequently reacted with a renewed outburst of rage. In one session, as he experienced rage toward me, he associated to times that his father had depreciated him. This made him feel small and understandably enraged. This led to associative fantasies of outdoing and defeating me and his sadistic father. I wondered if, out of the dread of destroying me/his father, he needed to inhibit all forms of aggression, and he then could not let himself feel age adequately as big as me (and his father). He burst out, "If it was bigger, I would've killed him!" (I noted to myself the shift from, or the equation in his thought of, "being big" to "having a big penis.") A moment later, he suddenly burst out angrily again, "Why should I feel so guilty!" And with much pain, he went on, "This last year when I feel guilty—I sense—a shooting pain—a shock!" After this, he calmed, as if surrendering to the pain, and he said, "It's guilt! [Has] to do with my father and sexual feelings."

Here I want to draw attention to my patient's affecto-verbal description that, although triggered by a wish to destroy me—the father in the transference, whom he valued—the feeling of guilt arose within him like a shooting pain and so led to his outburst of rage; this was soon followed by the demand that I make the pain go away.

This rage toward me seemed, at least in part, produced by a strong residual conviction that I, the omnipotent transference parent, could make his painful guilt go away, could even prevent his obsessive guilt from emerging; but because he is so hateful, and therefore undeserving of love and protection, I refused to do so. This conviction of my omnipotence was tied to other convictions, including one arising out of his projection, that I would castrate him when he experienced sexual feelings toward his girlfriend. My understanding of his transference experience included, in addition to oedipal and preoedipal facets of it, the feeling that he was enraged with me because I did not stop his painful guilt.

I am acutely aware that how we interpret our patients' experiencing orients attempts to identify and make sense of their experience emotionally and cognitively, and it helps to organize and synthesize their past, current, and future experiencing. In the course of analyzing this young man's need to suffer as it interwove with phallic competitive feelings with me and his dread of feeling good and being big too, he burst out his wish: that if his penis were bigger, he would have killed his father. His reactive guilt—produced by his intense ambivalence—was then experienced acutely, and he described with secondary rage the shooting pain that he felt. He focused his rage toward me: "Do you understand what I am saying! Why can't I grow out of this? Why can't I just say my father and I are equal! Why?" I started to interpret: "I hear your plea that I make you feel and think differently, that I make your pain go away, but you feel I just won't." He interrupted me angrily, "Aren't you the doctor!" Because it was time to stop, I told him that, in large part, he was quite right but that we had to stop and that we should continue this next time.

He opened the next session with "I've been feeling relatively good for a relatively long period of time; I'm wondering why." Midpoint in this session, after an uninterrupted flow of associations, he said tentatively, "I do feel better but not good. If I feel too good, the guilt'll come back. I don't know why I feel better." He was silent for a moment and then painfully burst out, "Now I feel guilt! Why? Why? I sensed in my mind my father saying I can't have G [his girlfriend]." Confirming his association, I said, "Yes, we have often found that you feel guilty when you become aware that you feel good." Before I could go on to link it with his fantasy of my prohibiting his having a girlfriend, because many years before he had wanted to take away my girlfriend, he exclaimed, "So what!" (his current way of depreciating my interpretations).

After his saying "So what!" two more times to my interventions, I interpreted, again, his need to depreciate what I say to prevent him from feeling that I can help him, that I am "big" so to speak, a competent doctor, which then leads him to feel small and worthless. He retorted immediately, "I do feel *like* I hate you—and I hate my father!" Note my patient's recognition of the transference experience, that is, of the externalization onto me of his internalized hate feelings toward his father, the awareness that he experiences me as if I were his father. Gabbard (1991) rightly sees this as being critical for analyzability of such hate transferences.

In my interpretations, I wanted my patient to grasp the reasons for his rage reactions, one arising out of his feeling acutely the pain of guilt, the other arising out of his dread of humiliating defeat in phallic competitiveness and feeling small, narcissistically devastated, which then resulted in his hating me. Both, of course, are experiences that produce marked excessive unpleasure.

Repeatedly analyzing his rage reactions over several years, a task made possible by his increasing trust, his stabilizing positive transference, as well as my ongoing self-analysis, this young man quite ably analyzed his rage toward me, toward his narcissistic mother, his highly ambivalent father, as well as the guilt associated with these and with his sister's death, the sister that he felt his oedipal wishes pressed him to destroy. His ego functioning improved dramatically; his superego became much less sadistic; he terminated analysis significantly better able to adapt to the demands of quite a good life. Five years later he was married, a professional, and on last hearing from him, he has a child.

It is especially in working with patients like this young man that I came to recognize a therapeutic strategy that I have come to use over the years, especially, it seems to me, when I work with adults in the analysis of their hostile destructiveness (their hate and rage in particular), a strategy that lies outside of what I understand to be analytic interpretation. Because, like many colleagues, I know that there are aspects of our work with patients in psychoanalysis that have not been sufficiently identified and described in our quest to explicate "what cures" in psychoanalytic treatment, I want to try to define and detail this strategy.

ON THE THERAPIST'S BENIGN
TRANSFERENCE ENACTMENTS

Benign transference enactments may seem to some a rather elusive and murky concept; it has been so for me for some time. We know that many neurotic and most borderline transferences are more difficult for us to analyze, in large part, because these are burdened with high levels of hostile destructiveness. I have held for a long time, as have others, that we will not help our patients sufficiently if we do not analyze their hate, which is best done in the context of their ambivalence (Mahler emphasized this in her teaching). This, of course, requires their ability to love the object they hate, and it means that they must be capable of experiencing ambivalence—that is, that the anxiety that their hate activates does not make or no longer makes splitting obligatory (as defined by Kernberg 1966, 1992), as was the case with the twenty-five-year-old patient.

I have found that the process of working through benign enactments in the context of the patient's transference can make analysis more bearable to such traumatized patients and thereby facilitate an analytic therapeutic process. What I am proposing pertains to the concern expressed by Sandler (1983), namely, that we all use strategies in clinical analysis seemingly not yet accounted for in clinical theory. We use these strategies from an intuitive experiential conviction that they facilitate the analytic process. Indeed, in agreement with Kantrowitz (1995) that it is traditional in psychoanalysis to search for what brings about change toward better adaptation in our patients, in the last twenty or so years, there has been a flurry of theorizing about what beyond the interpretation of transference and resistance makes analysis work, as we know that it does. It is to this effort to conceptualize in greater detail what we do clinically that we believe works, and that has not yet been spelled out in clinical theory that I am addressing myself. Let me make clear what I mean by *benign transference enactments.*

First, there is still substantial disagreement about the meaning of the concept of enactment (Panel 1992). We all assume that reactions by the analyst to the patient's transference are both conscious and unconscious, be they enactments (Boesky 1989, as cited in Panel 1992; Jacobs 1991; McLaughlin 1989, as cited in Panel 1992; Chused 1989, as cited in Panel 1992) or countertransferences. I assume that to engage in an analytic process, the analyst must lend himself or herself to the patient as transference object and must be as tolerant as feasible to be buffeted by the patient's transference experiencing. On this, with regard to hate, there is much agreement among us (Winnicott 1947;

Modell 1976; Epstein 1977; Kernberg 1991). This is in the nature of the subjective experience essential to being a psychoanalyst, to getting "inside" information about the patient's experience.

But let me be more specific. As the analyst is buffeted by the patient's transference experiencing, he or she is trained and disciplined to become conscious of his or her own experiencing as well as the patient's. From this dual experiencing, the analyst decides which therapeutic strategies will be best effective at a given moment to increasing the patient's tolerance for self-experience, for gaining insight, for tolerating the internal forces, especially so, for conflicts of love and hate (ambivalence) and wishes and prohibitions against them, as well as punishment for these (ego versus superego), and, most important, for the issue that I am addressing, for optimizing working through—that is, the process of changing stabilized intrapsychic modes of experiencing and coping. To gain insight where hostile destructiveness is intense, the analyst's strategy must effect a progressive diminution of the distorting defenses then at play to eventually rid of distortion the ego's experience of the moment in the transference. This is essential for transmutations of stable reactivities and patterns of coping.

I have found that where transferences are heavily laden with hostility and hate, moments present during the working-through process when I believe that I have facilitated both transference and genetic interpretations by a benign enactment on my part reactive to my patient's here-and-now painful and distorting transference experiencing. In the 1989 panel "Enactments in Psychoanalysis," chairman J. T. McLaughlin noted that "the word enactment suggests an action whose purpose, force, and intention . . . is to persuade, or to force the other into a reciprocal action. The message is carried in words . . . and particularly [in] nonverbal communications" (quoted in Panel 1992, 827). McLaughlin's definition is congenial to how I see the strategy that I am describing here. Boesky defines it differently, emphasizing that the term should be used to denote "inner experiences of patient and analyst, . . . and [that it] might be confined to behaviors that derive from the actualization of wishful fantasies" (840). McLaughlin prefers "to reserve the term . . . to refer to events within the analytic relationship experienced as interpersonal happenings coconstituted by both parties in consequence of shared regression" (828). We all agree that enactments have unconscious determinants. It is not discussed whether an enactment may be essentially consciously determined (though as I read him, McLaughlin certainly implied. Boesky speaks of enactments as being "often unconsciously" determined. But this is just what I have in mind here, that the benign enactment I am speaking of is a spontaneous but conscious strategy.

For example, in the course of analyzing my twenty-five-year-old young man, on a number of occasions, I said to him, when he was in the throes of a sadistic attack on himself, that his conscience makes demands for punishment that the adult world would not allow, let alone demand. In essence, I protested that people cannot be and are not punished by law for thoughts and feelings that they have but only for their actions. Furthermore, being aware of psychic development, I added, "Three-year-olds [which my patient, by then, knew referred to his oedipal years] can't be held responsible for wishing to violate moral laws when the development of their own moral code doesn't begin to settle in until about five or six years of age!" I intoned these statements with the sound of protest. At other times, enactments can help in getting the patient to question the conviction of his projections. For instance, on occasion, when he complained that I did not want him to have sexual feelings and a girlfriend, I affectively challenged the truth of these feelings and asserted that my patient was externalizing onto me his hostile conscience, about which I in turn complained, because it robbed him of the feeling that he has a right to his penis and the reasonable gratifications that it can bring him.

Now, these are neither interpretations of transference nor those of defense, nor are these genetic interpretations. Each was presented as a challenge to, as an argument with, the patient's ego regarding the immaturity and sadism of his conscience. Of course, one does not argue with a patient. What I did here was enter into the transference experiential context of my patient and confront his sadistic and unreasonable conscience at a moment when the patient himself (ego) seemed not up to doing so. It may be clarifying and theoretically accurate to say that interpretations of transference are made from the periphery of the transference. That is, while experienced, it is looked at as if from above while still within, to gain a view or picture of the transference dynamic being experienced. Benign transference enactments, however, are made as the transference object within the transference. One might argue that I acted as an auxiliary ego, in a conscious benign enactment of what I repeatedly perceived to be his intrapsychic experience; but I prefer to hold the concept of auxiliary ego for affectively intoned transference object experiences that do not engage in the intrapsychic conflict but that act in support of the faltering ego in a moment of excessive strain for the patient. I would occasionally use this type of benign (conscious) enactment in association with the dynamic interpretation that he needed to beat himself down to alleviate the guilt that his increasing current successes engendered. When optimal, I added such enactment when interpreting his need for punishment, which was especially reactive to sexual and hostile transgressive wishes activated in the transference. In speaking with J. Sandler regarding this strategy, he thought that it falls within the kind of intervention that he views as pertaining to the analyst's "free-floating responsiveness" (personal communication, 1993). So, too, Tyson considered what I was speaking of as "confrontation" (personal communication, 1993). It may suitably be considered both, but of themselves, confrontation and the analyst's free-floating attentiveness are rather broad concepts. Because I see greater specificity in the strategy that I am describing, I am attempting to put it forth for consideration. I do so because I think it useful for analysts to be as specific as they can in their efforts to further elaborate psychoanalytic clinical theory.

It seems to me that benign or conscious transference enactments also touch on the much debated concept (Rangell 1989) of the analyst as a "new" or "real" object for the patient. Having learned (especially from analytically informed direct infant observational research) the various interactional avenues by which the libidinal object influences the development of the child's personality-determining biogenetic givens, Scharfman (1989) proposes, I think wisely, that we should allow these newer findings to influence our analytic therapeutic stance. I agree with Scharfman that "many global patterns [of coping] are not accessible to change by interpretation" alone. Scharfman examined this assumption and the rationale that it opens to us for therapeutic intervention complementary to, but other than, transference interpretation. Ascribing the locus of help that recent infant observational findings open to us to the domain of a "real object relationship," Scharfman believes that the better understanding we have of early childhood, the more it "can help us understand exactly what use can potentially be made of that relationship" (62–63). In this, Scharfman sees that what he is saying takes on the nature of a *corrective emotional experience*, a term that he, Wallerstein (1990), and Settlage (1993) want to reclaim for psychoanalysis by rendering it benign and to stand in contrast to the way Alexander and French (1946) used it— which was to accelerate analysis by nonanalytic manipulations of the transference relationsip.

Scharfman (1989) thinks that one area brought into particular focus by much analytically relevant infant research "is the role of the therapist's emotional availablity and of the therapist's range of expressed emotion." He asks, "Should the therapist be free to indicate a range of emotional responses, not necessarily role playing, but allowing a full range of spontaneous demonstrated responses? Given their importance in early development, positive responses by the therapist may be a major factor in the therapeutic process" (58). Settlage (1993), too, in a somewhat different context, believes that "for some patients, . . . [the analyst's] empathy needs to be explicitly conveyed, affectively and verbally. Experiencing the analyst's empathy is a necessary factor in the patient's emotional conviction about the correctness of the analyst's understanding" (24). Settlage's clinical conviction in this regard has a place in what I am calling *benign trasference enactments*, in that these enactments cannot be useful to the patient where the analyst's reading of the patient's experience is inaccurate. I want to add here that as I read them, Scharfman and Settlage are pointing to aspects of the analyst's view of his or her work that matter greatly to the patient's transference experience. This is highly relevant to the central concern that we all have about analysis, that is, what will optimize a good treatment outcome. It is pertinent that the best psychoanalytic treatment outcome research findings available to us (Bachrach et al. 1991) substantially support Freud's assertion (1912, 1913a) that a positive transference is highly facilitating of the conduct of a psychoanalytic treatment and, furthermore, of a positive treatment outcome (see also, Luborsky et al. 1988; Kantrowitz 1993, 1995).

I agree with Scharfman, and I applaud the actions that he took in his treatment of eight-year-old Donny. But I conceptualize what he did differently from what Scharfman does. Rather than conceptualize Scharfman's being a "real" object in his relationship with Donny, I conceptualize his making use of himself in Donny's experience of him as a transference object who in benign transference–embedded enactments provided Donny with self-object interactional experiences that challenged his past average-expectable interactional experiences, thereby restructuring old, patterned object-expected reactivities with much more reasonable, realistic, growth-promoting reactivates. This responsivity by the transference object may provide the mirroring (Kohut 1977) and social referencing (Emde and Scorce 1983) experiences that we now know to be crucial for self-experience affirmation and verification in orienting to life events, whereby in the treatment, old maladaptive expectations and reactions may be replaced by better adaptive ones, in the manner of internalizations of experience well described by Stern's concept of RIGs (intrapsychic representations of interactions that have been generalized; Stern 1985, 97).

   I think that I can explain how I came to use benign transference enactments. Its origins probably lie in my analytic work with children where, in general, analysts likely use benign enactments quite routinely. There are moments in the analysis of prelatency-age and early-latency-age children—in fact, I have treated young adolescents who in moments of regression enact being a prelatency-age child—when, either by direct acting (pretend) or in puppet or doll play, they act out (enact) a scene that by the children's action invites my participation. There were many such moments in my work with Glen, when I entered into his fantasy play and became a participant of it, either with or without ongoing sportscasting commentary. This strategy differs from the child's direct invitation, such as, "Let's play puppets," or when the child's puppet that he or she is manipulating addresses me directly, thereby inviting a play-acting (enacting) response on my part, such as "Did you see what that duck did?" (hump my whale), in that benign transference enactments are not invited by the patient, at least not consciously. These child therapy events occur within a child's metaphoric presentation of her or his associations. With a more disturbed child like Michael, for instance, the analyst must consider allowing the hating child to feel effective in that hate; this can be achieved by such enactments as pretending (in a serious-enough manner) to be frightened by the justifiably angry child. Then the integrative effect of the feeling of power contained in the hate can be used in the work of helping the child understand the genesis of the hate experienced here and now in the transference, for example, as having my puppet say as I did with Glen, "Please tell me what did I do that makes you so angry with me now?" This, in turn, can lead to the verbalization of an already uncovered interactional experience that has been reconstructed to be a source of excessive pain. The affective coloring in the pretending can give the analyst's enactment a quality of experiencing not contained in interpretation. Enactments, of course, must naturally rise out of the analyst's experiencing himself or herself as transference object; they come from the real object embedded in the transference object, and these enactments provide in the transference an experience of gratification that can enhance the positive transference, that powerful ally needed to enable the analysis of excessively hostile transferences. Of course, clear lines of transference gratification must be drawn; for example, in structural terms, no id and superego gratifications should be granted.

I want to emphasize again that benign transference enactments should occur only during the working-through episodes and phases of analysis. Side by side with transference and genetic interpretations, their ultimate aim is the effectance of intrapsychic change. Enactments are best implemented after transference interpretations are being assimilated and are meeting internal resistance to their fuller assimilation. Benign enactments cannot be used during the uncovering episodes or phases of analysis.

In summary, new hypotheses generated by the clinical situation and by the data of direct child observation have led a number of psychoanalytic theorists to independently reformulate aspects of the psychoanalytic theory of aggression on which there is striking agreement. Changes in theory, because they bring with them views that influence and may change our understanding of our patients' experiencing, ultimately bring with them changes in our therapeutic interventions. I have made clear the changes in the theory of aggression that our observational and clinical research, as reported in this book, has led me to. In reintroducing this book, intentionally unchanged from its original printing, I wanted to update its theoretical surround and give brief evidence of its clinical cogency and application.

In this second section of this extensive introduction, I tried to illustrate from patients in analysis some of the implications for treatment of the central hypothesis that excessive unpleasure generates hostile destructiveness (EU $\rightarrow$ HD). I have found that this hypothesis gives us an experience-near dynamic explication of the nature of the hostility and hate that we encounter in our patients' transferences and that it can usefully help us shape the content of our interpretations and facilitate our patient's self-understanding.

This brief look at some implications of the EU → HD hypothesis for our clinical work does not exhaust its relevance for it. For example, what are the implications of this hypothesis for the emergence and the nature of psychopathology? Does it not challenge some far-reaching explications of pathogenesis and psychopathology that some among us hold derive from the death instinct–based theory of aggression?

I want to note that I have not explored here the implications from our clinical work of the hypothesis that a major trend in aggression is inherently nondestructive. I have not emphasized that I hold the view that assertiveness and strivings for autonomy are not invariably or solely the product of a "neutralized" self-destructive drive or a sublimation of the sexual drive. Rather, assertiveness and strivings for autonomy that fuel our goals and make us overcome obstacles to them are generally, inherently, fueled by an inborn nondestructive trend in the aggressive drive.

I readily confess that I have been overtaken in my work by the promise of the hypothesis that EU → HD holds for the reduction of hostility and hate in the world (Parens 1993d, 1996a, 1996b, 1996c, 1999b, 2007a, b, c; Parens, Giacomo, McLeer 1982; Parens et al. 1987; 1997). The fact that this hypothesis gives us guidelines to the reduction of excessive hostility and hate—key co-determiners of intrapsychic and interpersonal conflicts and the major determiners of malignant prejudice (Parens 1999a) and violence—makes it a hypothesis that warrants inclusion in a model of aggression that we propose. It is to maintain as much clarity about the genesis of this hypothesis as I could bring to it that I want this book to continue unmodified from its original presentation.

NOTES

1. Stechler (with and without Halton) on a number of occasions participated and presented in the biannual Interdisciplinary Colloquium on Aggression, sponsored by the American Psychoanalytic Association, then chaired by Isaiah Share, MD, and Gerald Brown, MD. They also presented their views to

one of the Margaret S. Mahler Psychiatric Foundation's Research Colloquia, which were chaired by Calvin F. Settlage, MD, and myself.

2. Freud had written to Marie Bonaparte in 1925, following on the criticism of a number of analytic colleagues that he no longer could think of aggression in any other way.

3. In his theory building, Tomkins apparently aimed at correcting and improving on what Freud had conceptualized of the nature and role of affects and drives in psychic life and personality formation. In this sense, although Tomkins's work does not come from the psychoanalytic research or clinical setting, his effort was made in dialogue with and is pertinent to psychoanalytic theory.

4. As Freud defined the drives in 1915, he said that they require an object for their gratification. It was one of the four characteristics/requirements for definition as a drive, and he made it clear that he considered the libido to be object seeking. This, in fact, has been disregarded by analytic theorists as well as theorists of attachment. That is, when Bowlby (1958) presented Anna Freud's view of the structuring of the libidinal object (Spitz, 1965) as being dependent on the feeding experience, a view that Anna did emphasize, both Anna and Bowlby failed to recognize Freud's conceptualizing of the libido as being biologically programmed to be object seeking. The fact is that libido theory is much more congenial to attachment's being built into the newborn's adaptive abilities than has been recognized by many. Yet, both Spitz (1946, 1965) and Mahler (1975) duly recognized the built-in character of attachment in libido theory.

5. Four categories of behavioral manifestations of aggression are unpleasure-related destructiveness (paradigm: rage reaction of infancy), nonaffective destructiveness (paradigm: sucking and chewing), nondestructive aggression (paradigm: pressured exploration and manipulation), and pleasure-related destructiveness (paradigm: teasing and taunting).

6. I believe that trauma is universal; no one escapes it. But we are not all traumatized equally, nor do we have equal capabilities to cope sufficiently self-protectively and constructively with potentially traumatic events or situations. Like everyone, I assume that traumatization results when the individual cannot emotionally adequately cope with the trauma, that is, when the ego is overwhelmed and the defenses required to deal with the trauma are psychically costly to adequately constructive adaptation.

7. I want to emphasize that in the model of aggression I have proposed, hostile destructiveness is generated to protect the self against the destructiveness of a perceived noxious agent.

8. This colleague asked to not be identified.

The theory of instincts is so to say our mythology. Instincts are mythical entities, magnificent in their indefiniteness. In our work we cannot for a moment disregard them, yet we are never sure that we are seeing them clearly.

—Freud, *New Introductory Lectures*

THE DEVELOPMENT OF
AGGRESSION IN
EARLY CHILDHOOD

INTRODUCTION

To expose aggression in its simplest forms and pare away some of the existing confusion about its nature, this work focuses on the emergence of aggression in the first three years of life.

In our longitudinal research, a ubiquitous finding of the normal infant's strivings toward assimilating and mastering the self and the outer world, with a quality of drivenness akin to libido, led us to question some basic assumptions of current psychoanalytic theory in this area. We consistently found that nondestructive aggression, like destructive aggression, appears prior to the structuring of the ego as agency and therefore has an autonomous origin; it is, furthermore, capable of being defined according to Freud's 1915 criteria for instinctual drives. Later, during the second six months of life, all the children in our study except one whose development was delayed by a prenatal brain disorder showed a more or less sharply delineated biologic upsurge of aggression. We saw this upsurge as a major force in initiating the separation-individuation phase; it motivated a powerful thrust for autonomy, for sensorimotor action, and for mastery of self and environment—activities which we have seen as paradigmatic for differentiation. In addition, finding rage reactions in our infants demonstrative of the most primitive form of hostility and occurring only in association with what we inferred to be excessively felt unpleasure, we asked, Does hostility emerge spontaneously or does it require the precondition of excessive unpleasure? These and other findings from the developmental phenomenology of aggression have important implications for psychoanalytic theory.

From the beginning of psychic functioning, the libidinal and aggressive drives coexist at all times, with greater or lesser influence upon each other according to the character of experience. However, because psychoanalysts have tended to view aggression as following a path of development coincident with and dependent upon the libido, aggression theory has not been as well formulated as libido theory. Psychosexual theory seems not to correctly reflect the epigenesis of aggression as a drive in its own right. In teasing out the red threads of aggression in the complex fabric of psychic functioning, to avoid the bias imposed by libido theory on aggression theory (A. Freud 1972, Solnit 1972) and yet retain the vital interaction of the drives, ego functioning, and object relations, we have elected to employ the sequential developmental phases proposed by Mahler's theory of *symbiosis and separation-individuation* as our frame of reference. Mahler's theory easily absorbs Spitz's formulations (1950, 1965) of the development of the libidinal object—a development that plays a central part in the vicissitudes of aggression in the child.

To facilitate visualization and description of the varying manifestations of aggressive discharge in the children, we gradually developed four categories which encompassed them, allowing for a most useful phenomenology. In the order in which these manifestations of aggression emerged from birth, we named them (1) *the unpleasure-related discharges of destructiveness,* (2) *the nonaffective discharge of destructiveness,* (3) *the nondestructive discharge of aggression*, and (4) *the pleasure-related discharge of destructiveness.* The categorization itself helped us organize our findings and thoughts into the two main areas of concern in this book: the theoretical elucidation of the aggressive drive and the epigenesis of aggression in the first years of life.

TOWARD A REFORMULATION OF PSYCHOANALYTIC THEORY OF AGGRESSION

Both the progressive formulation of an epigenesis of aggression, and, in time, the devising of the various categories of manifested aggression with their specific attendant dynamic, affective, and qualitative characteristic discharges have led to the hypothesis that each category represents a trend in the aggressive drive. Against the background primarily of Freud and Hartmann, I reformulated a set of psychoanalytic hypotheses regarding aggression and destructiveness as a unitary instinctual drive. The category that first was so striking in our children's behavior—*nondestructive aggression discharges*—describes a trend in the aggressive drive, the aim of which is to assert the self upon, control, and master both self and environment. In this trend we saw no aim to destroy structure. On the other hand, *nonaffective destructive discharges* (such as sucking and chewing) do evidence a trend deriving from *prey aggression*, a condition lucidly demonstrated in carnivores, which is not, in origin, influenced by an affective state and the aim of which is destruction of structure for the purpose of self-preservation.

From birth on, we also found the category *unpleasure-related discharges of destructiveness* manifested especially in the rage reactions of our infants. Was this evidence of a destructive drive, the aim of which is destruction of the self, a drive that would confirm Freud's 1920 hypothesis? In time we concluded that such rage discharges did not occur spontaneously; that is, they did not arise, as do libido and the other two trends in aggression mentioned above, from biologic vegetative cyclical activity. Rather, we found that *excessive unpleasure* seemed to be a precondition necessary for the emergence of our infant's rage reactions—the earliest evidence and the prototype for this category of destructiveness. We found, furthermore, that this type of destructive discharge could be prevented or stopped very early in life not by the child's destroying an object but rather by the mother's arresting the unpleasure which caused the infant's rage. Drawing a parallel with the cell protoplasm's irritability response to noxiae and the consequent self-protective mechanism to destroy or eject noxiae from it, we hypothesize that when an agent causes excessive unpleasure in the child, it is experienced as too painful, and attempts are made by the infantile somatopsychic organization to destroy or eject it from the self-surround. From the dynamics of this discharge of destructiveness, we inferred that the affective state created by excessively felt unpleasure causes an all-important modification in the aggressive impulse, the aim of which becomes to inflict pain, to harm and destroy the object in order to rid oneself of the psychic pain incurred.

Hostile destructiveness does not arise spontaneously but requires the precondition of excessively felt unpleasure, the aim of which, while self-protective in origin, can become the inflicting of pain or harm upon, or the destruction of, the object for the sake of doing just that. I also propose that the manner by which the trend of hostile destructiveness becomes *automatized* makes it appear as an instinctual drive, though it is not, since no absolute vegetative generation of hostility exists which must be discharged. That is, life's earliest experiences determine patterns of mobilization, accumulation, and discharge of hostile destructiveness which in time intrapsychically attain *secondary* autonomy, hence automatization. Hostile destructiveness can be mobilized to a greater or lesser degree in the child's psyche by the degree to which excessive unpleasure is experienced, especially in early life. From this viewpoint, the child's earliest object relations are the final common pathway by which the automatization of hostile destructiveness takes place. In addition, the infant's earliest cathexes of self and object are the prime determiner of the ego's gradually developing ability to *neutralize* destructiveness.

The last type of destructive discharge manifested epigenetically in our children was the *pleasure-related discharge of destructiveness,* the prototype of which is *teasing and taunting, sadism in the broad sense.* This type of discharge we found not to emerge until well into the last part of the first year of life after ample evidence had appeared of the structuring of the libidinal object and the beginning functioning of the ego as agency. From their dynamics and affecto–qualitative characteristics, we inferred these discharges to be originally unpleasure-related destructive impulse accumulations *delayed* in their discharge by the action of the child's ego. In these discharges, we also inferred such defenses as displacement onto another instead of at the mother and especially making-a-game with mother of hostility toward her. Most important was the growing ego's capability to change the affect associated with the discharge: the unpleasure experienced earlier at the time of arousal being changed into pleasure associated with the actual discharge of hostility. Therefore, we hypothesize a trend in aggression, sadism, in the broad sense, which is a variant of hostile destructiveness by the action of the ego on the hostile destructive impulse. Like hostile destructiveness, this last trend does not arise spontaneously, although the mechanisms for its arousal are constitutionally built into the neonate's psyche. As with hostile destructiveness, the degree to which this trend is mobilized and automatized in the psyche is largely determined by the child's earliest object relations. Our observations strongly suggest that the extent to which the intrapsychic modification of hostile destructiveness is achieved in the child is the history of his or her object relations.

In brief, we found sufficiently distinguishable categories of aggression manifestation to infer component trends in the aggressive drive. From their earliest appearance these trends tend to form a spectrum—one end manifesting destructive, and the other nondestructive, aggression. We found also a number of instances when it was difficult to place the inferrable impulse in one trend or the other, the observed behavior seeming to straddle aggression-manifestation categories. This phenomenon, we felt, rather than weakening the hypotheses advanced on aggression as a drive, may, in fact, lend strength to the view that there is a *continuum* between these trends, thereby adding weight to the possibility that these various impulses derive from the same source and that they are component parts of a single aggressive instinctual drive.

EPIGENESIS OF AGGRESSION

Employing the categories of manifested aggression as vehicle, we found our way through the epigenetic unfolding of aggression using Mahler's symbiosis and separation-individuation theory as landmarks.

Normal Autistic Phase

From birth to about twelve weeks, we observed in our infants one major class of events from which unpleasure-related destructiveness could be inferred—rage in reaction to somatically painful stimuli. With the exception of one of our infants whose neonatal cerebral-palsied state heavily dampened her reactivity to painful stimuli, all of our children readily went into a rage if their mothers allowed discomfort to go unattended long enough. At this period, too, of course we found infant sucking activity which we have come to see as a manifestation of nonaffective destructive discharges.

From the first days of life, individual differences vis-a-vis tolerance of painful stimuli were clearly discernible. Of the twins, for example, Cindy would waken from sleep abruptly, and her reaction to mounting unpleasure would rapidly crescendo into rage, greatly distressing her mother. Candy, on the other hand, would waken more gradually, fuss benignly, and due to her innate disposition, as well as to the well-tuned, well-timed mother-child interaction, show no rage reaction at all. We found ample evidence of the *unpleasure-related discharge of destructiveness* and the *nonaffective discharge of destructiveness;* weak evidence of *discharges of nondestructive aggression* and no evidence of *pleasure-related discharges of destructiveness.*

Symbiotic Phase

A monumental maturation in psychic organization occurred around the second month in all our infants except, again, cerebral-palsied Anni. Their social-smiling responses became more and more discriminating, thus gradually evidencing the progressive specificity of the nurturing object, the mother. At about five to six months, the infant's intrapsychic structuring of her as libidinal object could be inferred. During the same period as the symbiosis and structuring of libidinal object progressed, separation and stranger responses emerged.

All (except Anni) also exhibited successful-enough signaling for the mother to answer his or her needs. But Vicki especially showed us that the mother at this phase is not simply the protector against experiences of excessive unpleasure and rage; Vicki's painful progressive anaclitic depression dramatically showed, in fact, that the mother, albeit unintentionally, may be the foremost inducer of rage. Here the mother's unconscious hate attached to past objects was displaced onto her child. This displacement took the form, for example, of rationalized pulling out of the nipple at midsucking, painful nose cleaning, brusque handling and a lack of affectionate interaction.

As the part-object became specific, it was increasingly apparent that at this time the infant was laying down the groundwork for the *first conflict of ambivalence.* This dyadic conflict emerged during the early part of the separation-individuation phase and seemed to be significantly determined by the quality of the infant's symbiotic life experience. The degree to which excessive unpleasure and rage were felt determined the degree to which hostile destructiveness was mobilized and irrevocably amalgamated into the infant's symbiotic self-object representation.

Manifestations of nondestructive aggression appeared more frequently from the beginning of the symbiosis. Although a few of our infants engaged in persistent exploratory activity from the second week of life, this trend in the aggressive drive became activated in most from about three months of age. The intensely pressured, constant, and seemingly obligatory busyness and drivenness of our children led us to question Hartmann's concept that this activity was motivated by neutral ego energy (which he postulated in the stead of self-preservative instinct). We concluded rather that their primary ego apparatuses are fueled here by instinctual energy—by nondestructive aggression. In line with Hartmann and Loewenstein (1965, pp. 43–44), we saw both libido and aggression as contributing to self-preservation, that is, to adaptation. Hartmann believed that this adaptive confluence occurs only after neutralization of the drives, hence after the structuring of the ego as agency. We, on the other hand, saw this nondestructive current of the aggressive drive as having an inherently neutral relation to the ego (although it is essential for the ego to gradually gain control over it), and as being available to its primary apparatuses from birth since it does not require neutralization. Hartmann further theorized that neutralized energy might be available to the ego even prior to its structuring as agency; for this to be possible, though, we would have to postulate a process of primary neutralization. Rather, it appears that neutralization must await ego structuralization. Our findings suggest, as do those of Spitz (1965), that neutralization of destructiveness does not occur before the last quarter of the first year of life. In addition, we found that sufficient structuring of the libidinal object is prerequisite to the emergence of this function in the ego.

Beginning Separation-Individuation Phase—
The Differentiation and Practicing Subphases
The process of separation-individuation begins from about five months on, at the peak of the symbiosis. Several critical phenomena cluster here. Hand in hand with maturation in ego and libido, we found a striking biologic upsurge in the aggressive drive which showed itself

in the three categories of manifested aggression already evident in the infants. In the libidinal, oral phase of development, with the concomitant eruption of teeth and biting behavior, we saw ample evidence of oral-aggressive, nonaffective destructive, as well as cannibalistic activity. At this time aggression also strongly influenced the structuring of the libidinal object, and hence the wish to possess the mother and, by extension, the environs. In the case of our twins, Cindy and Candy, for instance, Cindy fought for the toy Candy was holding while next to her was her own identical toy. (Mother had gotten one for each in an effort to avoid such rivalry.) Driven by a confluence of nondestructive aggression and libido, taking possession was complicated by peer resistance and led to the arousal of hostile destructiveness and the earliest form of peer rivalry.

Concomitantly with this upsurge of aggression, the maturation of the sensorimotor organization now accomodates the large locomotive efforts of the toddler in his pressured strivings for autonomy and mastery of self and environment. Characteristic practicing-subphase behavior such as obstinacy and sadism (clinically associated with the anal phase) began to emerge long before the mothers or the children made any effort toward toilet training. Significantly, the libido shift from the oral to the anal phase followed by several months the maturational upsurge of aggression which led to this obstinacy and sadism.

With the child's sharp thrust for autonomy and new locomotive efforts came the mother's repeated protective limit-settings upon his many-faceted sensorimotor actions and explorations. Here then, the smooth mother-child interaction of the good-enough symbiosis was repeatedly punctured by the eruption of hostile destructive feelings toward the mother as a result of her many necessary prohibitions. In consequence of this interpersonal conflict we saw evidence that a more or less intense intrapsychic conflict develops within the child which is dyadic in object-relatedness—*the first conflict of ambivalence.* In this the first workshop of hostility in object relations, the child makes large and varied efforts to erect defenses to cope with the anxiety produced within him or her by the child's hostile destructive feelings toward the beloved mother. In several of the children in our project we could, over a period of time, begin to infer progressive structuring of bad and good representations of the mother. In addition, we could see the child working toward integration of these two sets of representations. Defenses such as displacement and primitive forms of repression and sublimation (such as making-a-game of anger toward the mother) were also amply evidenced. At the same time, internalization of maternal dictates, begun by the wish to retain mother's love and approval, sharply gained momentum. From these, of course, the first superego precursors crystallized. In this context, the momentous development of neutralization of destructiveness was also initiated.

Latter Part of Separation-Individuation Phase
and Entry into the Oedipus Complex
From about eighteen months to about thirty-six months, the same practicing-subphase child who had expanded his radius of pressured exploration so greatly as to worry his mother that her toddler was constantly out of reach, now reapproached the mother, observably making her the center of both his cyclic efforts at gratification and his ongoing exploration and mastery of self and environment. The ego's priorities sharply shifted at this time to focus on the child's relation to the symbiotic mother; this, over and above the fact that the mother's presence and responses had all along been the most important among the young child's existing object relations. This marked change in focus seemed in large part created by significant maturation and development in the ego as well as by the all-important maturational change of a considerable segment of narcissistic libido into object libido, a psychobiologic differentiation which greatly influences the vicissitudes of the child's destructiveness. Without this magnificent differentiation in the libido, the civilizing of the human being, as we know it, would be impossible.

During this period *the first conflict of ambivalence* in the children grew more complicated and in some much intensified. Importantly, however, in optimal circumstances the ambivalence became further resolved and less intense. Its further complication arose because the hostility mobilized toward the love-object during the practicing subphase might now be increased, both by a continuation of difficulty with mother's limit-setting as well as by the unavoidable, more or less excessively felt, unpleasure induced by the task of rapprochement (to resolving the wish to retain the mother, symbiotically tied to the self, and the wish to separate and individuate from her). As the ego's efforts to cope with these ambitendent wishes peaked in what Mahler and her coworkers call the *rapprochement crises,* love and hate feelings toward the love-object were sharply intensified. The child then greatly renewed efforts to protect the love-object against hostile destructiveness by further elaborating ego defenses and stabilizing neutralization as an ego function. Depending on the intensity of the conflict of ambivalence during the practicing subphase and the degree to which it may be further resolved or intensified during rapprochement, the resulting balance of love and hate feelings toward the love-object significantly influenced how the child fared in object relations in following years.

At about two years of age, our children's rapprochement type of behavioral and emotional closeness to their mothers decreased markedly—an indicator that the child was entering the working-through subphase *toward-object-constancy.* This period of comparative calm, more sharply defined in some children than in others, was observable in all. Nevertheless, within this calm, from about twenty-seven months or so on, three elements of the oedipus complex began to appear on the behavioral horizon of every child in the project (except again, Anni): (1) the castration complex, (2) observably heterosexual and rivalrous attitudes toward love objects according to gender, and (3) the girl's wish to have a baby. At about two and a half years, due to a constitutionally determined differentiation in the libido which results in infantile heterosexuality, all conditions requisite for the oedipus complex are operating.

One aspect of aggression encountered at this time, deriving from a differentiation in the aggressive drive, is what we identify as *phallic aggressiveness.* In addition to the emergence of phallic aggressiveness, a sharp upsurge of hostility occurs during this early part of the oedipal phase—on the part of the girl toward mother, on the part of the boy toward father. While phallic aggression seems to be a psychobiologi-cally induced differentiation in aggression, the oedipal upsurge of hostility toward the rival love-object is reactive in the dynamics of the oedipus complex. We found much evidence of phallic aggression in our boys but not in our girls. In general, the little boy's behavior had a quality of ramminess, at times including gorilla-like posturings as well as the chasing of a little girl with a hard object. By contrast, Mary, for example, who when she crawled had looked like a football tackle, at this developmental period began to look much lighter, much more feminine in appearance and movement. Because we did not find a dominance of phallic aggression in the girls, we postulate here a gender-related distinction between boys and girls. Indeed, we found striking differences between girlish and boyish behavior that preclude application of the term *phallic phase* to the girls. Their awed, adoring affects and actions at the sight of a baby were particularly impressive. This attitude dominated psychic activity in most of our girls for months and in some for years. Boys showed none of this near ecstacy at the sight of a baby. Similarly the boys' rammy, large muscle, heavy locomotor activities were not shared by the girls. In consequence, instead of the phrase *phallic phase* we substitute the term *first genital phase* for both boys and girls to emphasize the gender-uniqueness of their psychosexual development during the third year of life.

Another significant distinction between the psychic lives of boys and girls became apparent during what we call the *second conflict of ambivalence.* During *the first conflict of ambivalence* (the *dyadic* conflict which arose out of the separation-individuation phase) our normal-enough girls experienced their conflict of destructiveness and libido with their mothers, just as the boys did. During the *second conflict of ambivalence* arising out of the oedipus complex, the boys, of course, did not undergo the *triadic* conflict with the mother because their oedipal rival was the father. The girl, however, also had an additional conflict of ambivalence—this with mother, her rival for father's love interests. This ambivalence then and subsequently tended to make her ambivalence toward other females *much more intense* than toward males. In our boys, ambivalence toward objects in general was less biased by the heavy concentration of prime conflicts of ambivalence only with the all-important mother. We frequently found support for Freud's 1913 formulation that the threat of consummation of destructiveness toward the oedipal rival, in the face of strong love feelings for that rival love-object, leads to intense feelings of remorse. Due to this triadic ambivalence conflict, aggression plays a large and central part in structuring the ego's defenses and the superego (as in the dyadic conflict of ambivalence, it does in structuring superego precursors).

TOWARD PREVENTION OF EXCESSIVE DESTRUCTIVENESS

In our final chapter, toward furthering the development of that extraordinary capability to modify hostility in the child and therefore in the adult, we discuss some of the implications for primary prevention to which our findings point. Foremost, formal education for parenthood is the principal method by which prevention of excessive hostility and emotional disorders may be secured. Since even many good-enough parents readily admit to being in the dark about what is growth-promoting and growth-inhibiting in their vast input into the child-parent relation and in their child-rearing efforts, we underline this need as urgent. Indeed, more parents in our community called for such help then we could accomodate. Our project mothers responded eagerly to our attempts to educate them, resulting in a significant facilitation and improvement in their parenting; the extent to which good-enough parents learn to recognize their children's needs, the meaning of their behavior and absorbing knowledge on child development is impressive. We also see the necessity to educate our children in human psychic development and parenting from as early as the first grade.

Part I

PSYCHOANALYTIC THEORY
OF AGGRESSION

Chapter 1

THE CONTINUUM
OF AGGRESSION

DESTRUCTIVE AGGRESSION

In the introduction, it was noted that this study of aggression was compelled by unexpected evidence of nondestructive aggression in human infants. This evidence, derived from direct observation of infants under six months, raised questions about some aspects of the currently accepted psychoanalytic hypotheses regarding aggression and wrested from me the comfortable confidence I had gained from the classical formulations on aggression of Hartmann, Kris and Loewenstein (1949).

In a preliminary publication (Parens 1973a) I advanced the view that while there is evidence from earliest infancy of innate destructive trends in humans there is another trend in the aggressive drive which seems to be innately *non*destructive. I postulated that the instinctual aggression drive has two inherent, currents—to stay with a metaphor Freud used with regard to libido (see Parens and Saul 1971). It might be more accurate, however, to posit a spectrum of aggressive tendencies—one end of which fuels nondestructive self-assertiveness and mastery of both self and environment, and the other which fuels hostile destructiveness and rage (see Marcovitz 1973).

Before beginning our reexamination of this problem with a brief exposition of the spectrum of destructive and nondestructive trends in aggression inferred for earliest infantile behavior, a comment is in order. In moving from observation to theory, I make a leap some may question. As I worked with the categories of aggression manifestation, the conviction grew more and more that each category may represent an inherent trend in aggression. Once this inference was made, it not only clarified why there has been so much difficulty formulating theories of aggression, it also opened the door to the formulation of hypotheses which seem to be both theoretically and clinically useful. While the hypotheses advanced in this work derive from and retain many of those long established in psychoanalysis, some differ to such a degree that it has become necessary to propose a reformulation of aggressive drive theory.

UNPLEASURE-RELATED DISCHARGE OF DESTRUCTIVENESS

While one may question the nature of the psychic content of neonatal rage reactions—at a time when diacritic function is not possible and the psyche functions at the coenesthetic level (Spitz 1945, 1965)—one is justified in inferring from such drive discharges inherent, innate destructive tendencies in the psyche. In other words, it is difficult, as Spitz (1953,1965) has implied, to infer destructive intent in the mouthings and motor activities associated with the earliest efforts at exploration and nonnutritive assimilation of the external environment, but it is not difficult, when observing infants, to infer the primitive, omnipotent intent to destroy when enraged. The rage reaction is among the earliest unequivocal manifestations of a destructive drive in the first four months of life (Parens 1973a, p. 52).

Most analysts work with the assumption that there is an innate instinctual destructive drive in humans. Doubts as to the innateness of destructiveness have come largely from other disciplines. The present observations of infants leave no room for doubt that derivatives of a destructive drive are manifest at birth, and that its discharges have a *primary* character. It is difficult to reconcile with this Spock's (1965) suggestion that there is an "innate inhibition of aggression" in human infants. No infant ever waited to be taught, or to imitate, rage. Many infants come out of the uterus with what is viewed benevolently as a lusty cry; however, within a few hours of birth , what was viewed earlier as a lusty cry will show itself to belong to the family of affective discharge phenomena we identify in other instances as rage.

Direct observations of normal infants reveal that the trend

manifested in unpleasure-related discharges of destructiveness operates from birth. In observing infant rage reactions, we invariably found in them evidence of an antecedent condition of cumulative *sufficient unpleasure* (Parens 1973a). For such a destructive discharge, this antecedent condition may be necessary even after the earliest infantile period.

Rose (just twelve weeks old) visually explores a brightly colored, six-inch felt block for about one minute. She continues to look at it, seemingly becoming more and more activated: her arms move more and more, her legs kick rhythmically, her mouth opens now and then, her hands exhibit discharges of the grasp reflex. She seems to want to reach that block. Her affect appears pleasurable and she becomes more excited, her total motor activity increasing in energy and rate. She is also salivating and thus presumably exhibiting concomitant libidinal excitation during this mounting exploratory, motor excitation.

In spite of all her motoric activity, Rose cannot obtain the object upon which her attention cathexis is turned; for all her effort to grasp and mouth the block, she stays put and cannot achieve any tactile-mucosal exploration. At the peak of this activity, unpleasurable affect appears on her face, and she begins to cry. She is, in our judgment, frustrated and angry. After two or three minutes, the intensity of her valiant effort to reach the block peaks and is followed by evidence of frustration. Unpleasure and destructiveness are manifested (see Freud 1915, pp. 120–121). The unpleasure seems to arise not from any autonomous activity of the protoplasm, as sucking and exploring-integrating do, for example. Rather it occurs when frustration seems to have mounted beyond a certain threshold, gratification having been held off too long.

No doubt an intimate relation exists between mounting unpleasure and the destructive drive. Focusing on the use of the word *hate*, Freud stated in 1915 that "unpleasure seems to be the sole decisive [factor]. The ego hates, abhors and pursues with intent to destroy all objects which are a source of unpleasurable feeling for it.... Indeed, it may be asserted that the true prototypes of the relation of hate are derived not from the sexual life, but from the ego's struggle to preserve and maintain itself. As an expression of the reaction of unpleasure, ...[hate] always remains in an intimate relation with the self-preservative instincts" (pp. 138–139). Unpleasure plays a large part in the arousal of destructiveness, and observation seems to confirm that unpleasure provides the condition in the somatopsychic continuum for the emergence of this type of destructive impulse. While unpleasure is not autonomously initiated, once it attains a sufficient level of intensity it activates a mechanism whereby destructiveness is induced or mobilized in the psyche.

I do not believe the reactive nature of unpleasure—the sine qua non of the rage reaction in infancy—excludes this type of destructive impulse from instinctual drive status; it does not, in other words, justify the view that destructiveness is secondary in nature, that is, acquired or learned. This type of destructive impulse does not, however, seem to accumulate in the psyche by the kind of mechanism that generates libido and other trends in aggression which seek discharge cyclically. This issue is further taken up in chapter 4; suffice it to say here that sufficient unpleasure(in infancy, painful somatopsychic tension) activates an inherent tendency within the soma to discharge a destructive impulse. Without the postulation of a primary mechanism which mobilizes this type of destructiveness, we cannot explain rage in infancy. From such unpleasure-related destructive discharges, a specific destructive trend in aggression is postulated. But it is not the only destructive trend we found.

NONAFFECTIVE DISCHARGE OF DESTRUCTIVENESS

As our observation proceeded, it became necessary to account for the type of data to which Eissler (1971) and Simmel (1944) addressed themselves. We were at first little drawn to the destructiveness inherent in sucking, biting, and the breakdown of food, but Eissler's thesis made us well aware of it. There is unequivocal evidence that a *cyclical, spontaneously* arising, *nonaffective destructiveness* is occuring in the infant's sucking and other feeding activities. Although the feeding process of the human infant, like that of carnivores, and indeed all animals, requires the nonaffective destruction, or breaking down, of animate structure, be it animal or plant, I am keenly aware, as was Eissler, that this destructive trend in the aggressive drive serves self-preservation and is not in essence aroused by unpleasure experiences or affects per se. These destructive impulses have a somatopsychic origin that is constantly, cyclically activated by internal vegetative processes.

This trend in the destructive drive, amply evident from birth, is essential to the survival of the organism and active throughout its life.

I do not want to oversimplify the destructive-drive manifestations we found. Complications set in for the observer, particularly with the psycho-biological upsurge of the aggressive drive which induces the practicing and differentiation subphases. Occasionally such complications occur earlier, but they become common during the practicing subphase.

We could readily see that in rage reactions, affectively experienced unpleasure is the sine qua non for the mobilization of destructive impulses which press for discharge. However, as with the nonaffective destructive trend, this does not seem to be the case for certain other acts which appear to be destructive. In the practicing subphase particularly, no affective experienced unpleasure is manifest in many innocent acts which nevertheless must be examined from the vantage point of their apparent destructiveness. For example, Bernie, at fourteen months, swings a pull-toy widely, striking Candy who is nearly three years old. Candy reacts momentarily as if Bernie had struck her intentionally, but what we see in Bernie is the picture of innocence. For him the object of discharge was the toy and not Candy, and he seems unaware of having struck Candy. This lack of *intentionality* (Hartmann 1939, 1952) and *object-directedness* with regard to Candy makes us reluctant to place this act into the same category as rage, as evidence of an affective, and essentially object-directed, destructive drive discharge. *Intentionality* and the *object* of the instinctual impulse must be clearly discerned in our effort to understand any drive-determined event. The intentionality as well as the object-directedness (object-choice) were focused on the toy, not on Candy, and thus we found it more convincing to consider this a nondestructive impulse discharge.

Mary's bursts of aggressive drive discharge were also puzzling. From about seven months, when the practicing-subphase upsurge of aggression began, she would excitedly strike the floor with her arm, in a shower of several blows. At those times, she usually exhibited pleasurable affect. When she exhibited pleasure, we tried repeatedly to trace if the pleasure and excitement had led to the aggressive discharge or vice versa. We could not answer this question despite repeated direct and film examination of this phenomenology. In brief, we concluded again that this pleasureable aggressive discharge, rather than falling in a category of destructiveness, belonged in the nondestructive category.

It has also been difficult to assess Cindy's innocently tearing pages of a magazine or Jane's tearing a sheet of paper on which she was crayoning (both at eighteen months)—especially difficult regarding the nature of the aggressive impulse which motivated them. Regarding these acts, we vascillated between a destructive element and a nondestructive element. Long debates in our research conferences could not resolve or, more correctly, could not simplify the inferrable aspects of aggression here involved. Are these acts in fact destructive drive discharges? While such discharges do resemble destructive acts in certain respects, they are nonetheless of a different order of destructiveness—one which can most simply be differentiated as *non-hostile* as compared to unpleasure-derived destructive manifestations which are *hostile*.

PLEASURE-RELATED DISCHARGE OF DESTRUCTIVENESS

Throughout our study, we found a large category of *pleasure-related destructive drive discharges* which were the outcome of displaced and delayed discharges of antecedent *unpleasure*-related, hostile destructive impulses. This type of discharge—*sadism* in the broad, but also in the narrow, sense—would find a place along the destructive side of the spectrum of aggression. Here it is well to draw attention to the part played by ego functions in the displacement, delay, modulation, and particularly in the neutralization of aggression, especially as it determines the quality of this drive discharge and where along the spectrum of aggression such impulses fall. With respect to this category, we are no longer dealing with aggression in pure form, a consideration of much importance to understanding the nature of the drive.

In summary, early infant observation reveals that there are sufficiently distinguishable categories and hence, in my view, component trends in the aggressive drive. From their earliest appearance these tend to form a spectrum—one end manifesting destructive and the other nondestructive aggression. We also found a number of instances when it was difficult to place the inferrable impulse in one trend or the other, the observed behavior seeming to straddle aggression-manifestation categories. This phenomenon, we felt, rather than weakening the hypothesis that the aggressive drive is a spectrum of trends, may, in fact, lend strength to the view that there is a *continuum* between these trends, thereby adding weight to the possibility that these various impulses derive from the same source and that they may be component parts of a single aggressive instinctual drive.

I leave this introductory discussion of destructive aggression for the time being and will return to it for elaboration in chapter 3. We turn now to the cardinal finding of nondestructive aggression, which requires exposition and documentation before it is possible to fully address the question of aggression in the human child.

NONDESTRUCTIVE AGGRESSION

THE PROTOTYPIC INFANT OBSERVATION

In "Aggression: A Reconsideration" (Parens 1973a), I employed a brief running commentary of a film taken from our project (Parens and Prall 1974) to illustrate the nondestructive-aggression data which had led to the formalization of our study. As was indicated in the subtitle of this commentary, it was and continues to be a "Problematical Observation Commonly and Frequently Made in Normal, Well-Cared-for Infants Three-Five Months of Age."

As Jane 0–3–19,[1] is being fed by her mother, she makes her first attempts to control the spoon that mother is putting into her mouth. One can see the effort invested in self-feeding, the early motor effort to control the feeding process. The mother integrates her feeding efforts with those of her daughter. Jane then sleeps for twenty-five minutes lying on a cover spread on the floor. During the next thirty-minute period, much occurs worthy of our attention.

Within minutes of waking Jane begins to look at objects—her mother and observers. She smiles broadly, already (at this age) focusing on her mother, and then looks around at articles on the floor, looking at several quite intently as she briefly fixes her attention on them in passing. She now turns her attention to a set of plastic rings on

1. Age stated in terms of years-months-days.

a string, which she very busily explores. She begins by pulling them apart, mouthing them. The sensorimotor effort is visible on her face, and one soon hears vocal concomitants of that effort. She moves the rings back and forth while she looks at them, a serious expression on her face, and a good deal of pressure can be inferred from the way she seems to be working. She waves her arms as she attempts to reach the rings which she has inadvertently just pushed out of reach. When mother (cooperating with us) then advances the rings so that Jane can reach them again, she does so promptly, her attention continuing to be focused on those rings. The affect which bespeaks the effort she makes to bring the rings to her mouth, the effort with which she pushes and pulls them, suggests that this pressure is in the service of assimilating the rings.

The activity is of course interrupted by physiological needs, as well as by socialization. She looks around and smiles at her mother. She then returns to the rings. Notable is the intense, work-like affect—the constancy of the effort she invests in exploring the rings and the inner-drivenness of that activity. Much energy seems to be invested in the exploratory mouthing, pulling, and pushing of the rings. While she explores these rings, there is no thumbsucking activity. Repeatedly she mouths the rings, sometimes with simultaneous pulling movements of her arms and lifting of her torso, and her legs are activated as well; indeed, her entire body is involved in her effort. Her facial expression and entire body posture indicate the tension of, and the large effort invested in that protracted activity.

After eighteen minutes of nearly continuous effort, she pauses, lying down on the mat. One sees she is tiring. She pauses for about fifteen seconds, looks up at her mother, smiles softly, and returns to the rings, at once very busy. Soon she pauses again, and one begins to see signs of unpleasure on her face. She cries as if annoyed and stops her exploratory activity, rings in hand. Now, for the first time in a twenty-minute period, she puts her thumb in her mouth and lies quietly. Has her oral exploratory activity aroused her oral mucosa? Has this arousal, together with tiredness and frustration, led to the need for libidinal gratification, at least to the use of her thumb? She returns to the rings. The effort continues to be strong, but one now senses unpleasure as she seems to experience some frustration, presumably arising from her activity in relation to the rings.

From here on she alternates between exploration of the rings and thumbsucking. While she sucks her thumb she lies rather quietly on the mat, giving the impression that she is recovering from her tiredness and unexplained frustration. Her body curls up again, her legs kick up, and she sucks rather vigorously, experiencing some frustration in that too. She stops the thumbsucking, cries momentarily, and looks up at her mother. She pushes the rings away from her. The noise of the rings being pushed away seems to make her turn her attention again momentarily to those rings. She spits up a bit, and her mother picks her up to comfort her. Jane has now been awake for about twenty-five minutes and has been continually busy.

This type of pressured, driven, exploratory activity was observed from the ages of eight to sixteen weeks in eleven of our twelve infants during periods of wakefulness and physiologic and psychic comfort. In some infants it was of greater intensity than in others; with some these activity periods were of greater duration than with others. In Jane, the strong pressure, and duration of this exploratory activity from the time she was nine weeks old, was impressive. When she was awake and her physiologic needs were relatively quiescent, she looked constantly—at her mother's face, at observers, at a bell, at the lighted window, at the source of a noise. The persistence of this looking, exploring activity was compelling. Jane, like our other children, did not elect to look; she seemed driven from within to look, and I would add, to gratify the push from within to assimilate, control, and master her visual experience.

What calls for classification are the inner-drivenness and constancy of this sensorimotor activity—the pressure to master the inner-outer environment (at a time when internal and external, self and object are by no means differentiated) and the attention cathexis commanded by this inner drivenness.

I will return to this issue after first detailing the evolution of this prototypic activity. I am not satisfied to say that what we see here is just the epigenetic unfolding of ego functions or of physiologic maturation. Such a position would take no account of the drive activity this type of datum reveals.

Here, I want to try to extract from Jane's developmental history that one aspect of the differentiating aggressive drive which I have been compelled to assume sets the type of activity described above into motion. In my sketch of this evolving activity, attention is drawn to the fact that manifestations of nondestructive aggression are only one element in psychic activity. This component of the instinctual drive can be discerned only if one keeps its red thread in focus as it occurs naturalistically, interlocked (Lorenz 1953) with physiologic function (especially the sensorimotor-muscular apparatus in which aggression is embedded) with evolving ego function, and with the vicissitudes of the libido.

The description of our prototypic observation illustrates those details in Jane's activity from which I infer nondestructive aggression. Already at fifteen weeks of age, we found the following features of such activity. Early manifestations of aggression appear in activity which occurs during states of good-enough physiologic comfort and libidinal (oral need) gratification. It is now well known that the infant is not then in a state of nirvanal quiescence. Rather we find, as in fifteen-week-old Jane awakening from sleep, a gradual alerting to the outside world— which we assume is not yet psychically experienced as outside. First we find a visual exploration of the environs, an *active* effort. There are also *reactions* of alertness to strong-enough auditory stimuli. The large motor musculature is quite still. Such large-contrast phenomena as light/dark seem particularly influential. Second, in rather short order, an overall busyness sets in. By *busyness* I mean activity that is continuous, as if turned on by a switch. Infants seem to have an ever-present curiosity under these conditions (Prall 1970). Anything can become an object of exploration, if at first only a visual one—*scanning* Pacella (1973a, 1973b) calls it. Third, the hand-mouth and motility apparatuses, the striate musculature, following the visual apparatus, become engaged by some underlying force which effects this *directed activity*, as Spitz (1965) so rightly calls it. Fourth, there is, within the limits of individual endowment, a clearly manifest pressure from within, an inner-drivenness, which propels this activity and sustains it, while the budding ego apparatuses begin to direct and organize it.

Winnicott (1950), understandably at a loss to integrate what he inferred from observations of infants with existing psychoanalytic theories of aggression, suggested that the underlying impulse in question derives from a *life force* (p. 26). He considered but retreated from the view that aggression is the motivating force in this behavior. This inner force leads to the *busyness* of which we speak. In this busyness we can see so well what Waelder noted when considering the relation of aggression and mastery in such behavior as the child's play: "A drive toward mastery *or something equivalent to it* would have to have a place in the normal equipment of living beings....If we make room in our theory for such a tendency and classify it, presumably, among the *ego activities,* we have to recoginize that this involves *a measure of aggressiveness*" (1960, p. 140n, italics added). No doubt this is conflict-free ego activity at its fountainhead. But it is not just ego activity; it is also id activity, for there is an energic, a motivational factor at work here. Indeed I assume that, as do Freud's old self-preservative instincts and the functions of the ego, energic-motivational (id) and adaptive (ego) factors work hand in hand here.

From beginnings such as those described in Jane's activities at fifteen weeks—from the period when *directed activity* (Spitz 1965) begins to be observable—follows a long, continuous history in the evolving of this activity, from its very modest beginnings to extremely complex id-ego activity that underlies learning and the development of ego functions and skills.

These observations have, in fact, also raised questions from just this corner. There is an assumption in psychoanalysis particularly relied upon by those of us who work with children, that learning in school results from the neutralization and sublimation of drive derivatives. A frequently used corollary clinical assumption of great merit is that where the neutralization and sublimation of drive energy is insufficient, learning will be poor. And the further step then taken is: it is insufficient neutralized aggressive energy available to ego functions that accounts for this poverty in learning. I had put this assumption to much clinical use in the past and found no need to question it. A related hypothesis which Joseph (1973) questioned as a result of clinical psychoanalytic data, is that all aggressive activities, such as participation in sports, must derive from sublimations and neutralized, destructive drive derivatives.

I submit now, from direct observations deriving from our project, that there is a direct line from such activity as that in our prototypic observation to school activities and motor skills necessary for sports, work, etc. While clinical experience amply shows that much aim-inhibited activity enters into and molds the process of learning—learning both skills and content—there is also a path which is a direct continuation from the preneutralization activity detailed above. While neutralization and sublimation play a central, all-important part in learning, there is also a line from the earliest infantile activity to complex learning which is motivated and fueled by energy that does not require neutralization and sublimation—although it is necessary that it come under control of the ego (A. Freud 1952).[2]

I follow now, in brief outline, the developmental line (A. Freud 1965) of this activity in Jane. Even prior to the age at which the prototypic activity was observed, from age 0-2-11 on, Jane showed the noteworthy busyness in exploration which to a lesser or greater degree are found in the other children as well. At this age, during states of alert wakefulness which lasted about seventy-five minutes, Jane looked about her continually. Aggression and libido endowment were considered moderate. By 0-2-29 we had been seeing clear evidence of directed activity for some time, but in the directed activity on this day particularly, we began to note the tension evident in her effort and could infer a compelling inner-drivenness. At 0-3-8, the tension, the effort, and the inner-drivenness were evident in her steadfast looking-exploring, in her reaching for and grasping things, in her oral-tactile explorations, and in her newly acquired capability—rolling over. Her effort to make her body tip over in the rolling-over activity was contagious; observers and the mothers could empathetically experience the pressure from within the body and the persistence of that pressure to achieve the act, possibly to master the newly acquired capability. The prototypic observation recorded above was made when Jane was 0-3-19, and we have stressed in that commentary the constancy and *inner-drivenness* of the activity in question.

When Jane was 0-4-17, we noted in our records that as usual and

2. Let me say for the moment that, while I have come to different conclusions, Hartmann's (1950a, 1950b, 1952, 1955) view that the ego has neutral energies available to it from early days of life can also well explain this hypothesis.

predictably there was much visual exploring; more and more now, however, there was locomotoric exploring. Hand-mouth integration (Hoffer 1949) was turned on by some inner force. She now held and self-fed a cookie, held and directed the bottle to her mouth. Her reach, arm out-stretched, was greatly extended, and where it was insufficient to reach the object of her search-exploration, she crawled. While there was, no doubt, pleasure-in-function in crawling, this newly acquired capability seemed at least enhanced by some inner demand to get from point A to point B in order to take hold of something upon which Jane's attention cathexis had fallen. At this time in development, mastery—if we can call it that— is compelled; it is not elective, but is compelled by some inner force which fuels it. (The thoughts of Hendrick (1942, 1943a, 1943b) are of considerable interest here.) As we have noted before (Parens 1973), this energic phenomenology cannot be explained by physiological energies alone; a drive to get the toy and act upon it pushes the motor apparatus to effect crawling.

At 0-4-24, after a morning nap, Jane crawled excitedly from one thing which she explored to another; she socialized intermittantly well, interrupting her nonsocial explorations; she took four ounces of juice at the one-and-a-half-hour point. The directedness of her explorations was apparent. In the midst of the exploratory activity, we removed all the toys. Jane promptly became fussy and cried. She was comforted by her mother, but remained fussy. When we returned the toys to the floor, she stopped fussing, her mother put her down, and she returned to her prior busyness. It should be noted that this child's object relations were developing well—that while, as will be shown, she was an active child and was actively engaged in exploring toys, furniture, etc., toys did not acquire undue value to her. Her sources of comfort (in the sense of the transitional object) were her mother's thumb, her bottle, and the adroit, normative use of her own thumb. At this date, she stood well on her legs with maternal hand support, and took four or five steps with that support.

When Jane was 0-5-0, we noted that sensorimotor development was extensively exercised. Crawling was readily available to the ego, and Jane would now get on her knees and rock, showing thereby autoerotic aspects of this sensori-motor activity. Now a dramatic phenomenon appeared, one observed repeatedly in all our children beginning at this developmental period. With this first degree of mastery of autonomy, in her exploratory push, she has grabbed a toy from Temmy. This important phenomenon, we thought, lends support to the view that *aggression* plays a part, is in fact the motor-fuel for the earlier activity (at age fifteen weeks in Jane) from which we inferred aggression. An act of aggression was evident. We could not infer *intent* to take *from Temmy*, only intent to take hold of the toy which was located there, in Temmy's hands.[3] While we did not infer *intent* to take *what Temmy has*, we saw here a precursor of the kind of activity from which, very soon, we would all agree we could infer aggression—in a form with which we were more familiar. We had not expected to find this event, but more important, we were impressed with its frequency of occurrence. More and more it led to conflict between the children. Within two months, Jane's taking a toy from Temmy became *intentional*. From this trend in the aggressive drive, which represents just one aspect of the vicissitudes of nondestructive aggression, ensues a complex dynamic which has all-important implications for us.

What dynamic factors lead to this direct continuum from the nondestructive aggressive activity of Jane at 0–3–19, as detailed in our prototypic observation, to her grabbing the toy from Temmy at age 0–5–0–?

1. The contribution from the libido is great: the urge to take possession of the *newly structured libidinal object* and all its derivatives, all things in the environment.

2. There may be an *innate releasing mechanism* (Lorenz 1935, 1953), as proposed by Spitz (1965) for the smiling response, which activates imitation and insures primary identification as well as later identifications. This mechanism may have played a part in Jane's preferentially taking the toy which Temmy held rather than others available to her.

---

3. Movement attracts the visual apparatus, as Spitz (1965) found in smiling-response enhancement by movement of the visual percept. Bernie at 0–10–14 like the other children, showed a magnetic attraction to a younger infant asleep or awake on the floor mat; he had to be prevented, like all our children, from grabbing at the baby's face, particularly the eyes. Several times, a sudden movement of the quiescent baby startled Bernie. Thus Temmy holding a toy, in her movements may have led to Jane's attention falling more readily on the toy she held. Of course, the same happened to Temmy when Jane held some particular item.

3. A primary *nondestructive* trend in the *aggressive drive* propels the infant to explore, take hold of, and manipulate. Perhaps it motivates the human's life-long efforts to master the unknown thing, environment, universe, and with it the objects he comes to value. In this, aggression and libido work hand in hand.

What consequences soon arise from this aggressive phenomenon?

1. Resistance is aroused on part of Temmy and of Jane's mother, that is, on the part of the environment.
2. Self-assertiveness follows from this. If sufficiently fueled by aggression, it will mount with successive efforts to take hold of and master the object in which the infant's attention cathexis— aggressive and libidinal—is invested. The nondestructive trend in the aggressive drive determines and fuels *self-assertiveness* in the child.
3. Hostile destructive aggression (Freud 1915, Winnicott 1950b, Spitz 1965) is mobilized in Jane by the *unpleasure* aroused by persisting environmental resistance to the gratification of the exploratory-mastery effort.
4. Conflict develops in a matter of months now, with the ascendence of *intentionality* (Hartmann 1952)—at first, interpersonal conflict, but soon, into the second year of life, intrapsychic conflict.
5. Ego defenses are, in time, instituted against her mother's resistance to such actions as Jane's taking the toy which Temmy held. These defenses include internalization of the mother's dictates; therewith the earliest precursors of the superego evolve.

Thus at this developmental period, from nondestructive manifestations of the aggressive drive, we observe the emergence of self-assertiveness; libido also plays its large part through narcissism; where environmental resistance persists, destructiveness is mobilized, or activated, through mounting unpleasure and this later trend in the aggressive drive overtakes and influences the further elaboration of self-assertiveness into affective and motoric destructive wishes. From this developmental period on, wishes (Schur 1966) and intentionality (Hartmann 1952) are evident in behavior. Also note the confluence of nondestructive and destructive aggression here which shall be discussed further below.

Returning now to tracing the path taken by nondestructive aggression, we find that Jane's nondestructive aggressive activity was vigorous. At 0–5–7 she was sitting. At 0–5–24 she pulled herself up to standing position. By 0–6–27 she was mastering pulling herself up. Her exploratory activity, her working with toys, was a predominant activity during her visits with us.

When, at age 0–7–7, her mother worked outside of the home for a period of seven days, ten hours a day, Jane became affectively low-keyed (Mahler and McDevitt 1968) and her exploratory, nondestructive aggressive activities visibly slowed down. One could readily presume the turning inward of her psychic energies. As in the case of Temmy, who for months experienced excessive stranger anxiety, when Jane was low-keyed, nondestructive aggressive energies seemed to enter into the service of ego functions that preempted conflict–free–sphere mastery and development. As our film evidence shows, at age 0–7–11, when her mother was back at home taking care of her family and home, Jane's conflict-free-sphere activity quickly returned to its normal ever-expanding level.

At 0–8–1 she took a solid step alone. Here we could see, as we had with regard to her rolling over and crawling, the effort made by Jane to control her body. From this point on, she made progressive efforts to walk which she achieved at nine months. Her busyness was extensive. We noted again, in a summary statement, that Jane's object relations were developing well, at a good pace; a meaningful dialogue (in Spitz's sense) was characteristic of Jane and her mother. We also noted at this age that in association with her high level of activity, Jane tolerated well the gratification of passive yearnings. She was an easy child to feed, and when she was in the mood, was easy to hold, with good mutual molding by the dyad members. When adverse events occurred, she readily sought comfort and was easy to comfort. She ate well and slept well. Jane was not and is not a hyperactive child.

From about 0–10–10, Jane's self-assertiveness increased. She would be quite bossy and resist her mother's limiting her exploratory activity, which had acquired a wider range and area due to her stabilizing her upright locomotion and her even greater aggressive thrust. I inferred this to be associated with the upsurge in aggression which makes for the practicing subphase. This greater ego autonomy, an ample source of energy and self-assertiveness, led not only to a fruitful and differentiating busyness, but also to the peremptoriness of her demands on her mother and peers.

I noted at 1-0-29: She is constantly busy exploring and "playing" with things. This constantly leads her to want what others have—including my coffee. When I did not let her have my coffee cup, she turned to her mother and got juice. But, it is not so easy with her peers. She becomes more demanding and angry, pulling and holding onto things. She screamed twice and shouted in anger at Temmy and Vicki. But while she is more aggressive she is also more cautious, more *aware* of the conflict situation this creates. While I have called attention to increasingly skillful self-assertiveness, I should also mention its application in getting what she wanted in her explorations. She was tenaciously pursuing the purse that Temmy held. Temmy held on for about one minute, but Jane pressed her demand, kept pulling, and vocalized angrily until Temmy let go of her end and cried, standing in place. Jane's mother intervened. Our notes show that at age 1-1-9, she was also tenacious and persistent in doing things herself. She was squeezing a paper cup from which, with mother's help, she was drinking; the squeezing came from her effort to pull the cup from her mother's hands.

At age 1-2-0, Jane now played with a pull-toy as a pull-toy. That is, she pulled it carefully so that it stayed upright, looked at it, and exhibited her achievement, looking at others as she passed. She also tried to get the telephone jack-in-the-box to pop out by pushing the buttons. She perservered in this task, using the tip of her index finger (small movement control). At 1-2-7 we remarked on Jane's notable development in affects, each affect becoming not only broader but each also having more points on its spectrum curve. Just as the development of small motor movements (coordination of legs and arms) improved, so did the length of her attention and her persistence in efforts to master activities pertaining to the conflict-free ego sphere. At 1-2-28 she played with a ball, was very busy, and even pulled an electrical plug from the wall—for which her mother promptly and vigorously scolded her. We were impressed with Jane's effort, persistence, patience at 1-4-2 in trying to put into a box, blocks of different shapes that would fit only in certain similarly shaped openings. She frequently returned to this challenge during this period. In this task her mother helped her. Jane's characteristic busyness, self-assertiveness, and demandingness were amply evident. As she walked down the hall she looked into nearly every room; many items were looked at and some were touched. To be certain that the data is properly described, I must say that this was exploratory curiosity and persistence, not compulsive behavior. At age 1–4–16 we recorded that systematically, at her mother's feet, Jane had put round donut blocks on a peg. Surprisingly, they were in proper order of decreasing size. This she did for about fifteen uninterrupted minutes, putting them on the peg, then slipping them off and starting anew. She was intent in her work and well controlled. Later, in the same systematic, work-like manner, she stacked a set of Chinese boxes, stacking each within the next size, busily, interestedly. From all indications, she also tried to repair the broken leg of a toy dog, using alternately toy screw driver and wrench. After several attempts she gave up trying, frustrated. Mrs. K informed us that Jane was using those tools as her father had done recently.

At age 1–5–29, due to the hospitalization of mother who then delivered Anni, Jane was again low-keyed affectively, and her conflict-free-sphere activity again decreased. This affective and conflict-free activity low-keyedness was relieved when Mrs. K. returned home; Jane's busyness returned to its characteristic level. At 1–7–9 she, and two of her older siblings, were brought to the project without their mother who was ill. At times Jane settled down to work in the toddler area but in the course of one and three-quarter hours went back and forth between the toddler and infant areas many more times than was usual. Every now and then her work with toys and utensils was interrupted to search for and call for her mother. This day in fact she explored for her mother a great deal. Her play-work activity was not as well organized as usual: she was restless, and her attention to toys and utensils was comparatively brief and scattered. When she arrived home and her father greeted her, she cried. At the next visit her mother was in our infant area and hence available to her; Jane was her usual busy and competent self.

I would mention here, that when Jane was low keyed, self-assertiveness was notably weak for her as we had seen on several occasions by now. By contrast, as recorded at 1–7–19, whenever she was in her usual cheerful, comfortable, pleasant mood, she might show behavior from which one could easily infer a strong level of self-assertiveness. She could even be grabby and take things against resistance, being also vocally demanding; at times she would be outrightly pushy and bossy. This of course we saw in all our children. Jane would also many times yield to such aggression against her by others.

By this developmental period, Jane again spent much time in the toddler area. (*Again* refers to that period which we considered transitional, during which the later part of the rapprochement and the object constancy subphases overlapped; the first time much activity away from her mother to the toddler area occurred was during the practicing subphase proper.) Now, at age 1–8–16, Jane would spend nearly the entire two hours in the toddler area. Activity there consisted of play-work with paper, crayons, construction materials, clay, puzzles, paper scissors, glue, toys, etc. Snack was served halfway through the period. Games are played as the children could progressively activate such and participate in them. Children could freely move from the toddler area to the infant area and, when the mothers permitted (that is, in most instances), from the infant to the toddler area at will. The children's busyness, attention span, interest, and multiple skills in handling these preschool materials followed an ever-increasing level of development of much complexity.

Because of its implications for nondestructive aggressive activity, I will follow the course of Jane's reactions to object loss and its influences on her activity. When Jane was 1–9–21 we recorded the following: "Jane has not been with us for three visits (ten days), until today, due to her having had measles and to her mother's being in the hospital much of the time with Anni who has had pneumonia. Mrs. K. goes to the hospital at 5:00 A.M. and returns there every two hours for feedings except during the night when Anni sleeps. Anni has been in the hospital for six days now. Jane is brought to the session by E.S.[4] who carries her. She is showing her now well-known intermittant low-keyedness. Jane is soft and moulded into E.S. She remains there for

---

4. E. Scattergood, our very skilled project coordinator, has known Jane from birth and has often been used by Jane as auxiliary object when, for example, her mother was occupied with Anni. Jane's affection for E.S. was reliable; since E.S. never pushed herself on Jane but rather let interaction be guided by Jane's wish or necessity, Jane has never rejected E.S. and we have inferred that E.S. has been experienced by Jane as a derivative of the good-mother representation.

about fifteen minutes; then she suddenly perks up and joins sister S. at ironing play, smiling. Jane pulls, self-assertiveness somewhat soft for her, to retain the iron against Terry's efforts to take it from her. She then goes to the toddler area where she interacts with E.H. (staff) and Temmy in clay activity. Intermittantly, she comes back to E.S. in the infant area, low-keyed, and stays on her lap for up to ten minutes for *refueling*. (Furer, according to Mahler 1968). We can infer that she misses her mother deeply, that she is sad; but she can also move to pleasurable feelings, to smiling, working, and to playing with peers." When her mother was with her the next visit, Jane's low-keyedness in affect and conflict-free-sphere activity again lifted.

We noted that Jane at 2-2-1 had long ago quietly entered the anal phase. Although she was not being toilet trained (Mrs. K. wanted to let her daughter dictate her own toilet training time, something she did easily with Jane), Jane was making things and bringing them to mother for approval, was enjoying clay, putting order in her games (work), repetitively stacking the Chinese boxes, and at presnack wash time washing and drying her hands attentively.

At age 2-2-26 Jane attempted to further master the use of scissors. She started to cut a sheet of paper, but at midpoint she pulled and tore the sheet the rest of the way. Bringing such nondestructive aggressive impulses under ego control is one of the significant tasks of the ego. At age 2-3-12, Jane matched wooden puzzle pieces into their form-fitting cut-out segments. She carried out a five-minute dialogue with her mother.[5] At this age, two years, four months, Jane spent about 85 percent of her two hours with us in the toddler area [6] where much ego control over the drives and much ego, or work, skills were already visible: the use of tools (paper, crayons, pencils, scissors), task-type toys (puzzles, pull toys, machine toys, telephones), dolls and clothes, carts, and games (balls, taking-turn games) were extensive.

---

5. We have not drawn attention here to the complex progressive development of preverbal, paraverbal, and verbal communications, which interdigitate with that of pretend games (enacted fantasy) and other developmental lines—all of which derive in part from the nondestructive aggressive drive.

6. I strongly feel that we were no more seductive in attracting the children to the infant area than to the toddler area; rather we followed the tide. Snack was, however, eventually served in the toddler area where, it could thereby be argued, the children were drawn. But snack occurred at the one hour mark (10:30 A.M.) and lasted only fifteen minutes. On the other hand, the mothers generally stayed in the infant area during snack.

At age 2-4-29 Jane spent most of the morning in the toddler area. She had worked with wooden puzzles. As was often the case, she brought to her mother the collage she had made this morning. Coming down the hall, she shouted peremptorily, as she did customarily, and with self-assertiveness, "Mommy!" All the while, she was coming to her mother with her achievement of the morning.

As was noted above, the development of self-assertiveness had a history that begins with the infant's first peremptory demands—a beginning in which narcissism (libido) and aggression play a part. Aggression plays a part basically in its nondestructive aspect, but where delay of gratification or objectal resistance persists, via unpleasure and narcissism, destructive trends of aggression are mobilized which heighten self-assertive claims. An especially salutary self-assertive trend seen from even fifteen weeks of age on in Jane (when she tried to feed herself), one in which nondestructive aggression is clearly evident, is: *I want to do* it. We also noted beginning self-assertiveness in wanting what the peer has from about seven months of age on in Jane. Now at 2-7-1, Jane wanted the toy Candy had. With her mother, she indicated that she wanted to take her coat off by herself. She showed a good deal of pressure in wanting to do things herself, to the point that her father showed some impatience about it.

When Jane was 2-7-4, Mrs. K. told her it was time to pick up Anni at the hospital. Jane responded with "I wait here, mommy." Mrs. K. accepted that, since it was her plan to return in about half an hour. For the first time, we had the opportunity to find no affective reaction of low-keyedness or longing on Jane's part to her mother's absence. We then also saw that Jane continued at her usual level of busyness. She separated with comfort, did not become depressed, and her conflict-free-sphere activity was not victimized (reduced). Although this separation was understood by Jane not to be of long duration, just several months before Jane had not volunteered such a separation and was taken along. The difference lay in Jane's achievement of a sufficient degree of self- and object-constancy, so that separation did not mean intrapsychic object loss and the ego could continue to function in the conflict-free sphere at its usual level. We felt this to be an important development for the future: that retaining the object intrapsychically permitted separation from it without encroaching (due to depression and turning cathexes internally) on energies needed by the ego for conflict-free-sphere function. The implication for school readiness and work was clear.

Intentionally I have presented much of the direct, continuous evolution of activities of the primary autonomous apparatuses, ·in which, according to the view advanced here, aggressive drive energy is used which does not require neutralization. While there are many instances where sublimation already plays an important part quite early in learning, energies involved in learning and the development of ego skills also come from sources other than sublimation.

It has been my intention here to show that there is activity fueled by drive energy which is neutral with respect to primary autonomous ego apparatuses and later with respect to the ego as agency. All our data might also support the view postulated by Hartmann decades ago that the ego has innate neutral energies available to it. I was brought to question that part of Hartmann's hypothesis which holds that this energy is noninstinctual and stands apart from libido and aggression by the repeated presentation of observable phenomena which I have detailed here.

I advanced the hypothesis, alternative to that of innate noninstinctual, neutral ego energies, that this activity is fueled by aggression which has an inherent nondestructive current and which does not require neutralization by the ego. Rather, this aspect of aggression has an inherently neutral relation to the ego, although it is essential for the ego to gradually gain control over it, and organize and influence the mode and distribution of its discharge.

The most compelling reason for advancing this alternative hypothesis is that the activity in question *phenomenologically, qualitatively* gave the impression time and time again of being aggressive. The qualitative aspect of the effort on fifteen-week-old Jane's face, of the push of her entire musculature upon the rings for example, was of the type one empathically experiences as aggressive but not destructive, as one might experience pushing a wheelbarrow, or in the intellectual sphere, struggling with a theoretical problem. Indeed the knowledge that analytic child therapists presume good skill and performance in school and at work to be dependent upon neutralization of the aggressive (destructive) drive also played a part in this reformulation. Repeatedly I felt that at fifteen weeks, before the structuring of ego as agency and before the capability to neutralize destructiveness, Jane was doing what at twelve, eighteen, twenty-four years of age and beyond would be considered good work—something many of us have ascribed solely to sublimation and particularly to neutralization of aggressive drive energy. This observed, clinical impression, repeated many times in all our children, was the foremost factor which for me jarred at their foundation the hypotheses that noninstinctual innate neutral ego energy was at play, and that aggression was inherently only destructive.

TWO CURRENTS OF THE AGGRESSIVE DRIVE—POINTS ON A SPECTRUM OF AGGRESSION

As was noted at the beginning of the chapter, one can infer from behavioral manifestations widely different ends of the aggressive drive spectrum, with a number of distinguishable areas along that spectrum. That there are intermediate points at which it is difficult to place an inferred impulse in one or the other category of drive manifestation, it was noted, rather than weakening the hypothesis advanced, may in fact strengthen the view that there is a continuum between the polar trends of aggressive impulse—nondestructive and destructive currents—and, hence, add weight to the assumption that these various trends may derive from the same source.

While these impulses all pertain to the aggressive drive, they represent inherently different qualitative aspects of that drive, perhaps just as there are inherently different qualitative aspects of libido, not just the oral, anal, and genital, but particularly that which is *affectional, sensual,* or an admixture thereof (Parens and Saul 1971). The somatic source of aggression is the muscular apparatus (Parens 1973a), but the various aspects of aggression do not seem to exist by virtue of a *shifting dominance* of somatic excitation as is the case for the libido; nor, as a result, does aggression have the unique sequential phasic developmental nature that the libido has, although it is well known that psychosexual development plays a significant part in giving to aggression its familiar libido-derived characteristics of oral sadism, anal sadism, and phallic aggression.

This subject, however, may not be as fully developed as is sometimes assumed. As I will try to show, more emphatically, it would seem than others except Peller (1965) have, perhaps the anal phase of the libido is essentially a phase the character of which is determined dominantly by a dramatic differentiation of the aggressive drive. In this psychosexual phase, as Freud implied by calling it the sadistic-anal rather than the anal-sadistic (according to Peller), the libido is anaclitic with regard to aggression.

Very much to the point here is a remark by Storr whose two volumes on aggression (1968, 1972) are serious inquiries and contributions to psychoanalytic investigations on the nature of the aggressive drive. Reflecting just what I am reporting here, Storr, concurring with Schilder (1964), remarks, "It might be thought that confusion could easily be avoided by inventing or appropriating some term to designate 'active striving toward', whilst reserving the word 'aggression' for 'unprovoked attack.' Unfortunately, that cannot easily be done; for, as in other semantic dilemmas, the double usage indicates that there is an area of experience in which the two concepts *are* connected, and that to try to separate them might make confusion worse confounded" (Storr 1972, p. 16).

Chapter 2

THE PRESENT STATE
OF PSYCHOANALYTIC THEORY
OF AGGRESSION

Does the aggressive drive have an inherent, primary adaptive trend? In Freud's first instinctual drive theory, aggression is subsumed under the self-preservative (ego) instincts, and thus would inherently have an adaptive trend. Freud indicated in 1905 and 1915 that cruelty and destructiveness arose from a mastery instinct—a position modified in 1920 when he postulated the death-instinct-based aggressive drive. Freud noted that under the influence of the libido and of the ego, the self-destructive drive is turned outward from the self onto objects, subsuming a mastery instinct (1924) alongside aggressiveness and destructiveness (1930). The *primary* adaptive aspect of aggression found in the first drive theory is lost in the second, where self-preservative instincts are subsumed under Eros, and hence represented by libido. It is due to the influence of the libido and the ego on destructiveness that aggression is used in the service of adaptation. Hence, in the second drive theory, adaptive aspects of aggression are secondary.

Hartmann, Kris, and Loewenstein (1949) did much to further elaborate our understanding of the *adaptive* aspect of aggression. Their view of aggression, based with some reservations on Freud's second instinctual drive theory (they did not accept the death-instinct basis of aggression) also postulated the adaptive trend in aggression to be secondary. That is to say, the adaptive trend derives from the influence of the libido (externalization, and as Freud described in 1923, neutralization by fusion) and especially, according to these authors, from that of the ego (neutralization).

I cannot reconcile the inferences deriving from our direct observations with the hypothesis that all the children's aggressive behavior is inherently destructive *only*. There are still many psychoanalysts, especially in Europe and South America, who adhere to the death-instinct basis of aggression; however, Bibring (1941), Fenichel (1945), Hartmann, Kris, Loewenstein (1949), and Waelder (1956), as well as the large majority of analysts in North America, have rejected that hypothetical basis for the destructive drive. Nonetheless, even without theoretical death-instinct underpinning, current clinical usage suggests a retention of the second instinctual drive theory, especially as it is elaborated by Bibring and by Hartmann, Kris, and Loewenstein (see also Brenner 1971).

The earliest manifestations of aggressive behavior do not support the hypothesis that the contributions of aggression to adaptation and self-preservation are secondary only. With large justification, we are all puzzled by the relation of aggression not only to adaptation but also to the development and functioning of the ego, to mastery, and to activity. It is equally difficult to conceptualize what the interrelations are among self-assertiveness, strivings for mastery of self and environment, adaptive destructiveness (as in prey aggression or the destruction of animate structure for the purpose of self-preservation), and, foremost among our clinical concerns, hostility and hate.

Standing knee-deep in a stream of observational data, how does one reconcile with the views of Hartmann that prototypic aggressive behavior detailed in chapter 1, from which I have inferred a neutralized (i.e., nondestructive) form of aggression prior to the ego's structuring as agency, in other words, prior to its capability to neutralize destructiveness? Or, if this prototypic datum for nondestructive aggression cannot be a manifestation of neutralized destructiveness, then how does it reconcile with Hartmann's proposition that the ego is equipped with innate *noninstinctual* neutral ego energy?

What compelled Freud to propose that aggression is inherently only destructive? How did Hartmann come to propose the difficult-to-integrate concept of noninstinctual psychic energy? When, in clinical practice as well as in direct child observation, any one of us has met a finding irreconcilable with existing theory of aggression, how have some of our foremost colleagues dealt with such an encounter? These are the issues of this chapter. In sequence, I want to present an historical and theoretical survey, first, of Freud's writings on aggression, then an attempted reconstruction of Hartmann's evolving thoughts that led him to noninstinctual ego energies, and, lastly, a selected and limited survey of the psychoanalytic literature from 1949 to the present.

FREUD ON AGGRESSION

Freud evolved two dual instinctual drive theories, in both of which aggression played a significant part.[1] It is noteworthy that although the two theories are significantly different in character, Freud was attempting, from 1905 through 1939 (1940), to bring together the same elements of the aggressive drive relevant to our present discussion. By detailing sufficiently the characteristics of Freud's two instinctual drive theories, I shall show how the postulated spectrum of aggression, with destructiveness at one end and nondestructiveness at the other, may reflect essentially a reordering of his first drive theory. From this point of view, the second instinctual drive theory contains the important dichotomy which places aggression on a par with sexuality as one of the two essential drives subsuming all instinctual impulses. The aggression hypothesis advanced in this work is thus not original in psychoanalysis—even without taking into account the views of Storr (1968, 1972) and others; rather it is a reconsideration (Parens 1973a) of some of Freud's views found in his two drive theories. It is indeed because the death instinct determined the second drive theory and because this concept has met with persistant rejection from many quarters within psychoanalysis that one is justified in reordering the elements of the aggressive drive in accord with observable data gathered psychoanalytically.

---

1. Jones (1935, p. 164) rightly notes that Freud's instinctual drive theory evolved in three stages: first, the contrast between sexual and ego instincts, (2) the contrast between object-love and self-love (see Freud 1914), and (3) the contrast between life and death instincts. As I shall show, while the second formulation in "On Narcissism" troubled the first duality, it did not lead Freud to a reformulation of the first drive theory. Indeed as Jones suggested, it was only in 1920 that Freud was able to resolve "the dilemma he had produced in 1914" (p. 162).

The antecedents of the first dual instinctual drive theory are contained in "Project for a Scientific Psychology" in Freud's remark that "endogenous stimuli...have their origin in the cells of the body and give rise to the major needs: hunger, respiration, sexuality" (p. 297). The Q concept, best understood as a precursor to *psychical energy* (1895, pp. 392-397), is employed pertaining to *endogenous stimuli*. Thus, psychical energy and the *self-preservative* and *sexual instincts* of the first drive theory, still years away, are nonetheless anticipated in these early thoughts.

In 1905 in *Three Essays*, Freud first explicitly spoke of the sexual instinct, but not of self-preservative instincts (the reference to self-preservation there, p. 182, was added by him in 1915). The first drive theory began to emerge here but it would only become clearly established in writing, to the best of my knowledge, in the Little Hans paper, in which Freud referred to the "*familiar* instincts of self-preservation and of sex" (1909, p. 140, italics added). The rightly-admired editors of the Standard Edition also found no prior reference to the self-preservative instincts as such; indeed, the earliest reference they cite is from 1910, "The Psycho-Analytic View of Psychogenic Disturbance of Vision" (see introductory Editor's Note, 1915). We must assume, therefore, that the first dual instinctual drive theory became "familiar" between 1905 and 1909, before it appeared in writing.

Freud first addressed himself explicitly to aggression, also in *Three Essays* (1905b). In an examination of sadism and masochism, the avenue by which he first explored aggression, Freud implied that in his view there is a connection between *aggressiveness, activity/passivity,* and *obtaining mastery.* He remarked that "the sexuality of most male human beings contains an element of aggressiveness—a desire to subjugate; the biological significance of it seems to lie in the need for overcoming the resistance of the sexual object by means other than the process of wooing. Thus sadism would correspond to an aggressive component of the sexual instinct which has become independent and exaggerated." And here Freud notes that the aggressiveness may be "characterized by an *active* or *violent* attitude to the sexual object" (pp. 157-158, italics added). While in most of this section Freud uses the concept *active* in relation to the direction of the aggressive sexual impulses in sadism (in contrast to a passive direction in masochism), his use of the words *active* and *violent* may be read as contrasting the ideas of acting upon versus destroying.

Having already commented on a connection between the "aggressive element of the sexual instinct...[and] the apparatus for obtaining mastery" (p. 159), Freud later observed, "The cruel component of the sexual instinct develops in childhood even more independently [—than do scopophilia and exhibitionism—] of the sexual activities that are attached to erotogenic zones. Cruelty in general comes easily to the childish nature, since the obstacle that brings the *instinct for mastery* to a halt at another person's pain—namely a capacity for pity—is developed relatively late.... It may be assumed that *the impulse of cruelty arises from the instinct for mastery* and appears at a period of sexual life at which the genitals have not yet taken over their role" (pp. 192–193, italics added). A most relevant footnote tells us two things: (1) that the last sentence was added in the 1915 revision of this 1905 opus and (2) that in 1905 it had read: "It may be assumed that *the impulses of cruelty arise from sources which are in fact independent of sexuality*, but may become united with it at an early stage owing to an anastomosis near their points of origin'" (p. 193n, italics added). Here then, we find that in 1905 Freud had felt that cruelty arises from sources separate from the sexual instincts, and that he clarified this in 1915 by saying that "the impulse of cruelty arises from the instinct for mastery."

In 1905, he added a further note on *activity*, and the *instinct for mastery*, and the *musculature*. Speaking of the sadistic-anal organization, and of one relation of activity/passivity to masculinity/feminity, Freud noted, "Activity is put into operation by the instinct for mastery through the agency of the somatic musculature" (p. 198). Although while commenting on ambivalence (p. 199), Freud spoke in 1905 of "the opposing pair of instincts" (sadism and erotogenicity), he added that the origin of the component instinct of cruelty "is not yet completely intelligible" (p. 201).

Again in 1905, Freud drew attention to an existing connection between the sadistic instinct and muscular activity: "We are all familiar with the fact that children feel a need for a large amount of active muscular exercise and derive extraordinary pleasure from satisfying it.

Whether this pleasure has any connection with sexuality, whether it itself comprises sexual satisfaction or whether it can become the occasion for sexual excitation—all of this is open to critical questioning.... One of the roots of the sadistic instinct would seem to lie in the encouragement of sexual excitation by muscular activity" (pp. 202–203).

Thus beginning in 1905, Freud introduced the view that there are connections between a sadistic (cruelty) instinct which he directly connected with aggressiveness, activity, a mastery instinct, and the musculature. This complex of interconnected elements remained problematical and resistant to integration, in the opinion of this writer, because of the step Freud took in 1920, the introduction of the death instinct. Even beyond that time, as in 1924, Freud would ask what the connections are that link these psychic elements together.

In 1909, in "A Phobia in a Five-Year-Old Boy," Freud made several remarks relevant to our present concern. Here, as is well-known, he rejected Adler's assertion "that anxiety arises from the suppression of...the 'aggressive instinct,'" to which the latter had ascribed "the chief part in human events, 'in real life and in the neuroses'" (p. 140). Although Freud concluded that Hans's repression of his "aggressive propensities" toward his mother and father were responsible for his phobic anxiety, he stated, "I cannot bring myself to assume the existence of a special aggressive instinct alongside of the familiar instinct of self-preservation and of sex, and on an equal footing with them" (p. 140). This, of course, he revised later. Thus in one stroke, in reaction to Adler's challenge, Freud in 1909 established the first dual instinctual drive theory. He was compelled by prior views, and perhaps by his argument with Adler, to subsume aggression under the self-preservative instincts, a relation already suggested in 1905. When Freud eventually did ascribe instinctual drive status to aggression, its nature and the part it plays in psychic life did not coincide with that formulated by Adler.

Freud then added a remark of more than passing interest to us: "It appears to me that Adler has mistakenly promoted into a special and self-subsisting instinct what is in reality a universal and indispensable attribute of *all* instincts—their instinctual and 'pressing' character, what might be ascribed as their capacity to initiate movement. Nothing would then remain of the other instincts but their relation to an aim, for their relation to the means of reaching that aim would have been taken over from them by the 'aggressive instinct.' In spite of all the uncertainty,...I should prefer for the present to...[leave] each instinct its own power of becoming aggressive" (pp. 140–141).

Our interest in this note derives from two sources. First, during the course of our observations, and in the thoughts which derived from them, no single point troubled me more than this all-important fact, that an instinctual drive has its own force, its own pressure—a point asserted by Freud on more than this occasion (see also 1915, 1933, 1940). In the nature of the push to explore which we found universally in our infants—the prototypic activity detailed above—did we see a primary libidinization of the external environment? Is it the libido that pushes this activity, or is there first aggressive drive pressure which *initiates* and *fuels* this activity, following which the libido is selectively invested in things as they become valued? Or, does the libido influence the mode of exploration (oral), but ride the wave of aggression which compels the exploration? It would seem that the latter explanation is the most plausible.

Second, this note holds at least one source of the seemingly unavoidable confusion about the nature of aggression. It is the equation of *activity*, or *initiating movement*, with aggressiveness. Spitz (1965) particularly made this point, as did Greenacre (1960, 1971) and Winnicott (1950). So, it seems to this student, did Freud. Of the *instinctual, pressing* character of drives, of their *capacity to initiate movement*, he said, "I should prefer for the present to...[leave] each instinct *its own power of becoming aggressive*" (1909, p. 141). This point, already drawn to the reader's attention, remains to be clarified.

At the height of his formulations of the first instinctual drive theory which would yield the invaluable "Instincts and Their Vicissitudes" (1915), during the first and essentially only examination of narcissism (1914), Freud discovered the achilles heel of his duality of self-preservative (ego) and sexual (libidinal) instincts. While some unclarity in the concept *ego*, which Hartmann (1950) has since clarified, may have played a part [it may mean at times "self" and at other times "ego as agency," which was soon to be spelled out (Freud 1923], it was nonetheless the parallelism of ego (self-preservative) instinct with narcissistic libido (self-invested instinct) which led him to note in 1920, in *Beyond The Pleasure Principle*, as he had in 1914, that "narcissistic libido was of course a manifestation of the force of the sexual instinct...and it had necessarily to be identified with the 'self-preservative instincts' whose existence had been recognized from the first" (1920, p. 52). Eventually, in *Beyond The Pleasure Principle*, Freud placed both libido and self-preservative instincts under Eros, the life instincts, which came to be represented by libido.

This problem did not yield to a quick solution. He discovered that the self-preservative and sexual instincts, as regards narcissistic drive investments (i.e., self, 'ego' at that time), have not only a conflict relation—a view derived from the treatment of the neuroses which pitted ego instincts against sexual instincts—but also have a syntonic, if not identical, relation (character). This discovery led to the necessity to bring them together. However, Freud would then have had to find a place for the aggressive, cruelty, and mastery instincts, heretofore troublesome instinct components, which, each time their discussion came up (1905b, 1915), became subsumed under self-preservative instincts. Freud solved this problem when he formulated the death instinct (1920). For this and other reasons (noted in Parens 1973a) one cannot do justice to Freud's solution to his instinctual drive theories without due consideration of the introduction of the death instinct (see Bibring 1941). One might ask, however foolish such an exercise would be, what would Freud have done had he not been so deeply convinced of the existence of a death instinct, as many of us are not? It is also to be emphasized that it was the death instinct that made *destructiveness* preempt other aspects of the heretofore implied aggressive drive, indeed a mastery drive from which cruelty arose (see Freud 1905, pp. 192–193, for his views both in 1905 and 1915).

Before turning to the death instinct, we must examine much that is of interest to us in "Instincts and Their Vicissitudes." There the instinctual drive criteria were set down, and Freud (1915) continued to hold to the dichotomy of sexual and ego instincts, at least as "a working hypothesis." However, after the problem encountered in "On Narcissism" (1914), he claimed no finality for that dichotomy despite the support it derived from the biological view that certain forces ensure the survival of the species while the others ensure the survival of the individual (pp. 124–125).

Also relevant to our present concern are the following notes from "Instincts and Their Vicissitudes." First, in discussing the characteristics of instinctual drives, Freud noted that "by the source (Quelle) of an instinct is meant the somatic process which occurs in an organ or part of the body and whose stimulus is represented in mental life by an instinct" (p. 123). It is of large interest then that in this same work while speaking of sadism, Freud noted that "in sadism *the organic source ... is probably the muscular apparatus* with its capacity for action" (p. 132, italics added). In this remark, prior to the postulation of the death instinct, a source for aggression was suggested by Freud. It is noteworthy that this view is seldom expressed and to my knowledge it is repeated nowhere else by Freud, although erotic aspects of muscular function are taken as a matter of course in psychoanalysis. This bias derives at least in part from the problematic vicissitudes of aggression during the course of the first instinctual drive theory which I shall highlight while making the next two points. (1) Sadism comprised aggression, mastery, and inflicting humiliation and pain on objects. (2) In both the *Three Essays* and in "Instincts and Their Vicissitudes," while sadism was *initially* viewed as belonging to the sexual instincts, in the course of his exposition Freud *concluded,* in both works, that aggression (cruelty in 1905, hate in 1915) pertains to a mastery, (1905b), or to ego (1915) instincts.

First, in a brief note on sadism-masochism, while speaking of sadism, Freud wrote, "This instinct, side by side with its general aim (or perhaps, rather, within it), seems to strive ... not only to *humiliate* and *master*, but, in addition, to inflict pains. Psychoanalysis would appear to show that the infliction of pain plays no part among the original purposive actions of the instinct. A sadistic child takes no account of whether or not he inflicts pains, nor does he intend to do so" (Freud 1915, p. 128). This last is readily observable in toddlers up to eighteen or so months of life. But, had he not postulated a death instinct, where would Freud have gone with aggression? For in characterizing at least one aspect of aggression he said: "The infliction of pain plays no part among the original purposive actions of the instinct," the general aim of which seems to be "to strive ... to master."

Second, when speaking of "the change of the *content* of an instinct into its opposite," Freud found it "in a single instance only—the transformation of *love into hate*" (1915, p. 133). However, this assumption is raised into question by the conclusion Freud reached following an extensive note on the problem. As I indicated above,

Freud began his discussion of aggression-as-sadism under the sexual instincts, but ended up, as in 1905, by placing aggression under the self-preservative instincts. Thus at the end of his note on love and hate, Freud closed with: "It is noteworthy that in the use of the word 'hate' no ... intimate connection with sexual pleasure and the sexual function appears. *The relation of unpleasure seems to be the sole decisive one.* The ego hates, abhors, and pursues with interest to destroy all objects which are a source of unpleasure feeling for it. ... Indeed, it may be asserted that the true prototypes of the relation of hate are derived not from the sexual life, but from the ego's struggle to preserve and maintain itself" (p. 138, italics added). He concludes that as an expression of the reaction of unpleasure evoked by objects, "hate" always remains in an intimate relation with the self-preservative instincts; so that sexual and ego instincts can readily develop an antithesis which repeats that of love and hate" (p. 139). And of utmost relevance to the question of drive origin and of drive undifferentiation at birth (see Spitz 1965, Jacobson 1964), Freud affirmed: "So we see that love and hate . . . . do not stand in any simple relation to each other. They did not arise from the cleavage of any originally common entity, but sprang from different sources, and had each its own development before the influence of the pleasure-unpleasure relation made them into opposites" (p. 138). This of course stands in clear contradistinction to Freud's questioning in "On Narcissism," where he found the problem of the first instinctual drive theory reported above: whether there is in origin one "indifferent psychical energy."

THE SECOND INSTINCTUAL DRIVE THEORY

For Freud's drive theories, *Beyond the Pleasure Principle* is of utmost importance. Its importance derives equally from the fact that it permitted Freud to solve the problem introduced in "On Narcissism" and to propose the second instinctual drive theory. Since it is the foremost postulate of Freud's which many analysts have not accepted, the solution that it yielded seems to have been maintained with insufficient formal theoretical underpinnings.

For some of us, Freud's argument advancing the death instinct by way of the repetition compulsion and the seeking of unpleasure—beyond the pleasure principle—is not convincing. The reexperiencing of a painful situation in child's play, or in the traumatic neuroses, can be explained, as Freud noted (see 1920, chapter 2), alternately by the postulation of a death instinct-derived repetition compulsion or by the ego's efforts to master a situation of helplessness (anxiety). Certainly manifestations of self-destructive trends, or masochism, can be explained without postulating a primary trend toward self-destruction deriving from an impulsion to return to an inorganic state.

While the death instinct has been rejected by numerous analytic writers, the hypotheses this postulation yielded are retained— principly, the concept that the aggressive drive is a primary destructive drive. While every analytic case is a confirmation that such a destructive drive exists, it is possible that some of that drive's inherent complexities may have been masked by the very useful concept of neutralization of destructive impulses, which, while its application is no doubt correct in certain spheres of aggressive drive activity, may not have an influence over *all* of that drive's activities. The assumption that all aggression derives from the destructive drive may indeed be incorrect.

Another death instinct-derived postulate, that may be questionable altogether, is that of primary masochism. More recent knowledge advanced on the state of psychic nondifferentiation of the neonate (Spitz 1965, Hartmann 1939) would indicate that with the rejection of the death instinct, the concept *primary masochism* can now be based solely on the assumption of primary narcissism, where one may consider that all impulse discharges not only emanate from but are directed toward the *self*. But primary narcissism is a state in which self-object representations have not yet begun the long process of differentiation, where the boundaryless object is experienced as part of the all-encompassing *narcissistic self*—perhaps better called the *autistic self* (a condition which developmentally precedes the evolving of the *symbiotic self-representation*). In the autistic self, the newly coenesthetically and diacritically experienced self and non-self are bound together within a metaphorical symbiotic membrane (Mahler 1952, 1968), thus: I–not–I (Parens 1971a). Jacobson (1964) and Piaget (1937) rightly cautioned us to bear in mind this too often unrecognized difficulty inherent in the concept of primary narcissism. We must note that in a postulated primary masochism not supported by the death instinct, narcissistically discharged destructive impulses are directed inside and outside as one. Therefore, primary masochism would here be synonymous with primary sadism. Thus since in the infant, there is no self-as distinguished from object-directionality to drive discharge, there is no more primary masochism than primary sadism. If we do not accept a death instinct, we then cannot retain the view that there is a trend, primary masochism, which precedes sadism.

Let us return to the line of thought central to our present concern. When Freud (1920) developed the argument that "an instinct is an urge inherent in organic life to restore an earlier state of things" which is "an expression of the *conservative* nature of living substance" (p. 36), he concluded that "'the aim of all life is death,... and everything living dies for *internal* reasons—becomes inorganic once again" (p. 37). Here Freud reordered drive priorities, but note that he continued to hold specific instinctual drive components together: "The hypothesis of self-preservative instincts, such as we attribute to all living beings, stands in marked opposition to the idea that instinctual life as a whole serves to bring about death. Seen in this light, the theoretical importance of *the instincts of self-preservation,* of *self-assertion*, and of *mastery* greatly diminishes" (p. 39, italics added).

From 1920 on, the duality of instinctual life is based on the life and death instincts. "The original opposition between ego instincts and the sexual instincts proved to be inadequate.... Sexual instincts— probably alongside others—operated in the ego" (1920, p. 52). On the other hand: "We suspect that instincts other than those of self-preservation operate in the ego" (p. 53). (Ego here does not mean ego as agency of structural theory.) Freud noted that the polarity advanced by the second instinctual drive theory is exemplified in object relations by "love (or affection) and hate (or aggressiveness)" (p. 53). Here he reminded us that he had considered a sadistic component in the sexual instinct in 1905. Again, but with more finality, the sadistic instinct is separated from the sexual instinct in its origin and derived not from Eros but from the death instinct "which, under the influence of narcissistic libido, has been forced away from the ego and... emerged in relation to the object" (p. 54).

The postulation of the death instinct sharply reordered the elements of the first instinctual drive theory. In a footnote added in 1921, Freud for the first time set the "libidinal instincts" in opposition to the "destructive instincts" (1920, pp. 60–61). The sexual drives which preserve the species were now set side by side with the self-preservative drives under Eros, the life instincts. The death instinct, inferred clinically principally from the compulsion to repeat (see p. 59) subsumed destructive trends. Thus this second instinctual drive theory created a wider split in the instinctual trends than did the first instinctual drive theory—that is, in destructiveness, cruelty, aggressiveness, mastery, self-assertiveness, and their relation to the muscular apparatus. The self-preservative aspects of aggression, a principal source of adaptation in animal life, were placed in a very uncertain position.

It is well to note that at the time of their formulation, Freud was "not convinced...of the truth of the hypotheses" he advanced in 1920. He cautioned that this "third step in the theory of the instincts...cannot lay claim to the same degree of certainty as the two earlier ones—the extension of the concept of sexuality and the hypothesis of narcissism." He concluded that he may have overestimated the significance of the regressive character of instincts, a view which rested on observations of the compulsion to repeat (p. 59).

In *The Ego and the Id*, Freud restated what he had advanced in 1920 and the second instinctual theory seemed more readily accepted by its author. The sexual and self-preservative drives aim to preserve life (1923, p. 40). Of "the second class of instincts," this a death instinct, "we came to recognize sadism as its representative" (p. 40). Freud elaborated: "The death instinct of a single cell can successfully be neutralized and the destructive impulses be directed on to the external world through the instrumentality of...the muscular apparatus; and the death instinct would thus seem to express itself...as an instinct of destruction directed against the external world" (p. 41). Freud also affirmed here that the death instinct operates silently (p. 46).

Quietly, however, in the economic problem of masochism, the new instinctual dichotomy still holds together certain previously connected instinctual components in which we are interested. "In...organisms the libido meets the instinct of death, or destruction, which is dominant in them and seeks to disintegrate the cellular organism...into a state of inorganic stability.... The libido has the task of making the destroying instinct innocuous, and it fulfills the task by diverting that instinct to a great extent outwards...with the help of...*the muscular apparatus.* ...This instinct is then called the *destructive instinct,* the *instinct of mastery,* or the will to power. A portion of the instinct is placed directly in the service of the sexual function.... This is *sadism* proper" (1924, p. 163, italics added). Here Freud again explained how he believed primary self-destructiveness (death instinct) by the action of narcissistic libido is turned outward. While he did not say so here, we know that in 1923 Freud also ascribed to fusion with libido the detoxification of destructiveness toward objects. But no explanation was given as to how the *mastery instinct* is derived from the death instinct.

It is pertinent just to this point, that in *Civilization and Its Discontents,* Freud, attempting to trace the influences to which civilization owes its origin, observed: "The communal life of human beings had...a two-fold foundation: *the compulsion to work,* which was created by external necessity, and *the power of love....* Eros and Ananke (Love and Necessity) have become the parents of human civilization too" (1930, p. 101, italics added). How easily this two-fold foundation could have been assimilated into the first instinctual drive theory, and how readily it too would have forced the view that the old sexual and ego (self-preservative) instincts were not invariably in opposition, as indeed Freud found in 1914 and affirmed in 1920. While it is easily confirmed that work is created by external necessity, could such a "compulsion to work" have an instinctual origin? It would not be difficult to recognize such tendencies as self-preservative trends. How interesting that Hendrick (1942, 1943a, 1943b) also found a connection between what he called a mastery instinct and work. In chapter 6 of *Civilization and Its Discontents* Freud repeated that "the sadistic instinct, stood out from" the other object-instincts. "It was obviously in some respects attached to the ego-instincts: *it could not hide its close affinity with instincts of mastery which have no libidinal purpose*" (p. 117, italics added). Here Freud noted again what he found in 1905, "that the impulses of cruelty arise from sources which are in fact independent of sexuality, but may become united with it at an early stage," and in 1915, that "the impulse of cruelty arises from the instinct for mastery."

It is not clear why in a number of instances Freud spoke of "an instinct of aggressiveness *and* destructiveness" (1930, p. 119, italics added). I cannot discern if such a statement was intended to distinguish destructiveness from aggression which may or may not be destructive.

Again, a little later in the 1930 opus, Freud writes his well known: "I can no longer understand how we can have overlooked the ubiquity of non-erotic aggressivity *and* destructiveness" (p. 120, italics added). And again pointing to the derivation of a mastery-type instinct from the destructive and aggressive instinct, Freud (1930) remarks: "the instinct of destruction, moderated and tamed, and, as it were, inhibited in its aim, must ... provide the ego with the *satisfaction of its vital needs and with control over nature*" (p. 121, italics added). On the other hand, there is of course little question that Freud often used *aggression* and *destruction* interchangeably, and hence little can be made of his occasionally using these in combined forms—for example, "The aggressive instinct is the derivative and the main representative of the death instinct" (1930, p. 122).

The editors of the *Standard Edition,* in their introduction to *Civilization and Its Discontents* note that Freud, in a letter to Marie Bonaparte dated May 27, 1937, alluded to an "originally" outward-directed aggression. "We should have a neat schematic picture if we supposed that originally, at the beginning of life, all libido was directed to the inside and all aggressiveness to the outside" (1930, p. 63). This dichotomy may have its paradigm in the view that all pleasure is experienced as coming from within and all unpleasure as coming from outside and as being turned outward. But while Freud had only tentatively put forward the death instinct in 1920, by 1930, despite the resistance met with "even in analytic circles," he noted that the assumption of the death instinct had "gained such a hold on me that I can no longer think in any other way" (p. 119). Hence the thought expressed to Bonaparte seems to have gone no further.

Again, in *Analysis Terminable and Interminable,* Freud alludes to difference in the term *aggression* as compared to *destruction.* Thus he noted of masochism, the negative therapeutic reaction, and the sense of guilt: "These phenomena are unmistakable indications of the presence of a power in mental life which we call the instinct of aggression *or* of destruction *according to its aims*, and which we trace back to the original death instinct of living matter" (p. 243, italics added). Several lines later he repeats this unelaborated distinction: "an instinct of death *or* of destruction *or* aggression [which] claims equal rights as a partner to Eros ... has found little sympathy ... even among psycho-analysts" (p. 244, italics added).

In *An Outline,* Freud continued to hold to the view that the instincts "are the ultimate cause of all activity." He traced the "numerous instincts" back to "only two basic instincts, *Eros* and *the destructive instinct.* (The contrast between the instincts of self-preservation and the preservation of the species, as well as the contrast between ego-love and object-love, fall within Eros.)" Freud notes of the destructive instinct that "we also call it the death instinct" (p. 148).

Freud noted again that the death instinct, so long as it operates internally, does so silently. "It only comes to our notice when it is diverted outwards as an instinct of destruction. It seems to be essential for the preservation of the individual that this diversion should occur; the muscular apparatus serves this purpose" (p. 150). Freud never returned to the view of 1915, that "in sadism the organic source ... is probably the muscular apparatus" (p. 132). Rather, after the postulation of the death instinct—although he had also expressed a similar view before 1920—the muscular apparatus is considered an instrument for the discharge outward of primary self-destructive impulses. Thus while he asserts that the libido has somatic sources, "that it streams to the ego from various organs and parts of the body" (p. 151), the aggressive drive has the important distinction of having no stated somatic source, a problem that has been of repeated concern for some of us.

The aim of this survey has been to show the vicissitudes in Freud's writings of that spectrum of instinctual trends which pertain to a primary aggressive drive. Through the vicissitudes of Freud's two instinctual drive theories, certain instinctual trends are invariably connected: destructiveness (including cruelty and sadism), aggressiveness, a mastery instinct, self-assertiveness—these being furthermore connected to the somatic musculature. A presentation was made of Freud's two instinctual drive theories to show that these instinctual trends remained interconnected despite the changes in drive theory. In the first instinctual drive theory, aggression—first viewed through sadism and hence briefly at first considered to derive from the sexual instincts— was subsumed under the self-preservative, or ego, instincts. At this time, cruelty (and sadism), destructiveness, aggressiveness, self-assertiveness, mastery, and activity were viewed as deriving from self-preservative instincts, their common discharge pathway and vehicle being the muscular apparatus. Further exploration of libido in "On Narcissism" (1914), in which Freud noted that the self (ego) can be taken as an object, disturbed the first instinctual drive theory. Freud remarked that self-directed libido and self-preservative instincts pertain to the same instinctual trends (1914, 1920, 1930). But it was the postulation of the death instinct that provided a framework for a drive theory revision of remarkable attractiveness which reordered the components of the first drive theory. Freud's provisions for the externalization and outward-directedness of impulses deriving from the death instinct—destructiveness or aggressiveness—added to the notable attractiveness of his 1920 postulate. One weakness of the second instinctual drive theory lay in the undue but necessary generalization of the libido into life instincts.

It is well known that the second dual instinctual drive theory consists, on the one hand, of life instincts which subsume sexual and self-preservative instincts, and on the other hand, of the death instinct which is represented by destructiveness. In this context, it can no longer be maintained that destructiveness or mastery and self-assertiveness derive from self-preservative trends. Self-preservation now pertains to the life instincts, to the much broadened, and weakened, concept of libido. It is the task of self-preservation by way of the libido to inhibit and influence destructiveness so as to "provide the ego with the satisfaction of its vital needs and with control over nature" (1930, p. 121). Hence while self-preservative trends play a part, nonetheless, mastery and self-assertiveness derive from the destructive drive. We note too that the death instinct operates silently while its psychic derivatives, destruction and aggressiveness do not.

The most significant problem deriving from the second drive theory for our present findings from direct infant observations is that destructiveness preempts the aggressive drive. The inferences which we derive from observations do not confirm that assumption. I believe that our data permit the inference that there is an innate trend of the aggressive drive which is not destructive and would comply better with primary self-preservative, adaptive trends. For this reason it is here advanced that (a) with regard to this last point, the first instinctual drive theory comes closer to the inferences derived from observation than does the second drive theory, and (b) that it was the postulation of the death instinct which led to the view that the primary nature of the aggressive drive is *only* destructive. The first drive theory would have readily permitted the inclusion of innate destructiveness and nondestructive trends. But it must be added that although any conclusion must be on the side of destructiveness, Freud clearly and openly left areas of doubt regarding the question of "destructiveness or aggressiveness" as the representative of the death instinct.

The significant contribution of the second drive theory to our concerns is that it brought the aggressive drive into its own, on a par with libido. This new duality is strongly compatible with structural theory (Freud 1923) and solves well the problem of self-preservative instinctual trends as against the task of self-preservation which is assigned to the ego (Hartmann 1948, Parens 1973a).

HARTMANN'S INNATE NONINSTINCTUAL NEUTRAL EGO ENERGY

Observation and inference recommend the proposition that the type of activity described in chapter 2 is a manifestation of aggression. If so, then aggression must play a part in fueling the primary autonomous ego apparatuses. I have, therefore, questioned (a) if I am ascribing to aggression the motive force Hartmann ascribed to innate noninstinctual ego energies, and (b) what relation this energy may have to Freud's old self-preservative instincts, drives he placed under libido in 1920 and retained from their initial formulation in 1905 through 1939.

More and more I felt that Hartmann had disposed of the self-preservative instincts with difficulty and then had to postulate innate noninstinctual ego energies in their place. Lantos (1958) felt that Hartmann's "Mechanism of neutralization explained some of the changes from the instinctual into the ego mode of activity." But she was troubled, as I am, by Hartmann's suggesting the "possibility of an originally neutral, noninstinctual energy in the ego." She suggested that "among others ... Hendrick (1943b) ... must have had similar misgivings, for, in exploring the nature of the executant ego, he insisted on the instinctual motivation of ego activities. Lantos stood close to where I stand now: "It would fill a gap in analytical theory and dispose of the idea of the non-instinctual origin of some of the ego energy, if we assume that our primary ego activities [derive from] *self-preservative aggressive* animal instincts" (p. 117, italics added).

One is hard-pressed to explain the character of the energy which fuels the prototypic activity described in chapter 2. The energy seems, indeed, neutral in relation to the pre-ego; it fuels primary autonomous ego apparatuses. But is the activity here evidence of an instinctual drive? There is good reason to examine this problem—which has been of concern to Buxbaum (1970), Hendrick (1942, 1943a,b), Spitz (1965), White (1963) and Winnicott (1950x)—because it imposes the necessity to choose between at least two explanatory concepts: either (1) this early activity is fueled by a primary "neutral" ego energy as advanced by Hartmann (1950a, 1952, 1955), a stable reservoir of *noninstinctual* ego energy to which sublimated libido and neutralized aggression are later added, or (2) an instinctual drive is at work, indeed a component of the classical instinctual drives, which in its primary state serves the ego (or rather the pre-ego) and is syntonic, and hence neutral, with respect to it.[2]

Because I was compelled by observations to question Hartmann's hypothesis that the primary autonomous ego apparatuses are fueled by noninstinctual psychic energy, I felt obliged by my respect for his work to explore the origins of his hypothesis, and have attempted to reconstruct stepwise the route taken by Hartmann.

In his 1939 monograph, Hartmann established the innate, constitutional origin of the ego. Hartmann felt that while Freud had implied such "inherited ego apparatuses" as early as the *Three Essays* (1905), it was in "Analysis Terminable and Interminable" that he (1937) for the first time spoke of inborn ego characteristics (Hartmann 1939, pp. 105–106). Prior to this time, at least as of 1923 (*The Ego and the Id*), Freud had held that the ego differentiates out of the id. Although Freud alluded to innate characteristics of the ego in 1937, he returned again, in 1939 (1940), to an undifferentiated ego-id, noting that the id is the "oldest ... of the agencies which ... contains everything that is inherited, that is present at birth, that is laid down in the constitution" (p. 145). Hartmann's hypothesis was advanced despite pressure to retain old positions of the master, who perhaps was not himself altogether convinced of the new proposition he had made in 1937. It remains that Hartmann's advance was most important: the ego

---

2. I would dispose first of all of a third possibility which might be suggested: this activity does not result purely from the discharge of physiologic neuromuscular energies (Applegarth 1971).

is brought on a par genetically with the id and has innate, constitutional predispositions; primary autonomous ego apparatuses are ready to function at birth. Following Freud's long held position that the ego has the task of self-preservation (1923, 1940, p. 145), Hartmann suggested that the ego has the task of adaptation.

Hartmann (1939) upheld the view that adaptation "involves both processes connected with conflict situations, and processes which pertain to the conflict-free sphere" of ego functioning (p. 10). By drawing attention to the conflict-free sphere, he widened enormously the scope of analytic investigation and concern.

Hartmann again followed Freud, in part, on a significant, closely related phylogenetic consideration. He felt that where adaptation in animals lower than humans on the phylogenetic scale is determined by instinctive structures (the old *instincts* of biology), in humans the adaptational role of such instincts is assumed by a differentiated id and ego. While Freud held that the ego has the task of self-preservation (1923, 1940), he nonetheless ascribed self-preservative instincts (drives) to the id. Hartmann, however, was reluctant in 1939 to ascribe self-preservative activity to the id and advanced the view that in humans, the ego takes over the self-preservative task assigned to instincts in lower animals. In contrasting humans and other animals, Hartmann noted, "It is just this sharper differentiation of the ego and id ... in human adults which on the one hand makes for a superior, more flexible, relation to the external world, and on the other *increases the alienation of the id from reality*" (p. 48).

This last note holds the key to those of Hartmann's evolving views in question here. In 1939, Hartmann repeatedly points to an inherent, *primary antagonism between the ego and the id* (e.g., pp. 28, 48, 105, 106). It is my impression that under pressure to make a place for the ego's innate dispositions he had to preempt territory already held by the id, and eventually overstated the id-ego antagonism. For example, Hartmann rightly noted that intelligence is "at least partly determined by inherited dispositions" and that intelligence plays a role "in delaying motor discharge and in fulfilling a *general inhibitory function*" (italics added). From this last step, which is of course subject to interpretation, he proceeds: "From this vantage point we can obtain a new outlook on the problem of *the ego's primary antagonism toward the instinctual drive,* which was raised by Anna Freud (1936). Since many of the ego apparatuses are inhibitory, and ego achievements are determined not only by mobile ego tendencies but also by ego apparatuses, it would follow that 'the ego's distrust of the demands of instinctual drives' is the expression of *a primary factor."* Hartmann also suggests here that the phylogenetic view of a "partial antagonism between the survival of the individual and the survival of the species" is another, although lesser, factor, from which the ego–id antagonism derives (pp. 105–106; italics added).

In 1939, Hartmann noted that the id–ego conflict had been the earliest model for psychoanalytic investigation, because problems of id–ego conflict underlie symptomatology. In 1948, he again emphasized the antagonism between drives and ego: "Freud's approach to the position of the drives in human personality comprised from the outset the consideration of conflict (between the drives themselves, or between drives and other psychic tendencies), and ... this element has remained central in psychoanalytic psychology through all its stages" (p. 373). It must be remembered that Hartmann's emphasis on psychoanalytic concern with intrapsychic conflict derived from his efforts to bring attention to conflict-free psychic activity, to the part the latter plays in adaptation and development, and specifically, to the conflict-free sphere of ego development and function; for in underlining the antagonism between id and ego, Hartmann strengthened his position that certain of the ego's adaptive functions cannot derive from the instinctual drives (p. 101).

Hartmann (1939) did note in regard to syntonic functioning "the superego is not only in antithesis to the ego and the id" (p. 52). The three agencies function syntonically: for example, "The ego may take up and sanction the superego's demands" (p. 67). Referring to sexual activity, Hartmann also notes that there are "ego-syntonic drive-actions" (p. 93); he seemed, however, to consider these *secondary* developments. Of course we can speak of ego–superego relations only in terms of secondary developments, since the superego differentiates out of the ego's relation to the id and reality and no innate predispositions are assigned to the superego (see Freud 1923, 1933, 1940). Regarding the secondary relations of the id and ego, Hartmann (1939) stated: "Instinctual drive processes and the ego mechanisms arise from a common root prior to the differentiation of the ego and the id; though after they have structuralized, they may *secondarily* enter into the most varied connections with each other" (p. 102, italics added).

Thus, it seems to me, Hartmann held that a *primary* antagonism exists between id and ego, and there is evidence he viewed their syntonic relations as *secondary* developments. This is a pivotal point in what follows. This last assumption is supported by Hartmann's view that self-preservation is the domain of the ego and not the id. While Freud even to the last, in *An Outline,* held that the ego has the task of self-preservation which the id neglects, the libido nonetheless subsumes the self-preservation instincts (drives) (see Freud 1923, p. 40, and 1940, pp. 145, 148). As I have noted before (Parens 1973a, p. 40) Freud was not troubled by this *seemingly* paradoxical state of affairs. Hartmann's view of the role of the id in self-preservation on the other hand was uneasy. Hartmann held, as I think Loewenstein rightly implies (1965, pp. 43–44), that both libido and aggression contribute to self-preservation (adaptation) but only after the drives can be neutralized, hence only after ego structuralization.[3] This seems to be the only condition that can overcome the primary antagonism of id and ego which he has asserted. In other words, if the id is primarily antagonistic to the innate dispositions of the primary autonomous ego apparatuses and functions, the instinctual drives cannot inherently contribute to self-preservation (adaptation).

Hartmann, I must quickly add, did not clearly spell out what I am noting here; I advance it in an effort to reconstruct why he rejected the assumption that the instinctual drives have a primary role in the conflict-free ego sphere and in the function of its primary autonomous apparatuses. In fairness to him and to me please note that Hartmann held cautiously that "on the average the whole ensemble of instinctual drives, ego functions, ego apparatuses, and the principles of regulation, as they meet the average expectable environmental conditions, do have survival value. Of these elements, the functions of the ego apparatuses ... are 'objectively' the most purposive" (1939, P. 46). Nonetheless, there is an undercurrent, which I have tried to show in this reconstruction, of a *primary* antagonism or enmity between the

---

3. The difficulty caused Hartmann by the problem under scrutiny here was such that in 1955 he suggested that perhaps neutralization can occur even prior to the structuralization of the ego, in which case, neutralized energy would be available to the ego even earlier than he postulated heretofore.

drives and the ego. In this regard, it is particularly in the era prior to ego structuralization, prior to neutralization, that difficulties in this line of thought emerge.

It would serve the theoretical establishment of innate endowments of the ego if the innate impetus to self-preservation could be shown to come, not from the self-preservative drives, but from the ego. Freud of course could rely on the drives fulfilling this function and indeed did so; he thus found no need to postulate innate ego tendencies and did so only in 1937 and perhaps ambivalently in 1939 (1940). Hartmann, however, had to show the part played by innate ego tendencies in self-preservation. In 1948, Hartmann remarked that sexual and aggressive drives did "obviously contribute to self-preservation.... But I should hesitate to speak of whatever such contributions toward self-preservation there are as constituting an independent and definite drive" (p. 381). Of particular interest to my theoretical presentation is Hartmann's view that "the tendencies whose aim it is to master the environment and which show a definite relation to self-preservation had a rather indefinite position in psychoanalysis; today we rather tend to stress the *aggressive elements we find in them* and the role ego-tendencies play in their setup.... It is the functions of the ego, ... which become of primary importance for self-preservation in man.... Whatever the part played by the drives in this setup, there can be no doubt that other important elements participate in it" (pp. 382–38). Shortly thereafter he notes: "Neither the aims of sexuality nor of aggression, as we use the terms today, suffice to account for the mental mechanisms which serve self-preservation in man" (p. 386).

While another reader may come up with a different reconstruction since emphasis is critical in reconstruction and interpretation, I wish to note again my impression that the postulation of a primary antagonism between id and ego is a significant determinant of Hartmann's subsequent hypothesis development.

As noted above, in 1948, Hartmann advanced the view that postulating a self-preservative drive, whether or not subsumed under libido, was unwarranted metapsychologically; the drives consisting of libido and aggression contribute to self-preservation when the structuralized ego can effect neutralization, and are inherently antagonistic and alien to the ego and to reality (Hartmann 1939). Hence, prior to the ego's capability to neutralize aggression and libido, there is no psychic energy available to primary autonomous ego apparatuses, since at that time the drives—while they are said to be undifferentiated, an assumption of no help in this dilemma—would be antagonistic to those ready-to-function ego apparatuses. Although in my readings of Hartmann, I have not encountered this dilemma presented, the next step in the evolution of the theory under scrutiny seems to me, retrospectively, to require Hartmann's awareness of it.

While Hartmann well knew that there are motivational forces in psychic life other than those deriving directly from the drives (for example signal anxiety), he could not presume that any force other than some form of psychic energy could fuel primary autonomous ego apparatuses and their functions for at least the first six months of life prior to ego structuralization and drive neutralization.

He postulated, then, that the ego has a source of psychic energy of its own, that the ego has at its disposal from birth innate energies that are *noninstinctual.* I believe that this assumption, that the energy is *noninstinctual* was imposed by the assumption that the ego and the instinctual drives are in primary antagonism.

Thus in solving the problem of the ego's preneutralization source of psychic energy, he exchanged one problem for two new ones: (1) What in fact is the nature of noninstinctual energy; what are its characteristics and what is its origin? We know only that it is neutral in relation to the ego and that it fuels primary autonomous ego function. (2) What relation does this energy bear to the instinctual drives? Here a difficult problem may arise from Hartmann's assumption that *deinstinctualized* instinctual energy resembles or works like energy that is noninstinctual in origin. Does deinstinctualized energy, then, become noninstinctual energy? The concepts of sublimation and neutralization of instinctual energy do not contain the proposition that deinstinctualized energy becomes noninstinctual energy. Would this metamorphosis not have to be assumed to support the propositions of Kris (1955) and Hartmann (1955) regarding energy that is entered into the stable reservoir of ego energy? Is it sufficient to assume that deinstinctualized and noninstinctual energies coexist in that reservoir?

Hartmann (1955) did suggest that perhaps neutralization may occur even before structuralization of the ego. However, unless one postulates a primary neutralization—which Hartmann did not suggest—one is more secure in proposing that neutralization of drive must await sufficient ego structuralization, even though it is difficult to pinpoint when the latter occurs. Hartmann (1952, p. 43) suggested that intentionality—which emerges at about six to eight months—marks the beginnings of ego as structure. Spitz (1965) helps further in this regard by proposing that neutralization cannot occur before the development of the libidinal object (six months of age), not even perhaps before the last quarter of the first year of life (p. 289). Our research supports this timing. Our observations of infants under six months of age, prior to the ego's capability to neutralize, sublimate, or modify psychic energy, may, similarly, help clarify further the nature of this early energy in question here.

INSTINCTUAL DRIVE ENERGY

As I noted above of the detailed prototypic infant observation, what calls for classification is *the inner-drivenness and the constancy of this sensory-motor activity, the pressure to master the inner-outer environment, and the attention cathexis commanded by this inner-drivenness.* Is this early, primary autonomous ego activity fueled by noninstinctual neutral ego energy, or by the energy of an instinctual drive?

Ego energy would not have the pressure and motivational characteristics inherent in instinctual drives. Being 'potential' rather than 'kinetic,' ego energy would be available to the ego for function but would not dictate the course taken by the ego. This view is consonant with those of Hartmann (1955) and Kris (1955) that in subsequent development, instinctual energy is deinstinctualized and added to the stable reservoir of ego energy. That is, the *peremptoriness,* to use Klein's image (1967), is taken out of the instinctual impulse, leaving that aliquot of energy to be used by the ego at will.

Freud (1915) observed that an instinctual impulse is experienced as a need, that it is peremptory, and that it cannot be escaped since it arises from within. Furthermore, the drive is constant. Indeed, the prototypic activity here in question has the singular characteristics to be found in the manifestations of an instinctual drive (Loewenstein 1940): *inner-drivenness, intrapsychic origin,* and *constant activation.*

In accord with Freud's 1915 formulation, the instinctual drive inferred may have a source, an aim, and an object. In fact, the characteristics of inner-driveness and constance of this prototypic activity are so impressive that they propel exploration of the *source, aim,* and *object* of the impulse they infer.

Bearing in mind Freud's view (1905, 1915) on the somatopsychic nature of an instinctual impulse, I suggest that the *source* of the impulses in question could be the sensori-motor apparatus—the central nervous system, with its peripheral sensory receptors and its motor end organ, the musculature. To the best of my knowledge, only once did Freud (1915) propose that "in sadism the organic source ... is probably the muscular apparatus" (p. 132). Infants from nine weeks of age on, and earlier, who are reasonably well gratified physiologically and libidinally, reveal long periods of exploratory sensori-motor activity. Such activity occurs during feeding and seems quite important there in organizing the libidinal object from the environment (Spitz 1965). Such activity during waking states may be continuous; it is spontaneous, but also responsive to stimuli from outside. (Removing the object of exploration often leads the infant to look at another and yet another object.) The *aim* of the impulse is achieved when it spends its energy in apprehending, assimilating, and bringing the environment under control. In this, it abides by the pleasure principle. (Unpleasure is also evident in the nine to sixteen-week-old when sufficient gratification is not forthcoming.) The direct relation this aim bears to mastery and ego function is self-evident. The *object* is that which serves as vehicle for the gratification of the impulse; the object attracts the impulse from the receptor apparatus and serves in the activation of the motor apparatus.

The nature of the energy which fuels primary autonomous ego apparatuses meets the criteria for instinctual drive proposed in 1915, criteria recommended and used by Bibring (1941), Loewenstein (1950), Simmel (1944), Fenichel (1945), Hartmann (1948), Hartmann, Kris, and Loewenstein (1949), Waelder (1956, 1960), and others. This force which motivates the activity in question has an inner-drivenness, is constantly activating, and is readily observable during states of wakefulness when physiologic and libidinal needs are sufficiently or even in the process of being gratified. Its source, aim, and object can be postulated. It thus warrants classification among the instinctual drives. Since it arises from and is represented in the id, but also, in origin, fuels primary autonomous ego apparatuses, the energy would be neutral with respect to the ego.

SOLUTION TO THE PROBLEM CREATED BY THE CONCEPT
OF NONINSTINCTUAL NEUTRAL EGO ENERGY

Hartmann strongly recommended direct infant observations for the verification of reconstruction-derived hypotheses and for the opening of areas closed to reconstruction (see Hartman 1939, pp. 6, 8, 9–10, 12; 1950b, pp. 7–8, 10; 1958a, p. 135; 1958b, p. 121). Such observations recommend that we view the energy fueling primary autonomous ego apparatuses as instinctual, but nonetheless neutral with relation to the ego. In other words, drive and ego function syntonically, the fueling energy deriving from the libido and the nondestructive current of aggression (Parens 1973a). (This is in contradistinction to the libido's gradually 'libidinizing' primary ego apparatuses.) This hypothesis rejects the assumption of a *primary antagonism* between the instinctual drives and the ego, an assumption which I believe compelled Hartmann to postulate noninstinctual neutral ego energy. I do not mean that there is no conflict potential between the drives and ego (reality), but that it is not necessary to postulate a generalized, or primary, antagonism between id and ego.

In Freud, the id and ego are not simply antagonistic, and the vicissitudes of drive theory help highlight the point. In the first instinctual drive theory (see Lantos 1958), a relation of antagonism exists between ego and drive, as reflected in the prestructural view (prior to 1921–1923) that conflict arises from a clash between the sexual and ego, self-preservative instincts. As Hartmann (1939) reminds us, this antagonism was contributed to in part by the antithesis: preservation of the self versus preservation of the species. Even in 1914, however, Freud found in his study of narcissism that the sexual and ego instincts are not always in opposition. Here of course we speak of ego as it was understood prior to the *ego* of structural theory.

The second instinctual drive theory (1920, 1923) formulates a more complex relation of id and ego. Here the self-preservative instincts (the old ego instincts of the first instinctual drive theory) are subsumed by the life instincts, represented in the id, and cannot be construed to be antagonistic to the ego, to which the task of self-preservation is assigned (Freud 1923, 1940). Hence while in the second drive theory antagonism between drive (id) and ego can and does lead to conflict, an area of syntonicity exists between the self-preservative elements of the libido and the ego.

From the first extensive formulation of structural theory (1923), Freud adhered to the view that regarding the cathexes which proceed from the id, "the ego ... either acquiesces in them or tries to fend them off by the process of repression" (p. 29). Much of life consists of the nonconflictual pursuits by the ego of needs it experiences which derive from id cathexes. Indeed infant observations seem to suggest that the ego becomes antagonistic to id derivatives not by some primary disposition but under the influence of the ego's relations to objects (reality). (See chapters 8, 9 and 10 regarding those factors that lead to the erection of defenses by the ego against destructive impulse derivatives.)

Hartmann emphasized that psychoanalysis had, from its earliest history, advanced theories derived from a conflict-based antagonism between id and ego (and superego) and he was the foremost theorist to advance the conflict-free sphere of psychic function. It is puzzling, therefore, that when Hartmann (1939) quoted Anna Freud's classic *Ego and the Mechanisms of Defense* (1936) regarding a primary antagonism between ego and id, he did not hold in account that she was concerning herself there principally with the conflict relations of the ego and id, for she clearly indicated that areas of conflict-free function between these agencies also exist. Most important is her note that in nonconflictual function, boundaries between the agencies cannot be discerned, par excellence a statement of syntonic functioning. There are times when "the two neighboring powers—ego and id—are peaceful. ... Differing instinctual impulses are perpetually forcing their way from the id into the ego, where they gain access to the motor apparatus, by means of which they obtain gratification. In favorable cases the ego does not object to the intruder but puts its own energies at the other's disposal and confines itself to perceiving; it notes the onset of the instinctual impulse, the heightening of tension and the feelings of 'pain' by which this accompanied and, finally, the relief from tension when gratification is experienced.... The ego, if it assents to the impulse, does not enter into the picture at all" (1936, pp. 6–7). At this time in the history of psychoanalysis, with the emphasis on the nature of pathology and conflict, the ego was viewed as a passive participant in the context of nonconflictual phenomena. Although this view was soon to be extensively modified under the impetus of Hartmann's monograph (1939), Anna Freud's remarks left room for syntonic, nonantagonistic ego discharge (action) of id cathexes, or of instinctual drive derivatives.

Of course Anna Freud amply examined the conflictual aspect of id-ego relations: "Unfortunately the passing of instinctual impulses from one institution to the other *may be* the signal for all manner of conflicts.... On their way to gratification the id-impulses must pass through the territory of the ego and here they are in an alien atmosphere. In the id the ... 'primary process' prevails; ... in the ego, [the] 'secondary process' .... Peaceful relations between the neighbouring powers are at an end" (p. 7). The modes of function differ—primary versus secondary process—but that of itself does not necessarily create enmity or even dystonicity. Hartmann himself noted that Freud (1926) held that "the ego must treat [*only*] *certain* instinctual drives as dangers" (Hartmann 1939, p. 28, Hartmann's addition).

Hartmann was to draw our attention to the fact that a large segment of psychic function life is conflict-free. But I would add that there is not only a conflict-free ego sphere, but *in normal developmental process there is also a non-conflict-inducing drive (id) sphere.* In fact there is a large segment of psychic life in which a mutual and syntonic relation exists between drives and the ego, as for example, when the ego secures from the environment the gratification of drive demands which it, the ego, experiences as needs (Freud 1923). The drives do not at all times make conflictual demands of the ego.

I have the impression that the old, but extremely important, conflict-based dichotomy of ego versus drives was retained unilaterally by Hartmann. He saw the conflict-free sphere of ego function, but in certain respects retained the view that drives have an influence only in the conflict sphere of psychic function. The point is, *had Hartmann brought the drives into the conflict-free sphere, he would not have had to postulate noninstinctual neutral (i.e., nonantagonistic) ego energies.*

The developments which the drives induce in the ego—such as the all-important formation and functioning of the superego—do not derive only from the conflict sphere of psychic life. I advance the thesis that from birth the drives also induce ego developments from their conflict-free relations to the ego: that the nondestructive current of the aggressive drive and libido fuel primary autonomous ego apparatuses and functions from birth without the necessity for neutralization; that an important part is played by the libido in libidinizing evolving functions of these apparatuses prior to any capability of the ego to modify instinctual impulses; that aggression may even play some part in the libidinizing of these primitive apparatuses. In addition, we can assume that neutralization only becomes necessary for aggressive and libidinal drive derivatives that pertain to the conflict sphere of psychic function.

In the conflict-free sphere, ego and id (libido and aggression)—even from their primitive, relatively undifferentiated beginnings—function syntonically, inherently making possible that complex of functions that subserve self-preservation (Parens and Saul 1971, p. 78, pp. 118-119; Parens 1973a, p. 44). As Hartmann remarked: "No instinctual drive in man guarantees adaptation *in and of itself,* yet on the average the whole ensemble of instinctual drives, ego functions, ego apparatuses, and the principles of regulation, as they meet the average expectable environmental conditions, ... have survival value" (1939, p. 46).

It is plausible to ask whether such an ego-syntonic instinctual drive—a nondestructive current of the aggressive drive—reflects some of the characteristics Freud early ascribed to the self-preservative instincts. The formulation of aggression advanced in this work would do away with the problem of self-preservative instincts, since both libido and aggression contribute to it inherently, and its postulation as a separate instinctual drive would be, as Hartmann suggested (1948, 381), unnecessary (p. 57; see also Bibring 1941).

In summary then, *a non-conflict-inducing instinctual drive (id) source* provides the drive energies which the primary autonomous ego apparatuses employ, and it is not necessary to postulate innate ego energies of a *noninstinctual* nature. We can postulate that since such energies come from the aggressive and libidinal drives from their earliest state of relative undifferentiation, they are available to the ego from birth, prior to neutralization and the structuring of the ego as agency. Furthermore, these fulfill the characteristics ascribed by Freud to self-preservative drive trends; hence self-preservative drive components are contained in aggression and libido, and it is unnecessary to postulate an independent self-preservative drive.

FURTHER SELECTED LITERATURE REVIEW

An impressive number of psychoanalysts have raised questions about existing psychoanalytic theory on aggression. The list is so extensive that I shall focus only on those who have played some part in influencing my formulations. Several authors, from their own direct infant observations, have tried to explain the nature of the drive which fuels the activity we have considered prototypic for nondestructive aggression. The rest have tried to explain the nature of aggression from other clinical and theoretical perspectives. Among the former the work of Winnicott (1950x), Hendrick (1942, 1943a, 1943b), and Spitz (1953, 1965) is of central relevance to my work. In the latter category, the list is much longer. In addition to Freud's views on aggression, there are those of Hartmann, Kris, and Loewenstein (1949), Waelder (1956, 1960), Lantos (1958), Greenacre (1960, 1971), and more currently those of Solnit (1966, 1970, 1972), Storr (1968, 1972), Joseph (1973), Marcovitz (1973) and Stone (1971). In chapter 3, a most interesting note is added from neurophysiology (Reis 1973).

WHAT FUELS THE PROTOTYPIC ACTIVITY
DESCRIBED IN CHAPTER ONE

Finding activities akin to those ascribed to neutralized aggression observable *prior* to the development of the ego's capability to neutralize instinctual drive energy, I have presumed that these activities derive from a primary aggressive trend. Both Spitz and Winnicott, who in direct infant observations explored the early activity in question also, independently, consider it to pertain to the aggressive drive.

Winnicott (1950x) observes that: "Baby kicks in the womb" and a few weeks after birth "thrashes away with his arms" and "chews the nipple with his gums." He concludes "*At its origin aggressiveness is almost synonymous with activity*" (1950, p. 204; italics added). This view resembles that taken by Spitz (1965) and Greenacre (1971). But Winnicott overgeneralizes here: "In so far as behavior is purposive, aggression is meant" (p. 205).

Five years later finding his earlier position untenable, Winnicott (1955) advises that we examine the "prehistory of the aggressive element (destructive by chance) in the earliest id experience. We have ... certain elements which date from at least as early as the onset of fetal movements—namely motility.... The environment is constantly discovered and rediscovered because of motility" (p. 211). What Winnicott had in 1950 ascribed to *aggressiveness,* in 1955 he ascribed to *motility.* "The summation of motility experiences contributes to the individual's ability to start to exist" (p. 214).

Like Winnicott, Mittelmann (1954, 1960) has expressed the view that a motility drive would explain well the nature of the push to motor activity one observes in infants and children. This view advances the position that a drive, some instinctual force, underlies the pressure and constancy of sensorimotor activity readily observed during states of wakefulness where there is sufficient psychologic and physiologic comfort. Reversing the course taken by Winnicott (who first suggested *aggressiveness* for such drive activity and then retreated to *motility*), I would suggest that such a motility drive would have to be a component of the nondestructive current of the aggressive drive here proposed.

Probably because he could not reconcile his views on aggression and motility with existing aggression theory, Winnicott yielded in his observations to a conclusion of questionable merit: "We need a term here such as *life force*" (p. 216; italics added). He suggested then that spontaneity of action or impulsiveness, which derives from this life force, becomes aggressive when opposition is encountered (p. 217). In my formulation, opposition leads to intensification of primary aggressive trends at the level of self-assertiveness; sufficiently persistent opposition leads to mounting unpleasure and the mobilization of hostile destructiveness—a point that will be developed further in the next chapter.

It is striking that Greenacre and Spitz independently came to views quite close in character to those of Winnicott. Taking a position already hinted at as early as 1960, Greenacre (1971) ties the origin of aggression to some energic force inherent in growth: "I would see aggression as having its origin in the enormous pressure of growth—in the expansion and differentiation of the organism during the parasitic period of fetal life.... The force of growth would appear of necessity *a nonhostile form of physical aggression* and will later contribute to the core of the autonomous ego, as the body ego develops into the psychic ego" (p. 197, italics added).

In 1965, speaking of the beginning of what he calls *directed action*—activity observable in infants about eight to sixteen weeks of age—Spitz said, "Energy charges evoked by incoming stimuli can now be discharged in the form of directed action and no longer only as random diffuse excitation.... In the literature this function of directed activity, of actions as such, in promoting development during the first year of life has not been duly considered" (p. 106). Then he remarks, "It is rarely spelled out that the aggressive drive is not limited to hostility. Indeed, by far the largest and most important part of the aggressive drive serves as the motor of every movement, of all activity, big and small, and ultimately of life itself" (p. 106).

I cannot go the distance traveled by Winnicott, Greenacre, and Spitz in this regard. Both Winnicott and Greenacre, in particular, cross over to biological beginnings which, while plausible inferences seem to be contained in their views, are not within the capability of analysis to assess. Like Bergson's *élan vital,* and Freud's life and death instincts, they may be useful concepts, but it is in the realm of biology to spell out such formulations. From Winnicott's and Greenacre's formulations I nevertheless extract, as relevant to instinctual drive theory, the view that some nondestructive, *nonhostile,* form (Greenacre) of aggression seems to operate at a *primary* level in the psyche.

While Winnicott and Greenacre conceptualize a basic organic force in which aggression has its origin, Spitz (1965) departed from specific observable units of behavior, "directed action," and generalized that "the aggressive drive serves as the motor of every movement, of all activity, ... and ultimately of life itself" (p. 106). This generalization requires clarification. It could imply that no action derives primarily from libidinal sources, a view which we are certain Spitz would not hold. It might imply that aggression plays a part in all directed action, in the sense that aggression is instrumental in attaining libidinal gratification, in which case its role would be of a secondary order. While this view of achieving libidinal gratification against resistance applies in many instances, there are, as Freud noted in 1905, instances in which libido sets the *physiological* motor apparatus (in contrast to the aggression-fueled motor apparatus) into motion; aggression may play no part in this "directed action."

Three notes more to the point for our present concern can be extracted from Spitz's remarks: (1) "It is rarely spelled out that the aggressive drive is not limited to hostility." Indeed, Spitz noted, "When I speak of 'aggression,' I do not imply hostility or destructiveness; although at times these may be among the manifestations of the drive" (p. 285*n*). (2) Spitz implied that much directed action is fueled by a nonhostile form of aggression, indeed, an adaptive, life-preservative aggression. In 1953, Spitz noted that aggression fuels grasping, holding, and exploration of the environment. (3) There is an inferrable spectrum of aggressive activity which spans from nondestructiveness to destructiveness. His inclusive sweep from constructive "directed action" through destructive action is stated at the outset of his *The First Year of Life*: "Freud conceived of aggression as the other fundamental drive operating in the psyche. ... This aggression serves to approach, to seize, to hold, to overpower, or to destroy the object— and by extension things. It is expressed or carried out 'through the instrumentality of a special organ ... the muscular apparatus'" (Spitz 1965, p. 9).

In 1969, in an imaginative and astute essay supporting his earlier views (1953, 1965), Spitz concurs with Lorenz (1966) that aggression is "one of the most important of the forces that lead to adaptation, if note *the* most important." Spitz goes further: "Without aggression, without the energies and the tools derived from it, no evolution would be possible" (p. 81).

Thus, while there are notable differences in the formulations of Winnicott, Greenacre, and Spitz with regard to this problem, there are nonetheless important similarities. First, a nonhostile, nondestructive form of aggression is inferrable from the behavior of infants prior to the advent of neutralization of drive by the ego. Second, there may be a primary nondestructive form of aggression. Third, this aspect of aggression bears a relation to hostility and destructiveness in that they pertain to the same basic aggressive drive.

Hendrick's very relevant formulations, also derived from direct infant observation, propose another viewpoint. The inner-drivenness, the constancy of the exploratory, mastering type of prototypic activity I detailed in chapter 1 lead Hendrick (1942) to propose an "instinct to master" by which Hendrick means "an inborn drive to do and to learn how to do" (p. 41). He rightly emphasizes that this tendency determines a significant part of infantile activity and notes that "the objective of the instinct to master is the alteration (sometimes the cognition) of an external situation. ... Its simplest manifestations are the use of the sense organs, the peripheral muscular apparatus, and the rational association of ideas" (p. 41). Hendrick makes a notable effort to find a place for this instinct other than with the sexual instincts and sadism (destructiveness, aggression), an effort which bears some resemblance to the formulation of nondestructive aggression advanced here: "Most manifestations of the instinct to master cannot be empirically differentiated from sadism [aggression]" (p. 54). The reader will recognize that in his formulation, Hendrick comes rather close to postulating innate neutral ego energies, but his insistence on considering it instinctual makes his view incompatible with that of Hartmann.

Hendrick's (1943b) formulations of the work principle also are extremely interesting. "Work pleasure is not, primarily, displaced or sublimated sensual pleasure." According to Hendrick "The work principle is an expression of an instinct to master" (p. 327). This view he derived from observable data like that which so impressed us: the pressure "to learn how to do things, manifested in the infant's practice of its sensory, motor, and intellectual means for mastering its environment, is at least as important as pleasure seeking mechanisms in determining its behavior and development during the first two years of life" (1942, p. 34). While I question Hendrick's contrast of this activity with pleasure seeking mechanisms, his observations and his data are no doubt the same as ours. Hendrick (1942, 1943b), like Storr (1968), feels that this activity (manifesting the work principle in Hendrick's view and nonhostile aggression in Storr's) is not governed by the pleasure principle. This view I cannot share with them; indeed, nondestructive aggression, as I see it, is very much governed by the pleasure principle—as amply evidenced by the reaction of unpleasure which generally follows on obstruction of its gratification. It must be said for Hendrick, however, that this particular position derives from his use of the concept *pleasure* to mean strictly sensual pleasure, and not the decrease of drive tension due to impulse gratification (see 1942, pp. 40–41). This view he later modified, "The work principle holds that primary pleasure is sought by efficient use of the central nervous system for the performance of well-integrated ego functions which enable the individual to control or alter his environment" (1943b, p. 311).

While I question Hendrick's arrangement of the pieces of the puzzle, the elements he found seem to be those I found in the course of longitudinal direct observations, the particular juxtaposition in psychic activity of (nondestructive) aggression, mastery, and work. Waelder (1956, 1960), too, disagreed with Hendrick's formulation although he believed that some formulation was required that would link together mastery, ego function and aggression. Freud's constant efforts to bring together self-preservative instincts, a mastery instinct, and a cruelty instinct, all of which would function through the muscular apparatus, also bear a relation to the effort made by Hendrick. It is of interest that in a letter responsive to criticisms of his "instinct to master," Hendrick (1943a) remarks that "Karl Menninger … while wholeheartedly accepting the 'work principle,' prefers to ascribe it to those forces already described as aggressive instinct" (p. 564). While this comes closer to the position adopted by this author, I cannot, however, share Menninger's view that aggression derives from the death instinct.

That Winnicott, Spitz, and Hendrick approach aggression from the vantage point of direct infant observations makes their reports of vital interest to this presentation. It is especially relevant that they found questions regarding existing psychoanalytic theory of aggression very similar at their core to those I have raised.

Equally relevant are the views of some analysts who have come to similar questions about aggression from data derived from psychoanalytic clinical work.

COMPLICATIONS IN UNDERSTANDING AGGRESSION

Certain conceptual interrelations enormously complicate our efforts to understand and explicate the nature of aggression. One interrelation pertains to adaptation, self-preservation, and destructive and nondestructive aggression. These concepts interdigitate about the central issue whether the contributions aggression makes to adaptation are primary (innate) or secondary (acquired). A second interrelation, which Freud, like many analysts since, especially held to, pertains to aggression, assertiveness, mastery, nonhostile and hostile destructiveness, and the muscular apparatus. In essense this second conceptual interrelation concerns manifestations of aggressive activity which consist of a spectrum extending from motility, exploration, and self-assertiveness to hostility and hate. To complicate matters more, these two sets of interrelated concepts further interdigitate with each other.

In addition to these complications, we must consider what the relations are of aggression to the ego, including the view that aggression serves the ego, is instrumental, which again brings us back to the relation of aggression to mastery. A special interest also exists regarding the relation of aggression to the muscular apparatus and to motility. And lastly, pertinent to this study, is the relation of frustration and unpleasure to destructiveness, especially to what I label *hostile destructiveness.*

ADAPTATION AND AGGRESSION

There is little question among psychoanalysts that aggression serves adaptation. There is debate, however, concerning whether that adaptive trend in aggression is primary (innate) or secondary (acquired). In Freud's first instinctual drive theory, aggression is subsumed under the self-preservative (ego) instincts. In 1905 and 1915, Freud proposed that destructiveness and cruelty arose from a mastery instinct, the adaptive trend in aggression at that time being considered primary in nature. The advent of the second instinctual drive theory induced by Freud's postulation of the death instinct disrupted the readily assumed connections linking the ego instincts, self-preservation, a mastery instinct, and destructiveness. The aim of the aggressive drive, the representative in the psyche of the death instinct, is now destruction of the self to effect a return of its component parts to the self's original inorganic state. If we assume that adaptation means the preservation of the self by securing the gratification of needs ensuring survival, then aggression in the second instinctual drive theory undermines adaptation. Freud inferred this much by two explanations: (1) This trend in aggression is turned away from the self by the libido and the ego. (2) The old self-preservative instincts (to which he adhered to the end) are ascribed to the libido (life instincts) rather than to aggression. Mastery is now separated from self-preservative trends, Freud suggesting that strivings for mastery arise from the modification of the destructive drive. In the second instinctual drive theory, aggression serves adaptation *secondarily,* by the action of the libido and ego on destructiveness. The theoretical connections between the ego, self-preservation, adaptation, mastery, and destructiveness are now much more complicated. The key factor affecting this greater complication is the postulation of the controversial death instinct.

Hartmann, Kris, and Loewenstein (1949) did much to further our understanding of the adaptive aspects of aggression. While they rejected the death instinct basis of the destructive drive, they adhered to its second instinctual drive formulation in holding adaptation to be secondary, determined not only by the influence on aggression of the libido but especially, according to the thesis they so well developed, by neutralization of the inherently destructive drive. But in discussing the aims of aggression, Hartmann, Kris and Loewenstein (1949) doubted the assumption that "total destruction of objects, animate and inanimate" is their original aim. They remarked that "at the present state in the development of psychoanalytic hypotheses the question as to the specific aims of the aggressive drive cannot be answered" (p. 18). Nonetheless, they considered the contributions of aggression to adaptation to be secondary. These contributions, they noted, were of larger consequence to psychic life than analysts had tended to acknowledge in 1949. Emphasizing that the tendency in psychoanalysis had been to examine only the destructive trend in aggression, these authors wanted to supplement this traditional view by an alternative: "It seems that the plasticity of aggression manifests itself in *the control of the body,* in *the control of reality,* and in *the formation of psychic structure"* (p. 18, italics added). These contributions to adaptation are of course enormous.

At the same time as Hartmann, Kris and Loewenstein reported their classic observations on aggression, B. Rank (1949), from her work with atypical children, suggested at least two aspects of aggression, an adaptive one—"aggressive behavior means adaptation," as a reaction to frustration (p. 47), a point Solnit would emphasize twenty years later—and a destructive one. It is not clear from Rank's remarks, however, that adaptation derives from the inherent character of the aggressive drive itself.

In 1956 and 1960, Waelder, after a rigorous exploration, noted that only with difficulty could he accept the proposition of an "essential" (primary) destructiveness, meaning hostile destructiveness. He not only contrasted it to adaptive aspects of aggression but also drew attention to the relation of aggression to the ego and mastery. As I shall detail below, while he criticized Hendrick's (1943a) proposed mastery instinct, he called attention to such a drive to which he felt aggression must contribute.

After a number of papers on the subject, Lantos summarized her bold and innovative views in 1958. Objecting to Hartmann's disposition of self-preservative instincts and his hypothesis of innate noninstinctual ego energies, she called for a reassessment of both self-preservative instincts and aggression. She proposed that there are two primary categories of aggression. First she pointed to a primary adaptive aggressive trend. As would Lorenz (1966) and Storr (1968, 1972), Lantos pointed to infrahuman animals to document the generalization that in animals, aggression is self-preservative or adaptive.

Once she had rejected innate noninstinctual neutral ego energies, Lantos proceeded "to make good [the] neglected connection between self-preservation and aggression." She asked: "Does it explain every human manifestation to assume, in accordance with the Second Instinct Theory, that all aggression is directed, primarily, against the human object and turned only secondarily, by neutralization, toward non-defensive ego activities?" (p. 118).

While I do not agree with every step Lantos took from here, it may be useful to briefly state her formulations. She noted "that animal aggression makes sense biologically and follows two patterns: it is either aggression against the food animal, the prey; or it is aggression against the fellow animal, the rival" (p. 118). The first is determined by "objective aggression," the second by "subjective aggression" (p. 118). Thus she felt that humans "have a prey aggression and a rival aggression." The first is without affect, and is therefore objective aggression. This she felt "is the neutralized aggression to which Hartmann (1955) refers when stating that 'the highest degree of neutralized aggression is shown in nondefensive ego activities.'" Lantos continued, "Human ego activities, aiming at procuring from the environment all the objects for the gratification of innate or culturally acquired needs, use the neutralized energy of the self-preservative, aggressive, animal instincts, sublimating them, by identification with the love object, into human activities. This aggression does not originate in aggression directed primarily against the human object. We should make a point of calling this neutralized animal aggression *activity,* and differentiate it metapsychologically from that aggression which is primarily directed against the human object, working on the other pattern of animal aggression, namely, on rival aggression" (p. 118). Lantos developed this view further by noting among other derivations from this hypothesis, that "for the human, we must extend the animal pattern of rival aggression to include aggression against the frustrating object" (p. 119). She stated explicitly that she was speaking of an "original primary aggression" even where there is reactive aggression (p. 119). While I cannot share Lantos' particular phenomenologic-dynamic view of aggression, elements of this formulation come quite close to that presented in this work—a view which derives not from deductions from animal behavior, but from longitudinal direct infant observation. It is particularly interesting to compare the thesis advanced by Lantos (and later Lorenz) regarding the duality of aggression with the findings from neurophysiology reported by Reis (1973) which I shall detail in chapter 3.

In 1960 in a very different style and from the vantage point of years of clinical analytic experience and casual child observations, Greenacre remarked, as she would again in 1971, "We must look for the primordial origins of aggression as well as of libidinal pleasure in the early processes of maturation" (p. 576). She believed that aggression has its roots "in the force of growth" and the physical activity of the organism. She came close here to the views of Winnicott and Spitz. She noted that *activity,* at first physical activity, is tied to pleasure in functioning (pp. 576–77), and remarked that "the raw aggression of infancy and the concomitant pleasure in functioning [are] important in the formation of the ego and later are utilized by it" (pp. 578–79). In discussing the "antecedent stages in the development of aggression," Greenacre at this date remarked that "from the biological angle," the aggressive drive may be considered to be largely "in the service of the continuation... of the individual," that is, self-preservation.

Our own observational data strongly support Greenacre's views. During the course of maturation, Greenacre saw "spurts of aggressive behavior [in] growing motor executive abilities rather than as simply increasing destructive urges threatening to the infant and to the property around him". In this she echoed a view expressed in terms of secondary adaptation by Hartmann, Kris and Loewenstein (1949). She saw the "utilization of the energy of the aggressive drive in the biologically creative formation of new body skills" (p. 581).

In a series of three papers (1966, 1970, 1972) Solnit addressed himself particularly to the adaptive aspects of aggression. In the first two papers, Solnit presented and discussed two fascinating clinical findings: (1) Aggressive, irritable behavior in young infants (ages five to twelve months) was the first sign of recovery from a life-threatening infectious diarrhea associated with a degree of anaclitic depressive reaction resulting from separation (due to hospital isolation procedures) from mother, an already specific libidinal object (Spitz 1946). (2) In a group of children placed in foster families following institutionalization in infancy, aggressive, irritable, naughty behavior emerged when they began to form a libidinal tie with the foster parents. "Observations indicated that such behavior served adaptive functions" (1966, p. 169).

There was a shift in Solnit's view. In the first two papers, he had particularly emphasized Hartmann's formulations on the secondary adaptive aspects of aggression—especially the part played by neutralization of destructiveness—and used these to explain his findings. Although in the 1970 paper he referred in passing to Spitz's (1965) view that aggression is not inherently only destructive, he had assumed nonetheless that aggression *is* destructiveness, and that its adaptive aspects derive from the neutralizing actions of the ego and libido (fusion) on destructiveness.

In the third paper, however, Solnit (1972) hinted at further developments in aggressive drive theory, developments which seem consonant with several aspects of my own formulations (Parens 1973). Solnit emphasized that "the usual pejorative meanings attributed to aggression or aggressiveness are too narrow and not sufficiently descriptive" (p. 436). He held the view, deriving from the second instinctual drive theory, that aggression is inherently destructive and that its fusion with libido and neutralization of destructiveness are the factors operative in its becoming available to the ego for constructive purposes. Solnit added, however, the concept that aggressive energies "serve the attaching, clinging recovering functions of the young child, especially at various phases of deprivation and in recovery states from such deviant conditions. This, of course, is *in addition to the more commonly held view of aggression as a destructive impulse.*" And quoting Greenacre (1960), Solnit suggested "Perhaps, therefore, it is useful to define aggression by its literal meaning...: to approach, to step, to go, to attack, to undertake" (p. 441).

From his observational and clinical data, Solnit (1972) described manifestations of aggression from which one can infer primary destructiveness but, at the same time, aggressiveness of a different order. He described two infants in the first weeks of life who are "very active and nurse energetically, sucking and jawing vigorously." Following the developmental line reflected in this behavior (A. Freud 1963), Solnit noted about these children at seven months of age: The child "enjoys his mastery, the outcome of aggressive efforts.... Aggressively derived behavior has played an important role in the relationships, the differentiations, and the elaborating development of each child" (p. 445). While he did not say it, Solnit showed that one can trace the beginnings of this adaptive behavior deriving from the aggressive drive to a period prior to neutralization of aggression, to the first weeks of life, which would thus demonstrate an adaptive trend in aggression that is primary. This type of knowledge seems also implied by Weil (1970) who spoke of "the vigor and forcefulness with which the infant expresses his delight in human contact, or his preferences and dislikes, or his mood.... There is a balance within the aggressive drive, namely, between vigor and assertiveness on the one hand and negative moods on the other" (p. 457).

Most exciting, it has seemed to me (and evidently also to Konrad Lorenz who wrote a preface to *Human Aggression*) is Anthony Storr's significant study of aggression. In two small volumes, entitled respectively *Human Aggression* (1968) and *Human Destructiveness* (1972), Storr proposed that aggression, which he attempted to distinguish from (hostile) destructiveness, is inherently adaptive and self-preservative. Because his views were in noteworthy sympathy with those of Paul Schilder (1964), he drew on Schilder's views in support of his own. Storr developed more easily than did Lantos a duality of aggression and destructiveness which resonates well in many respects with the formulations I shall detail in chapter 3.

In 1972 Storr asserted, "If we are to understand man's destructiveness, it is vital that we distinguish between aggression as 'active strivings,' the drive toward mastering the environment, (which is both desirable and necessary for survival: and aggression as 'destructive hostility,' which we generally deplore, and which seems to militate *against* survival, at least of the species, if not of the individual.) Self-preservation and the preservation of the species demand that we actually strive toward obtaining food, space, and the acquisition of a mate with whose cooperation we can reproduce ourselves. In the pursuit of what we need for survival and self-realization we are necessarily competitive, and thus 'aggressive'; but there is no obvious reason why we should be destructive, provided we can gain satisfaction for our basic needs" (p. 20).

Storr's attractive theory is capable of pulling together those interrelated concepts assertiveness, self-preservation, mastery, non-hostile destructiveness (prey aggression), and hostile destructiveness (sadism in the broad sense). In rejecting the death instinct basis of aggression, he, Schilder, and Lantos, as do I, also shed the restrictions imposed by it which have led to the view that primary aggression is (self-) destructive only and that the contributions aggression makes to adaptation and self-preservation are secondary in nature. Storr's theory is based principally on Freud's first instinctual drive theory except that it considers aggression on a par with libido. It does, however, need further development to achieve metapsychologic status. That he comes to his views from a vantage point notably different from mine—his from clinical practice and a psychoanalytic philosophical stance, mine from psychoanalytic longitudinal direct child observation—points toward consensual validation of findings and explanation.

Also pertinent to an examination of the adaptive trend in aggression is Marcovitz's (1973) view that aggression is "an 'umbrella' term covering a ... kind of spectrum of ... various aggressive activities and relationships" (p. 227). These range from curiosity and exploration, self-assertion, the assertion of dominance, and exploitation. He then describes various types of hostility, instrumental (to hurt someone in order to accomplish some other goal), the intent to hurt or destroy the source of frustration, self-defensive hostility, and hatred. He concludes this spectrum by noting the use of hostility for the attainment of pleasure, sadism in which sexual excitement plays a part.

This author's presentation is psychodynamic and in it he makes no effort to state his views in metapsychologic concepts. As a result one cannot be certain that he speaks of a primary or secondary adaptive trend in aggression. The following summarizing quote, however, reflective of the tone and valuable aim of his communication, leads me to read it as a primary trend: "Pleasure, aggression, and the processes of mastery of the self and of the environment are inseparable at every stage of libidinal and ego development. We may deplore violence but we cannot deplore aggression. Without aggression there would be no survival, no active drive toward learning, nor to the mastery of our inner drives and of the challenges of the world around us" (p. 231). He noted that "human dignity depends on aggression. A healthy feeling of one's own worthiness depends on the ability to meet the difficulties, obstacles, and challenges that are inevitable in the process of living" (p. 232).

A number of other psychoanalysts, such as Brenner (1971), Rangell (1972), Heimann and Valenstein (1972), and Joseph (1973), have drawn attention to the difficulty in formulating the various conceptual interrelations of aggressive drive theory. As Rangell (1972) stated in his Presidential Address to the Twenty-Seventh International Psycho-Analytical Congress: "Aggression is to be differentiated from activity or mastery or forcefulness." He advised that "certain dichotomies" require clarification: "constructive versus destructive aggression; ... aggression as an instinctual discharge or aggression in the service of the ego," that is, "instrumental" aggression (p. 5). Rangell also asked "What is the role of aggression in the process of adaptation, in sublimation, in creativity?" (p. 5).

At these Vienna meetings, Stein's distressing remarks (see Lussier 1972), echoed by individual presenters, highlighted the diverse views held by analysts with regard to aggression. Several presenters at the Congress, as reported by Heimann and Valenstein (1972), drew attention to the problem of the exclusive focus on destructiveness in aggressive drive theory. This point, which harks back to Hartmann, Kris and Loewenstein's classic 1949 opus, was also emphasized by Joseph (1973) who felt we are overlooking other manifestations of aggression of equal or greater consequence that play important adaptive roles in both human development and human interaction (p. 198). Heimann and Valenstein noted (p. 32) that Freud was not unequivocal on this point. As I tried to show above, in both his first and second drive theories, Freud went beyond aggression *qua* destructiveness and pointed to relations among destructiveness, assertiveness and self-actualization through personal initiative" Valenstein duely remarked that "probably only after Hartmann's addition of an explicit adaptational point of view to ego psychology did the concept of aggression find its connection with such terms as assertiveness and self-actualization through personal initiative" (p. 32).

Heimann and Valenstein (1972) summarized that from the clinical view of aggression, it is recognized that "normally every child has a thrust toward activity, toward asserting himself and toward mastery; it need not necessarily become an overweening urge toward destructiveness." They referred to Winnicott's work which was presented by Masud Khan (p. 34). This normal thrust was emphasized by Joseph (1973) who concluded his communication with the view that "nonhostile, nondestructive ... aggressive [thought and] behavior in the broader sense of the term, ... leads to important adaptations in the interrelationships between an individual, the objects in his environment, and the total environment" (p. 212).

At present, the question as to the primary or secondary nature of the adaptive trend in the aggressive drive remains unresolved.

EGO, AGGRESSION, AND MASTERY

The Ego and Aggression
Both in the writings of Freud and in Hartmann's furthering conceptualizations of the ego (1939, 1950a, 1952) and of aggression (with Kris and Loewenstein 1949), an all-important adaptive relation is understood to exist between ego and aggression (id). The nature of this relationship, however, has undergone change over time, as new findings and new conceptualizations of psychic functioning have emerged. As I just noted above, at present, of course, there is no common agreement among psychoanalysts on the nature of that relationship.

Prior to the formulations of the second instinctual drive theory (Freud 1920) and of psychic structural theory (Freud 1923), self-preservative instincts were equivalent to the ego instincts. Among these was sadism (in 1905 especially in the form of instrumental aggression achieving the aims of the libido). This arose from a primary mastery instinct and included cruelty and destructiveness. In 1915, in drawing a distinction regarding the origins of love and hate and ascribing love to the libido, Freud made aggression more than instrumental, noting that hate (a derivative of destructiveness) could only arise from the ego instincts. In the first instinctual drive theory, ego instincts, mastery, and aggression were connected by virtue of their common origin, operating hand in hand on a primary basis. Most interestingly, after the advent of the structural model of the mind, Freud (1923), still holding to self-preservative instincts, now ascribed them to the libido (life instincts) and separated them from the mastery instinct (*Bemaechtigungstrieb*). Reversing the order of origin between aggression and mastery, he now proposed that mastery derived from the primary destructive drive. In addition, he now distinguished the concept ego from instinctual drive, ascribing the executive-effector apparatuses to the ego while assigning primary psychic motivational forces to the instinctual drives and to the id. Nonetheless, Freud (1940) held one area of primary syntonicity between id and ego: while the self-preservative instincts are represented in the id, the task of adaptation which they impel falls in the domain of the ego. Furthermore, while he did not state it, we can infer from his writings that mastery, also being a task of the ego, received input from a drive toward mastery which in 1924 he had noted arose from the destructive drive. Therefore, in the second instinctual drive theory, Freud held to but reordered the connections of ego, mastery, and aggression; now a *secondary* syntonic relation existed between them which was effected by the libido (fusion) and the ego (neutralization).

In their classic paper on aggression, Hartmann, Kris and Loewenstein (1949) took particular interest in the relation of aggression to the ego. They approached it by way of the relation of aggression to the skeletal musculature and to *action,* an interest Hartmann had already expressed in 1939. In 1949, these authors observed that "since the ego exists as a functioning organization the relation between aggression and the skeletal musculature implies a particularly close tie between the ego and aggression" in a number of important areas of psychic life (pp. 22–23).

The authors noted that "however clinically important assumptions concerning the internalization of aggression are, we cannot, in establishing general hypotheses on the vicissitudes of aggression, be satisfied with the dichotomy of self-destructive and externalized aggression. *Not all internalized aggression leads the way to destruction of the self,* no more than all internalized libidinal energy leads necessarily to self-infatuation. Freud was used to comparing the relation between narcissism and object-love to that between self-destruction and destruction of the object.... However, ... he neglected to take account of the fact that he had established a more complex concept of narcissism, which includes not only 'self-love' but also other cathexes of the self; one of the forms of these cathexes is the cathexis of the ego with neutralized "de-aggressivized" psychic energy, that does not lead to self-destruction but supplies the ego and superego with motor power and equips particularly the ego for *its function in action"* (p. 22, italics added). In 1939, Hartmann had pointed out that *action* is central in the domain of ego function. Now with Kris and Loewenstein (1949) he noted that "where aggression is involved means and ends are more highly differentiated than where libido is involved.... These means and ends comprehend a development that has led from the use of the body itself to its extensions by the tools of modern technology and to the 'conquest of nature'." Most importantly, they added: "It seems that *their importance led Freud to retain the assumption concerning the identity of ego drives and aggression* even at a time when his definition of the structural organization already implied that the controls of means and ends are to be considered as important functions of the ego as a system" (p. 23, italics added). Here the authors seem to point to two things regarding Freud's views on aggression and the ego. (1) Perhaps Freud remained influenced, even after the second instinctual drive theory was in use, by the common origin he had ascribed to ego instincts, aggression, and mastery in the first instinctual drive theory. (2) When Freud assigned the task of adaptation to the ego he nonetheless held the motivation for adaptation (self-preservation) and mastery (deriving from destructiveness) to derive from the drives. Hartmann especially, by assuming a primary antagonism between ego and id (drives), could not reconcile these relations on a primary basis, although he was not without reservations about the postulate that the destructive drive meant total destruction of organismic structures. As I described above, Hartmann accomodated to these difficulties by proposing innate noninstinctual ego energies and, with Kris and

Loewenstein, was instrumental in further developing the view that neutralization of primary self-destructiveness rendered to aggression its adaptive (self-preservative) trend. In their 1949 paper, these authors detailed extensively the large contributions aggression makes to ego development and the means by which aggression becomes available to and is implemented by the ego.

In concert with the view of Hartmann, Kris and Loewenstein is Greenacre's suggestion (1960) that aggressive is invested in ego apparatuses and functions and that in the very young child "spurts of aggressive behavior" are discernable in "growing motor executive activities." She believed, however, that the energy of the aggressive drive is utilized in the *primary* biologically creative formation of new body skills (p. 581). In this, in contradistinction to Hartmann, Greenacre saw this constructive relation of the ego and aggression to be primary.

Joseph (1973), adding his interest in *action and thought* to that of Freud, Hartmann, and others, suggested that activity in thought (which Freud regarded as trial action) partakes of more aggression than is often stated. He concurred with Hartmann, Kris and Loewenstein not only in regarding action and thought to be in the domain of the ego, but also in feeling that we have overemphasized the destructive aspects of aggression and understated the implementation of aggression in action that is adaptive and mastering. Drawing attention to Hendrick's (1942, 1943a, 1943b) postulation of a mastery instinct, Joseph noted that "it could be considered a diversion of aggressive tendencies in the service of learning, experience, maturing ego functions, and so forth— that is, in adaptation to the child's environment" (pp. 205–206). Joseph's referring to Hendrick is apt, since Hendrick noted that his concept of an "instinct to master ... was suggested to provide a dynamic explanation of the force impelling the development and exercise of ego functions" (1943a, p. 561). There is consensus among psychoanalysts that aggression plays a large part in thought, sublimation, and creativity, but, again, that relationship is variably formulated, often only sketchily.

Rank (1949) and Solnit (1966, 1970) viewed the aggressive behavior of children under varying conditions of experiencing excessive pain and unpleasure as adaptive to such experiences; they therefore ascribed the activation of such aggressive (destructive) behavior to the ego organization. Lantos (1958), Schilder (1964), and Storr (1968, 1972), especially, rejected the death instinct basis of aggression and ascribed to aggression a primary self-preservative trend. In consequence, they suggested that a syntonic and primary relation exists between adaptive (especially nondestructive) aggression and the ego.

Thus there is wide consensus among the analysts whose work is touched upon in this review, that a significant relation exists between constructive, adaptive aggression and the ego, but that relation is variably conceptualized. The tendency seems to be growing among the more recent authors quoted to ascribe a primary syntonic relation between the ego and at least some adaptive, especially nondestructive, trend in the aggressive drive, to which is added a secondary syntonicity arising from both fusion with libido and ego neutralization of self- and object-destructiveness. Since Freud's formulation of the second instinctual drive theory, Storr's reformulation of aggression and destructiveness seems to me the most extensive.

Aggression and Mastery

All these writers who proposed that adaptation is served by aggression and the ego, in turn, acknowledged the ego's task to master self and environment. This would follow, of course, but again, their formulations as to the nature of the link between aggression and mastery varied. Despite large difficulties created by the shift from the first to the second instinctual drive theory, Freud held to an intimate relation between aggression and mastery, assuming in the latter theory that rather than destructiveness and cruelty arising from a mastery drive, mastery derived from the inherently destructive drive, by means of the latter's fusion with libido and neutralization by the ego. While the libido (primary naricssism) protected the organism against its own self-destructiveness from birth, especially by turning that destructiveness outward, the ego effected its influence only after it differentiated out of the id. While Hartmann assumed that id and ego differentiate from a common matrix and that some primary autonomous ego apparatuses can function from birth, he nonetheless also inferred a delay in the ego's capability to neutralize the destructive drive. Along with Kris and Loewenstein, Hartmann proposed that neutralization of that destructiveness could begin only with the sufficient structuring of the ego as agency—although in 1955 he questioned whether neutralization might occur even prior to that point in the differentiation of psychic structure. In 1949, Hartmann, Kris and Loewenstein believed that the modification of aggression (destructiveness) by ego defenses is a "most important prerequisite of mental integration and of mastery of the environment" (p. 22).

Stone (1971) in examining the possible relation of the destructive drive and mastery asked, most interestingly, if mastery is a "tamed version" of the destructive drive, or if the latter is a "regressive variant" which appears when mastery and/or gratification fail. Stone, furthermore, felt that "the role of the drive toward mastery (*Bemaechtigungstrieb*) merits separate and extended discussion. It is mentioned by Freud as one of the major alternative modalities of aggression." Stone, who doubted that aggression is an instinctual drive, noted that mastery "lies close to the functional center of the aggressive complex" (p. 239).

The views of Hendrick and Waelder especially are of interest because they focus on the nature of mastery strivings in psychic life. As I detailed above, Hendrick (1942, 1943a, 1943b) admirably labored to propose an autonomous instinct to master, "an inborn drive to do and to learn how to do" (1942, p. 41), distinguishable from the libido—a drive which he eventually suggested was subject to the pleasure principle (tension reduction). The link of this mastery instinct to aggression was not established by Hendrick, although he noted that "most manifestations of the instinct to master cannot be empirically differentiated from sadism [aggression]" (1942, p. 54). Significant also was the derivation of *the work principle* from the instinct to master. This last step also reflects a different relation from that proposed by other analysts between aggression, the development of ego skills (Hartmann, Kris and Loewenstein 1949, Greenacre 1960), action and thought (Stone 1971, Joseph 1973), work or school, failure and success (Schilder 1964, Storr 1972), and other elements of mastery (Rank 1949, Solnit 1966, 1970).

While Waelder had criticized Hendrick's postulate of an instinct to master (1943a, p. 562), a decade later he came rather close to Hendrick's views. In 1960 Waelder rejected the hypothesis that mastery arose only from modification of the destructive drive, the latter being an unavoidable conclusion from Freud's second instinctual drive theory. Waelder believed that "the drive toward mastery displayed, e.g., in the child's play, does not in itself make [the assumption of a destructive drive] unavoidable. *A drive toward mastery or something equivalent to it would have to have a place in the normal equipment of living beings, regardless of whether or not there is an inborn need to destroy.* If we make room in our theory for such a tendency and classify it, presumably, among the ego activities, we have to recognize that this involved *a measure of aggressiveness*" (160, p. 105n, italics added).

Aggression as Ego Function
The relations of aggression to the ego raise one further large question. At a panel on the Theory of Aggression which he chaired, Waelder (Ostow 1957) asked whether aggression is an ego function. This is to be distinguished from the related issue raised by Rangell (1972) among others, indeed from Freud (1905) to the present (Stone 1971), namely, that aggression serves the ego or is *instrumental,* for example, in fueling motility to achieve libidinal gratification and other ego tasks. One gets the impression that those who suggest that aggression fuels all activity (Spitz 1965, Winnicott 1950x, Greenacre 1960) mean it in the sense that the aggressive drive is instrumental in achieving not only its own aims but also those of the libido and the ego as well as environmental demands. None of the writers referred to in this literature survey doubt that aggression serves the ego instrumentally.

The question Waelder asked, whether aggression is an ego function, however, has received little attention. Recently, Stone (1971) again raised this question. Following Freud's first instinctual drive theory and the post-1920 relations of the id and ego with regard to self-preservation, as well as Hartmann's views on the ego's implementation of instinctual drives for the purpose of adaptation, Stone suggested that "one must still think of aggression as playing an important role in the system of ego functions" (p. 224). This was also Waelder's view. Stone added: "Certainly the ego aspect holds true if one speaks, as Freud did, to the instinct for mastery, *Bemaechtigungstrieb,* as a manifestation of primary aggression. ... The impulse to mastery is an integral part of even the most complex ego activity, even in solving a problem in calculus" (p. 225). The writers surveyed here would agree with Stone that an intimate relation exists between mastery, aggression, and the ego; however, his conclusion that aggression may be an ego function is not supported by them. Rather all the other writers consider aggression an instinctual drive on a par with libido.

Through the length of his writings Freud noted a special relation between aggression and the skeletal musculature. For the most part that "preferred relationship" derived as Hartmann, Kris and Loewenstein (1949), p. 17) noted from the aggressive-discharge capability of the motor (muscular) apparatus. While the libido too is discharged by motor activity, these authors noted the greater tendency of the ego to effect the discharge of aggression via the musculature.

However, in one instance, Freud proposed a very different relation of aggression and the musculature. In 1915, in addition to its pressure or impetus and recurrent inner activation, Freud established three criteria for defining an instinctual drive, its *source, aim,* and *object.* In speaking of aggression, Freud said: "in sadism [aggression] *the organic source* ... is probably *the muscular apparatus* with its capacity for action" (1915, p. 132, italics added). With two exceptions of which I am aware, namely Solnit (1972) and Parens (1973), little has been made of this view either by Freud or other analysts.

Hartmann, Kris and Loewenstein (1949) addressed the musculature strictly as an apparatus of the ego. They emphasized the discharge function of the musculature, a function over which, in healthy development, the ego gradually gains control. In addition, they noted that "the relation between aggression and the skeletal musculature implies a particularly close tie between the ego and aggression since this organization normally controls motility" (pp. 22–23). They observed the important part played by the musculature and motility in *action*. Particularly from the fact that action is carried out by the ego via the musculature, these authors noted that (a) a preferred relation exists between the musculature and the discharge of aggression, (b) aggression "supplies ego and superego with motor power and equips particularly the ego for its function in action" (p. 22), and (c) aggression fuels the ego's control of the body and of reality (p. 18).

The relation of the musculature, aggression, and motility has been considered by several other writers as well. Winnicott (1950x), in formulating the drive he inferred from direct infant observations, at first proposed that aggression fueled the sensorimotor activity of the type I have detailed in chapter 1. Due to the difficulty of integrating this idea with existing theory of aggression, he replaced the concept aggressiveness with *motility*. Like Winnicott, Mittleman (1954, 1960) expressed the view that a motility drive would well explain the nature of the push to sensorimotor activity one observes in infants and toddlers.

Of special interest to the findings and formulations I shall detail in this work, Greenacre (1960) theorized "on the biological beginnings of aggression as it is involved in skeletal muscle maturation, and the relation of this to the development of the ego" (p. 583). She reported an upsurge of aggressive activity—skeletal muscle activity and oral aggression—at about five months of age (p. 583), a finding in our own observations that impressed us sharply and which I postulate represents a biological upsurge of the aggressive drive, concomitant with somatic neuromuscular maturation. This upsurge in aggression, which I will detail, induces the practicing subphase of separation-individuation and gives it its character. Interestingly, Greenacre noted particularly the "differentiation" aspect of this "aggressive" activity which occurs simultaneously with the first part of the practicing subphase (Mahler 1972a, 1972b, 1975). Greenacre writes: "By the end of the first six months, there is the appearance of *actively asserting pressure against* the mother as part of the growing maturational separateness" and notes the now "much more powerful thrust of body movements.... The *physical aggression* in this behavior is striking even though one cannot think in terms of motivation, but rather of a degree of biologically autonomous againstness.... In this activity there may be an increasing sense of physical power and of the ability to initiate motor activity and to control it to a degree" (p. 580, italics added). At variance with Mittleman, and reversing the course taken by Winnicott, Greenacre considered the organization of body motility to be determined by the aggressive drive (p. 581). This too was the view implied by Schilder (1964, p. 283) and Storr (1972, p. 17).

Also of large interest to the findings and formulations I shall detail in this work, is Freud's note that "the organic source" for aggression (sadism, as Freud then identified it) is the muscular apparatus (1915, p. 132). So too is the view of Solnit (1972) who, in examining the aggressive drive from the vantage point of Freud's 1915 criteria, suggested its *source*. Solnit's formulations on the source are virtually the same as my own (Parens 1973, pp. 42–43). Solnit said, "The sources could be the neuromuscular apparatus and selected major perceptual equipment (e.g., visual, tactile, and auditory)....In aggression, motoric characteristics and patterns (...reflecting...neuromuscular functions) are more emphasized than those characterized as sensuous (...erotic characteristics of engorgement, expansion, suffusion, and explosive or climatic discharge, followed by satiation)" (p. 438).

It is appropriate to conclude these notes on aggression and the muscular apparatus with Solnit's remarks regarding the part physiology research may play in clarifying further our assumptions about aggression: "For example, the skin and neuromuscular apparatus will become increasingly the window through which to observe psychoaggressive phenomena, just as the mucocutaneous junctions have served as a window to psychosexual, erogenous-zone phenomena....I would hazard a guess, along this line, that the elaboration of our knowledge about the adrenal and certain anterior pituitary gland hormones will enable us to identify more specifically the chemical messengers for aggression that will be analogous to testosterone, estrogen, progesterone, and the gonadotropic hormones in regard to biological counterparts for the libidinal drives" (pp. 443–444). Pertinent to this thought are remarks by Reis on ongoing neurophysiologic research which I briefly detail near the end of the next chapter.

FRUSTRATION, UNPLEASURE, AND DESTRUCTIVENESS

I can only briefly touch on the interrelation of frustration, unpleasure, and destructiveness. That frustration and unpleasure are directly connected to the experiencing of destructiveness has been of interest to psychoanalysts since Freud. Regrettably I cannot deal here with the limited but important frustration-aggression hypothesis (Berkowitz 1969a, 1969b) but would note as Waelder (1960) did, that any theory of aggression has to take into account the frustration and unpleasure induction of destructiveness.

Frustration and unpleasure are, of course, not equivalent. Frustration, the denial of gratification, is a large determinant of unpleasure, the mounting of stimuli to a level of experienced pain. Excessively mounting stimuli causing pain can come from sources other than frustration, such as physical pain, injury, or attack. While frustration in humans features significantly in our clinical work, in psychoanalytic theory the more basic and lower common denominator ￼ concept *unpleasure* has been found to have a greater heuristic value than frustration.

In 1915, when attempting to explicate the destructive drive derivative *hate*, Freud remarked that "unpleasure seems to be the sole decisive [factor]. The ego hates, abhors and pursues with intent to destroy all objects which are a source of unpleasurable feeling for it....It may be asserted that the true prototypes of...hate are derived...from the ego's struggle to preserve and maintain itself. As an expression of the reaction of unpleasure...[hate] always remains in an intimate relation with self-preservative instincts" (pp. 138–39).

Spitz (1965, p. 137) and Rank (1949) concurred that unpleasure plays a large part in the arousal of the destructive aspect of aggression. Winnicott (1950x), Marcovitz (1973, and in personal communication), Trilling (1973), and others suggest that resistance (opposition) to self-assertion upon an object, animate or inanimate, is the decisive factor in the arousal of aggression. I am more inclined toward Storr's conclusion (1972), one he stated while asserting the value of making a distinction between aggression and hatred: "When a man goes hunting for food, or cuts down a tree to make himself a dwelling, he is actively striving towards gaining from the environment the food and shelter which he needs. It may be alleged, with reason, that he feels no hatred toward the animal he kills or the tree he sacrifices; yet he is making an unprovoked attack upon each. It is true that, if the animal eluded and exhausted him, or the tree proved particularly resistant to his axe, the man might well come to 'hate' both, and to show undue violence to both, since frustration undoubtedly increases aggression although it does not, in my view, cause it" (pp. 18–19).

Pertinent to one aspect of the formulation I shall detail in the next chapter is Sandler's notion of "the *capacity* to be aggressive" which, according to Lussier (1972), Sandler considered "as a given, inherited by the species. This capacity is mobilized and used by the ego in ...its attempts to avoid unpleasure and pain....Anything experienced as unpleasurable mobilizes this capacity to attack. Consequently, we should distinguish between the *capacity* to be aggressive on the one hand and the drive impulses on the other, because there are not only outer stimuli to aggressive behavior but also inner stimuli which represent a drive" (Lussier 1972, p. 14).

In his searching, scholarly reflections, Stone (1971) asserted that one significant problem with postulating a primary destructive drive is that there is no conclusive evidence that destructiveness is spontaneous and can be stopped only by its gratification. In this, aggression "does not evidence one of the most important criteria for instinctual drives stated by Freud in 1915—operation as a constant force" (p. 198). As I shall note in this work, the question whether or not destructiveness is spontaneous requires a further breakdown of the question along such lines as: Is *self*-destructiveness spontaneous? Is the destruction of animate and inanimate *objects* spontaneous? In questioning the spontaneity, that is, the constant inner activation of destructiveness, is nonhostile destruction of objects to be distinguished from their hostile destruction? Such a further breakdown of this question also applies to the second element in Stone's assertion: "Can destructiveness be stopped only by its gratification?"

At the 1971 Vienna meetings, Sandler addressed this last-stated point. He expressed the view that satisfaction of the aggressive impulse is not invariably the end point of its arousal. "Essentially...it is that such reduction is achieved mainly by the feed-back information that one has fulfilled one's aim, the mental representation of having fulfilled the wish that one had" (Lussier 1972, p. 14). Sandler rightly noted that the discharge of an aggressive impulse may not lead to satisfaction, if the wish which aroused the destructiveness is not thereby satisfied. He suggests that what leads to the reduction of instinctual tension is the feed-back information that the target (of the wish) has been reached: "What seems to allow for a reduction of instinctual tension is the identity of perception between the wish and the fantasy of perception of having accomplished that wish" (Lussier 1972, pp. 14–15).

This review of the literature and the thoughts delineated in it is intended only to trace in limited detail the course taken by the psychoanalytic theory of aggression. The varying viewpoints we have inherited reflect a critical state of flux in the conceptualization of aggression. This condition is not limited to efforts by psychoanalysts to understand and explicate aggression; much disagreement and variance in findings exist as well in other disciplines that address aggression. From Freud to the present, a number of psychoanalysts' papers and books have not been included here only due to the limits of this author's energies. In what follows, I will attempt to formulate hypotheses on aggression, or to reformulate critical aspects of the psychoanalytic theory of aggression, which derive from our own direct child observational work and which find support in some of the views of others I have summarized here.

Chapter 3

AGGRESSION:
A REFORMULATION

The observational data reported in this work recommend that we consider aggression to span a spectrum whose trends extend from the inherently nondestructive to the destructive. I now want to explore each trend using as a frame of reference Freud's 1915 criteria for the determination of an instinctual drive. While the hypothesis that there may be biological life and death instincts is unsettled (see the papers presented at the Vienna Meetings, 1971, particularly the presentations of Stein [Lussier 1972] and Anna Freud [1972]), psychoanalysts as a group continue to rely on the 1915 criteria for instinctual drive confirmation (see Stone 1971, Lussier 1972).

In formulating his two instinctual drive theories, Freud was struggling to organize the same manifestations of psychic activity as those we examined in our study—namely, the various manifestations of aggression, from self-assertiveness through mastery, rage, and hate. Numerous psychoanalysts have found from their varied clinical experiences, as did we in direct observation, much evidence of an inherently nondestructive trend in human aggression. In consequence of the strength of these findings, an attempt is made here to revise the presently extant psychoanalytic formulations of aggression.

The hypotheses which follow interdigitate with certain aspects of psychoanalytic theory on aggression as developed by Hartmann (1948, 1950b, 1952, 1955, with Kris and Loewenstein 1949). What the present formulation particularly retains are Hartmann's views regarding the destructive trend of aggression—namely, his formulations on fusion with libido and on the ego's neutralization of destructiveness, the influence of object relations on the vicissitudes of the destructive trend in the aggressive drive, and the role of destructiveness in the evolving of ego defenses and in the structuring of the superego. All these our observations support and our formulation adheres to as it does to the view emphasized by Hartmann, Kris, and Loewenstein that the aggressive drive plays a large part in adaptation. On the other hand, our findings compel disagreement with the concept of *noninstinctual neutral ego energies* and with the view that adaptive aspects of aggression derive solely from the tranformation (neutralization) of destructiveness—a view necessitated by Hartmann's assumption that aggression is inherently, as instinctual drive, only destructive. As I proposed above, neutral ego energy originally derives from inherent nondestructive aggression and libidinal strivings that do not encounter resistance (prohibition) from within or without.

NONDESTRUCTIVE AGGRESSION

The term *nondestructive* has been selected over others, such as *constructive* (Rangell 1972, p. 5), or *nonhostile, adaptive,* or *benign* (Stone 1971), simply because it best represents that trend in aggression the aim of which is not destruction of self, object, or environment, but rather their control, assimilation, and mastery. It is that trend in aggression which Spitz, Greenacre, Winnicott and others believed serves *inherently* adaptation, self-preservation, and growth. As Hendrick (1942, 1943) and Waelder (1956, 1960) suggested, it *serves* mastery—an activity effected by the ego. This view is in accord with that of Freud, derived from the second instinctual drive theory, in which an energy source (self-preservation instincts) serves the ego in its task of self-preservation. Joseph, Lantos, and Storr also implicitly or explicitly suggest a primary nondestructive trend in the aggressive drive. While Solnit, Rank, and Marcovitz do not say so, they also hint at this possibility.

Continuing investigation upholds the hypothesis that the nondestructive trend in aggression can be defined according to the 1915 criteria for instinctual drives. On this subject my views and those advanced independently by Solnit (1972, regarding aggression in general) are notably close, if not indeed the same. It was from the nature of the *impetus;* the constancy and inner-drivenness, and the *aim,* that is from the qualitative character of the drive manifestations, that this study and this hypothesis regarding nondestructive aggression came into being.

The *impetus,* the constancy and inner-drivenness, of the prototypic activity are compelling evidence that this activity is the manifestation of an instinctual drive. During all the children's development, the character of the activity in question—compelling, peremptory exploration, examination, and manipulation of everything within reach—recommends that we categorize it among manifestations of aggression. I am convinced that in children ten years older such activity would in large part be attributed to neutralized aggression. That this drive manifestation occurred in infants under four months of age, however, precludes the ego's capability to neutralize aggression. The assumption was developed that this drive manifestation pertains to aggression rather than to noninstinctual ego energy. From its outset, this drive activity seemed to have as its *aim* the exploration, asserting oneself upon, control assimilation, and mastery of the self and environment. From its aim, the *object* and the *source* of this drive activity were deduced.

The *object* is that toward which the impulse is directed and becomes attached; from the first months of life on, it includes the child's own body, that of the object, and the environment. Observation permitted the inference that from the outset the object (including the self) is the passive recipient of the impulse. The object is a stimulus to the impulse in the sense of directing the attachment of that impulse, rather than in the sense of arousing it. The impulse is ready-to-attach and seeks out the object. In the first months of life the object is not yet differentiated from the narcissistic self-object—in other words, it is not a libidinal object. In the first months of life the concept *object* refers to that which becomes object by virtue of the attachment of instinctual impulses to it.

The last criterion of an instinctual drive, the *source,* was more troublesome to discern. Relying on observations and inferences which could be drawn from them, I postulated that the drive might derive from the somatic sensorimotor organization, particularly from its effector, motor aspect. I concluded that the musculature, especially the striate musculature, noted by Freud and Hartmann to be connected preferentially with the discharge of aggression, might not only be the preferred discharge pathway but, more importantly, might be the somatic origin and source of the aggressive drive. Solnit (1972) too has come to this conclusion. Indeed Solnit goes further, suggesting that more insight will be gained as knowledge increases about the hormonal mediation of the aggressive drive. He suggests that the aggressive drive may have hormonal mediation analogous to those gonadotropic and gonadal hormones known to be the "biological counterparts for the libidinal drives"(1972, p. 444). While confirmation will be no simple matter, I think Solnit is right.

It should be noted that the nondestructive trend in aggression has a spontaneous origin. From the first weeks of life, the awake, sated infant explores, searches visually more or less intently, in what may be inferred to be his first efforts to control and assimilate the environment. This spontaneity, the nonstimulated internal origin of this activity, is characteristic of an instinctual drive (Freud 1915). It is however, particularly in this feature that the hostile destructive trend of aggression is problematical.

DESTRUCTIVE AGGRESSION

A NOTE

We found much difficulty in ascertaining the nature of destructiveness in and from our infant's activities. This study in no way has helped to ascertain or reject the hypothesis that there is a death instinct from which the destructive drive derives. On the other hand, neither can, of course, our findings reject Freud's assumption that the operation of such a drive is silent—that is, not inferrable from direct observation. A distinction might be helpful here. Although our finding that nondestructive aggression is manifest in infant life before the ego, as agency, is capable of neutralization, can refute Hartmann's hypothesis that the ego has innate noninstinctual energies at its disposal, this finding, viewed from the slightly different vantage point that the ego as agency is not required to deflect the postulated destructive drive from the self, does not rule out Freud's hypothesis of a death instinct. This is so because in Freud's hypothesis, at the beginning of life the libido, not the ego, counters the influence of the destructive drive and deflects it outwardly. The libido at first achieves this end under the impetus of narcissism and the aegis of primary autonomous pleasure-ego functions, not under that of adaptive ego functions, and it can do so from the beginnings of psychic life. Although our finding cannot be used as evidence against Freud's hypothesized death instinct, it is possible to formulate hypotheses regarding our findings without relying on a death instinct to explain the nature of aggression.

Our observational data dictated three categories we took to be manifestations of *destructive* trends in the aggressive drive. As these destructive trends emerged, two were strongly evident, *unpleasure-related discharges of destructive impulses* and *nonaffective discharges of destructive impulses*. The third trend, however, *pleasure-related discharges of destructive impulses* emerged later and its nature was more troublesome to ascertain. Each trend is taken up now in turn.

NONAFFECTIVE DESTRUCTIVENESS

Eissler (1971) has argued that the sucking reflex—and the process of eating (the aim of which he asserts to be the disappearance of the object)—can be considered the prototype of aggression. In presenting this view, he acknowledges that "the neonate's survival seems to make necessary [this] act that amounts objectively to the most complete destruction possible" (p. 39). From there he generalizes: "It is possible that all acts of destruction ultimately have in the unconscious, the meaning of devouring" (p. 40). The sucking infant breaks down or destroys the food he takes in and eventually assimilates into his own body. This act manifests the tendency in animals to destroy their prey—to track down, control, capture, kill, tear apart, and finally digest that prey—thus breaking its tissues down to their molecular level. Since, as Eissler notes, this destructive process serves self-preservation and adaptation, there may be some uncertainty in discerning the aim of the impulse in question. Its aim must be, as Eissler acknowledges, perceived as destruction of the object but also as self-preservation.

Held to be *both* destructive and self-preservative, this aspect of aggression cannot be reconciled with a death-instinct-derived destructiveness, the aim of which is the destruction of the self. The aggressive drive in Freud's second instinctual drive theory clearly has as its aim the dissolution of the self; only deflection of that primary aim explains destruction of objects and the environment. It is not possible, it seems to me, to show that a drive which leads the newborn to devour milk can derive from the death instinct.

It is not necessary to develop a sophisticated argument or presentation of data to support the assumption that nonaffective destructiveness—what Lantos (1958) called "prey" aggression (destructiveness) and which is amply discussed by other disciplines (see Lorenz 1966, Reis 1973)—is an adaptive, self-preservative type of destructiveness. This destructive trend is readily documented in the animal kingdom, where all carnivores[1] survive on animal prey and all (we assume with the exception of man) have developed complex instinctive structures to insure successful adaptive nonaffective destructiveness. It is plausible to hypothesize that an instinctual drive, with evolutionary roots in such infrahuman instinctive prey destructiveness, exists in humans. While its existence may be inferred, as Eissler believes, from the beginning of extrauterine life, some may argue that prey destructiveness does not become sufficiently observable in human infants until the second half of the first year of life when teething and biting become manifest and participate in the breakdown of particulate, solid food. But it seems to me plausible to infer this drive to be at play from the first hours of extrauterine life in the breakdown of even nonsolid foods such as milk—when for the purpose of digestion and assimilation into the self milk is broken down to its molecular level—as well as from the muscular activity inherent in sucking.

The hypothesis advanced by Eissler (1971) and Marcovitz (1973), that there is a drive to destroy animal (and plant) tissue for the purpose of the eating and assimilation of vital materials, seems to me well supported by observation. In our theorizing we must account for a destructive drive arising spontaneously from within the soma, the gratification of which is compelling and unyielding. I would insist, as do Eissler and Marcovitz, that this destructive trend serves self-preservation *inherently,* in its *aim,* and that it is not necessary to assume it derives from a death instinct; rather, it has its roots in biophysiological survival mechanisms.

---

1. It is questionable if destruction of plant life is essentially less destructive than destruction of animal prey. Plants of course do not *resist* attack as do animals, or at least not in the same way, and this factor makes for a large difference in the character of the destructive effort involved.

One is compelled to propose what is well known from other behaviors in humans as well: there are destructive trends in the aggressive drive which in their aim and in their outcome serve adaptation. Hence, adaptive aggression comprises both nondestructive aggression as well as trends in destructive aggression. It would, furthermore, be plausible to suggest that a continuum may exist between these currents. This could be ascertained if the *aim*, in particular, of each drive trend could be established. This, however, is not an easy matter. It could be advanced that the *aim* of nonaffective (prey) destructiveness is described by the following sequence: *exploring* and *tracking down, asserting oneself upon* and *catching even against resistance,* bringing under *control,* and finally *tearing down structure* in order to make the process of *assimilation* possible. The aim is destructiveness. We note, however, with much interest that this destructive trend includes elements also found sequentially in nondestructive aggression: *tracking down (exploring)* and bringing the object under *control, asserting oneself upon* it, *mastering* it, and even *assimilating* it into the self.

It would seem, then, that the *aim* of nonaffective aggression is the same as that advanced above for nondestructive aggression: that is, acting upon, control, mastery, and assimilation of the self and the environment (including the object). It may be presumed that in prey aggression, tearing tissues down, breaking down structure, is acting upon in a specific manner to bring the object under control of the self, to make assimilation into the self possible. I readily concede that some unclarity may result from this formulation of the *aim*, in that it goes beyond tearing or breaking down structure, which is the legitimate paradigm of *destructiveness;* nevertheless, it is agreed by many that tearing or breaking down structure is not a sufficient paradigm for aggression. It seems to me that *acting upon, asserting oneself upon, controlling,* and *mastering* are at the center of this aspect of the aggressive drive, which, along with libido, as well as reality and the superego, makes the ego its servant.

It is not difficult to presume, therefore, a continuity between nondestructive and destructive trends in aggression. We may postulate, from the economic and adaptive points of view, that certain aspects of nonaffective destructiveness (prey aggression) have become less explicit in humans than in other carnivores, due to the civilization and industrialization of food production (there is now no need for most humans to hunt and kill prey for survival). Some aspects of that destructive aggressive trend have been modified in the course of evolution into those trends here identified as nondestructive aggression, trends which have served to expand enormously human adaptation and the achievement of control and mastery over the environment. It is not, however, necessary to presume that this evolutionary change in the aggressive drive derives from the longitudinal standing influence of the ego upon these dirves—an influence which might be invoked to explain the change from destructive to nondestructive trends since we can assume that aggression served survival and adaptation equally if not more explicitly before such large advances were made by civilization.

HOSTILE DESTRUCTIVENESS

The cumulative data in the category *unpleasure-related discharge of destructive impulses* is most impressive, both in its early appearance and in its overriding unavoidability. It appears even in what seem to be excellent child-endowment and child-object circumstances.

Of much interest is whether evidence of destructiveness of self, object, or environment (possibly deriving from a death instinct) can be found in early life. Such destructiveness deriving from an internal tendency to destroy the self, to return to an inorganic state (Freud 1920), would have to be compelling and arise *spontaneously*. Even if one does not ascribe it to a death instinct, does one find in human children from birth on evidence of a *spontaneously* arising hostile destructiveness for its own sake toward self, object or environment. Stone (1971) and Sandler (see Lussier 1972) have explicitly questioned that hostile destructiveness arises spontaneously. Stone asserts, on this basis, that destructiveness may not meet a basic requirement for consideration as an instinctual drive according to the criteria of 1915, and doubts that such destructiveness has constant, inner activation, that it has an *innately determined* internal spontaneous impetus.[2]

2. In infantile psychosis, as in less deviant development, and indeed *in normal development*, a secondary (i.e., acquired, experiential) inner activation of hostile destructiveness develops out of internalized hostile object- and self-representations.

Amply observable in neonatal life are states which permit the assumption that the normal-enough neonate is born with a capacity to experience and express rage, that he is born with a ready-to-function organization of rage experience-discharge, which is not acquired. As I have remarked, rage discharges are compelling observable evidence that the normal newborn is capable of discharging affect-laden destructive impulses; these, however, in the first six months of life do *not* appear spontaneously, but only under given conditions. The normal-enough, sated, awake four-month-old, who spontaneously discharges libido, nondestructive, and nonaffective aggression, does not seem to discharge rage spontaneously. It may rightly be argued that preconditions are also essential for the accumulation of drive tension and its spontaneous, compelling discharge with respect to libido, nondestructive and nonaffective destructive aggression. In these, however, the conditions required are determined by biological cyclical somatopsychic activity—that is, by automatic inner-determined, cyclical accumulations of libido, and nondestructive and nonaffective destructive aggression. The condition required for a rage discharge, on the other hand, is unique, as I shall note in a moment.

We sought again and again to find whether aggression identified as hostile destructiveness, or a destructiveness for its own sake, appears *spontaneously* in the first few months of life. There are some threads of evidence, but they do not inspire the confidence that they derive from an instinctual drive as do manifestations of libidinal and nondestructive aggressive tendencies. For instance, 3 month olds pull their hair or mother's hair, or scratch their faces. But in our infants these seemed to be unsustained, discontinuous, *adventitious* movements, rather than movements motivated by some psychic aim-directed energic source, with which libido and nondestructive and nonaffective destructive aggressive discharges can already be characterized.

During our continual efforts to ascertain the nature of infant rage reactions we had to conclude that there is no satisfactory evidence that these emerge *spontaneously*. We found no evidence which would lead us to infer that these destructive discharges have a somatopsychically induced, spontaneous (by virtue of biological vegetative cyclical activity), inner activation.

In speaking of biological cyclical process activity, I mean those rhythmic changes in internal equilibria which lead to the accumulation of tensions. In the psyche these are represented in the id, for example, the cyclic waxing and waning of libido. While disequilibria of the *milieu intérieur* (Claude Bernard), if sufficiently large, may lead to rage reactions, they do so by the mechanism I want to describe in a moment. Whether they arise from inner or outer origin, such large disequilibria are dealt with by the good-enough auxiliary ego on whom the neonate is absolutely dependent (Winnicott 1965, Parens and Saul 1971). At this level of consideration—the problem of the relations of biological cyclical vegetative process activity, the disequilibria of the *milieu interieur,* and the *spontaneity* of instinctual drive accumulation and discharge—one readily recognizes that no drive accumulation or discharge occurs truly spontaneously. This is, of course, understood in instinctual drive theory, where an instinctual drive is especially intended to contrast, on one hand with instincts (see Hartmann 1939, Lorenz 1935, 1966), and, on the other, with motivation which is acquired or learned.

Despite these technical difficulties, because a most important consideration arises from it, I believe it worth while to continue for the present to speak of *spontaneous* drive accumulation and discharge arising out of vegetative biological process. I feel that a critical drive accumulation and discharge occurs which differs from that induced by vegetative process and which, thus (for this discussion), does not arise spontaneously. Rather, this seems to be a drive accumulation which arises from a special *extra-vegetative reactive somatopsychic* process. Whereas we may assume libido, and nondestructive and nonaffective destructive aggression to be creative and growth-inducing somatopsychic *urges* of vegetative origin, the drive impulses under consideration here—that is, hostile destructiveness—seem *extra-vegetative reactive* in nature.

In the infant under six months, at no time were we able to assume from its phenomenology a rage discharge occurring *spontaneously.* We found that a unique condition seemed required for rage to appear: *the internally-felt experience of excessive, sufficient, unpleasure.* Not only could a cause of excessive or sufficient unpleasure be ascribed to be the instigator of rage, but we could confirm this to be the causative factor by altering the environment not to gratify the rage but to arrest the underlying, known or inferred, cause of the unpleasure. The data supporting this observation dictates the hypothesis that a source of sufficient unpleasure mobilizes destructiveness which is discharged in rage, and that gratification of such destructive impulses is a more complex matter than is the case for libido and nondestructive aggression, that this rage requires not fulfillment of itself, but rather the elimination of the unpleasure which instigated it. Hence, I advance the view, here as before (Parens 1973a), that in the first four or so months of life, the unique condition of *sufficient unpleasure—* experienced first in somatopsychic irritability—is the sine qua non of the infantile rage reaction, the first clear manifestation of hostile destructiveness in the human child.

This formulation rejects the view expressed by some that the rage discharge of infancy is no more than a patterned neonatal *somatic* reactivity; rather, it would seem that already in the neonate, *psychic* elements participate in the experience and expression of postneonatal rage. This formulation also holds that there is some basic degree of drive differentiation at birth in the human, a view I have asserted before (Parens and Saul 1971, Parens 1973a) in attempts to clarify the point that the concepts *undifferentiation* (Hartmann 1939) and *nondifferentiation* (Spitz 1965) are not absolute but relative; and that hence there is a relative degree of differentiation of psychic structure (primary autonomous ego apparatuses and functions) and of drives in the human neonate. This, of course, is consonant with the views of Hartmann (1939, 1950b, 1952).

It is relevant to our hypothesis regarding the uniqueness of unpleasure in psychic life—an all-important governing principles of psychic functioning in psychoanalytic theory (Freud 1915, Schur 1966)—that the experience and expression of unpleasure is available to the neonate (see Spitz 1965), while by contrast the expression of pleasure may not differentiate until three to six weeks after birth, emerging with the social smiling response. Wolff (1963) has found smiling responses to occur prior to the social smiling response described by Spitz (1946b, 1965), and closer exploration is required of thèse two presumably pleasure-related findings. But there is no debate that explicit expressions of unpleasure appear from birth on.

THE AIM OF HOSTILE DESTRUCTIVENESS[3]

No doubt the expression of unpleasure has a somatic root: irritability of the protoplasm. By virtue of the irritability of the protoplasm, in accord with Freud's views, the noxious accumulation of tension in the cell (organism) is experienced psychically as unpleasure. This sensory reactivity of live matter serves to protect against the destruction of the cell and acts primarily to rid the cell of noxious tension. From the adaptive point of view, it may be said that this experience of pain-unpleasure, on hand since birth, is the first workshop of the hostile destructive trend in aggression which from the outset becomes deflected toward the outside (to rid the cell of noxiae) onto the environment. The somatopsychic force in this riding activity is aggression. The activity is effected by primary autonomous *pleasure-ego* functions under the aegis of primary narcissism.

Insured by this vital somatopsychic protective mechanism, the aggressive-ridding impulse is brought about *reactively* to rid the self of the noxious agent which instigates the excessively-felt unpleasure (irritability). Near birth, of course, the specific noxious agent is not diacritically discerned; the attachment of aggressive-ridding impulses to a specific agent (object) requires sufficient ego development. Nonetheless, the existing mechanism or process of ridding oneself of whatever causes unpleasure is activated. It is, furthermore, amply inferrable from observation that in earliest life these aggressive-ridding impulses in due time first attach to the representative of the *outside*, the symbiotic partner.

I have spoken so far of aggressive-ridding impulses rather than hostile destructive impulses, because a further step has first to be elucidated before I can do so. I return to a specific observation-derived hypothesis.

Unlike libido and nondestructive and nonaffective destructive trends in aggression, hostile destructiveness does not seem to accumulate within the somatopsychic continuum due to vegetative biological processes; rather, it requires an underlying excessively felt

3. For especially helpful discussions of this point I am grateful to Dr. Eli Marcovitz (during a meeting of the Colloquium on Aggression of The American Psychoanalytic Association, chaired by Dr. Leo Stone, Dec. 1974), as well as, to members of the Child Analysis Section of the Duke-UNC Psychoanalytic Society during a presentation of parts of this study, May 1975.

unpleasure experience for its mobilization. Of critical importance, we found again and again that, as Stone (1971) and Sandler (see Lussier 1972) have noted, destructiveness of this type does not essentially require gratification in and of itself. It is true, however, that given certain dynamics, such as occur with the erotization of destructiveness (that is in sadism in the broad sense),hostile destructiveness, once unleashed, may come to require gratification. We found evidence that in certain circumstances the gratification of such destructive impulses seemed to derive strictly and simply from their discharge upon an object; in many other instances such a discharge was displaced upon a substitute object. But in many instances, a hostile destructive discharge would stop as if turned off by a switch, or even prior to its being unleashed, when the instigating source of unpleasure was successfully counteracted. For example, the imminent attack by Jane upon Temmy who was intruding in her activity would cease without fruition of that attack when Temmy retreated from intrusion. This type of behavior is well-known in the animal kingdom (Lorenz 1966, Goodall 1971, 1973, Hamburg 1973).

Now, by what step does the aggressive-ridding impulse become a hostile destructive impulse? It would seem that the important factor which modifies the aggressive-ridding into a hostile destructive impulse is the part played by unpleasure. From observations we infer that *excessively felt unpleasure introduces an all-important qualitative character into* (even the most primitive self-protective) *aggression: this painful affective condition changes qualitatively the aim of aggression, the end point of which then becomes a hostile ridding impulse, or a hostile destructive impulse. Aggression modified by excessively felt unpleasure acquires the qualitative aim of inflicting pain and harm upon and of destroying the object.* This goes beyond the self-protective ridding mechanism, becoming destructiveness for the sake of doing just that. It is in this sense, *because this aspect of aggression is anaclitic and requires the precondition of excessively felt unpleasure for its mobilization, that it does not appear spontaneously, and that its gratification is not peremptory if the source of unpleasure is eliminated.*

Widespread destructiveness, then, need not be considered to derive in humans from a primary drive to destroy for its own sake, to destroy the self or the object, or to serve a death instinct. Obviously, the problem of eliminating that widespread destructiveness is not lessened by this formulation: *since unpleasure is unavoidable from the beginnings of human life, so is the mobilization of affect-laden destructiveness.* Freud made this point clearly. In *Civilization and Its Discontents* (1930), he spoke extensively of the ways in which humans struggle to secure gratification of instinctual needs. Speaking of the process of civilization, Freud remarked: "Most important of all, it is impossible to overlook the extent to which civilization is built upon a renunciation of instinct.... *It is the cause of the hostility against which all civilizations have to struggle.*... It is not easy to understand how it can be possible to deprive an instinct of satisfaction" (1930, p. 97, italics added). He spoke of "the familiar instinctual dispositions of human beings, to satisfy which is, after all, the economic task of our lives" (p. 96).

It is necessary to quickly add that the avoidance of unpleasure, which is "the economic task of our lives," ought not to be the goal of parenting and child rearing. First of all, it cannot be achieved. Secondly, dealing with unpleasure is not only essential for survival, but induces much growth in the individual. It would be as futile and dangerous for the self to eradicate unpleasure as to eradicate anxiety, pain, and irritability of the soma, phenomena which enhance the development of adaptation, and as regards unpleasure and anxiety particularly, the development of not only the ego but the psychic structure as a whole. What is required, as with so many matters of psychic development, is to take a course between the Scylla and the Charybdis of instinctual life, between excessive gratification and excessive frustration, to insure an age-adequate balance between gratification and frustration such as will enhance the development of psychic structure.

Lantos (1958), arguing against a unilateral destructive aggression deriving from a death instinct, turned to infrahuman animal aggression for an examination of this problem. She proposed two trends in the drive, a *prey* aggression, and a *rival* aggression. Storr (1968, 1972) too came to a related view that there is aggressiveness which is inherently nondestructive and aggressiveness which is essentially destructive. Rangell (1972) asked that we compare *constructive* and *destructive* aggression. We also have recently learned of a most impressive finding from neurophysiology.

Reis (1973), in a paper circulated for the first of a series of Interdisciplinary Colloquium on Aggression[4] sponsored by the American Psychoanalytic Association, summarized the findings of a number of neurophysiology investigators—findings which are of notable interest to the hypothesis advanced here regarding distinguishable trends in destructiveness. He advanced the view that various biochemical compounds "believed to function in the central and peripheral nervous system as neurotransmitters may serve to modulate the expression of aggressive behavior. These agents are synthesized, stored, and released *by specific and discrete neural systems* in the brain." These compounds are norepinephrine, dopamine, serotonin and acetylcholine. Reis presents "evidence suggesting that each of these agents may have selective and independent actions mediating the expression of *two neurologically* distinct classes of aggression: *affective* and *predatory* aggression" (p. 1, italics added). It should be noted that Reis is speaking of two neuroanatomically, neurophysiologically, and neurologically "distinctive patterns underlying the expression of aggression or attack behaviors" (p. 2) which are found in higher vertebrates (also p. 17). "These two classes of aggression differ in their mode of expression, the provoking stimuli, the neuroanatomical substrate, and... their neurochemical modulation" (p. 2). They also differ in characteristics which makes them behaviorally distinguishable. The terms *affective* and *predatory* are particularly interesting to us. It is my impression from the characteristics of the aggression of which these terms are descriptive, that Reis's *predatory* aggression is equivalent (or nearly so) to what I have termed nonaffective (or prey) destructiveness; while his *affective* aggression is equivalent (or nearly so) to hostile destructiveness which is, of course, affect-laden. The term *affective* used by Reis is attractive because it implies the most singular factor which influences the character of that destructiveness, *unpleasure,* which leads to and becomes reflected manifestly at its farthest reaches in hostility, rage, and hate.

Reis notes that "the bulk of evidence suggests that neuronal release of neophorine facilitates or possibly initiates affective aggression" (p. 7). There is some suggestion, according to Reis, that the agents

---

4. Held in New York, December 1973, Chairman, Leo Stone.

which facilitate affective aggression inhibit predatory aggression, although not all studies are in accord on this point (pp. 11, 13). Cholinergic (acetylcholine) mechanisms particularly mediate predatory aggression, but may also facilitate affective aggression; serotonin tends to inhibit both types of aggression.

Reis's paper addresses itself to neurophysiological (and behavioral) work deriving principally from cats and rodents. He believes, however, that with due caution these findings may have implications for higher vertebrates, including humans. He notes too that the neural system which mediates predatory aggression must be particularly developed in predators. It is a moot question how much such a system is developed in humans.

These findings from neurophysiology (Reis 1973) support the assumption that there is a basic difference between aggression that is essentially nonhostile and that exemplified by infantile rage, which I consider prototypic of hostile destructiveness. In 1973 I suggested two essentially different currents of aggression, noting then that unpleasure played a unique part in their essential difference. Additional consideration, made especially clear by the thesis advanced by Eissler (1971), in compliance with the findings of our longitudinal observations, recommended the additional category *nonaffective destructiveness.*

I suggested above that the aim of the trend identified as nondestructive aggression and that of nonaffective (prey) aggression can be found along the same continuum: to act upon, assert oneself over, control, master, and breakdown for the purpose of assimilating into the self. This aim of aggression, emphasized by the authors whose views I have presented in chapter 2, is responsible for the dissatisfaction expressed by them with some aspects of existing psychoanalytic theory on aggression. Because the *aim* of these two trends can be hypothesized to be on the same *aim* continuum, we can postulate that these two trends themselves are on the same aggression continuum. It is suggested furthermore, that their somatic *source* (Freud 1915) is the same: the skeletal musculature. This musculature is not only the preferential pathway for the discharge of aggression, but in the case of nonaffective (prey) aggression contains the substrate from which, for example, tearing and masticatory impulses may be presumed to arise.

It is furthermore possible to advance the view that the *aim* of hostile destructiveness can be found along the same spectrum as that formulated for the above two trends. In this case it is: to act upon, assert oneself over, control, master, and break down unpleasure-inducing noxiae. The psychobiological influence of unpleasure is the decisive factor which warrants, however, the distinction of this current from the others. By introducing its affective character into the aggressive drive, excessive unpleasure changes the aim of the aggressive impulse, the end point of which can become *destructiveness for its own sake*. The *aim* of the modified aggressive impulse becomes: *to inflict pain* or *harm upon,* and *to effect the hostile destruction of the object* (including the self as object). Unpleasure also makes for the finding that this trend in the aggressive drive does not arise spontaneously and that its gratification is not imperative if the source of unpleasure is eliminated in sufficient time.

These basic trends in aggression are on a continuum. It is sufficient unpleasure which induces a modification in the *aim* of the aggressive drive, a modification induced by the affective tension state, by which the aggressive impulse can become autonomous from its survival value, serving destructiveness for its own sake.

AUTOMATIZATION OF HOSTILE DESTRUCTIVENESS

Some colleagues are reluctant to speak of a *hostile* destructive impulse existing in neonatal life. Freud noted that hate does not exist in the neonate, that it arises in the psyche on the way from (primary) narcissism to object love (1915, p. 136). That, of course, did not deter him from later proposing the existence of a primary self-destructiveness (1920) which in no way, however, is to be viewed as self-hate. Our findings, formulated in terms of primitive hostile destructiveness and conflicts of ambivalance, in part support these views.

In order to hold in clear focus the point I want to delineate, I will not enter here into a discussion of the rather wide spectrum of hostile destructiveness, namely its ranging from anger through hostility to hate—a crucial problem handsomely sketched by Marcovitz (1973). I am satisfied to propose for the present that the unpleasure-valenced, aggressive-ridding impulse is the first and most primitive hostile destructive impulse and that the neonate-psyche is capable of experiencing it. Whether one accepts the view that it is a primitive form of hostility or simply that it is aggressive and unpleasure-valenced, when the neonate experiences excessive unpleasure this impulse motivates or energizes action to rid the self of the noxious agent and its attendant painfully felt unpleasure. The hostile aggressive impulse, by virtue of primary autonomous pleasure-ego function, becomes attached and discharged to the outside. Because of psychic immaturity (ego undifferentiation) the impulse attaches to the *outer rind* (Mahler 1968, Mahler, Pine and Bergman 1975) of the archaic autistic (narcissistic) self. During symbiosis, with evolving ego differentiation, under conditions of excessive unpleasure experience, the hostile-ridding impulse attaches to that part of the outer rind of the self, so to speak, which becomes the symbiotic partner, the part-object of the symbiotic dyad.

In a symbiotic dyad in which excessive unpleasure is experienced too often—each child's ego having its own threshold of unpleasure—hostile destructiveness becomes mobilized accordingly and, so valenced, attaches to the evolving cathexis of the symbiotic partner. By virtue of immaturity, and hence limited differentiation of self-object, that hostile cathexis also attaches to the part-self of the symbiotic dyad.

It is, however, at the point of sufficient diacritic self-object differentiation, during the second part of the symbiosis and the beginning of separation-individuation (six to twelve months, well prior to the attainment of libidinal object constancy), that true hostility and hate begin to emerge in the psyche. Observation makes it amply clear that hostility (and hate) emerges most singularly in the child's relations to objects. When the object becomes libidinal object (Spitz 1965), attachment of hostile destructive impulses occurs first and foremost to that object.

Due to its large importance to the infantile psyche, the valence of the cathexis invested in the symbiotic partner (libidinal object) during the symbiosis and the separation-individuation phases becomes prototypic for and most influential in all subsequent object relations. So too does the valence of the cathexis of the evolving self-representation. Because of their earliest and all-important epigenetic status (in his last major work Freud [1940] noted that the earliest cathexes are indelible), these internal representations of the object and the self will spawn object relations modeled upon them. Because of this indelible and omnipresent influence, the hostile destructiveness invested in the earliest object- and self-representations becomes the fountainhead of hostility in the psyche. From this psychic structuralization, hostile destructiveness becomes part of repetitive, automatic, patterned modes of functioning in intrapsychic dynamics and in object relations. By this means, hostile destructiveness—anger, hostility, rage, hate, revenge (Marcovitz 1973)—achieves an apparently automatic spontaneity, and indeed, autonomy.[5] In consequence, I believe, one often gains the erroneous clinical impression that hostile destructiveness is an omnipresent instinctual drive which, like the other aggressive trends and the libido, is produced by vegetative life processes and must be discharged.

PLEASURABLE DISCHARGES OF DESTRUCTIVENESS—
SADISM IN THE BROAD SENSE

In the course of our observations certain data emerged, from the second half of the first year of life on, that could not be satisfactorily placed in the three categories of aggression manifestation which had up to then served us well enough. It was necessary to distinguish these data from the first three categories and, trying to devise as clear and simple a nomenclature as possible, I labeled this last *pleasure-related discharges of destructiveness*. As I noted in chapters 7, 8, and 9, this category showed two types of data, each of which is of special interest.

The first type represented by Mary's gleeful floor-pounding at seven months of age (see chapter 7) is of special interest because by its characteristics it had to be examined from the vantage point of its apparent destructive potential—the seemingly gleefull smashing of things—and from the fact that it arose spontaneously. I have been especially concerned to ascertain whether destructiveness for its own sake arises spontaneously, since it would affirm the existence of destructive impulse and that the neonate psyche is capable of destructive drive. The closest we came to such an assumption occurred during the practicing subphase when we found the type of data

5. I am indebted to Dr. Joseph Slap whose comments became invaluable suggestions.

demonstrated by Mary, or by Bernie's vigorously swinging a pull-toy which struck Candy. But under close scrutiny we felt that these instances could not satisfy the assumption that such spontaneously emerging acts represented destructiveness for its own sake. Bernie discharged aggression not just through, but upon the toy, not upon Candy. From what we could determine, Candy was not an intended target (the object of the impulse). The toy was; it was swung around, 'acted upon,' not destroyed. So too it seemed with Mary's floor-poundings. Nevertheless, I found this phenomenon most difficult to ascertain and explain. In the case of Mary's poundings, it was proposed that this discharge more correctly represents a derivative from the nondestructive trend of aggression rather than a destructive trend. In addition, pleasure-in-function seemed to play a large part in her mounting excitement. It is necessary to note that this discharge occurred at a time, during the practicing subphase, when such motoric excitement is identified not only by its pleasure aspect (its libidinal and omnipotence derivation) but equally important by the aspect of mastery of the body (especially of the musculo-locomotor apparatus), indeed by its mastery of the total self and the environment. Here the part played by the nondestructive trend of the aggressive drive in the emergence of the practicing subphase was found to be central.

From the end of the first year of life on, however, we began to find the second type of data which could be especially well distinguished by three features: *destructiveness* discharged in association with *pleasure* affects and which seemed to appear *spontaneously*. By virtue of our sufficient knowledge of these children's psychic life—having observed and known them since birth—and by the latent content inferrable from the manifestations of these aggressive drive discharges, it became apparent that a complex dynamic brought about this type of destructive discharge. It was destructive; but what of its affective condition and its spontaneity?

When Jane (1–1–12) sat on Renee's (0–6–27) head, when at 1–3–0 she playfully made as if to bite her mother, when Candy (1–7–18) smilingly pushed her head hard into her mother's face, did these discharges arise spontaneously, as did Mary's floor-poundings? We were led by the children and their material (data) to infer a pre-existing condition which determined this type of destructive discharge. It was similar to when fourteen-month-old Candy seemed to just walk up to two and-a-half-year-old Donnie and strike him one rather solid blow on the arm. It appeared to be spontaneous. But it was not at all. Three days before Donnie had struck her harshly,. She had cried but we then saw no manifest discharge of destructiveness except onto her twin Cindy and on toys. Now, three days later, with the ego in control, it seemed that Candy calculatedly unleashed destructive impulses toward Donnie. Many a time, from the end of the first year of life on, such delayed destructive discharges were encountered in all the children and it could be determined that these discharges were *not* spontaneous, but indeed had *an intrapsychically registered antecedent.*

Similarly we found the *pleasurable* affect associated with such discharges to be suspect. Teasing and taunting—and by extension, bullying, scapegoating and ultimately persecuting—which seem to emerge at the turn into the second year of life, appeared in all instances to be determined by the antecedent experience of psychic pain, that is, of sufficient unpleasure. It became necessary to assume that in such instances unpleasure-related destructive impulse mobilized by an earlier psychically painful event were antecedent to and determined the discharge of these destructive impulses now under ego control and modified affective, that is, pleasurable conditions. In these instances, the ego's growing capabilities play a most important part in delaying the destructive drive discharge and modifying its affective expression. In some instances, as in biting, nonaffective aggression and libidinal modes of discharge serve as models for these destructive drive discharges.

The first type of data—Mary's gleeful floor-poundings—I ascribe to nondestructive aggression. The second—Jane's squatting on an infant's head, or making as if to bite her mother while playing—pertains rather to a destructive trend in aggression. At an observational level, this latter type of aggression-manifestation required separate categorization: the *pleasure-related discharge of destructive impulses.* We understand the dynamics of these discharges as the delay of an *un*pleasure-related destructive discharge, modified by the ego's emerging capabilities not only to delay but also to inhibit, displace, effect reaction-formations, make-a-game-of (presublimate), and discharge under ego control. This type of data represents, therefore, the pleasurable discharge of *hostile destructiveness* and is but a variant of that trend in aggression. For this reason, being the pleasurable discharge of hostility, it warrants labeling as *sadism*, in the broad sense. In contrast, sadism in the narrow sense refers to the discharge of hostile destructiveness aroused as a precondition to erotic gratification. We take the view that, like the direct expression of hostile destructiveness, it does not arise spontaneously. Again, then, it is by virtue of early life experiences, the degree to which hostile destructiveness is mobilized and attached to self- and object-representations, by the indelibility of these earliest cathexes, that sadism becomes automatized in the psyche (see Automatization of Hostile Destructiveness, above) and may give the impression of being primary—of being an instinctual drive which inherently requires discharge.

These formulations, advanced to deal only with data observable in normal human infants, hold that the aggressive drive is a unitary drive with discernable, relatively identifiable trends, the identification of which may serve not only theoretical clarification but, more importantly, clinical understanding. Like Marcovitz (1973), I have found it "useful in therapy to differentiate the various forms of aggression in order to help a patient recognize that self-assertion does not necessarily mean the destruction of another person, or that repudiation of destructive violence need not require renunciation of curiosity or rivalry, or of other forms of aggression" (p. 232). Like Marcovitz and others (Trilling 1973), I too feel that "human dignity depends on aggression. A healthy feeling of one's own worthiness depends on the ability to meet the difficulties, obstacles, and challenges that are inevitable in the process of living" (Marcovitz, 1973, p. 232).

VARIABLE ACCUMULATION AND TRANSMUTATION
OF DESTRUCTIVENESS

Destructive impulses, it is long established in psychoanalysis, are modified by the action upon them of the libido and the ego. We presume that during the earliest weeks of life, whatever destructiveness is mobilized in the psyche is turned outward by the action of primary narcissism and perhaps even by primary autonomous pleasure-ego precursors. In these very early days, primary narcissism may already lead to the fusion of narcissistic libido with destructiveness. At this age, on the other hand, it is most likely that the primitive pleasure-ego acts only to eject destructiveness from the vegetative core of the autistic primitive self without mitigation of the impulse.

During symbiosis and the early part of the separation-individuation phase, the progressive valuation (cathexis) of the differentiating self-object leads to both fusion of destructiveness with libido, and to action by the emerging ego (as agency) to variably protect the object against the self's destructive impulses. Largely influential in average-expectable circumstances regarding the degree to which the ego safeguards the object against destructiveness is the quality of self-object experiences and the resultant valence of the object- and self-cathexes. All other factors being equal, the more positively valenced the libidinal cathexis of the object and self, the more effective and influential the fusion and neutralization of destructiveness. (For a detailed study of the vicissitudes of destructiveness in development, of its fusion and neutralization, see Part 3.)

Equally as important as the qualitative cathexis of self and object in effecting the mitigation of destructiveness is the anaclitic libidinal condition and marked ego (adaptive) immaturity of the human infant. For a long time, the young child requires the object for the gratification of his basic vegetative and emotional needs. When destructive impulses are directed to the progressively stabilizing libidinal object—from about six months of age—not only does the libido invested in the object play a large part in compelling the ego to mitigate this destructiveness, it also, due to the threat of object loss and the condition of its helplessness (anxiety), effects protection of that object, especially by the development of its neutralizing capability.

One gains the impression that fusion and neutralization act complementarily, neither being sufficient to mitigate hostile destructiveness. We infer that the young ego's capacity to progressively neutralize destructiveness depends fully on the quality of the infantile cathexes. It is well known clinically that where an insufficiently positive libidinal object cathexis is established, insufficient fusion with libido will occur, and defenses additional to neutralization will be employed by the young child to protect the anaclitically required object. For example, in cases where the object is minimally gratifying, the ego will evolve to excess the defense of splitting good and bad representations of the object to safeguard that object against the child's destructive impulses (Kernberg 1966, Mahler 1968). In such instances the destructive impulses are only held in abeyance, they are not mitigated in their qualitative aim—which is to destroy the object and/or the self. Without a sufficiently positive object cathexis, as our observations in the project and in analytic treatment have amply documented, neutralization by the ego will not effect the optimal mitigation of destructiveness which comes from its influence when it is complemented by fusion with libido.

What has been said so far adds nothing new to what is currently held regarding the *mitigation* of mobilized or activated destructiveness. The reformulation of aggression advanced in this work proposes that experiences of excessive unpleasure, when too numerous, too frequent and too harsh, lead to *increases* in the mobilization of destructive impulses in the human child. In other words, while the potential for the mobilization of hostile destructiveness is part of every child's psychic apparatus and constitutional endowment, the *actual* mobilization and accumulation of destructiveness within the psyche derives most importantly and singularly from the child's experiences of excessive unpleasure. While such excessive unpleasure may derive from varied physical and congenital sources—as in children who have significant allergies or as we found in Cindy who has minimal brain dysfunction— its most common and most important source seems to be libidinal object relations (see Freud 1930, chapter 2). Our findings on this question support and are supported by clinical experience (see the data reported in Part 2 particularly on Vicki, and the epigenetic unfolding of aggression presented in Part 3).

Hostile destructiveness, rather than being a constitutionally determined drive which obligatorily presses for discharge, is activated by specific experiences which have a common denominator, excessively-felt unpleasure. This view then must carry with it the hypothesis that the vicissitudes of destructiveness are not only determined by the degree to which its fusion and neutralization are effected *but equally by the degree to which hostile destructiveness is mobilized and accumulates in the psyche by less than optimal life experiences.*

AGGRESSION, MASTERY AND THE EGO

A singular relation exists between aggression, mastery and the ego. The beginning history of this relationship is traceable to Freud's 1905 and 1915 views that cruelty arises from a mastery instinct which pertains to the self-preservative, ego instincts. After the 1920 dichotomy, Freud still held to a relationship between the destructive drive, a mastery instinct, and a self-assertive drive (will to power) (1924, p. 163). In 1923 and in 1939 (1940), he held that there are self-preservative instincts in the id while the task of self-preservation falls to the ego. Waelder (1956, 1960) suggested that "a drive toward mastery or something equivalent to it" must exist, that it pertains to ego activities and involves "a measure of aggressiveness" (1960, p. 104n). Waelder may not have been satisfied with Hartmann's concept of noninstinctual ego energies, since that concept could easily have been fitted to suit Waelder's connecting the ego with an energy which insures mastery. It would seem that Waelder looked for an instinctual drive to fulfill this role.

Of particular interest, on another occasion, Waelder (see Panel in Ostow 1956) asked if aggression is an ego function. Other than an extensive discussion by Stone (1971), this question has created little debate. It seems to me from its effector character and from its instrumental actions, the question arises: is aggression an ego function? Aggression is par excellence the effector drive; but Freud (1909, pp. 140–141) questioned and rejected the view advanced by Adler that aggression is the motor force of all instinctual gratification. Freud held that by definition an instinctual drive has its own force, its own *impetus*. It is, however, true that aggression acts as the effector force in many instances, specifically, in many instances where instinctual gratification encounters sufficient resistance, as Winnicott (1950) and others have suggested. In 1905, Freud ascribed to aggression the task of insuring the gratification of libido, observing that aggression serves to make the object submit to the subject's libidinal claims. This implementation of aggression to obtain gratification of libidinal and narcissistic wishes is clearly instrumental (Stone 1971). Where unpleasure is experienced, the pressure, or instrumentality, of aggression may increase; and where unpleasure mounts to pain, aggression will become hostile and destructive and serve not only to achieve libidinal and narcissistic gratification, but to cause pain in and of itself; indeed, the original libidinal wish may temporarily be lost in the heat of gratifying hostile destructiveness.

Aggression becomes instrumental especially when it provides the ego with the energies required to obtain the gratification of libidinal and narcissistic claims against resistance, or to redress the ego's condition of helplessness, that is, to bring the self, the object, or the environment under control. Where this end is excessively frustrated, excessive unpleasure is experienced and hostile destructiveness mobilized. This is how and where Rochlin's (1973) view that narcissism so largely motivates aggression comes to light. Unpleasure, the activator of hostile destructiveness, is significantly determined by the vicissitudes of narcissism. There is a close connection here to Stone's significant observation (1971) that helplessness of the ego often if not invariably mobilizes aggression.

There is also room to believe that aggression, while not being instrumental in a given action, nonetheless generally or often puts its stamp on libidinal strivings. For example, the sucking characteristic for a given child, essentially a libidinal and aggressive phenomenon (Eissler 1971), is influenced not only by the pressure or *impetus* of the libido—a matter of libidinal drive endowment—but also carries with it the pressure from the characteristic aggressive drive endowment of that child. The muscular play of the mouth on the nipple is aroused in many instances by spontaneous *erotic* mucosal activity. The musculature here acts *anaclitically* rather than *instrumentally*, thus adding its weight to the impetus inherent in the libido. The sum activity we see in *erotic* sucking results from the cumulative impetus deriving from the libido (erotic trends) and an anaclitic aggressive trend.

Our findings and formulations recommend the view that aggression is an instinctual drive and not an ego function. Our findings lead to the proposition that aggression inherently serves and motivates the ego's task to master and to adapt; this can be seen as a realignment of Freud's view that certain drive trends aim at self-preservation while the ego has the task of achieving that end. It is also evident that Freud's pre–death–instinct formulations of aggression, mastery, and their inherent relation to the ego—the post–1923 ego—represent a hypothesis in many respects compatible with the findings reported here. It is possible, were it not for the formulation of the death instinct, that the new structural theory (1923) might have led to the evolving of a drive theory which, I would like to think, might have come close to the formulations advanced here that aggression hand in hand with certain threads in the libido fuel the ego's functions which in turn insure mastery and adaptation.

Part II

THE EMERGENCE OF AGGRESSION

Chapter 4

METHODOLOGY

PSYCHOANALYTIC DIRECT CHILD OBSERVATION

I elected to approach this study of aggression from the vantage point not of the psychoanalysis of young children but from that of psychoanalytic longitudinal direct observation in the spirit of the remarks of Kris (1950), Hartmann (1950a, 1958a) and Anna Freud (1958, 1965). Our model has been Margaret S. Mahler's early child development project, carried out at the Masters Children's Center (see Mahler, Pine, and Bergman 1975). We have relied not only on the directly observed phenomenology of infant and mother activities but on viewing this phenomenology as the manifestations of intrapsychic functioning, of the drives, ego, and superego. This approach, of course, derives from the posture and methodology employed by the psychoanalyst in the psychoanalysis of children. We approached our subject committed to follow the manifestations of the aggressive drive wherever these would take us, compelled by the provocative data to which I have alluded, and believing as many before us have, that our understanding and metapsychologic conceptualizations of aggression must stem from its phenomenology.

Some psychoanalysts have questioned the validity of psychoanalytic direct observational findings for psychoanalytic metapsychology (for example, see Brenner 1971, p. 140). Kohut (1971) is an example of a prominent psychoanalyst who finds himself at variance with this method. He noted that while his conceptualizations "are in comformance with the metapsychological viewpoints of psychoanalytic theory," those of psychoanalysts who employ the method of longitudinal direct child observation belong in a nonspecific "sociobiological framework of direct child observation" (pp. 218-9). As Kohut seems to be saying, psychoanalytic direct child observation does not permit metapsychologic inference and conceptualization. However, he ignores a large body of metapsychological conceptualizations which have already come to psychoanalysis from that methodology (particularly the work of Spitz and Mahler).

Other prominent psychoanalysts have opposed the view expressed by Kohut with strong conviction. In 1950 Kris pointed out that "the value of observational data has never been in question in Freud's mind. He deplored that, while writing the *Three Contributions*, he had not been able fully to utilize observational data.... Freud's interest in this problem area extended over many years.... There are ways to establish a decision but none—he argued later—is more decisive than the study of the disturbances of the child during childhood.... In speaking of childhood neuroses, Freud does not mainly refer to the psychoanalytic technique of study but to observational procedures" (pp. 38-9). Kris insisted that "the two approaches, the one by reconstruction, the other by observation, are bound to overlap but cannot be made to substitute for each other" (p. 42).

During the same period Hartmann spoke as convincingly on this issue as did Kris; he did so first in 1939 (see pp. 6, 8, 9, 10, 12) and again in 1950: "The conclusions about childhood which we reach on the basis of analysis with adults have the disadvantage that we gain them through a complicated system of reconstructions only, and through many detours of thought. This gap could be closed in part, but not completely, by child analysis. Therefore the combination of the direct longitudinal observation from early childhood on, with the reconstruction data furnished by analysis, is of paramount importance" (1950a, pp. 7-8). Hartmann felt that psychoanalysis introduced new factors into the direct observation of children, factors which are absent in "other psychological methods. Direct observation by nonanalysts...missed many central developmental positions and trends" because they did not concern themselves with observable aspects of unconscious, instinctual, and conflictual activity. Hartmann noted the necessity of an "interpenetration" of reconstructive and observational findings. Speaking of "the undifferentiated phase," he remarked, "Direct observation here helps first of all to discard hypotheses which are not consistent with behavioral data. But it is equally relevant in giving positive cues for the formulation of our developmental propositions" (p. 10).

Hartmann was firm in his stand. In 1958 he underlined again the views he had expressed in 1950 when he commented on the relevance of "prediction, or predictability" in psychoanalysis: "Developmental predictions, to be valid, presuppose a general theory of growth and development. This is probably the simplest reason why data of direct observation of children are a necessity also for analytical thinking in general. The handicap of so many analytical and nonanalytical theories of development was time and again that they were built on too narrow a base. The bridge between reconstructive data and data of direct observation is mostly to be found in ego psychology *which has developed concepts that are equally meaningful in both approaches.* ... The two series of data have to be translated into each other" (1958a, p. 121, italics added; see also 1958b, p. 135, where Hartmann affirms the same view).

On the occasion of the 1957 Ernst Kris Memorial Meeting, Anna Freud (1958) pleaded for the legitimacy of direct child observation within the framework of psychoanalytic investigation (p. 93). She hoped that her remarks would serve "to reduce the reluctance of many analysts to accept child observation and prediction of development as relevant concerns and convince them of the bearing of such clinical and diagnostic work" (p. 115).

In *Normality and Pathology in Childhood,* Anna Freud (1965) again turned to this matter. Devoting the first chapter of her book to a discussion of these two complementary psychoanalytic research methodologies, she suggested the rationale for some psychoanalysts' misgivings about accepting longitudinal direct observation as a second, sound, psychoanalytic research method. In doing so, she observed that the question whether direct observation, "namely, direct scrutiny of the surface of the mind, can penetrate into structure, functioning, and content of the personality has been answered ... especially so far as insight into child development is concerned, with increasing positiveness" (p. 11). She then suggested that some psychoanalysts have misgivings about scrutinizing surface phenomena because we have had so arduous a struggle to give unconscious life its due. In illustrating and discussing where "direct scrutiny of the surface of the mind" can permit access to latent content and inference of subsurface phenomenology, she noted that a "multitude of attitudes, attributes, and activities is displayed openly by the child...in whatever setup is chosen by the observer. Since each item is tied genetically to the specific drive derivative which has given rise to it, they permit direct conclusions to be drawn from the child's behavior to some of the concerns and conflicts which play a central role in his hidden mind" (pp. 21-).

Of course, we all recognize that studies in which direct observation and analysis can both be worked in combination on a given child, provide an immeasurable advantage for the validation of each method. Such studies, for example, are reported by Ritvo and Solnit (1958) and by Burlingham (1963).

Finally, it should be noted that Lustman (1963), too, addressed himself to this question in a report on research in psychoanalysis. He considered first and most important the method to be provided by the process of psychoanalysis. About psychoanalytic direct child observation, he pointed out that it has been "particularly fruitful in infancy and early childhood....Its contributions to psychoanalytic theory have been rich and extensive" (p. 54). Lustman rightly, however, cautioned that there are significant limitations to the yield from this method, that there are always "risks in speculation" and the danger "that one may 'lend too much depth' to the observation...to support one hypothesis rather than another" (p. 66).

This limited review is closed with the note that according to Lustman, Albert Einstein, in speaking of the thorny path from empirical data to postulation, said: "The way is so difficult that no methods whatever must be barred; no source of meaning whatever, imaginative, theoretical of whatever kind, are [sic] to be excluded" (Lustman 1963, p. 68). To the best of my knowledge, every psychoanalytic writer who has employed or advanced the usefulness and potential of longitudinal direct child observation has advanced it only to complement the unique method available to us in the psychoanalytic process.

I concur with Kohut's (1971) view that "the core area of psychoanalytic metapsychology...is defined by the position of the observer who occupies an imaginary point *inside* the psychic organization of the individual with whose introspection he empathically identifies" (p. 219n). The best path to that core area is the transference; it is from the transference that most of what has entered into the theoretic domain of psychoanalytic metapsychology has done so. However, the transference is not the only entry way for metapsychologically valid observation and formulation. Much evidence shows that direct observation, too, may yield invaluable *metapsychologic* conceptualization.

THE EARLY CHILD DEVELOPMENT PROJECT—EPPI-MCP[1]

The frame of reference of this project is classical psychoanalytic metapsychology. The investigative method employed is that advanced by Ernst Kris (1950), Hartmann (1950a, 1958a), Anna Freud (1958, 1965), Spitz (1946a, 1965), and brought to its most successful evolution to date by Margaret S. Mahler (1965, 1968, and with Pine and Bergman 1975).

Research Approach

Our research approach is *observational;* but by a commitment to the mothers and children, we also make efforts to educate the mothers regarding their children's behavior and needs. Occasionally we intervene vis-a-vis a child when it is indicated—which will be touched upon below. Twelve infants and their mothers are the subjects of this study which continues to be part of current and ongoing research started in 1969. We intend to continue to observe each child for as many years as circumstances will allow. To date, we have met as a group twice weekly, for two-hour periods, in the large living room of Henry House, in the Children's Unit of The Eastern Pennsylvania Psychiatric Institute. The mothers bring all their children who are not

---

1. This project is part of the Early Child Development Program and Project, Henri Parens, M.D., Director and Principal Investigatyor; Eastern Pennsylvania Psychiatric Institute, Robert C. Prall, M.D., Director Children's Unit; Medical college of Pennsylvania, Selma Kramer, M.D., Chief of Section of Child Psychiatry and Project Consultant. The Project described and reported upon in this work is Project No. 2: *Toward an Epigenesis of Aggression in Early Childhood.*

in school, but it is those children whom we have seen since birth who are our research subjects. The infants are cared for by their mothers, the staff observing. The preschool children, including our now five-year-old subjects, meet in an adjacent toddler area equipped and staffed to meet their preschool needs—personnel, paper, crayons and pencils, games, puzzles, and mid-morning snacks. The children are free to move between the infant area, where the mothers tend to stay, and the toddler area. Participation by all families is, of course, completely voluntary. Our contract with them simply states that if they permit us to observe naturalistically the development of their children, we will attempt to the best of our ability to answer any questions they have pertaining to the meaning of their children's behavior and to their rearing.

Functioning in the project as *participant observers,* we do not use one way mirrors. The word *participant* takes on a limited meaning here. Each research staff member is constrained to not interfere with mother-child interactions or with the child's spontaneous activity. Taking the stance of the child analyst who responds to the child's use of objects, the research staff member attempts not to impose his particular needs, wishes, or interests on the child. Despite the fact, however, that we prefer to act primarily as a recording instrument, we do become engaged by the children and their mothers within certain permitted parameters. Even though we respond variably to the children and their mothers, our first and sole research task is to observe them, keeping our focus on the several areas under investigation.

While our research approach is observational, our method is also *interventional* in several ways. First of all, we participate in the mother-child interaction just by being present when these interactions occur. While we try to set the mothers and children at ease, they inevitably modify their conduct because we are with them. Secondly, we answer the mothers' questions about their children's behavior in terms of psychic development. In addition, at times we draw their attention to a behavior which warrants discussion either to enhance understanding of it or to note its importance for their overall knowledge of their child.

We have tried to avoid transference induction; nonetheless, some elements of transference-like relations have developed which have disadvantages and advantages for our research aims. We do not psychotherapeutically treat the mothers in the project; we do not address ourselves to the mothers' dynamics or affects. Where we have seen the need for treatment in a mother, a therapist has been assigned to work with her outside of the project.

Neither do we treat the children in our project. Where we have seen trouble brewing we have intervened with an occasional insight-promoting comment and rarely with an interpretation. (The rare interpretations have been made only by the principal investigator who is a child analyst.) In two instances, it became necessary to institute individual psychotherapy for a child due to the emergence of unyielding symptomatic behavior. With regard to both mothers and children, as clinicians we feel bound to recommend and institute therapeutic intervention where sufficient disturbance appears.

The Subjects

All but one of our subjects considered in this study were volunteered by their mothers *before* they were born; the single exception was volunteered at seventeen weeks of age. Families from the lower and lower-middle socioeconomic population, white and black, they were among a group that had participated in a community summer nursery program. Only pregnant mothers were recruited. Four volunteered; one of the four delivered twins. None were clinic patients. Soon after our observations began, one mother from our clinic population was accepted into the project when her infant was seventeen weeks of age. We thus started with six infants who were close to the same age. Two more mothers also joined the project, each with a newborn, within one year of the onset of our observations. In addition, four of the seven mothers have had another child since the project started, and these also have become research subjects.

As it evolved, ten of our twelve subjects are normally endowed constitutionally, both in terms of somatic and psychic dispositions. One subject is a moderately cerebral palsied child, and another, from close to birth showed evidence of minimal brain dysfunction. These conditions were determined by pediatric, psychological, and psychiatric evaluations ongoing during the course of our investigations.

Collection and Recording of Data

Data collection was done by two basic means and two methods of recording were employed. The basic and fully relied upon means of data collecting was *the direct observation of each child* in our nearly-as-possible naturalistic setting. Each child could be seen for two hours twice-weekly from birth. Attendance was, of course, not ideal, but it was notably good (see table 1).

The second means of data collection, much less relied upon but enriching of direct observation, was the casual conversational gathering of information (by professionals) as to the child's activities outside the project arena, that is, at home and elsewhere.

Data recording from the outset of the project consisted of extensive note-taking for each visit which was then entered into a chart on each child. It was focused on specific lines of psychic development and on the defined areas of investigation. In addition to charted notes, the principal investigator, filmed from one hundred to two hundred feet of data each visit with a 16mm. movie camera. In addition, at scattered monthly intervals, our masterful Audio-Visual Media Director, Mr. Jacques Van Vlack, took several hundred feet of sound film. Since September 1973, upon the acquisition of video taping equipment, Leafy Pollock, M.S.W. has been taping a half hour of each visit of data pertinent to the areas under investigation. Twice-weekly research conferences have served to verify data collected and provide opportunity for critical discussions of the data and all research-related matters.

SOME PROBLEMS IN THE METHOD

The first and foremost problem inherent in the method of direct observation lies in the limitations to which one can infer latent content, so to speak, from manifest data. This problem is well recognized by psychoanalytic investigators as I pointed out at the beginning of this chapter. The assumption is made that inferences deriving from this method gain strength from two sources: (1) validation by data from reconstruction, and (2) consensual validations advanced by other psychoanalytically trained investigators and/or by the reproduction of data and inferences from further, repeated psychoanalytic investigation. Interpenetration, as Hartmann meant it (1950a), and mutual validation of data and inferences derived from observation and reconstruction provide a rigor and discipline which, for our field, is surpassed by no other existing investigative method.

The second problem is that while the psychoanalytic process is particularly limited in the reconstruction of preverbal development

Table 1

Research Subjects

Child's name	Age at time of this writing * (years-months-days)	Time attended (%)**	Comments
Jane	5–6–3	98	
Anni	4–0–7	90	
Candy	5–4–10	95	attended project until age 3–10–30, then observed in day-care center intermittently
Cindy	5–4–10	95	attended project until age 3–10–30, then observed in day-care center intermittently
Temmy	5–6–4	75	
Bernie	3–7–22	75	
Harold	4–8–3	95	Attended except for 6 month period, from age 3 to 9 months, when not seen at all
Doris	2–1–21	95	
Mary	4–3–28	75	
Vicki	5–3–18	50	
Renee	4–11–16	40	
Louise	1–4–14	70	

* All the children but one have been seen as project subjects since their birth; the exception is Temmy who joined the project at 17 weeks of age.

** Sessions are held twice weekly, Tuesday and Friday, from 9:30 to 11:30 A.M.; project closed during the month of August.

and experience, we must note that direct observation has its serious limitations here, too. When we examined behavior during the perverbal period of development, we were often frustrated that the children could not verbalize what they experienced, that they could not by verbal means add weight to what we inferred from their behavior. To a significant degree direct observation is frustrating too then, in as much as it cannot provide assured means to break through the nonverbal barrier from the behavior to the experience of the very young child. In spite of this limitation, however, much data *is* available. We relied on all those indices of intrapsychic life manifested in behavior and affects, indices we avail ourselves of in the analysis of children: their social, play, and skill-related actions, their affects, their direct and indirect nonverbal and preverbal communications, their responses to communications from the environment, their manifestations of defenses, etc. We proceeded from the assurance of Hartmann and Anna Freud that "there [has] emerged over the years 'a growing awareness of the sign- or signal-function, behavior details may have for the observer' (Hartmann 1950). As a by-product of child analysis many of the child's actions and preoccupations have become transparent by now so that, when observed, they can be translated into the unconscious counterpart from which they are derived" (A. Freud 1965, p. 18). We found this particularly to be the case where observations on the same small group of children are carried out extensively, regularly, and frequently enough from birth over a period of years. One gains the impression that technical-analytic acquaintance with the child's innate endowment and evolving psychic functioning along the three lines of structural differentiation can reach a noteworthy degree of confidence.

The third problem is an intricate one which remains to be assessed in detail—a task we cannot undertake now—and we will note only two aspects of it here. In time a special positive feeling developed among the children and their mothers vis-a-vis the staff, the project, and each other. The children (and mothers) came to recognize that certain attitudes and interests prevailed, that certain matters received attention in the project, that here they could enact and, when they got old enough, they could talk about matters of vital importance to emotional growth which were either suppressed or otherwise ignored elsewhere. Fortunately, this did not interfere with our observations or with the inferences deduced from them. Jane, for example, brought to the project her ambivalent feelings about giving up her bottle. Mary enacted her practicing subphase conflict in our midst. Even Donnie, the sibling of but not himself a research subject, would instruct his mother to try to find some helpful solution with Dr. P. to his having lost control over destructive impulses the day before. All child analysts have found and are aware of this phenomenon, that even three-year-olds know that certain events in psychic life can be talked about with the analyst as they can be nowhere else. For us, the great advantage was that the children presented material in the project which might otherwise not have reached the surface and, therefore, not have become available to us.

Underlying this same special positive feeling for the project was, of course, the attachment to the staff members which developed eventually on the part of the mothers and children. Since we did not engage in psychotherapy with them, these object attachments are best referred to as "transference-like reactions." Since we were participant observers a relationship inevitably developed, forged by mutual interests, by the reliable steadiness and character of our meetings, and by the interestedness of the professionals in the mothers and children. The "transference-like relationship" developed and with it a therapeutic potential emerged. In nearly all circumstances, however, interpretations were discouraged because of the stated purposes of our investigations. The rare therapeutic intervention in the project itself was carried out in the spirit of Anna Freud's remark (1958) that an analyst can, from the stance of longitudinal observation on a given child "combine past and present information for the purpose of analytic action...[and] dissolve [a symptom] almost immediately by means of analytic interpretation" (p. 99–100). It was clearly not in the format of our study to treat the children or mothers, nor to interpret analytically their behavior; while we rarely interpreted a child's troubled behavior, we at no time interpreted the mothers' behaviors or transference-like reaction.[2]

We feel, however, that there is large merit in the development of these transference-like reactions: they permit access to some latent

2. In one child, psychotherapy was instituted when a serious, unyielding depression appeared. The treatment of this child was carried out by a member of the project staff, Rogelio C. Hernit, M.D., while the mother was seen at first by Charlotte Blyn, M.D., then by Elizabeth Scattergood, M.A.

content which we might otherwise not as readily infer. The results of our rare interpretations have helped to confirm inferences which we have made from direct observations. Similarly, confirmation of some of our inferences have also come from the fulfillment of certain predictions which we have made on the basis of observational data and the explanatory psychoanalytic assumptions with which we work.

The fourth problem resulting from our methodology arises from the fact that we could study only a small number of children during any one longitudinal period of observation. This is not to pejoratively compare this psychoanalytic methodology with other formal psychologic and medical investigative models because I agree fully with Lustman's view (1963) that psychoanalytic methodologies have to develop from *within* psychoanalysis and seem not to succeed—at least as shown so far—when modeled on those of other scientific disciplines. It is so, nonetheless, that we can only study a small number of subjects at once over a relatively long period of time. One by-product of this limitation in subjects, and in our time and energies, is that we have not yet had the opportunity to examine in the manner of this methodology the vicissitudes of aggression in severe states of frustration, deprivation, malhandling, or pathology. Even the most extensive disturbances we observed in our subjects were limited in degree. Therefore, many data that should ideally enter into a study of aggression are not available to us at this time.

FRAME OF REFERENCE—SYMBIOSIS AND SEPARATION-INDIVIDUATION THEORY

Before proceeding to our findings, it may be useful to outline briefly the frame of reference used in our observations of aggression: Mahler's theory of *symbiosis and separation-individuation* (Mahler 1965, 1968, Mahler, Pine, and Bergman 1975). The stages of *libidinal object* development formulated by Spitz (1950, 1965) will be weaved into the fabric of intertwining developmental lines proposed by Mahler.

The theory of symbiosis and separation-individuation essentially covers the first three years of life. At birth, the child is in the *normal autistic phase.* Because of the immaturity of his ego apparatuses and his drives, he is in a state of primary narcissism wherein he perceives all experiences to derive from his amorphous, primordial self.

From the second month or so, he moves into the *normal symbiotic phase* during which he becomes progressively aware of the mothering person who becomes his libidinal object, but he experiences that object as if self and object are in a common symbiotic membrane, whereby the object is *perceived intrapsychically* as a part of the self.

From the middle of the first year of life, at the height of the symbiosis, the child begins the process of separation-individuation—a more-or-less life-long endeavor to resolve the childhood symbiosis. This process of separation-individuation in the first three years of life has distinctive features which cluster into what Mahler has called the *separation-individuation phase,* which begins at about five months of age and lasts on the average to the age of thirty to thirty-six months. The task of this critical phase is to differentiate and stabilize a conceptual and psychic representation of the self and of the object as two separate and individual organisms out of the fused self-object experience of the symbiotic phase. Because of the complexity of the work done during the separation-individuation phase, Mahler found it useful to detail it further into four overlapping but sequential subphases which she named respectively: (1) differentiation, (2) practicing, (3) rapprochement, and (4) toward self object constancy.[3]

NORMAL AUTISTIC PHASE

In the normal infant, the *normal autistic phase* extends from birth to approximately six to twelve weeks of age[4] when it gives way to the phase of *normal symbiosis.* The autistic phase is characterized by a primitive "state of sensorium" (Mahler 1968), of narcissistic self-sufficiency, when, it is postulated, the human infant experiences all satisfactions to arise from within himself. Due to the immaturity of his ego at this time, the infant does not recognize internal as opposed to external events, and does not experience the self as compared to the object (other). It is assumed that he experiences self and object,

3. The fourth subphase, so far defying simple nomenclature, has most recently been described under the title: "Consolidation of Individuality and the Beginnings of Emotional Object Constancy" (Mahler, Pine and Bergman 1975).

4. Emphasis is placed on the view that these dates are only intended to give an impression of the timing of emergence and the duration of these developmental phases. Normal children vary widely in their schedules of development.

internal and external, as continuous and as pertaining to the primordial self. This means then that the newborn cannot distinguish whether tension reduction arises from the self or the object. Mahler (1968) postulates that by means of *primary autonomous ego apparatuses*—the only relatively-developed neonatal ego mechanisms—the experiences that are pleasurable and good on the one hand, and unpleasurable and bad on the other, "the two primordial qualities of stimuli," are deposited in memory traces.

Until about six weeks of age, the id and ego are essentially undifferentiated (Hartmann 1939) and primary narcissism is absolute (Mahler 1968). From the time of her original formulations on the subject, Mahler (1952) has suggested that this phase is brought to an end when awareness dawns in the infant that help and nurture come from outside the self. An inextricable part of this dawning awareness is the beginning of the differentiation of inside-outside (internal-external) and I—not-I (self-object). "The task of the autistic phase is the achievement of homeostatic equilibrium of the organism within the new extramural environment" (Mahler, Pine and Bergmann 1975, p. 43).

This normal autistic phase coincides in psychic development with *the objectless stage* of Spitz's theory of the development of the libidinal object.

NORMAL SYMBIOTIC PHASE

This phase starts in the normal infant from about 6 to 12 weeks of age. The *nonspecific social smiling response* (Spitz 1965), a good index of its onset, indicates the dawning perception of the nonspecific, need-satisfying object. The symbiosis, generally extending to about ten months of age, reaches its apex in the child's psychic awareness and in intensity at about five months of age with the establishment of the *libidinal object* (Spitz 1965) and the first peak of separation reactions.

While her concept of normal symbiosis, according to Mahler, dovetails with Benedek's use of the term *symbiosis* with reference to the mother-infant relationship, it also differs from it in important respects. Mahler's concept does not, as does Benedek's, describe a psychobiological dynamic state of mutuality between two separate organisms. Mahler's term stands for the concept that the absolutely dependent infant *intrapsychically* experiences his mothering object as being enveloped with him in a symbiotic, unifying membrane; therefore, the symbiotic dyadic representation, as this theory assumes the child experiences it, can be said to be *I—not-I*. Infantile narcissism ensures this experience of oneness, of hallucinatory or delusional omnipotent fusion of the mother with the still undelineated primordial self.

The symbiotic phase runs parallel with the second and third stage of Spitz's formulation of the development of the libidinal object. With the advent of the *nonspecific social smiling response,* the infant enters the normal symbiotic phase of Mahler's theory, as well as the preobjectal stage of Spitz's theory. From this *nonspecific* reaction to *any object* which he encounters face to face over a period of three to four months, the infant progressively develops the ability to distinguish the partner of his symbiosis from other persons. Preferential, and increasingly *specific smiling responses* to this *specific object* evidence the infant's attaching libido most intensely and especially (in usual and optimal circumstances) to his symbiotic partner who gradually becomes established intrapsychically as his *libidinal object.* In association now with the evolving of the specific smiling response, one also finds somewhat lesser smiling responses to other familial and familiar objects, as well as the absense of such smiling responses and, indeed, the presence of *stranger responses* to unfamiliar objects. These varied responses evidence that the infant is beginning to develop a hierarchy of first-level object-relatedness. At the peak of the symbiosis, he or she has, according to Mahler and Spitz, intrapsychically established the *libidinal object.*

During the first part of the normal symbiotic phase then—from about the second to the sixth month of life—the infant moves from the point of psychobiologically perceiving objects as indistinguishable one from another, to attaching psychologically to one specific object, his symbiotic partner, whom he can now recognize and distinguish from others. From the sixth month through the remainder of the symbiosis, he essentially experiences that object as if attached to him in a symbiotic membrane.

From the peak of the symbiosis, occurring at about five months, the infant consolidates the libidinal relation to his symbiotic partner. The all-important gain made by establishing his symbiotic partner as libidinal object brings with it unavoidable occasional painful experiences associated with separation from that object. At this time too, reactions upon sighting strangers and on separation from mother are often intensified. During this latter part of the symbiosis—from about five through ten months of age—under the impetus of the thrust in the id and ego to develop, he begins the process of separation-individuation.

An unavoidable conclusion of the theory of symbiosis and separation-individuation is that an *"optimal human symbiosis"* is paramount for optimal psychic development (Mahler 1968). The normal symbiosis indelibly binds the individual child to his particular mother. The character of his symbiotic experiences, the pleasurable, reliable, stable relations to the symbiotic object, as well as the experiences which are unpleasurable and/or hostile, will leave their indelible mark in the development of his id, ego, and superego, and of course, in his object relations and individual personality. The theory also holds the view that a seriously pathological symbiosis is "the core disturbance" in infantile, adolescent, and even adult psychosis (Mahler 1968).

SEPARATION-INDIVIDUATION PHASE

During this phase the human infant differentiates out of his intrapsychic symbiosis with his mother (mothering person) into a relationship in which the child intrapsychically experiences the self and mother as actually separate, individual organisms, related by an indelible emotional bond. This part of the life-long separation-individuation *process,* extending from about five to thirty or thirty-six months, is a dynamic state in the child in which the fantasies and feelings of oneness with the object alternate and coexist more or less with fantasies and feelings of individuality and of separateness of self from the object. In the analogy of a reversible chemical equation, optimal progressive development induces an age-adequate shift to the right in the complemental series: symbiosis—separateness and individuation.

The separation-individuation process moves along two intertwining tracks: one of *separation* leading to intrapsychic awareness of separateness of self and object; the other of *individuation* leading to the evolving of the sense of self and of individuality (Mahler, Pine and Bergman 1975, pp. 63, 292).

This developmental phase, as noted before, is subdivided into four partly overlapping but sequential subphases: differentiation, practicing, rapprochement, and consolidation of individuality and beginning libidinal object constancy (or toward object constancy).

First Subphase: Differentiation
Beginning at approximately five months and extending beyond ten months, this subphase may be characterized by the child's earliest efforts at separating bodily and psychically from the mother, as evidenced in some pulling away behavior of the infant-in-arms. At this time, the child appears to be compelled from within to experience separateness, to put distance and space between himself and his symbiotic partner; and he experiences this as pleasurable. At this time too, however, separateness imposed on him by the necessities of everyday life may be felt by him as extremely painful, as manifested by separation reactions and anxiety and longing for the mothering person. During the evolving of this subphase, which overlaps with the second half of the symbiosis, the newly established *libidinal object* (Spitz) becomes fairly stabilized intrapsychically. Protracted, unsubstituted loss of the libidinal object, who is still the symbiotic partner, leads to that severe syndrome, anaclitic depression, which Spitz has described (1946a, 1965).

Second Subphase: Practicing
Launched in large part by locomotor maturation, the practicing subphase extends from approximately nine to fourteen or sixteen months. It is characterized by highly pleasurable exploratory motoric distancing of the self from the mother in a manner described by Greenacre's apt term *love affair with the world.* In many normal children, during this period of overlapping differentiation and practicing subphases, the pleasure deriving from mastering the locomotor apparatus and the environment is occasionally interrupted by unpleasurable fantasies and feelings of separateness with which the child deals by a visual or locomotor approach to the mother, an adaptive mechanism which Furer and Mahler identify as *emotional refueling.* Overall, however, during the practicing subphase many children experience long periods of obliviousness to being separate from the mother (while the mother is in the familiar surround) due to

the shift of the attention cathexis from relation to the object to the development and mastery of specific ego apparatuses, especially locomotion. This obliviousness stands in notable contrast to the prior and overlapping *differentiation* subphase, as well as the following *rapprochement* subphase, in which separations from the libidinal object are often experienced painfully.

Mahler further divides this subphase into two parts: "(1) the early practicing phase, ushered in by the infant's earliest ability to move away physically from mother by crawling, paddling, climbing, and righting himself—yet still holding on; and (2) the practicing period proper, phenomenologically characterized by free, upright locomotion" (Mahler, Pine, and Bergman 1975, p. 65).

Third Subphase: Rapprochement

This subphase extends from about eighteen to twenty-four months. The word is highly descriptive not only of the manifest behavior of the child, but especially and most importantly of the intrapsychic process which Mahler infers from that behavior. A new awareness of separateness seems to be experienced by the toddler who can now move away and approach the mother at will. There is a notable tendency again for the child to stay closer to mother, to draw mother into his orbit of activities, and to react more acutely to separation from her with more differentiated longing and grief, and with anxiety and rage. These affective reactions, indeed, the high increase in differentiation of manifest behavior (sensorimotor activities, fantasies, as seen in early symbolic play, affects, and new ego skills) indicate a sharp increase in differentiation of the ego, superego-precursors, and the drives.

According to Mahler, this subphase has particular sensitivities and a psychic organizing capability upon which subsequent psychic development heavily depends (in the sense of Rangell's view of the oedipus complex as psychic organizer, Spitz 1965). This is largely due to the difficult task and resultant conflict then imposed by development: on one hand stands the wish to separate and individuate out of the symbiosis against, on the other, the regressive pull of the normal symbiosis and the wish to remain one with mother. Appearing in more or less acute form, this conflict leads to what Mahler and her coworkers (McDevitt and Bergman) have identified as a rapprochement crisis.

Recently, Mahler has suggested that the rapprochement subphase can be subdivided into three periods: beginning rapprochement, the rapprochement crisis, and individual solutions of this crisis (Mahler, Pine and Bergman 1975, p. 89). From the polarity of wishes and psychic pressures characteristic of this subphase, a number of derivative anxieties may follow, such as dread of separateness, dread of the regressive pull of the symbiosis, and helplessness in the face of the dawning realization by the child that he is small and is not imbued with the omnipotence which he had narcissistically ascribed to the symbiotic partner from whom he is now separating and individuating.

Fourth Subphase: Toward-Object-Constancy
The last of these subphases extends from about twenty-four to thirty-six months of age. As Mahler has emphasized, the attainment of libidinal object constancy is not completed by the age of thirty-six or so months. The goal of the separation-individuation phase is to attain a sufficiently stable degree of object constancy and a sufficient beginning consolidation of individuality. These intrapsychic achievements are manifest in, and made possible by, the child's experiencing the relationship to his mother with enough positively valenced feelings toward her. Because he can now retain intrapsychically the image of his loving and protecting mother, even in her absence, he can separate from her without undue anxiety or longing and grief and without growth-inhibiting defenses against such affective reactions. This development indicates that the normal symbiosis has been sufficiently resolved with optimal differentiation of the self and the object, as well as the ego and the drives. Evidence of the child's age-adequate autonomy—not just of narcissism but of a beginning sense of self and individuality—appear in all aspects of his psychic functioning.

Following this brief exposition of Mahler's theory of symbiosis and separation-individuation I want now to present the method of data ordering we employed in this work.

CATEGORIES OF MANIFESTATIONS OF AGGRESSIVE DRIVE ACTIVITY

While observing our children when they were under four to six months of age, we found manifestations of aggression in their behavior which challenged the view that all aggression is, in origin, inherently destructive. Hypothetically based on the death instinct, the aggressive drive has been postulated to be in origin a purely self-destructive drive. According to this postulate, during infancy, by virtue of primary narcissism (the libido being all invested in the primordial self), destructiveness is turned toward the outside of the self, and later, by the influence of the ego, is respectively fused with libido and neutralized. By this, the ego achieves protection against self-destructiveness as well as mastery over the destructive drive.

The qualitative aspects of aggressive drive discharges in our work are determined by clinical judgment, the assumption that a discharge—whether in action or fantasy—is fueled by neutralized or unneutralized aggression depending on various manifest characteristics of the discharge. We assume, for example, that much unneutralized aggression exists in the psyche in which impulsiveness, undue intensity and pressure to discharge, lack of control over pain-inducing, or destructive action is characteristic of such discharges, as is found in harsh temper tantrums or rampaging cannibalistic fantasies. By contrast, where an aggressive discharge is characterized by the ability of the self to modulate it, to control it sufficiently, to discharge it in graduated doses and in a socially acceptable manner, we speak then of the ego's having to a greater degree neutralized aggression. And we have assumed that much constructive activity, including, for example, driving a truck, doing school work, and all forms of sublimation (artistic and scientific) implement neutralized aggressive energies.

Following especially from Hartmann's work, psychoanalysts assume that the neutralization of aggression is carried out by the ego. It seems plausible to presume that *neutralization of aggression is an ego function* which becomes operative only when the ego becomes functional as an agency. That is, the ego then begins to function at an organizational level capable of experiencing *anxiety* (Freud 1926), a *wish* (Schur 1966), and *intentionality* of action (Hartmann 1952). This occurs from about the latter half of the first year of life. At this time, the infantile psyche has structured, that is, invested emotionally in, a libidinal object (in Spitz's sense), this attachment to the object being specific and stably enough discriminating. In line with this thinking, one would expect to find neutralization of aggression to begin at the earliest from about six months of age on. Our findings on this question, which are reported in this work, support Spitz's belief (1965) that neutralization of destructiveness begins in the last third or quarter of the first year of life.

Hence, finding activity in infants *under four to six months of age* which had characteristics clinically inferrable as being motivated and fueled by neutralized aggression presented us with the dilemma already detailed. To investigate that dilemma, as we carried out our naturalistic observations of the children, we were prepared to look in their behavior for the manifestations of instinctual drive activity (Loewenstein 1940) along lines postulated by current psychoanalytic theory. I came to feel that, for the sake of a useful phenomenology, cumulative observations warranted our categorizing manifestations of aggressive drive activity into the following groups:

1. unpleasure-related discharge of destructiveness

2. nonaffective discharge of destructiveness

3. discharge of nondestructive aggression

4. pleasure-related discharge of destructiveness
These categories are now described.

UNPLEASURE-RELATED DISCHARGE OF DESTRUCTIVENESS

The interrelation of two features distinguish this category from the others. First, that one can infer *inherent destructiveness* from these behavioral manifestations. By *inherent* is meant that this type of discharge is not acquired ontogenetically; it is not learned, but is an innate disposition which we found to be ready to function at birth. By *destructiveness* is meant the tendency to tear down structure (an operative system, animate or inanimate); this is done against resistance since all structures (systems) have a greater or lesser degree of stability. Second, these discharges are invariably accompanied by, associated with, *an affective state of unpleasure.*

In this work the rage reaction of infancy is taken to be prototypic for this category of aggression discharge. While there is varied opinion on this matter, the rage reaction in infancy seems to have discharge qualities clinically characteristic of destructiveness. Although the human neonate can neither conceptualize nor has the capability to destroy an object, an unmitigated discharge of this type at a later age would readily be identified by the clinician as destructive. Repeated observation leads to the consideration that the rage reaction of infancy is a somatopsychic—not only a physiologic (Spock 1965)—discharge pattern in which destructiveness seems manifestly aroused by *sufficient unpleasure* in the infant. In this as in the other categories there is a range of drive discharge, the rage reaction being at one end of its spectrum. The intensity and duration of this type of destructive discharge, as well as the affect which accompanies it, tend to reflect, along with certain variable ego and drive dispositions, various intensities of excessive unpleasure from milder to unbearable unpleasure.

NONAFFECTIVE DISCHARGE OF DESTRUCTIVENESS

This category is distinguished from the others by three coexisting features. First, as with the category described above, is the inferrable tendency to *destroy,* to tear down structure which is unavoidably done against resistance. Second, this discharge is essentially devoid of an affective concomitant; it is essentially *nonaffective.* And third, it may arise *spontaneously* within the child, being determined by somatopsychic processes. It may be useful, following a line of thought suggested by Eissler (1971), to consider this category of destructive impulse discharge to be represented in early psychic life by feeding activity. Eissler and Simmel (1944), although from quite different vantage points, both equated the intake and assimilation of food (viewed by them, of course, as being the gratification of libidinal erotism as well as of the need for libidinal and physiological supplies) with making the object disappear by destroying it. Eissler suggests that sucking might be considered equally prototypic for libido—the gratification of mucosal erotism—as it could be for destructiveness, that is, the breakdown of animate structure. It must be noted, however, that such destructiveness serves to effect the assimilation of organismic products for the purpose of combining other cells with the self, a self-preservative trend which Freud eventually (1920) ascribed to the libido (Eros) and not to aggression. Here, the aggressive factor in neonatal sucking activity, and later of eating activity by biting and chewing, will be considered to be prototypic for *destructive* activity which does not have an essential *affective* component.

DISCHARGE OF NONDESTRUCTIVE AGGRESSION

This category is distinguishable from the others by virtue of its *not having an inherent destructive* character while it is recognizable by its characteristics to pertain to aggression. I mean such activity as determination to get hold of (pressured manipulation and exploration) and to assert oneself upon, control, and apparently master the self and the environment, including its animate and inanimate objects. The earliest form of this type of aggressive discharge appears during the symbiosis in pressured motoric activity. The compellingness, or inner-drivenness, inferrable in the activity and its constant appearance during states of alert wakefulness at this age, give the impression of drive activity and of aggression. At a manifest level beyond the first year of life, this category of discharge can become troublesome to distinguish from neutralized destructive (aggressive) discharges, the distinction of an inherently nondestructive from a neutralized destructive discharge being best assured when such a discharge emerges prior to the ego's capability to neutralize destructiveness.

PLEASURE-RELATED DISCHARGE OF DESTRUCTIVE IMPULSES

This category, the last we found to emerge ontogenetically, is distinguishable from the others by the interrelation of two features: *destructiveness* and a *manifest pleasurable affect*. We found pleasure-related destructive discharges of a convincing kind only from the latter quarter of the first year of life on. At that time, after the structuring of the libidinal object we found *teasing* and *taunting* by the child to best exemplify the category in question. As development proceeded, pleasurable and intentional causing of pain in others (sadism, in the broad sense of the word) emerged quite more convincingly. Its intentionality (Hartmann 1952) presupposes that the ego is structured as an agency before such destructive discharges occur.

I want to note from the outset that while it is useful to categorize the manifestations of aggressive drive discharges according to their phenomenology and discernable psychodynamics, such categorization is neither achieved with facility nor is it always satisfactory. Its greatest assets, which make its weaknesses tolerable, have been first, the order it lent to an otherwise rather bewildering amorphous mass of data; second, its pointing to hypotheses regarding trends in aggression. And third, its providing one more approach to the difficult problem of discerning metapsychologically and clinically the nature of aggression, its epigenetic evolving, the conditions for its discharges, and the character of its contributions to conflict, adaptation, and to the development of psychic structure.

Chapter 5

THE NORMAL
AUTISTIC PHASE
(Birth to 6 or 12 weeks)

Of the children's activities, the following seem to be the normal observable activities, behaviors, and affective states from which one can *infer* the discharge or motivational influence of an aggressive impulse during the phase of normal autism.

MANIFESTATIONS OF AGGRESSION

UNPLEASURE-RELATED
DISCHARGE OF DESTRUCTIVENESS

The earliest manifestations of a destructive impulse we inferred from observations are to be found in the rage reactions of infancy, which are prototypic for this category of aggression discharge. At this time in the child's development, we observed only one major class of events from which this type of aggression discharge could be inferred: behavior reactive to more or less intense and protracted somatically painful stimuli (experiences). Other precipitating events made their appearance in later developmental periods.

Somatically Painful Stimuli
Many sufficiently intense or protracted painful stimuli, physiological or physical, yield a mounting, although at times spasmodic, unpleasurable affectomotor discharge which can culminate in rage. These are well known phenomena such as protracted delay in

gratifying thirst and hunger, somatic irritations like excessive gut tension, skin urine burns, and malregulation of temperature. The role of *pain*-unpleasure is central in this category of phenomena.

Especially crowded and understaffed hospital nurseries are. a laboratory where every day a number of infants can be seen more or less gradually working themselves into a rage until they are picked up and cared for. Many infants who are cared for well enough tend not to experience such rage reactions since their expressions of unpleasure, fussing and crying, tend to mount gradually allowing time for the caretaker to assuage the pain-unpleasure at its source before rage appears. In other circumstances familiar to all clinicians who work with children, in which due to various difficulties in the caring, holding environment, the response to the infant's mounting crying is delayed, rage reactions are readily observed. There are, of course, many variations of responsivity in neonates (dictated by their constitutional endowment and somatic dispositions) which play a dominant part in their experiences of pain, unpleasure, and rage. From the first days of life, Cindy would tend to waken from sleep rather abruptly and very quickly; before preparation to care for her could be mobilized, her reaction to mounting unpleasure would crescendo rapidly into rage. This distressed her mother terribly. By contrast, her twin Candy would waken more gradually; her fussing was benign and due to her innate dispositions and to the smooth, well-tuned mother-child interaction, she showed no rage reactions at all.

During the first weeks of life, variations in drives and primary autonomous ego apparatuses notwithstanding, all the children in our project, except perhaps one,[1] we felt would (and some occasionally did) readily go into a rage if the mothers allowed their discomfort to go unattended long enough.

The earliest rage reactions occur within hours of birth. Some infants, of course, cry sharply and frenetically once out of the birth-canal— some due to the birth process itself, and some in reaction to such

---

1. Anni, whose neonatal cerebral-palsied state heavily dampened her reactivity to internal and external painful stimuli, went for hours without stirring for food and would require stirring by her experienced and skillful mother for even widely spaced feedings. Later in development she could well have shown rage reactions following upon excessive unpleasure; but I cannot be certain that within hours from birth such reactions would have followed upon prolonged deprivation of even basic needs for survival.

ministrations by medical personnel, as the treatment of their eyes with silver nitrate. While there may be some argument that the burst-like, sharp, or frenetic crying of the normal newborn seems insufficient evidence of marked unpleasure and rage, it is but a matter of hours from that time before a convincing rage reaction can be evidenced in a normal neonate who remains unfed for too long.

NONAFFECTIVE DISCHARGE OF DESTRUCTIVE IMPULSES

Some infants under twelve weeks are found to scratch their face or their mother, or to catch their nails in their swaddlings. At times, of course, such phenomena result from the motor discharge which accompanies rage reactions. At other times, however, these occur during motor discharges that seem not to be part of an unpleasurable experience. Are these acts then motivated by a destructive impulse? It seems necessary to ask whether, at this age, there is a category of behavior leading to self-object injury, however mild, which is not associated in origin with unpleasure—that is, behavior from which we can infer the motivating influence of *a destructive impulse which is not mobilized by unpleasure.* Such an impulse would then seem to arise *spontaneously,* namely from a cyclic somatopsychic source.

Whether or not to infer the *spontaneous* discharge of a *destructive impulse* from such face-scratching, is not a simple matter. Our research team felt that such activity was accidental and seemed to have *no psychical motivating content,* for example, when the nail made contact with the skin of the object during what seemed to be an adventitious physiological motor discharge. We know that the motor cortex is capable of spontaneous spike discharge and of spontaneous paroxysmal discharge (in seizures)—in other words that it is capable of what we believe to be purely physiological activity. On the other hand, we hold the view in psychoanalysis that the destructive drive acts by an inherent principle of constant activation which is capable of smaller or larger *spontaneous* impulse discharges, and that initially the neonate has little control of those impulses through primary autonomous ego apparatuses. It may be that some internal, somatic stimuli, without causing a discernible level of unpleasure, induce a motor discharge which can lead to a sweep of the arms with an adventitous nail to skin contact. Or, the discharge of a Moro reflex induced by an adventitious noise (an external stimulus) may under set circumstances lead to a scratch. However, such an externally induced startle reaction which has reflexive motor components must also be considered in terms of pain-unpleasure experience and may be a manifestation of aggressive discharges assignable to painful stimuli.

We found two of our infants to have a self-inflicted facial scratch. Such instances were rare; however, adventitious, grasping reactions which at times caught clothing were not rare. The facial scratches did not occur during observation by ourselves or the mothers, and we, therefore, could not determine whether they had been associated with a rage reaction or if they were of spontaneous, other-than-*un*pleasurable origin. In short, I could not ascertain nor infer with sufficient confidence that these scratches were motivated by a destructive (psychical) impulse.

Our way is clearer in another set of data of which we need hardly give examples. As we have noted, we owe to Eissler (1971) and to Simmel (1944) the consideration that *nonaffective destructive impulses* may best be represented by the *psychic determinants* of feeding activity. Eissler and Simmel, although quite differently, both equate the intake and assimilation of food with making the object disappear by destroying it. Eissler suggests that sucking might be considered the prototype of aggressive drive activity. The vigorous character of the sucking response in some of our infants (Jane and Temmy), and in one instance particularly (Anni) the lack of vigor, were strikingly suggestive of levels of aggression.

Two brief if contradictory remarks are in order here. First, when Freud struggled with a question along this line (1909, pp. 140–141), he concluded that libido was capable of variable pressure, since any instinctual drive, by definition, has an inherent force of its own. Hence powerful sucking may reflect high levels of libido without the influence of aggression. On the other hand, in support of Eissler's postulate is the belief extant in psychoanalysis that from birth the joint action of libido and aggression is postulated to occur in much, if not all of, psychic life.[2] In fact sucking could be equally prototypic for libido (the gratification of mucosal erotism) as it could be for aggression (in Eissler's view, the

2. While, in terms of their extrauterine history, the drives are in their most undifferentiated state at birth, there is evidence for the assumption that the libido and aggression are distinct, separate drives already from that time on.

breaking down of animate structure). As I have noted, however, such *destructiveness* serves to effect the assimilation of organismic products for the purpose of combining other cells with the self, a self-preservative trend.

While some may be skeptical that sucking activity is representative of a destructive impulse discharged upon the food that is ingested and digested, it is less doubtful that such tendencies exist in the psyche with the advent of teeth and the use of the biting, masticatory apparatus. Nonetheless, in both cases, the object is broken down, structure is destroyed, by the process of feeding. It is important to note that there is no constant affective component associated directly with the psychic determinants of feeding activity. The distress, and even the rage, reaction of the infant who cries for food is viewed in this formulation as part of the pain-unpleasure experience which arises out of excessive hunger in the face of infant helplessness, and is not in essence part of the motive force of feeding activity itself. In later years, the routine scheduling of food intake insured by the ego prevents the experiencing of excessive unpleasure arising from undue hunger and at this point, unpleasure *as a manifest affect* may play no part at all in the motivation to destroy for the sake of feeding the self.

DISCHARGE OF NONDESTRUCTIVE AGGRESSION

This category is distinguished by virtue of its *not having an inherent destructive* character while it is recognizable by its characteristics to pertain to aggression. This category of data is better represented by material from the next phase, the *normal symbiotic phase,* and especially the *practicing subphase;* its earliest features, those apparent during the normal autistic phase, only weakly demonstrate the characteristics of this type of drive discharge. The largest group of data from the normal autistic phase pertains to exploratory activities, mostly visual at this time, and to primitive efforts to assert oneself and motorically control the nipple, largely with the mouth and snout.

PLEASURE-RELATED DISCHARGE OF DESTRUCTIVENESS

This category of destructive discharge becomes evident from the latter half of the first year of life. We looked for discharges in which destructiveness seemed manifest in association with a pleasurable affect in infants under six to twelve weeks of age. First of all we found, as did Spitz (1965), that explicit pleasure manifestations in infants prior to the emergence of the *social smiling response* which emerges from about six to twelve weeks of age—are very meager as compared to the manifestations of unpleasure which are vigorous and many. Nonetheless, persistent in our effort, we found musculomotor discharge phenomena which appear to be accompanied by excitement, seem pleasurable, are often rhythmic, and may pertain to beginning libidinization of the motor-muscular apparatus. The infant may exhibit a series of short-arc, vigorous arm wavings which, at this period, seem to be spontaneous. The spasmodic stretching during yawning, for example, may be followed by an abrupt after-discharge of pendulum-like movements of the arms. The stretching of yawning and that on waking seem to have this affectomotor quality as well. Of course, all our infants showed this type of seemingly pleasurable musculomotor discharge. But after much deliberation on the question of their nature, much uncertainty remains. For the present I have to be satisfied with viewing these as physiologic discharge phenomena which do not have a primary psychic content and do not represent an aggressive instinctual drive discharge at all. The character of this seemingly pleasurable musculomotor discharge is notably different from that which emerges just beyond six months of age.

In summary, during this first phase of postnatal life we found clear evidence of two of the categories delineated: the *unpleasure-related discharge of destructive impulses* and the *nonaffective discharge of destructive impulses*. During the normal autistic phase *discharges of nondestructive impulses* were only very weakly manifest; these become observable and seem to emerge during the normal symbiotic phase which follows. We found no satisfactory evidence of *pleasure-related discharges of destructive impulses* during the autistic phase; these appear during the latter part of the first year of life.

Chapter 6

FIRST PART OF THE NORMAL SYMBIOSIS
(6 or 12 Weeks to about 5 Months)

Entry into the symbiosis (Mahler 1965, 1968) is effected by, and carries with it, the first large psychic changes after birth. Benjamin (1961a, 1961b, 1963) reported on a critical psychophysiological organizational shift in the postneonatal period which may underlie this large change in the six-week-old. The infant begins to recognize that help comes from the outside. Narcissism, while still *primary,* is now no longer absolute as it was during the neonatal weeks (Mahler 1968); gradually part of the libido becomes narcissistically invested in the symbiotic partner who is then experienced by the child as part of the self. The first experiences of object recognition, signalled by the social smiling response, lead gradually over the next four months, by means of progressive differentiation of the budding ego and the drives, to the intrapsychic structuring of *the libidinal object* (Spitz 1950, 1965). We see a progressive specificity of the smiling response complemented by increasing and intensifying stranger reactions. The structuring of the ego as agency begins during the latter part of this period (Spitz 1965, Parens and Saul 1971).

MANIFESTATIONS OF AGGRESSION

UNPLEASURE-RELATED
DISCHARGE OF DESTRUCTIVENESS

We looked for whatever possible data emerged from which we could infer a destructive impulse during the first part of the normal symbiosis.

Painful Stimuli
Painful stimuli effect such a discharge at this phase, as they do during the normal autistic phase. There is some differentiation in the affective manifestations from mild displeasure to rage reaction. Some experiences yield an explosive, sudden discharge of rage (as in acute abdominal distention), while others, like thirst and hunger, which mount gradually can be followed through a more progressive discharge pattern of vocal-and motor-muscular apparatuses. When an infant is four to five months of age, and in many instances earlier, many a mother can identify unpleasure reactions of a variety of origins by their already variable discharge patterns.

Undue Restriction or Interruption of Sucking, Nutritive and Nonnutritive, or of Contact Needs (Libidinal Gratification)
Little doubt was felt by Mrs. K. and the observers as to the cause of Jane's abrupt rage reaction (8-2-4) when mother pulled the bottle from her infant's mouth at a moment of rest in sucking. There was consensus that the rage was directed against the mother (symbiotic part-object) who has interfered with ongoing gratification. At the same time, the infant's peremptory demandingness suggested that the symbiotic part-object was expected to allay the tension over which the infantile ego had no control. At this level of development, this last remark relies heavily on assumption; later, there is no question whom the baby turns to for relief from unpleasure. Our assumption for this period, in this child, derived from the visible establishment of a good-enough normal symbiosis and on evidence of her healthy, resounding narcissism.

Libidinal nongratification may cause reactions of frustration and of rage at an even earlier age. Anni, at four weeks, fussed and cried as she seemed to waken. Her mother picked her up and, without feeding or other change in her condition, held her on her chest; the infant stopped fussing and slept. After about fifteen minutes of uninterrupted sleep in mother's arms, Anni was put down and within minutes started to fuss again. Once picked up again she slept peacefully on her mother's chest until they left, over a half an hour later. This demand for gratification by the object world can be expected from the normal symbiotic phase infant, who will express needs for libidinal nutriment, even though the object has not yet become specific, and will usually express unpleasure when these needs are unduly restricted or interrupted.

Acute Stranger Reaction

Our findings agree with Spitz's views (1950, 1965) on the timetable and formulation of the development of the libidinal object. During this first part of the symbiosis, which coincides with Spitz's preobjectal phase we found, earlier than we had expected, that as the *nonspecific smiling response* (which attaches to the *nonspecific part-object)* progressively differentiates into the *specific smiling response* (which attaches to the specific, libidinal object), stranger responses began to appear in some of our infants from as early as ten weeks. At 0–2–1, E.H. (staff member) picked Jane up and, facing her, chatted and cooed. Jane's mother, who was getting her coat, was not visible to Jane. Jane looked at E.H., and after a moment's hesitancy, smiled for two seconds. The smile stopped; she looked quizzically at E.H., then burst into a cry. This was repeated twice at a one minute interval. When the mother returned, Jane smiled broadly and excitedly. By this time we could classify her smiling response as *specific* since it suggested a preferential cathexis of her mother. At 0–2–29, she had a notable stranger reaction to a visitor; Jane screamed when mother left the room and the stranger remained in her field of vision.

Early stranger responses also occurred with Temmy who came to our program at seventeen weeks (see table 1, p. 135). She manifested not only the stranger responses that range from on-and-off smiling to sober-faced visual exploration of the stranger, but also, what seemed to be an acute, early form of anxiety-like stress reaction. She could reliably be calmed by physical contact with her mother. In this seventeen-week-old, who suffered sharply in our stranger environment with its stranger objects, it was early but clear that were the mother not to make herself physically and emotionally available, the child would soon become panicky and enraged. The mother did not permit the child's anxiety to become too sharp, and therefore, we did not see rage reactions. These, however, could easily be extrapolated from what we did see.

Traumatizing Object-relatedness

For some time, Vicki's mother was emotionally depleted and sadistic in her object relations. During Vicki's first six months of life and later, her needs for contact were often rejected. When she cried sharply for a bottle, her mother claimed that all Vicki wanted to do was eat. This depressed mother at this time cuddled her child poorly, and Vicki's rages arose many times from the frustration of libidinal needs. Since Mrs. V. could not gratify her infant's demands for normal symbiotic (part-object) libidinal gratification, Vicki adapted to her mother's efforts to make food intake do instead. Hence in those months she was our fattest infant, and her mother's complaint that she ate too much was justified. We postulated that during Vicki's first year, the mother's transient gratifications of her infant's libidinal and physiologic needs secured the infant's investment of libido and aggression in her mother sufficiently to structure a specific libidinal object, but an object whose mothering caused excessive unpleasure and aroused much destructiveness.

In addition to the frustration of libidinal needs, the sadistic treatment Vicki experienced at the hands of her overburdened and resentful mother was especially distressing. Too long delays in gratification, the pulling out of a bottle at midsucking, painful and enraging nose cleaning, brusque physical handling, while falling also in the categories of painful stimuli and frustration of needs, must also be considered especially as traumatizing object-relatedness. This separate category is warranted by the fact that the symbiotic partner, the protector against the development of rage, is also the inducer of rage by her own underlying, unconscious hate which has become directed against her child. Whereas Temmy's mother (and generally our other mothers as well) prevented rages from developing out of the child's acute stranger reactions, Vicki's mother unwittingly induced rages which she felt were the unavoidable result of her necessary care-taking methods.

Frustration of Nondestructive Aggressive Strivings

It is at this time in development, in the course of our observations, that we were confronted with that aspect of the aggressive drive for which we were not prepared. From nine to ten weeks of age on, some of our infants showed a remarkable degree of behavioral activity fueled by a nondestructive current of the aggressive drive.

We found that at times excessive frustration of such nondestructive aggressive strivings led to mounting fussiness, crying, and even rage. Renée, just three months old, had been visually exploring a six-cubic-inch, brightly-colored felt block, for about sixty seconds. As she continued to look at it she seemed to become more and more activated. More and more she moved her arms, kicking her legs rhythmically, her mouth opening now and then, her hands exhibiting discharges of the grasp reflex. Her affect appeared pleasurable and became more excited while her total motor activity became more energetic and increased in rate. We noted that she was also salivating and thus, we assumed, exhibiting concomitant libidinal excitation during this mounting exploratory-motor excitation.

In spite of all her motoric activity, Renée could not yet approach the object that held her attention cathexis; for all her efforts to grasp and mouth the block, she stayed put and could not achieve tactile-mucosal exploration. We then observed during the peak activity, the appearance of unpleasurable affect on her face; she began to cry, in our judgment, frustrated that she could not reach her objective. Her mother here intervened and comforted her. Renée's reaction is not uncommon.

Things become complicated rather early. At 0–2–29, Jane fussed when outside clothing was put on her. She was put in the carriage by E.S., still fussing but she quieted for a bit. When her mother came into view, she began her crying complaint sharply again from which we inferred: "Get these things off of me, I hate them." We postulated that her rage was aroused by the restrictive effect of the outer clothing which, among other things, inhibited her exploratory motor discharge.

DISCHARGE OF NONAFFECTIVE DESTRUCTIVE IMPULSES

As was noted for the normal autistic phase, during this early part of the symbiosis such specific acts as scratching one's face seem to suggest nonaffective self-destructiveness; but these acts are not cyclic, are not peremptory, and tend to appear adventitiously. For example, Renee had a face scratch which was associated with an accidential sweep of her arm. Similarly, self hair-pulling was found in several children. Cindy showed such activity in association with tension and irritability. Jane, Temmy, Renee and Cindy all rubbed their hair in what seemed a discharge of destructive impulses, but this seemed more commonly associated with affective and behavioral evidence of unpleasure.

The conclusion was sustained that nonaffective destructiveness is best represented at this time in development by oral activity which leads to the breakdown of animate structure derivatives for the purpose of eating and digestion.

NONDESTRUCTIVE AGGRESSION—ITS APPARENT EMERGENCE

We found in our infants from the early days of the normal symbiotic phase (in some as early as nine weeks) a remarkable degree of drive activity, the character of which we have been hard put to understand.

Jane, 0–3–1, had comfortable sleep and wake states. From the age of nine weeks (when we became impressed with this activity), when she was awake and hunger-sucking was relatively quiescent, she was *constantly* looking, be it at mother's face, at observers, at a bell, at the lighted window, at the source of a noise. The persistence of this looking, exploring activity was compelling; she did *not elect* to look[1]; she looked, driven from within to look, and, at the risk of thinking teleologically I would add, to gratify the push from within to master (synthesize, integrate) her perceptual field. If the item which she was exploring visually was removed, she followed it up to a point, not always when it disappeared, then just shifted her exploratory activity elsewhere. This child, and the others, taught us how very driven an infant can be to master inside and outside—not yet differentiated— and how indeed exhausted that infant can become from that activity. At ten to twelve weeks, when, after seventy-five minutes of *constant, driven* visual and motor exploration, Jane fell asleep, observers agreed that she was exhausted.

---

1. Infants, however, at times elected to look away from an observer when looked at in testing for early stranger responses.

At 0-4-17, Jane was beginning to crawl with good hip-leg integration. Hand-mouth integration developing successfully; she now held and fed herself a cookie; she held and directed the bottle to her mouth; her reach, arm-outstretched, grew longer daily and now where it was insufficient to reach the object held by her attention cathexis, she crawled to it. Her searching-exploring activity was rich; no destructive drive seemed inferrable by the quality of this activity; her mouthings seemed nondestructive. At 0-4-24, Jane crawled excitedly exploring nearly continually for two hours, taking four ounces of juice at the one and half hour point. The directedness of her exploratory activity was firm. Like Candy, Mary, Harold, Doris and Bernie, she approached her target with assertiveness. She exhibited frustration when we took away the toys she was exploring. She became fussy and cried, and was comforted by mother. Her fussiness stopped when the toys were returned to her, even when her mother put her down.

Having come to rely on Hartmann for the latest advances in our understanding of instinctual drive theory (1939, 1948, 1950b, 1952, 1955, with Kris and Lowenstein 1949), we at first put forward the explanation that neutral ego energies fueled this activity, and that libido accounted for some of its affective coloring and pressure. But the more we looked at it, the more we felt it to pertain to that aspect of aggression we expect to find where neutralization has had a sufficient influence: self-assertiveness, a pressure to explore, get hold of, assimilate, and master the environment. It was the pressure, the affect of determination to get hold of, grab, and to subject to constant, energetic exploration with pleasure, seriousness, excitement, and at times, frustration at failure, that made us doubt that the concept of neutral ego energies is sufficient to explain the character of the activity in question.

We found it necessary to put forward an explanation that could approach satisfying our experience of the children's behavior as aggressive without being at all, inherently, destructive, and this prior to the possibility of neutralization. In due course, we have found all our infants to show this type of pressured exploratory activity, some less pressured, less vigorous, some later than others, but with a realiable constancy.

We raised the possibility that the drive which fuels this activity, in line with the thoughts of Spitz (1965), Winnicott (1950), Storr (1968), and Greenacre (1971), may be a trend of the aggressive drive that is inherently nondestructive, that while it is represented in the id, it inherently serves the ego without requiring neutralization. In all other respects it serves the ego along the same lines as Hartmann (1950b, 1952, 1955) and Kris (1955) proposed of neutral ego energies.

It is well to note here that we found looking-exploratory activity in the neonate, during the normal autistic phase. Thus Bernie, at twelve days of age looked about a good deal when awake, and when held by his mother would already look at her face with attentiveness and persistence. However, it was especially during the beginning of the normal symbiotic phase that we began to see much activity which required the postulation of a current of inherently nondestructive aggression.

Again we found much complexity. At age 0-3-8, motor activity per se was added to Jane's repertoire of functions in which libido was invested. She was now able to roll from prone to supine positions, and return from supine to prone. The libidinal and aggressive energies invested in this activity led to interruption of her looking-exploratory activity. In addition, this looking-exploratory activity was interrupted by her rapidly growing interest in animate objects; she would smile and coo at faces. For the first time, she grasped her mother's pant leg, and a turtle soft toy which she mouthed. We saw here her efforts to reach the turtle, manifest now for two or three weeks, finally materialize. Indeed, she grasped the turtle and brought it to her exploring mouth several times. As we attempted to assess the character of manifest drive activity during periods of sufficient physiological satisfaction, we were impressed by the complexity and multiplicity of intertwining drive discharges: (a) nondestructive aggressive strivings—looking, exploring, motor apparatus discharge, and integration; (b) oral libidinal excitation with exploratory and erotic sucking; (c) socialization, with looking-exploring (nondestructive aggressive strivings) applied to libidinal object relations; and (d) large efforts and long periods in skill (ego) developing activity, as in gaining control of the motor apparatus.

COMMENT

With regard to aggression, the most striking finding during this developmental period is the manifestation of drive activity which, while aggressive—the pressured and peremptory exploration, hand-ling, self-assertiveness upon—is not destructive. While this drive trend seems generally to induce affectively neutral activity, the pleasure in function of the ego often gives to this activity a pleasurable affective concomitant. From here the manifestations of nondestructive aggressive impulses mount more or less rapidly depending on the congenital disposition of the child. This activity becomes preeminent during the practicing subphase, during which it is featured in a central dynamic role (in chapter 1, in an extensive discussion, this finding is explored theoretically).

Chapter 7

SECOND PART OF THE NORMAL SYMBIOSIS AND THE DIFFERENTIATION SUB-PHASE
(5 or 6 to 10 Months)

The second part of normal symbiosis overlaps with the first subphase of separation-individuation, that of differentiation. At this point in development, the structuring of the budding ego as agency is under way. In reciprocity with developments of the ego and the drives in the normal child (Spitz 1950, 1965), there is also now much evidence that the libidinal object is structured intrapsychically: the specificity of the smiling responses to mother, the emergence of stranger reactions to others, and separation anxiety in response to mother's leaving indicate sufficient psychic structuring of her as the child's libidinal object. While Piaget and some of his students (Piaget 1937, 1954, Gouin-Decarie 1965, Cobliner 1965, Bell 1969) have affirmed the emergence of *object permanence*[1] not to occur until sixteen or so months of age, our findings point to an impressive degree of specificity in the child's attachment to his particular mother by the age of six or so months (see also Spitz 1965). In our work, as in that of Mahler and Spitz, we found ample evidence that the mother is significantly emotionally invested by the normal six-month-old, that she indeed becomes his first love (libidinal) object. While there is no object permanence at the age of six months, there is evidence that the child values and recognizes his particular mother, that is, at this age he has developed the capability for *recognitive memory* (Fraiberg 1969). Even though no stable mental representation of the object is present at six months, some form of

---

1. The beginning of the child's capability to retain in memory the mental representation of an object, thing, or person, no longer in the child's visual field.

object representational schema, with some degree of stability and specificity, is already laid down and invested with libido and aggression.

Bearing in mind the caution advanced by Hartmann (1952) that we not overstress the importance of the object to psychic development, I am led to believe, by our findings and those of others, that the optimal development of the libidinal object is *vital* to, and reciprocal with, optimal development of the ego and the vicissitudes of the drives. This hypothesis is stated or inferred repeatedly in the work of Freud (1921, 1923, 1926, 1930, 1940), Mahler (1952, 1965, 1968, with Pine and Bergman 1975), Spitz (1946a, 1950, 1965), Jacobson (1954, 1964), and others. The task at hand propels me to focus on and delineate some of the influences which the development of the libidinal object has on the vicissitudes of aggression. Of much importance, for example, is the fact that during this period of development one finds the first manifestations of *superego precursors* and the emergence of a number of fundamental ego *defenses* resulting directly from the vicissitudes of aggression in relation to the object. In addition, there is a complex arousal of aggression which results from the wish to possess the object. These will be detailed in this and the two chapters which follow.

MANIFESTATIONS OF AGGRESSION

To maintain continuity with our epigenetic investigation I ask what are the normal observable manifestations from which one can infer an aggressive impulse in the child during the second half of the normal symbiosis, from five or six months to ten months of age.

THE UNPLEASURE-RELATED DISCHARGE OF DESTRUCTIVENESS

The conditions noted during the earlier developmental periods continue to arouse destructive impulses: *painful somatic stimuli, undue restriction or interruption of libidinal gratification, sufficient frustration of nondestructive aggressive strivings, and traumatizing object relations.* The final common pathway in all these conditions is the arousal of a sufficient level of unpleasure.

Separation reactions, including separation *anxiety* now, in addition to *stranger reactions,* become a further source of arousal of unpleasure which when carried too far lead to rage. All the children, including those who experienced a large degree of healthy narcissism and more than good-enough object relatedness with their mothers, readily showed reactions of anger in circumstances which caused them separation and stranger reactions. However, this was not always the case; these children at times exhibited no anger in their stranger reactions, rather, subdued, and immobilized, they would stare at the stranger, at times transfixed, at times turning their gaze away.

The anger mobilized by transient object loss can already, very early, have a complex influence on the budding ego. When Jane was 0-7-7, her mother worked for one week, ten hours each day, outside their home. Jane was well cared for by a young aunt, whom she had seen many times since birth. During that time, we saw no outer-directed manifestations of destructive impulses, which we presumed, nevertheless, were mobilized. Jane was strikingly *low-keyed* (Mahler and McDevitt 1968) in her mood and in her exploratory activity, where we had come to expect much vigor. In such low-keyedness we saw lucid illustration of the suppression of the ego's normally strong efforts to master the external environment as that ego struggles with internal matters—with feelings of rage toward the object or with affects of grief and longing for the libidinal object from whom the child had been separated. Aunt N. served as a workable substitute but one who did not succeed in taking the place in Jane's psychic life which Mrs. K occupied.

Also at this time, we recorded a further condition which aroused noteworthy unpleasure in Jane. Jane, at five months, was pulling herself up and could stand for long periods. She often enjoyed standing at the edge of the toy box, digging in and pulling out toys. At 0–5–24, she pulled herself up to standing, then moved her body over a greater radius than her legs could stably hold. She fell directly backward onto the carpeted floor. It was quite unusual for her to appear grossly distressed in the course of those early months, but this time she looked stunned, as though she had discovered for the first time, diacritically, the full shock of this unpleasant event. She screamed with outrage, much more hurt narcissistically, we thought, than physically. We were greatly impressed some eight months later when again her ego lost control over her body and she looked startled and screeched her feeling of helplessness and anger. While one might categorize this experience under *painful stimuli,* we find it more correct to point to the destructive impulse being aroused by the suddenly felt *helplessness of the ego* (see Stone 1971), a further experience in which sufficiently felt unpleasure leads to the arousal of destructive impulses.

Later, at fourteen months, we found Jane showing evidence that the loss of ego control over her body (equilibrium) caused her undue anxiety. We felt that it was in an effort to master unpleasure caused by such disequilibrium that for several weeks she would often walk about with her head tilted to one side or the other. Since she showed no neurologic problem, this was felt to be an effort at mastery evoked by the two stunning falls described above.

Similarly, Cindy started her walking efforts at eight months. She suddenly fell back once. From then on until she walked on her own, at twelve months, Cindy became anxious if her mother stood her up to walk; if her mother persisted, she would become angry.

These instances from our project illustrate and strongly support Stone's view (1971) that any excessive or protracted condition of ego helplessness causes not only the experiencing of anxiety, but may also arouse destructiveness. In the view of aggression advanced in this study,*excessive helplessness of the ego by causing excessive unpleasure tends to arouse and mobilize destructive impulses in the child.*

DISCHARGE OF NONAFFECTIVE DESTRUCTIVENESS

Evidence of cyclic recurrent nonaffective destructiveness associated with food intake, chewing and digestion, is, of course, ever-present from birth on. We need not comment on the ubiquitous and cyclic emergence of such impulses, which we have assumed to be representative of nonaffective destructiveness. With regard to adventitious self-injury—self-scratching, hair pulling, as well as object-injuries of that kind—from six or so months on we could no longer find evidence of spontaneous discharge of destructive impulses (unexplainable as to its motivation). By the time of the second half of the symbiosis and the differentiation subphase, and even more so subsequently, whenever a destructive impulse was discharged it was invariably possible to trace it to a sufficient stimulus, often in the immediate past. Soon, in the next subphase, such stimuli dated as far back as the evening before.

NONDESTRUCTIVE AGGRESSION

In most of our children during periods of sufficient physiologic and libidinal gratification, we observed the continuation of the large trend toward activity of the primary autonomous ego apparatuses which we had found during the first part of the symbiosis, with much exploratory activity and the manifestation of large discharges of nondestructive aggressive drive energy.

Jane's sensory-motor development was extensively exercised by the time she was 0-5-0. By then she showed an occasional autoerotic motor discharge, by getting her hands on her knees and rocking. By contrast, her outer-directed exploratory activity—fueled by nondestructive aggression—was constant and large. Her crawling was more and more facile. In her exploratory push, she grabbed a toy held by Temmy (age 0-5-1), which initiated important developmental sequelae: her vigorous nondestructive aggressive activity vis-a-vis a peer turned the corner into peer-related conflict and destructiveness. Here we were compelled to take note of that well-known phenomenon, to which Winnicott (1950x) drew attention: *resistance on the part of the environment* to gratification of the child's nondestructive aggressive strivings (and the ego's mastery) leads to frustration (unpleasure) in him and to the arousal of his destructive impulses. This is further discussed immediately below.

PLEASURABLE DISCHARGE OF DESTRUCTIVENESS

At this time we were alerted to the need for a new category of aggressive drive manifestation: that of affectively *pleasurable* discharges of *destructive* impulses. The following type of behavior forced us to consider this possible category of aggression manifestation. Mary (0-5-24) at the peak of the normal symbiosis, lay prone on a mat, eagerly looking around, her head and neck extended upward. For about one hour she had been exploring, grasping, and mouthing several toys—exhibiting in good fashion what we have come to identify as the discharge of nondestructive aggression (pressure or drivenness to explore and assmilate the environment). After about one hour of this activity, rather than tiring, she became, it appeared, more animated, her affect indicating excitement and pleasure. She stretched maximally to reach a toy just out of reach—her support slackened, her body smoothly collapsed back to the floor, and one of her arms struck the floor rhythmically several times. In one minute she tried again to reach the toy she could not reach. Her effort was strong, her pleasurable excitement mounted and she struck the floor vigorously several times, her arm extended. Her legs, too, flapped the floor rhythmically.

In contrast, when Temmy was upset, at four and five months, she would hyperextend her entire body, her stretched maximally arms and legs flailing, discharging what I inferred to be *destructive* impulses in an *un*pleasurable context. The motor discharge characteristics here described in these two infants seem similar, but their affective concomitant and the context of their dynamics are very different. In the instances described above, Mary did not become manifestly irritable, rather she retained a pleasurable affect throughout a series of such excited aggressive discharges. In some ways too, these discharges resemble those of our easily-excited Cindy, whose aggressive motor discharges at equivalent ages were not as stably controlled by the ego as those of Mary.

We found it difficult to categorize Mary's activity. Our choice lay between *the pleasurable discharge of destructive impulses* and the *discharge of those nondestructive aggressive impulses* that come closest to destructiveness in appearance. I found the latter of the two the more plausible. It may be that this type of activity is the manifestation of aggressive impulses that bridge two currents of aggression. It appears as though these discharges are a direct continuation of the pressured activity—nondestructive aggression— that all the children exhibit in exploring; but the level of excitation mounts and results in excited, rhythmical floor-banging. This mounting tension was not unpleasurable here as it was with Temmy or in the instance described with Renée (chapter 6). However, even without evidence of unpleasure, I placed this activity toward the more palpably destructive end of the spectrum of aggressive drive manifestations. I felt that here we were not dealing just with pleasure-in-function phenomenology, nor with simple erotization of the musculomotor apparatus.

Mary's behavior, however, alerted us to the need for a further category of aggressive drive manifestation: a destructive discharge associated with, and in the context of, a pleasurable experience. From observing older children, we knew to expect teasing, taunting, and sadism (in the broad sense of the word) which would necessitate such a category. However, I do not feel that Mary's behavior at this age, which I have just detailed, belongs in this category. Rather it seems better catalogued as the manifestation of a nondestructive aggressive discharge. Clear discharges of destructiveness associated with pleasurable affect seem to make their appearance within the next months, during the practicing and rapprochement subphases.

SOME DIFFICULTIES WITH THE AGGRESSION MANIFESTATION CATEGORIES

This discussion of Mary's behavior illustrates one major type of difficulty we encountered: sorting out even in simple behavior what is a discharge of aggression from other elements concurrently evident in psychic activity. In presentations and discussions of this material I found at times much disagreement on what is a manifestation of aggression. This problem comes at least in part from the difficulty in discerning whether a destructive *motive* or *intent* can be inferred from a particular behavioral discharge. Disagreement regarding such activities as Mary's is virtually unavoidable. On the other hand, some acts allow for inferences which, in disussions, are readily agreed upon and are more easily classifiable. This latter type of data encouraged the categorization of aggression-manifestations which forms the bulk of data on which this work is based.[2] Nonetheless, from the less clear-cut data—as in some examples cited here—come clues as to the nature of aggression. For example, does Mary's behavioral discharge *bridge* one trend of aggression (nondestructive) with another (pleasurable destructiveness)? Such a bridging manifestation would support the view that while aggression has various inherent trends, it is *one* instinctual drive. For an extensive discussion of some of these problems, see chapters 1 and 3 of this work.

---

2. In such presentations I also found that other aspects of psychic activity—as cognition, or ego function—drew the attention of some discussants. However, while we are cognizant of these other psychic activities which determine behavior, in this work I have limited myself to sorting out and following the various red threads of aggressive drive discharge.

Another type of data that caused us difficulty is exemplified in Jane's behavior at 0–5–24. While widely swinging a toy, Jane struck herself and others. Her nondestructive impulses were discharged upon the toy, not upon herself or the others who were inadvertently struck. Manifestly she seemed not to aim to strike an object, yet adventitiously did so. We catalogued this activity as an expansive, poorly-controlled (because of ego immaturity) discharge of nondestructive aggression which may give the impression of being a destructive aggressive discharge.

Still another problem emerges as the psychic apparatus becomes more and more organized. Already at this developmental period we were faced with much complexity in our search for the various threads of aggression manifestation. We expected and found that an inevitable concomitant of the sufficient libidinization of the mothering person into libidinal object would be the directing of aggression toward that object. I mean this in the sense equivalent to the libido's, on the way to becoming object-libido, attaching to the nonself partner (object) which is differentiating at this time out of the symbiotic self-representation (Parens 1971). As a result of this differentiation we found that in a number of observations the simpler categories of nondestructive aggression, unpleasure-related, pleasure-related, and nonaffective discharges of destructiveness failed to delineate enough. For example, in Jane's (0–5–0) grabbing Temmy's (0–5–1) toy—seen many times in all the children—we saw the overlapping of nondestructive and destructive components of aggressive drive. Pushed on the one hand by autonomous, nondestructive aggressive strivings, and, on the other, by the libidinal wish to possess objects,[3] Jane (0–5–24) wanted the toy that Temmy (0–5–25) had. Omnipotently, narcissistically, she proceeded to get it. But her course was blocked by Temmy's clearly expressed unpleasure and resistance. This led to consequent unpleasure in Jane which, in turn, led to the emergence of destructiveness in Jane and Temmy, albeit from different unpleasure sources.

Oral aggression also rears its complicated head at this time. Biting, as a concomitant of the eruption of teeth, is at times difficult to categorize along lines prescribed by our aggression-manifestation

3. The wish to possess objects (and things) is largely aroused by the development of *the wish to possess the libidinal object*, i.e., by the pressures of narcissistic- as well as emerging object-libido (see below).

categories. For example, Jane, at ten months, in a seemingly thoughtful state while reclining on mother's lap, is biting and pulling with her teeth at the nipple of her bottle. At times, biting behavior would follow her striking her head against the edge of a table, or her falling unexpectedly and hard, or, as we shall see later, in her having a conflict of wills with her mother. But at other times the biting behavior appeared spontaneous, even peaceful—a part of the ambience of thoughtful meditation, fantasy, a thinking about things.

What are we to make of this? Some infants approach the nipple as if ready to devour it, while others suck very softly, it is well-known that because of such discrepancies the line between libido and aggression is a troublesome one to draw. Freud (1909, 1915) cautioned us that each drive has its own pressure. From Freud's position then, intensity in libido may explain avid sucking without impugning aggression. Yet the expression of oral-aggressive, cannibalistic impulses of biting and tearing with the teeth, in accord with the observations of Abraham (1916, 1924), Freud (1933), and Erikson (1959), clearly emerge at this period of development. Our data support this view and timetable. Our findings, furthermore, suggest that when these biological and psychological developments are occurring (the emergence of teeth and the sufficient structuring of the libidinal object), they simultaneously set the stage for the emergence of cannibalistic impulses directed toward the newly structured libidinal object. At this juncture the hypothetical line between nonaffective and affective, between unpleasure-related and pleasure-related destructive impulse discharges becomes at times almost impossible to distinguish. One is then tempted to retreat from categorizing aggression manifestations and return to thinking in terms of a simple amorphous aggressive drive. That, of course, would take us no farther than we are to date.

In line with the reformulations of aggression proposed in this work, the following view is advanced. According to Eissler's note regarding self-preservative aspects of destructiveness, *nonaffective destructiveness* serves as the prototype for oral destructive impulses, and the experience of *sufficient unpleasure* is the determinant which adds to the otherwise nonaffective destructive impulse its quality of rage and hate in recognition of which we clinically call it a *cannibalistic impulse*.

Even when we found good grounds for the arousal of destructiveness, it was sometimes difficult to categorize destructiveness as being unpleasure- or pleasure-related. For example, Vicki at ten months bit the nipples of her bottles so hard that her mother, angry at her daughter's behavior, rationalized that Vicki no longer needed a bottle. Many times, at the moment Vicki bit the nipple, she did not *manifest* concurrent displeasure; she seemed instead to be affectlessly discharging tension. Because there was much evidence of excessively thwarted libidinal needs as well as at times harsh care-taking, and because Vicki progressively showed more and more pain-reactions and depression, we were compelled to infer that much unpleasure-related destructiveness was mobilized which was discharged in this seemingly affectively-neutral activity.

This brief presentation of some of the problems we encountered at this point in our study illustrates some of the obstacles in our way. Despite these and other problems, I did not consider them of such magnitude that they ought to prevent us from pursuing our exploration of aggression.

INFLUENCE OF AGGRESSION ON THE DEVELOPMENT OF PSYCHIC STRUCTURE AND OBJECT RELATIONS

Much psychic development derives from the mutual influences of structural (ego and superego) and object differentiations. These directly determine, and are in turn determined by, the vicissitudes of the drives. Much data reveals important developments in psychic functioning which are specifically determined by the vicissitudes of aggression emerging from the time the libidinal object is structured. In this and especially the next two chapters, some of these developments will be detailed. Attention is drawn particularly to the fact that, and the manner by which, the relation to the symbiotic partner in large part now begins to determine the vicissitudes of aggression in the child. First, however, I want to take a little detour to another aspect of the problem of aggression in earliest object relations.

ONE ROOT OF THE UBIQUITOUS PEER RIVALRY

By about five to eight months, our children have all (except Anni who did so later) experienced the type of behavior now to be described.

Long before Jane was capable of upright locomotion she was constantly very busy exploring many aspects of her environment. With notable frequency Jane, from age 0–5–0, was attracted to things which Temmy, one day older, was holding or playing with. In many instances, this behavior was found to occur with marked pressure. Twins Candy and Cindy did the same at this age, more frequently with each other than with the other children.

From the manifest character of Jane's approach to Temmy, like that of the others at this point in development, we could not infer a *destructive* impulse to be the motivating force at play; aggressive, yes, destructive, no. Rather it appeared as if Jane (age 0–5–0) expected Temmy's (0–5–1) toy to yield to her exploration as did the unattached toys. Many toys were available to the children. But it was soon very apparent that a preferential factor was operative: something led the child to want what another one had (see chapter 11 for a similar finding in Burlingham's twin observations). But Temmy was not compliant, she resisted Jane's wishes. At the outset, this type of encounter, repeated several times, led to progressively greater efforts on the part of both children, and in consequence, the earliest peer-directed destructive impulses were mobilized in each child. Because Jane's wish to possess the specific toy was resisted—thereby frustrating her nondestructive and libidinal strivings—she experienced unpleasure; and as Temmy's resistance persisted against Jane's progressively stronger efforts to take that toy, destructive impulses emerged in Jane against Temmy. In Temmy, in turn, Jane's threat to take her toy led to her being upset and retreating or holding on. This type of interaction precipitated the first exchange of blows between these peers. Sometimes the aggressor was the first to strike, sometimes the defender. Each responded according to her (or his) own present dynamic psychic state, one day by striking, the next day by retreating.

If this peer-related event were rare, not much could be made of it. However, in our population of children this wish-to-have and advance-to-take the other child's toy occurred with such frequency that it was at the center of the interaction among them at this developmental period. Every one of our infants had older siblings, and we may expect that they had each already had peer-related experiences of the type described here. The extent to which this phenomenon occurred was striking. With the twins, for example, Cindy was most often the aggressor, taking Candy's things; but when Candy's mind was set on it, she would not give up her possession. Each received an identical toy from their mother so that they would not continually take things from each other. To Mrs. G's dismay, Cindy insisted, with her own toy near her and available, that she wanted Candy's. The result, of course, was the emergence of destructive impulses and conflict (eventually intrapsychic).

Taking possession of objects is driven by a confluence of nondestructive aggression and of the libido. It has multiple influences, engendering adaptation pertaining to nondestructive aggression, narcissism, object relations, and superego precursors. The inevitability of this dynamic, its residua in peer (and sibling) rivalry, is well-known clinically.

Despite many efforts and discussions, our understanding of this wish to have another child's toy is sketchy (see also discussion in chapter 11); nevertheless, I wish here to note some of the ingredients which determine its emergence. At this age, the development of the ego, particularly in cognitive function, motor apparatus control, and in its integration into an agency, make this event —*wish* (Schur 1966) and *intentionality* (Hartmann 1952)—possible. The structuring of the libidinal object and narcissistic omnipotence underlie the wish to possess the object; hence this wish to take possession of the object interdigitates with what seems to be an *innate releasing mechanism* (IRM, Lorenz 1935, 1953) *for imitation* which becomes nuclear to the process of identification. The motive force comes from both libido and the nondestructive aggressive drive which fuel the budding ego.

Three months later, when Jane was 0–8–3 and Temmy 0–8–4, this activity had already become more complex. Now Jane pulled the pacifier from Temmy's mouth and put it in her own. When Vicki (0–6–16) touched her walker, Temmy began to whine and make gestures of pushing Vicki away. When Jane took a toy Temmy had played with several minutes before, Temmy whined and went to try to retrieve it. The wish to take possession and the reaction to loss of (inanimate) objects rapidly becomes more complex. And so do the related manifestations of aggression.

EARLIEST SUPEREGO PRECURSORS—
BEGINNING INTERNALIZATION OF MATERNAL DICTATES

During this period mothers often find it necessary to inhibit their child's getting an ashtray, tilting a half-filled coffee cup, or getting hold of a kleenex box. Many times, too, the mothers have to intervene when tugs-of-war over toys lead to blows. We have found that at seven to eight months of age, the children understand (react meaningfully and appropriately to) their mother's affecto-vocal admonitions. In many instances at this age, only several admonitions from mother are necessary to produce evidence of beginning internalization. Thus, Temmy (0–8–5) after receiving several reasonably toned admonitions would reach for an ashtray, stop her movement, look at mother, and at times shake her head negatively. At times Temmy's self-controlling effort would fail, and she would get the ashtray anyway; at other times she deflected her action and obeyed the combined internal-external admonition. We found such behavior in all our children during the subphases of differentiation and practicing.

When Jane was 0–8–1, we recorded the following note: For the past six weeks Jane had competed with Temmy for such items as plastic rings, carriage beads, and Temmy's walker. Temmy pulled these to herself, complained and fussed, and Jane occasionally struck her with her arm. When Mrs. K. called out to scold Jane, Jane responded by turning toward mother and inhibiting the destructive impulse in its trajectory. At 0–8–4, mother's verbal "be nice," said with a scolding tone from ten feet away, inhibited Jane's hitting Temmy.

Ego defenses erected to deal with object-directed destructiveness such as that just described begin to appear during this developmental period; however, they emerge especially in the dynamic context of the practicing subphase and become readily discernable at that time.

Chapter 8

THE PRACTICING SUBPHASE OF SEPARATION-INDIVIDUATION
(8 or 9 to about 16 months)

During the practicing subphase we find that the vicissitudes of aggression complicate sharply. *Maturation* of drives and ego apparatuses with consequent *developments of the ego and of object relations*—as these terms are used by Hartmann—are the large determinants of this growing complexity. Psychosexual theory holds that the epigenesis of the libido occurs sequentially, being determined by the maturation of its underlying somatic organization, with the sequential dominance at first of the oral, then, in turn, of the anal and phallic zones and modes of excitation and discharge (gratification). There are indications that the biologic maturation of the aggressive drive, other than for those elements that are anaclitic and concomitants of the libido, may not have the same attractive phases as are found for libido. There are indications that the somatic organization of the aggressive drive (Parens 1973a)—that is, the sensori-receptor-motor-muscular organization—is more fluid in its maturation and development. However, some peaks of excitation, based on a maturational schedule, are discernible. *One such peak which reflects dramatically on aggressive drive dominance occurs at the time of the practicing subphase.* Thus, while the differentiation of the sensori-motor organization begins in utero, a large peak of differentiation of its underlying somatic organization is reflected at this point in development, from about eight to sixteen months of age, in a marked upsurge of the aggressive drive, concomitantly with the maturation of the central nervous system and the motor-muscular apparatuses. Indeed this upsurge in the aggressive drive seems to be the principal energic biological determinant of the practicing subphase. The preexisting developments of the visual and auditory apparatuses, hand-mouth integration, preupright locomotion, for example, and evidence of infantile ego control over body and drives are prerequisites for the peak of development which we find in the practicing subphase. Thus differentiation of the drives and the ego—of the locomotor apparatus, of the prehensible-grasping apparatus (along with the continued emergence of teeth), all of which so significantly determine the discharge patterns of aggression—have a peak which begins during the last half of the first year of life. The vocal apparatus, which also mediates the discharge of aggression, differentiates significantly too, preverbally, at this time.

Within the developmental phase described in this chapter, one continues to find manifestations of aggression that fall within the simplified categories described for the preceding developmental periods. However, the increasingly complex differentiation of psychic content and intrapsychic dynamics often obscures the lines between these categories. Thus, for example, the increasing implementation of defenses on the part of the ego may yield a manifestation of aggression that would be categorized under pleasure-related discharge of destructive impulses, while the latent character of that discharge may belong to the category of unpleasure-related discharge of destructive impulses. In this case, in addition to ego defense, the increasing capacity of the ego for memory, delay of discharge, and the repetition compulsion play a part in modifying the impulse discharge from its character at the time of arousal. Some examples are detailed below under nondestructive aggressive strivings, and frustration of nondestructive aggressive strivings.

The vicissitudes of aggression, *especially object-directed aggression,* at this subphase determine significantly the development of the ego along a number of lines—including among others, reality testing, relations to objects, control and modulation of instinctual drives, and autonomous ego functions (Beres 1956). As I shall show in this chapter, in the ego's efforts to cope with and control aggression, several important defenses emerge including *inhibition, displacement, prerepression, presublimation, internalization* of parental dictates, *neutralization,* and *splitting of object representations.*

As is evident from the data presented for this subphase, we found in it a notable maturational upsurge of aggression in our children. This we found over and above the baseline of characteristic discharge patterns for each of these children conceptualized by Fries and Woolf (1953) as "congenital activity type." Indeed, as one would expect, we found a range in this upsurge of aggression to be superimposed on a range of already existing characteristic patterns of aggression discharge.

In this regard, we were interested to find that some of our children, such as Jane and Cindy, showed much evidence of a large disposition to discharge aggression already during the early part of the normal symbiosis; while others, like Candy and Mary, were placid and seemed disposed to discharge aggression at low levels as neonates and during the first part of the normal symbiosis. We found data to suggest that this holds for the discharge of both nondestructive and destructive aggression. This upsurge of the aggressive drive, which seems to give to the practicing subphase its unique character, varies according to constitutional endowment and schedule of maturation so that some children show a very sharp upsurge of aggression (Mary and Bernie), while others show one that seems more gradual (Candy[1] and Harold).

Secondly, whatever the pattern of upsurge of aggression, in all our children this upsurge was responsible in large part for the development of a characteristic conflict between child and mother which shall be documented and discussed because it has important implications for the mutual development of the ego and aggression in the child, as well as for his total psychic development.

MANIFESTATIONS OF AGGRESSION

I continue at this point with an attempt to illustrate and comment upon the various categories of manifestations of aggression found during the practicing subphase.

UNPLEASURE-RELATED DISCHARGE OF DESTRUCTIVE IMPULSES

That painful stimuli of internal or external origin may arouse destructive impulses is readily evidenced in the frequent manifestations

---

[1]There is room for question, and the need for further clarification, in that Candy and Doris who were basically low-level discharge children gradually proved to be strongly self-assertive in a quiet way, and each moved with much determination to achieve her ends, both features being fueled significantly by the aggressive drive.

of such aggression to which these stimuli lead. Furthermore, now with the structuring of the libidinal object—that is, with the earliest consolidation of the symbiotic partner as love-object—the inferred arousal of unpleasure-related destructive impulses seems often to be discharged against that love-object. We found now that often the mother, who appears to be experienced by the child as omnipotent, seems to be blamed for any rage-inducing painful experience, the discharge of rage being observably directed against her. Equally evident, however, we found that painful stimuli do not always lead to the discharge of destructive impulses against the omnipotent love-object. For example, at 1-1-19, Jane struck her head hard on a table. She screamed in sharp outrage and cried in obvious pain. She turned immediately to her mother for comforting. While she discharged hostile destructive impulses affecto-vocally, she did not seem to blame her mother and calmed quickly in mother's arms. Two minutes later, as if the memory of the blow had come back to awareness, she suddenly screamed (which seems to us an affecto-vocal discharge of destructive impulses), cried, and again responded positively to her mother's comforting. There was no locomotor-muscular discharge of a destructive type.

Many of the external and internal conditions which arouse destructive impulses during the earlier subphases continue to have a similar influence during the practicing subphase: *painful stimuli, undue restriction or interruption of libidinal gratification, traumatizing object relations, and sufficient frustration of nondestructive aggressive strivings.* But now, intrapsychic changes that result from both adaptation to (1) psychobiologic maturation, and (2) specific traumatizing environmental conditions (particularly traumatizing mother-child relatedness) lead to a change in the reaction to some of those conditions which earlier aroused destructive impulses. Thus, as an example of adaptation to psychobiologic maturation, in the preceding peak of the symbiotic phase (five-six months of age) and in the differentiation subphase, we find a peak for separation anxiety (Spitz 1950, 1965) and with it the potential for the arousal of destructive impulses. But at the height of the practicing subphase, the maturationally determined displacement of the large infantile attention cathexis from the libidinal object to the rapidly widening external environment—Greenacre's (1960) love affair with the world—tends to decrease transiently and intermittently the experience and influence of separateness, hence of separation anxiety.

Thus, in general, the influence of separation anxiety as a stimulus to the arousal of destructive impulses decreases during the practicing subphase when compared to its occurrence at the height of the symbiosis and of differentiation. We found this to be the case with Jane, Candy, Renée, Mary, and Bernie especially, whose separation-individuation subphases were among the clearest, the least interfered with by constitutional (as was Cindy's) or environmental traumata (as were Vicki's and Temmy's).

For an example of adaptation to traumatizing environmental conditions and the decrease in manifestations of aroused destructive impulses, we turn to Vicki. During the practicing subphase she was depressed and low-keyed in affect and activity (Mahler and McDevitt 1968). We found a notable inhibition in the large upsurge of practicing activity which we expected from her constitutional predisposition; evidence for this inhibition was readily ascribable to the traumatizing relation to her mother. And it was also due to this that she often did not react to separation with manifest anxiety. The danger signaled by the degree and character of her depression (see Spitz 1946a, 1965, Mahler 1963, 1966, 1968, Parens, Pollock, and Prall 1974) led to our instituting treatment for the child and mother. As the tie of the child to her therapist, and later to her mother, gained in libidinal investment, the manifestations of destructive impulse discharge increased significantly (Solnit 1971); the quality of these discharges at this time in development suggested levels of unneutralized aggression higher than that found in most of our other infant subjects.

Many observations of unpleasure-related discharges of destructive impulses support the view that helplessness of the ego may be not only the paradigm for anxiety, but that it may also be, as Stone (1971) has suggested, a prime causative factor in the arousal of aggression. It may be, furthermore, that this condition, helplessness of the ego, can arouse two forms of aggression: (1) it can arouse *destructive impulses,* even leading to rage[2], but (2) it can also mobilize *nondestructive aggression* which fuels the ego's mastery efforts. Of course, threatened helplessness of the ego does just that in the theory of signal anxiety (Freud 1926, 1933) and in children's play (Freud 1920).[3] This second kind of reaction to the ego's benign degrees of helplessness may play a part, complemen-

---

[2]Every clinician knows that it is difficult to distinguish anxiety from rage in panic reactions, one of the ultimate in the affective expression of helplessness of the ego.

[3]Hartmann might speak of neutral ego energies here.

tary to the inherent aim of the nondestructive aggressive drive, in the enormous amount of exploratory activity we have seen in our children from the earliest days of their symbiosis—the large push to assimilate, integrate, and master the progressively experienced internal and external environment. Examples of this benign state of helplessness of the ego, numerous in our daily lives from infancy through adulthood, it is here suggested, would mobilize nondestructive aggression and underlie some benign forms of learning.

Frustration of Nondestructive Aggressive Strivings

It is proposed in this work that nondestructive aggression contributes centrally to the motivation and fueling of self-assertive behavior and strivings for autonomy. In the normal child, in consequence of frustrating self-assertive and autonomous strivings, sufficient unpleasure may be experienced so that it mobilizes (hostile) destructive impulses. With her usual large exploratory push, Jane (0–10–3) reached for her mother's cigarettes on the coffee table. Her mother pulled Jane's hand away with reasonable insistance and moved the cigarettes and ashtray out of reach. Jane exploded unexpectedly into an outburst of anger directed at her mother, evidenced in a gesture, and followed through by hitting her mother with her hand. Simultaneously, she burst into tears. Then came the complex discharge of destructive impulses we had not seen in her before. For about one hour we observed the following: Within one minute after the above event, Jane permitted her mother to pick her up to comfort her. She stayed on mother's lap for ten minutes, overcoming slowly her angry feelings and tears. She then returned, with sober affect, to her characteristic exploring and mastering of herself and her environment. In a few minutes she stopped and after a moment of pensive stillness suddenly began to cry bitterly and angrily. Her mother picked her up to comfort her, but something from within Jane interfered and she did not quiet down as readily and quickly as usual. On her mother's lap, after a minute, she stopped crying and accepted the bottle offered by mother. She seemed pensive, sucking her bottle in a sitting position; she angrily rejected being reclined, and sat upright, pensively sucking; then she suddenly began to cry again, angry and despondent. Her mother's efforts to calm her fell short of their usual success, although they contributed to her calming after a delay of two minutes. Then Jane again pensively sucked; she seemed to be struggling against her tendency to fall asleep. Suddenly after five minutes she had another spasm of bitter, angry, despondent crying. Several times more, she repeated this alternating sequence of calming, being pensive, and then interrupting that state by discharging, via affective pathways, her mitigated, destructive impulses, inhibited in their aim and in their trajectory to the object.

We recorded the following note on Jane at 0-10-10: "Mrs. K. reports that Jane has been quite difficult, irritable, and dogmatic in her demands. She is clearly developing some conflict with her mother around autonomous strivings, insisting behaviorally, I wanna do this, when mother sets limits" (see p. 189). At 0-10-10, Jane was sitting upright on mother's lap, head hyperextended in order to get milk from the bottle she held. Mrs. K. tried just once to have Jane lean back against her, although Jane did look notably uncomfortable. Jane struggled with surprising anger to remain upright. Mrs. K. said, "She's fighting going to sleep." But, we also felt, she was fighting being put in a passive position at this moment, something she accepted readily at other times (see Nondestructive Aggressive Strivings for this period). In this instance, as well as when a toy was taken from her at the end of the session, Jane's expression of angry feelings (manifest of destructive impulses) was vocal and affective, but she did not strike out against the object, nor, at this time, did we see any displacement of these impulses.

In this sense, the frustration of strivings for autonomy, of exploration, and of testing control over the environment, which seem fueled by nondestructive aggression, tend to induce unpleasure, and if sufficient unpleasure is experienced, a destructive discharge often follows.

NONAFFECTIVE DISCHARGE OF DESTRUCTIVE IMPULSES

No comment is required here to indicate the everpresent ebb and flow of nonaffective destructive impulses which pertain to feeding in the context which has already been discussed in the earlier sections.

NONDESTRUCTIVE AGGRESSIVE IMPULSE DISCHARGE

A most important aspect of the manifestations of nondestructive aggression pertains to the evolving of self-assertion upon, as well as the control and mastery of, the self and the environment. This aspect of aggression seems to fuel strivings for autonomy (see Erikson 1959, whose discussion of autonomy is pertinent to our findings). In this too the vicissitudes of aggression make a large contribution to the development of the conflict-free sphere of the ego and the development of certain ego skills—cognitive, locomotor, and small motor functions—all of which effect control of self and environment (see the presentation in chapter 1 of the finding prototypic for this aggression manifestation category).

During the practicing subphase, with regard to self-assertiveness and strivings for autonomy, we found Jane from age 0-10-3 to become more and more engaged in a struggle for control with her mother. We do not want to convey the impression that strong narcissistically invested self-assertive strivings did not appear until this time; quite the contrary, they appeared earlier in all our children. But now, these self-assertive aggressive strivings led to an emphatic and protracted struggle for control with the mother in Jane, Temmy, Cindy, Harold, Bernie, Mary, Anni, and Renée. Such a struggle did not materialize to the same degree with Candy, Doris, Louise and Vicki, whose autonomous strivings during this period could more easily be deflected and guided by their mother. This should not be taken to mean that their self-assertive aggression was not powerful. It did seem that Candy and Doris, who were libidinally well cared for and of an easy disposition, were able to tolerate more than the others their strivings being deflected and guided. (This changed during Candy's rapprochement subphase.) On the other hand, in Louise and Vicki we felt that this mildness in the pressure of self-assertive strivings resulted from aggression inhibited due to the problems in their relation to their mother. The nature of these differences, some constitutional and some environmental, was found to have an influence on the early character formations of our children. In this regard, at this period, Jane and Candy, for example, whose psychic development were both very good, were at opposite poles of controllability in their self-assertiveness and strivings for autonomy.[4]

In speaking of the drive which could fuel such pressured, relentless

[4]One of the implications which may be read into this statement is that the child's strivings for autonomy are equivalent with nondestructive aggression. This cannot be the case since nondestructive aggression serves to effect a rapprochement with the object as much as it serves separation from the object. In the early manifestations of nondestructive aggressive activity, we find the infants explore the libidinal object to-be in the same general way as they explore the inanimate world. While it might be cogent to be able to say that aggression serves individuation (the separation of two organisms) in a form complementary to Freud's view that libido serves to bring two organisms together (which in its earliest form is the normal symbiosis), this formulation is not without problems. One less problem would be present to the applicability of that hypothesis if one were to hold that when aggression serves to effect a rapprochement to the object it acts instrumentally (Stone 1971), serving a libidinal need, or an anxiety-burdened ego.

strivings for autonomy, we must include aggression. No doubt infantile narcissism (libidinal investment in the self), and the omnipotence with which it imbues the evolving self-representation, directs and reinforces whatever inherent drive energy initially motivates that autonomous striving. Winnicott (1950x) called it *life force,* perhaps after Bergson's *élan vital;* Hendrick (1942, 1943a, 1943b) suggested a mastery instinct; Mittelmann (1954, 1960) thought of a motility drive; along with Spitz (1965) and Greenacre (1971), I think it is aggression.

Jane's reaction (0–10–3) to her mother's frustration of her exploratory activity, frustrating the discharge of nondestructive aggressive impulses, heralded and forewarned the onset of a struggle for autonomy which will now be described. Jane's reaction to her mother's not letting her get hold of the cigarettes was sharp; the ego dealt with the acute phase of that reaction for over one hour. For a child ten months of age, this was a long reaction; and the vicissitudes of the drive which motivated the activity in the first place—nondestructive aggression— were much complicated by the arousal of destructive impulses and the ego's efforts to control and modulate them. This occurred in large part, if for no other reason, because these impulses were directed toward the already well-structured libidinal object, her mother. It seems plausible to hypothesize that the degree of arousal of destructive impulses must correspond to the degree to which the ego experiences the frustration of the id cathexes (libido and nondestructive aggressive impulses). If this assumption is correct, we can presume from the character of the activity (its pressure and constancy), and from the reaction to its frustration, that a large push of libido and nondestructive aggression motivated the initial exploratory thrust. This large reaction at 0–10–3 was only the beginning of a marked struggle that lasted for weeks.

At age 0–10–17, Jane and mother were at an impasse. Jane wanted to go out the double door to where there is often a cleaning cart. Mrs. K. prohibited Jane's going out. Jane, pushed to gratify her strivings for autonomy, and went to the door about fifteen times, challenging mother's dictate not to go out. The first three times that her mother pulled her back, Jane had a benign tantrum. She screamed and resisted, but despite the arousal of large angry feelings, did not strike her mother, nor herself. While anger was clearly directed at the object, its motor expression was significantly obstructed by Jane herself.

One ought not to have the impression that Mrs. K. was weak in the statement of her prohibition; nor, was she unduly harsh. An experienced and talented mother, she seemed to have a nice grasp of the difficult situation that confronted her. Gradually, in a surprisingly smooth progression, Jane's reaction to her mother's repeated prohibition became less and less angry as she seemed to be coping, dose by dose, with the repeated frustration of her wish. In the project, this impasse remained at the forefront of Jane's relation to her mother for six weeks, until Jane was 0-11-18.

The harshness of this protracted experience led to dramatic adaptive attempts on Jane's part. At 0-10-20, Jane again wanted to go out the double door. When her mother fetched her, Jane clearly showed feelings of anger, but the tone of that anger was not as harsh as at the first frustration three days before. She permitted her mother to carry her back without the affecto-vocal struggle of the first day. On this day, because of good mutual interaction between child and mother, Jane made the fifth or sixth attempt to go to the door and her mother's prohibition into a playful situation. From that point on, she progressively mastered this nagging, recurrent striving to do as she wished.

At 0-11-1, Jane persisted in about twenty efforts to go out the double door. The strength and the pressure of the drive derivatives that called for gratification were evidenced not only in the repeated appearance of this behavior with each visit and its many repetitions during each visit, but also by the efforts made by the ego to adapt to the push of the drive and wish when this push came into conflict with the love-object; these efforts included the defenses of making-a-game of the conflict, inhibition, splitting the inferred representations of mother, and the internalization of those earliest dictates of the love-object which represent the earliest developments of superego-precursors.

At 0-11-18, Jane continued to show the residual wish to go out the double doors; the conflict between gratifying her autonomous strivings and complying with mother's dictate to retain her love was clearly evident. We then did not see Jane for one month due to vacations. When she returned to the project, we saw no evidence of the struggle to go out the doors and yet she did go out. It would not satisfy us to simply assume that mother now did not resist Jane's going out. The struggle seemed to have evaporated like one of Winnicott's transitional phenomena (1953). Jane's self-assertiveness and her strivings for autonomy and separateness did not lessen. At 1-0-29, she was determined to take possession of others' possessions, including the coffee of one observer, and proceeded in this path under a great head of instinctual pressure. At 1-1-19 our records indicate that Jane, like the other children, was persistent in wanting to do things herself. (We recall that Jane consistently grabbed the spoon mother brought to her mouth when feeding her at fifteen weeks of age. This effort at autonomy has not let up since. It has been safeguarded by her mother's reasonable handling and has also been age-adequately tamed.)

PLEASURE-RELATED DISCHARGE OF DESTRUCTIVE IMPULSES

This new category of aggressive drive manifestation was required by behavioral evidence of aggression which could not satisfactorily be included in the first three categories. The first set of data which compelled this fourth category has been described in chapter 6, and is again illustrated below where a behavior chronology from which we infer Mary's evolving aggressive drive is detailed (see pp.193–97). This is the floor-pounding behavior which, although it seemed to us to pertain to the category of nondestructive aggression, we had some difficulty in reconciling that activity with the other data representative of the nondestructive trend. The postulate was suggested that this type of discharge represents the sweep *toward* destructiveness of the nondestructive trend in aggression.

It was at this time that we encountered a further serious complication in deciphering the dynamics of certain manifestations of destructive discharges and their categorization. When Jane was 1-1-12, Mrs. K. was in the fourth month of her new pregnancy. On that day, to everyone's surprise, while we were talking of Mrs. K.'s coming new baby, Jane just sat on the head of Renée (0-6-27) who was asleep on the floor mat. Jane had never so treated an infant before. We noted that her affect seemed neutral. By contrast, one week later, at age 1-1-19, Jane exhibited parental behavior toward Harold (age 0-4-15). The character of her approach was notable: she wanted to pick him up, she looked at him and touched him gently in a new affective tone which we felt was parental, in identification with mother. We deduced from her behavior during this period that Jane was experiencing her mother's shifting cathexis to the infant inside her, and that Jane knew that her mother was going to have a baby. We considered Jane's sitting on Renée's head to reveal, along with other evidence, that destructive impulses were aroused by this knowledge.

It was noted that Jane's sitting on Renée's head had no precedent in Jane's one-year history and that it was enacted when her affect seemed neutral. We were satisfied, knowing this child well since birth, that this act was not innocent and that it did not arise as a manifestation of a nonaffective destructive drive discharge. Using our investigative and clinical judgments, we concluded from the data surrounding this act that Jane was discharging an *unpleasure-derived* destructive impulse, but that she did so without a currently manifest unpleasure affect. The ego, we postulated, was now capable of holding the unpleasure-related destructive impulse from immediate discharge. It was stored in the psyche, held in abeyance, and the ego could now delay its discharge and *disassociate the original instigative unpleasure affect from it.* When circumstances were favorable, the destructive impulse was discharged under affective conditions of a character very different from that which led to its mobilization. We deduced that sitting on Renée's head, carried out when manifest affects were neutral, was not innocent. It was instigated by an excessively protracted unpleasurable experience: the experience by the infantile ego that a new baby, as Jane told us one year later, was stealing her mother from her.

It is from this age on that we began to see this very important type of *pleasure-related discharge of destructive impulses.* This type of pleasurable destructive discharge derives from an originally unpleasure-related destructive impulse which is not permitted discharge by the ego, is modified by the ego, and is later discharged willfully, under some degree of ego control. This is *sadism* in the broad sense, the pleasurable discharge of destructiveness. While Jane did not gleefully sit on Renée's head, the process here described was inferred to be at work. Later in time, we began to find *teasing.* Several examples of this type of pleasurable discharge are presented in the material on Candy and Jane in the chapter which follows.

HYPOTHESES FOR THE PRACTICING SUBPHASE

BIOLOGICAL UPSURGE OF AGGRESSION

To point up the *upsurge of aggression* at this developmental period I shall now detail the manifestations of aggression in the behavior of two of our children.

Mary

When Mary was 0-1-12, we recorded the observation that her ego apparatuses seemed normal and well endowed, and that during states of "alert wakefulness," she would lie quietly and look about herself inquiringly. Her motor discharges were classified according to activity-type (Fries and Woolf 1953) as "moderate-low." When Mary was 0-5-10, we recorded the following note which sums up well what we had seen so far of her smoothly progressing development:

"Primary Autonomous Ego Functions: When awake she looks about herself continually, exploring things visually and tactilely. However, she appears less pressured in her need to explore, her area of exploration is smaller, and she does her work of exploring in a more placid manner than Jane. Yet she is as constantly engaged in this activity as Jane." A note on *Object Relations* indicated good development of specificity for mother, with age-appropriate stranger reactions to observers. Then under *Aggression,* we commented: "Discharges of non-destructive aggression are at *moderate-low level,* but a constant flow is inferred from her constant exploratory activity. We presume that because mother cares for Mary quite promptly when she fusses, we have seen few rage reactions in this infant. Nor is there any manifestation of self- or other-directed destructive impulses." We concluded that day's record with the remark that Mary seemed well endowed as regards libido, as evidenced in her socialization, affective responsiveness to mother, and oral activity.

At 0-5-13, our records indicate the beginning of a trend which would peak at about ten months of age. Regarding *aggression,* we wrote: "She is continually looking and busy exploring and socializing; activity is constant. Nondestructive aggression is at a quite higher level today— *moderate,* with waxing and waning discharges. During the waxing period, her entire body discharges—legs, arms, trunk, head—and she stretches in all directions. The accompanying affect is pleasurable and effort, drivenness, pressure are clearly visible on her face."

At age 0-6-14, we recorded a crescendo in manifestations of aggression: "Much nondestructive aggressive discharge present in her large exploratory activity of toys, faces. She also yells out sharply, with pleasure—a vocal aggressive discharge—seemingly associated with excitement. We also find that during exploration, she gets excited and pleasurably discharges mounting tension by rhythmically striking the floor with her extended arm; or she looks at an object, then with little apparent tension, strikes the floor several times; or while hyperextending to reach for something, she goes into another floor-pounding discharge. At times, the hyperextension associated with excitement or wanting to reach something itself has the quality for discharging nondestructive aggression. Three days later she is crawling."

About one month later, at 0-7-15, she crawled with reliability and tenacity, having achieved sufficient mastery to permit locomotion in a radius of from five to ten feet from mother. We consider this the beginning of the first part of the practicing subphase (Mahler 1972a, 1972b), the part of that subphase which overlaps with the differentiation subphase.

At 0-7-28 we noted that as soon as Mrs. W. put her daughter down upon arrival at the project, Mary sprang into exploratory activity, as though she had been wound up in readiness. Her energy level was vigorous. (This activity is the more startling in that the crescendo of the manifestations of the aggressive drive had not yet reached its peak.) At 0-9-0, Mary, following the same path the other children had taken, was encountering and reacting more and more to the resistance put up by the other children when she tried to take something from them to which she was attracted.

At age 0-9-10, she took several steps, supporting herself on a sofa. She loudly vocalized excitement. This upsurge in aggression was manifested not only in the conflict-free sphere of ego functioning. At this date, in object relations, we also recorded her aggressive reaction to separation anxiety: "Mrs. W. had reported that for several weeks now, Mary cried when mother left the room, but we had not seen such a reaction in the project. We did, however, see pleasure on reunion before. Today Mary's mother returned after a brief absence for an appointment. While mother was gone—even though she was held by a well-liked observer—Mary searched for her mother the entire time. Upon mother's return, instead of showing pleasure, Mary scolded her indignantly for a few seconds before she was comforted in mother's arms. Her mother held her for about ten minutes. Then when Mrs. W., responding to Mary's older brother's needs, put Mary down, Mary repeated the scolding, with the same reprimanding angry intonation with which she had greeted her mother upon reunion."

When we saw her after a five-week separation, we found Mary's object world expanding, coordination of her musculolocomotor apparatus advancing, and her drives continuing at the strong level we had come to know. She took her first unsupported steps at 0-10-28. At age 0-11-14, we recorded her entry into the practicing subphase proper. At 0-11-30 she reached what we felt to be the peak intensity of her evolving aggressive drive. Hereafter, she generally stayed at this level of aggression discharge and aggression-derived activity—a very busy, robust, self-assertive toddler. At this time, when she walked on all fours—a method she devised for crawling when she wore a dress—she "looked like a football player."

At this point in development, when her mother obstructed the sufficient gratification of her highly propelled strivings for autonomy, we began to see Mary's reactive frustration experienced at a new psychic level of functioning. When she was 1-0-13, we recorded the following:

"*Nondestructive aggression:* Mary's push to explore is urgent and large. When mother brings her in, as soon as Mary is on the floor, she takes off as if with a burst of stored-up energy which is readily discernable when she crawls—head down, rapid arm-leg movements, darting. But today she is also walking, and the novelty of that locomotor and ego mastery does not permit a rapid movement to her target. However, because libidinizing the locomotor apparatus carries with it the expenditure of aggressive energy, she can tolerate reaching targets slowly without frustrating aggressive impulses. She is busy continually for the entire one and a half hours of her visit.

"Again, the clearly discernable pressure, the drive-like quality, of her exploratory activity is striking. She does not determine that she will move from point A to B, she is propelled—like a bus pushed in motion by its fully-open engine—and the ego seems a little behind in controlling that powerful machine (Freud 1923).

"But today, we see a significant peak in one of the consequences of this pressured drive activity. Mary is constantly reaching for cups, ashtrays, other children's toys. Repeatedly she wants to push the toy cart which mother has been prohibiting her to do; now she looks at mother when she approaches it (superego-precursor) and at times redirects her trajectory to another target. She repeatedly goes into the hall where Mrs. W. feels it is not yet safe for her to go.

Hostile destructive aggression: Now, when mother follows her into the hall, picks her up, and tells her she is not to go out there, Mary complains angrily, her face flushing, muscles tense, shaking, and she yells. All can tell that she is frustrated and very angered by mother's interference. But she does not hit her mother, the object of that anger; indeed, she seemed at one moment to lightly hit herself in the nose. She does not bite, or strike her mother; she strikes the couch and the toy cart.

"Control of destructive aggression (superego precursor): Mary visibly works to control the actual discharge of destructive impulses toward mother, destructiveness aroused by mother's interference: she stands on her toes, tenses her whole body, shout-screams her objection; her face reddens. This discharge, partly expressed and partly contained, stops after two or three seconds. Several times she approaches the troublesome toy cart, turns and looks at her mother, then turns to a toy, thus changing the trajectory of her strong now-frustrated autonomous strivings. On several occasions, she goes into the forbidden hall for about five feet, stops, turns around to look for mother's prohibition, (we presume) even when mother does not see her and has said nothing, but she then gives in to the internal push and her mother has to retrieve her."

We can now see the *beginnings* of the internalization of maternal dictates, the displacement of drive discharge, and some inhibition of it. This is the beginning of a sharp conflict between Mary and her mother, one that will shortly come full blown. It will be detailed and discussed below (see pp. 202–210).

In the brief recapitulation of the evolution of Mary's aggressive drive, attention is drawn to the mounting of that aggressive drive activity, which high-lights by its marked rise what occurred less dramatically in the other children—but which we could now recognize.

At age 0–1–12, activity-type and aggressive drive manifestations were described as *moderate-low, quiet.*

At 0–3–20, these were again described as *moderate-low;* but there was a constant flow of visual-auditory exploratory activity when Mary was physiologically and libidinally gratified.

At 0–5–10, these activities were again found to be *moderate-low* in level; Mary was described as placid, but showing a constant flow of visual-auditory exploratory activity.

At 0–5–13, we recorded activities to be "at quite a higher level today," i.e., at a *moderate* level, waxing and waning, with musculomotor discharge.

From 0-5-17 until 0-11-4, when we recorded her entry into the practicing subphase proper, Mary's level of aggressive drive-derived activity mounted progressively to a *high normal* level, traversing nearly the entire range of normal levels of aggressive drive activity. Again at 1-0-20, her aggressive energy level was recorded as *high normal,* with much excitement present, much pleasure in function, and a strong and firm reaction of frustration and anger when mother prohibits specific acts of exploration, control, and mastery. On this day she reacted with short-lived anger at mother's prohibitions, directing that anger at mother. She seemed more determined and focused in her complaint. She did not strike her mother, herself or others; she yelled, tensed and extended her entire body, her face reddening. Her reaction of frustration and anger was greater as the two-hour period came toward its close, as the ego bore less well that frustration and hostility aroused by the excessive unpleasure she experienced.

I leave off the narrative on Mary's evolving aggressive drive—to return to it below in a discussion of the practicing subphase conflict—and present briefly a similar upsurge in manifestations of the aggressive drive in Bernie.

Bernie

Bernie showed much evidence of healthy ego apparatuses and a good aggressive drive disposition during the normal autistic phase. At twelve days of age when his mother held him he looked straight at her, clearly focusing attention on her face for thirty or sixty seconds; he repeated this several times in the course of thirty minutes. At age 0-1-2, we typed his activity level as *moderate*.

The following note, at 0-4-8, was characteristic of his smoothly evolving development: "Object relations differentiating well with specificity of the mother already clearly evident; so are normal reactions to strangers, including, as he shows on this day, the ability to use comforting by a stranger when mother is briefly absent (he reacted to mother's momentary separation by crying angrily). Regarding aggression and autonomous ego functions, we consider him of *moderate* activity level; there is a good deal of exploratory activity of all sorts of objects, animate and inanimate. When frustrated, in reaction to delay on mother's part to feed him or hold him, he cries rather quickly, loudly, demandingly, angrily, and soon moves into mild rage. Then he flails his arms, kicks his legs spastically, fists clenched; he does not pull his hair, strike mother or himself, reach to grab, etc." Ten days later, at 0–4–18, he indicated he wanted to stand and made surprisingly successful efforts to walk while his mother supported him, it seemed, only in terms of equilibrium.

At 0–8–27, again we noted Bernie's constant busyness, his continual explorations, his crawling with facility and speed. We noted his good expression of affects, preponderantly those of well-being, his age-adequate object relatedness, well-developing ego functions, and the good distribution of libido and aggression. Three days later, at 0–9–0, we entered the following note: "Sudden, remarkable upsurge of non-destructive aggression as evidenced in a marked increase in drive-derived activity, overnight. Bernie's upsurge is more sudden than that of the others, including Mary. The pressure of that activity is large: his face and body movements reveal this pressure, by its affect as well as the new power and velocity of his movements. These are not the result of a suddenly more powerful and capable musculature; rather it is as though a switch has been turned on which unleashes energy not available to him three days ago." We saw this turned-on power in Mary upon her entry into the practicing subphase. Here we marked Bernie's entry into the practicing subphase.

Four days later he was as active; the following note was entered: "Once his attention cathexis is turned on thing A, he grabs thing A irrespective of its location (as long as he can reach it). Thus, when he reaches for and takes the cracker in the hand of Renée, he seems not to know that Renée owns it. Visually, tactilely, orally, he takes hold of whatever rouses his attention irrespective of its attachment. It is not taking something from Renée that drives him, it is the pressure to take hold of, assert himself upon and control things. Par excellence, this is characteristic of the autonomous strivings that become so prominent during the practicing subphase" (see Peller 1965, and Hendrick 1942, 1943b).

This higher level of drive-derived activity became characteristic of Bernie's practicing subphase. Since Bernie was particularly strong physically, one could readily feel the play of aggression upon Bernie's musculature when he had grabbed something and then one had tried to pry open his hand to retrieve it. This was felt particularly by the mothers and observers during the brief period when he wanted to take hold of Anni's hair in his forceful exploratory grabbings. He entered the practicing subphase proper (Mahler 1972a, 1972b) at 1-0-6, when he took his first unaided steps and climbed onto the sofa three times under his own steam. The energy expended by him during the course of his practicing subphase, its ever present abundance and revitalization, is of course the history of youth. While I have several times raised an eyebrow at Winnicott's calling this source of energy *life force* (1950x, p. 216), I am now more timid about doing so; and I appreciate better Greenacre's enigmatic remark: "I would see aggression as having its origin in the enormous pressure of growth. . . . The force of growth would appear of necessity a nonhostile form of physical aggression" (1971, p. 197). And to close, from Spitz (1965): "Freud conceived of aggression as the other fundamental drive operating in the psyche. . . . This aggression serves to approach, to seize, to hold, to overpower, or to destroy the object—and by extension things. It is expressed or carried out 'though the instrumentality of . . . the muscular apparatus'" (p.9).

Pattern Variance
Drive patterns vary, a fact well-documented clinically, and in such publications as those of Alpert, Neubauer, and Weil (1956), Fries and Woolf (1953), and Escalona (1963). Weil (1970) has drawn attention to the fact that there is a very wide range of variance in the psychobiologic basic core of each child in an average child population.

With regard to levels of aggressive drive activity, for example, we found in Jane and Vicki an early disposition to a *normal-high* level discharge of aggression. Children like Jane (Charles too, whom we saw only from age three to six months) are busy physically from the outset, their entire body taking part in movements; they seem energetic; they are invariably described as active infants. Invariably too they suck well and vigorously, and often are easily responsive to maternal handling. We are not speaking of hyperactive children, but of normal levels of activity. In contrast, there are those children who show an early disposition to *normal-low* level discharge of aggression. Like Mary, Candy, and Doris, these infants look quite healthy and sturdy. But they move their bodies sparingly, except for their eyes; they seem to take in more than they act upon, or, they act upon the environment preferentially with their eyes.

Another pattern variance is found in the upsurge in aggressive drive manifestations and, hence we infer, in the upsurge of the children's aggressive drive which is associated with their entry into the practicing subphase. Thus Mary and Bernie showed an abrupt and marked upsurge; by contrast Candy, Jane, and Harold showed a gradual upsurge which escaped detection while it occurred but could subsequently be constructed from their protocols. These variances are spectral in character, of course, and not bipolar.

Upsurge of Aggression and the Practicing Subphase
In her early formulations of the practicing subphase, Mahler (1965, 1968) remarked:

"There is steadily increasing investment in practicing motor skills and exploring the expanding environment, both human and inanimate. . . . The main characteristic . . . is the great narcissistic investment of the child in his own functions, his own body, as well as in the objects and objectives of his expanding reality testing." Outstanding are the child's absorbtion in his own activities, his strivings for exploration, and his manifest 'love affair with the world'" (Mahler 1965, pp. 164-5).

In 1968, speaking of this period in development, Mahler remarked that there is a *"maturational spurt* of active locomotion, which brings with it increased pressure 'for action,' to practice locomotion and to explore wider segments of reality. . . . At that point, a large proportion of the available cathexis shifts from within the symbiotic orbit to investing the autonomous apparatuses of the self and the functions of the ego—locomotion, perception, learning" (pp. 18-20). A bit beyond, she notes that "through maturation of the ego apparatuses—and *facilitated by the flux of developmental energy* (Kris, 1955)—a relatively rapid, yet orderly process of separation-individuation takes place in the second year of life" (p. 21, italics added). In more recent formulations of this subphase Mahler continues to hold the impression that there is a spurt in ego functions, in practicing motor skills, and in exploring the expanding environment (1972b, p. 491).

We have found exactly this phenomenology. Psychoanalytic infant observation and the search for metapsychologic explanation lead me to propose that *these features of the practicing subphase are given their characteristics especially by the maturational upsurge of the aggressive drive,* which shows itself not only in the realm of nondestructive aggression. As will be shown below, the destructive trends too show a similar upsurge, further supporting the thesis that the various trends in aggression are part of the same basic instinctual drive.

Of course, such an upsurge may not be as readily detectable in some children. For example, in Jane, whose activity level was high from birth on, the practicing subphase was not as dramatically heralded by a sudden large outburst of drive activity as reported for Mary and Bernie. At the opposite pole, Anni's aggression was markedly dampened by a congenital brain disorder with a generalized muscle weakness: the increased activity of her practicing subphase had to be magnified by our senses to be observed, as did all aspects of responsiveness in this child.

It has been assumed in psychoanalysis that the drives differentiate in the sequence formulated in psychosexual theory, and that in the course of this evolving, the libido and aggression influence each other mutually. Attempting to tease out the differentiations of the aggressive drive from those of the libido leads me to underline again the hypothesis that it is the differentiation of the aggressive drive which gives to the anal phase its well-known character. I say *again* because Freud was well aware of this condition when, as Peller (1965) notes, he referred repeatedly to the anal phase as the *sadistic-anal* phase (not anal-sadistic) at a time when *sadistic* meant that drive which later became known as the *destructive* drive.

I question if the large maturational spurt in the aggressive drive at this time is matched by an equal upsurge in libido. Observations allow the inference that it is not. The shift in the libido from the oral to the anal phase seems to follow by several months the practicing subphase maturational upsurge of the aggressive drive. During the practicing subphase, this upsurge in aggression seems to dominate the trends in the ego. The libido tentatively invested in objects by the ego's attention-cathexis is in part withdrawn from the all-important symbiotic partner and becomes invested in those ego functions being exercised by, and the wide object-environment being explored under, the impetus of the upsurge in aggression. In other words, in line with a suggestion by Mahler (1968, with Pine and Bergman 1975), the libido seems more directed toward that aspect of the self which is its peripheral rind, especially its outer sensorimotor organization. At the same time, the libido extends now also omnipotently beyond the symbiotic orbit (and partner) to exploration and cathexis of the ego's widening horizons. Under the impetus of the upsurge in the aggressive drive, both libido and aggression are invested in ego functions that lead toward assimilation and mastery of the emerging self and the environment.

Along with the finding that the practicing subphase is launched by, and owes its character to, an upsurge in the aggressive drive, one also finds a consonant, large maturational upsurge in autonomous ego apparatuses which, fueled by the upsurge in aggression, becomes sharply exercised. In addition, it also seems that the upsurge in the aggressive drive is the powerful factor that gives to narcissism and omnipotence the thrust by which we know them so well during the practicing subphase, a thrust which contributes enormously to the child's remarkable autonomous strivings. While such autonomous strivings are evident earlier—as we saw in Jane's efforts at self-feeding at fifteen weeks of age (Parens 1973a, Parens and Prall, 1974)—they now acquire a momentum which is often difficult for the young ego to contain, one which leads to marked unpleasure and conflict when thwarted by the environment, a phenomenon to be described below.

PRACTICING SUBPHASE CONFLICT

In the section of this chapter on nondestructive aggressive impulse discharge, I detailed the development in Jane of a struggle for control which arose between herself and her mother, in which the intrapsychic pressure (strivings for autonomy) propelled Jane out the double door again and again despite repeated resistance on the part of her symbiotic partner. Mrs. K.'s efforts to protect her daughter by limiting in a reasonable way the periphery of her explorations led to what Freud (1915) has described as the rage induced by persisting environmental obstruction of drive gratification. In this instance it occurred at a time when an enormous upsurge of aggression made itself felt. The conflict which resulted took on the character of a battle of wills between child and mother. Where the aggressive upsurge is especially sharp, it may create an extremely difficult situation for the object (mother) and the child. This comes particularly from the fact that a sufficient frustration of nondestructive aggressive strivings often leads to the emergence of hostile (destructive) feelings in the child—a condition much complicated in those cases (unlike that of Jane) in which the mother's ambivalence toward her child is pronounced.

Such a focused and dramatic conflict as occurred in Jane was also found in Mary. We can conveniently pick up the chronology of aggressive drive manifestations in Mary which was interrupted above at age 1-0-13. As was noted, at this time we saw a significant phenomenon in consequence of the upsurge in aggression characteristic for this period. The mounting pressure of strivings for autonomy led Mary's mother to prohibit the gratification of those strivings because they presented some hazard, inconvenience, unsocial behavior, or the like. Mrs. W. did not want Mary to push the toy cart, go out the double door into the hall, or reach for cups of coffee or ashtrays or other children's toys; she often was brought to her feet to contain her daughter, who at this time seemed responsive principally to the pressure from within which propelled her in exactly these forbidden directions. I have asked numerous times why a child seems compelled at this developmental phase to push against the mother's prohibitions, which can only threaten the child with fear of loss of love. This will be taken up below.

It was observed that Mary reacted to her mother's restrictions with frustration, unpleasure, and the mobilization of destructive impulses toward her. We saw Mary complain angrily, her face flushing, her muscles tense, shaking and yelling; indeed, we saw her react with mild rage. Mary was visibly working to control the actual discharge of destructive impulses toward her mother, destructiveness aroused by her mother's interference. We saw evidence of the development of defenses and the beginnings of internalization of maternal dictates. Here we found then, the beginning of a sharp conflict between Mary and her mother.

The Conflict: Observations
At 1-1-3, I recorded that the conflict in Mary was mounting: "Today Mary's heretofore moderate objections, loud verbal complaints, and inhibited motor discharge of object-directed destructive aggression (body-tensing, shaking, face-reddening) gave way to a higher level of conflicted reactivity with the actual discharge of destructiveness toward her mother.

"When her mother brought Mary back from the hall, the first several times, Mary smiled and permitted herself to be passively returned to the infant area. But then progressively she complained more vigorously and vocally, contorting her body to extricate herself. Eventually she cried angrily, waved her left arm in a striking movement against her mother several times, kicked her, both from a distance but twice actually striking her mother with her arm. Once she also struck herself."

As we saw also in Jane and the other children, the encounter here between child and mother eventuated in thirteen-month-old Mary's showing evidence of intrapsychic distress. For the first time her crying could not be comforted by the good-enough efforts of her mother. The following was recorded: "Mary is crying angrily in her mother's arms, she seems to want to get out of those arms; her mother puts her down gently, without observable rejection, and Mary cries even more loudly and angrily. Her mother cannot hold her and cannot put her down. She does pick her up and continues to hold her while sitting in a chair, and Mary calms down some. As she sits on her mother's lap, she does not lean back into her mother's body—which she has always done easily— but rather sits upright, separated from her mother's torso. Mrs. W., wanting to comfort her more actively, reaches to touch Mary's arm; Mary pushes her hand away, in an unequivocal gesture of rejection. A moment later this is repeated. Mary's affect is sober and serious."

The narrative is interrupted to draw attention to the metapsychologic assumptions we inferred from the data here recounted, assumptions which indicate that the conflict between child and mother, an *interpersonal conflict*, led to the emergence of an *intrapsychic conflict* in the child, a two-faceted conflict: (1) a conflict of ambivalence (intrasystemic), and (2) a conflict between id-ego and superego-precursor (intersystemic).

When Mary's strivings for autonomy were thwarted by her mother, she progressively experienced more and more unpleasure; eventually hostile destructive impulses were aroused and discharged against the frustrating mother. But this state of unpleasure led the child to need comforting from the gratifying anaclitic object (the good mother), and Mary, crying and angry, turned for comforting to the same mother toward whom her destructive impulses were directed. The infantile ego—already burdened with frustrated autonomous (aggressive-libidinal) strivings—was now presented with antagonistic feelings toward the love-object characteristic of *ambivalence* and *intrapsychic conflict:*

Mary wished to destroy the frustrating (bad) object, and side by side with this, wished to be comforted by the gratifying (good) object. There was ample evidence that Mary seemed to then split object representations. When she was angry at her mother she related to the bad mother, investing her with a large cathexis of hostile destructive impulses; when she wanted to be comforted, she related to the good mother, protecting her against this destructive impulse cathexis by its inhibition. The presence and dominance of each representation seemed to alternate, or rather seemed to lead to a transient immobilization of the ego.

"Now, Mary sat on mother's lap, and as mother tried to comfort her, Mary seemed uncomfortable, but did not permit her mother to put her down. She seemed tense, anxious and restless. She gradually poised herself on her mother's lap, sitting on it but separated from the mother's torso. She rejected her mother's comforting hand twice, and her mother stopped actively trying to comfort her. After Mary's remaining thirty to sixty seconds so poised, Mrs. W. got up carrying her daughter and tried to distract her by going to the toy box. Suddenly, as Mrs. W. bent down, Mary began to cry as if she had been struck by a blow. Mother and observers were startled. When her mother returned to her chair, Mary calmed quickly and again sat upright on her mother's lap. Gradually, her body tone softened and she relaxed passively into her mother's body, thumb in mouth, where she remained, awake, for twenty to thirty minutes."

It is inferred from this second segment of behavior that the intrapsychic conflict of ambivalence (and splitting of object representations) caused the ego's immobility. It was possibly in the efforts by the ego to integrate these ambivalent feelings toward the object, in the work of splitting and integrating the dual representation of the libidinal object, that the ego could not be distracted. When the mother tried to prematurely distract her daughter's attention cathexis, and with it the ego, the interference was felt too unpleasurably by the child, it interfered too sharply with the ego's efforts to master the conflict it experienced, and Mary was suddenly again upset. Gradually, assisted by the mother's good efforts, the cathexis of the good mother representation seemed to gain the upper hand and Mary accepted the comforting offered to her.

That demands on the ego were made by an *intrapsychic* crisis, that indeed an intrapsychic crisis had occurred, seemed supported by Mrs. W's report—which was confirmed—that this same evening, Mary began to communicate with her mother vocally, using inflection and rhythms that sounded like words, except that this vocalization was preverbal. It was, however, a distinct step toward verbal communication, and a newly acquired ego skill. Recall that Mary had shown a significant level of libidinization of her vocal apparatus which she had selectively used early for the discharge of aggression; she was known to us all for her loud spontaneous yells. We hypothesized that the new skill arose out of the demands made this day upon the ego by the conflict in question, the drives, and the object (reality). An additional determining factor, arising from identification, might have been that mother made a point of communicating verbally her prohibitions of Mary's particular strivings for autonomy.

Three days later (1-1-6) the struggle between Mary's id-ego strivings and her mother continued at the same intensity, but Mary was more quickly responsive to her mother's verbalized prohibition, anticipating it more clearly. She went a step further in dealing with her mother's verbal no—and here lay another motivating factor to her new ego skill. She made a preverbal vocal argumentative complaint, all the while complying with her mother's dictate. In passing it is noted that the ego was progressively developing along a number of lines, one of which was its anticipatory function, one of the ego's great achievements. Thus as she walked from A to B, Mary saw a chair that was in her path from the corner of her eye, blinked and squinted, and swerved before she struck herself against it; the event so clearly showed the ego's recognition of the hazard before it occurred, and Mary's automatic, preconscious action to avoid it. This occurred of course at a time when anticipation of mother's prohibitions and disapproval was playing so large a part in her daily life.

Visit after visit, this struggle was evident, as it had also been with Jane and with the others. At 1-2-0, about one month after its onset, we felt that the conflict in Mary was slowly resolving, following a course that waxed and waned. On this day, it peaked slightly: "There was much nondestructive aggression discharged in exploration and continuing mastery of the environment and her body; many new skills were developing, including locomotor and fine hand movements. And with this, Mary also seemed very persistent in wanting the soft toys Mrs. J. had put in front of Charles (age four months); she wanted to take hold of many things, including coffee cups which, she gave evidence, she knew her mother would not let her have. The push of her vigorous strivings for autonomy was relentless. But the struggle was less, even at its height today, than it was three weeks before. Fourteen-month-old Mary continued to use her vocal apparatus to mediate and discharge aggression against her mother; while she complied more easily with mother's prohibitions, she was firm and loud in the expression of her wishes and complaints."

At 1-2-25, again the conflict peaked: "Mary was very self-assertive in wanting to go out the doubledoors, in wanting the sugar cup, etc. What she could have often gratified and gave pleasure, but at times was quickly discarded and some new item sought. Frustration mounted today to the point where she stopped accepting mother's limits and began to give in to the anger these prohibitions aroused. She at first expressed her anger by vocal sounds that had the quality of cursing and scolding. One observer thought she said damn. At one moment while walking away from her mother she hit out toward her in the air. This morning she managed to wake up the four children who were sleeping—that four were asleep was an unusual as the fact that she woke them all up."

Within the next two weeks further resolution of this crisis was apparent. At 1-3-1, about two months after its onset, "Mary approached her mother and conveyed to her the wish that mother relent in her prohibition against Mary's going down the hall to the toddler area. Here now, Mary was in control of her impulses, aware of mother's prohibition, but she modulated the pressure behind the wish well; she did not command, nor even demand. And she seemed to accept her mother's no. This was repeated one week later under conditions of renewed pleasantness between mother and daughter; Mary's affect and mood were good, cheerful. When she fell against a table, she readily accepted mother's comforting. Another week later, Mary's twelve-year-old brother, who was visiting, took her to the toddler area for snacks. One month later she was going there with her mother's permission. A number of factors relating to the mother's reactions to her strongly aggressive, growing daughter permitted Mary's movement to the toddler area."

This narrative is concluded here with the note that Mary's practicing subphase extended to age twenty-one months; since we recorded its beginning at about seven and a half months, we must—according to

Mahler's formulations—consider it protracted: about thirteen months in duration. It is my impression that the principal factor accounting for this subphase being long was the notably large upsurge in the aggressive drive which mounted from age five months on in a crescendo that peaked at about ten or twelve months. The breadth of this drive upsurge was such that the ego took much longer in gaining control over it and in preparing for the next subphase of separation-individuation.

When Mary was about eighteen months, Mrs. W. began to report that her daughter was showing an interest in sitting on the potty. The interest did not materialize in toilet training at that time. It should be noted, however, that this interest followed by a number of months the seeming resolution of the practicing subphase conflict. In the months which followed that conflict, there was little notable difficulty between child and mother, and Mary was a cheerful child. She remained so, rather unconflicted, until her rapprochement crisis when a transient sleep problem developed. She also had a full blown oedipal conflict in due time.

Interpersonal and Intrapsychic Conflict
While not all the children showed such focused and dramatic conflicts as did Jane and Mary, all the children (at the time of this writing) showed evidence of it. For instance, in Candy the strongest expression of this battle of wills between mother and child focused around touching the back of a television set or picking at plastic flowers; in Harold, it was around his touching an electrical cord. In Cindy, episodes were less benign, more protracted, and took the form of short-lived weak temper tantrums. We should note that in Candy and Harold the mildness of their struggle derived from them, from their greater malleability (a condition arising from a well-balanced relation of the ego and drives) and not from any particular meekness on the part of their mothers.

Unlike the phenomenon described by Mahler and coworkers as the rapprochement crisis (Mahler, Pine, and Bergman 1975), the conflict here described as characteristic for the practicing subphase *does not have an intrapsychic origin*. It arises from the marked upsurge of aggression and concomitant differentiation of ego apparatuses and functions (locomotor, cognitive, and object-related) encountering external objectal resistance. *It is in origin an interpersonal conflict.* But it has far-reaching consequences for such *intrapsychic* processes as the internalization of objectal dictates, the control and modulation of aggression, the erection of ego defenses (for example, the splitting of object representations with attendant distribution of libido and aggression in these representations), and without concluding the list of its influences, the confrontation by reality of the child's narcissism-omnipotence.

Thus while later in development some drive derivatives lead to conflict of intrapsychic origin, at this developmental period, drive derivatives lead to intrapsychic conflict secondarily, both by the internalization of the interpersonal conflict here described (between id and parental-introject/superego-precursor), and by the induction of ambivalence toward the libidinal object, the evolving good and bad object representations.

Observation recommends the assumption that the upsurge in strivings for autonomy found at this developmental period (see Erikson 1959) is effected by the large upsurge in the aggressive drive; the libido plays its part by cathecting the ego apparatuses and their newly evolving functions. The pleasure in function, so aptly described by Greenacre's (1960) metaphor, the child's love affair with the world, is evidence, in our opinion, of gratifications of both aggression and libido. It is the frustration of both by the more or less appropriately resisting, limit-setting object which leads now to striking rage in some children. For the ego, this libidinal-object-directed rage is a dramatic new experience, one in which the young ego becomes further acquainted with the power of the aggressive drive, a power it is in many instances helpless to contain. At the same time the newly evolving ego apparatuses and functions are sharply propelled by the push from the aggressive drive, they are also in the process of being libidinized; there is in addition, the concomitant shift in libidinal cathexis to those ego apparatuses and functions—a fact which imposes a lessening of attention cathexis invested in the libidinal object. We also find a marked heightening of narcissism and omnipotence, which, while not as absolute as the narcissism of the neonate, receives marked activation now by the heightened aggressive drive. In the practicing subphase the combination of these factors—the upsurge of aggression (with its push in strivings for autonomy, its heightening of narcissism-omnipotence, and its activation of ego apparatuses and propelling their functions) with the large investment of libido in these and with pleasure-in-function—gives the impression of an exhilarated, hypomanic-like state, the now famed love affair with the world.

It is in this phase that the average child encounters the good-enough (Winnicott 1953) object's first strong prohibitions; and it is here that the child's ego takes its first stand in a conflict between his own drives on the one hand and the highly cathected libidinal object's dictates on the other. The more benevolently cathected the love object, the more positive the ego's efforts to force compliance from the antagonistic drive derivatives, and the more the ego will make good use of the auxiliary ego (Spitz) in this task. It is readily recognized then, that this conflict opens most salutary possibilities for the development of psychic structure. This is where the ego's work to tame aggression begins. The young ego rendered anxious by the attitude of the object sets itself the great task of mediating between the drives and reality; it begins to internalize dictates from the highly cathected libidinal object and activates neutralization of hostile destructiveness toward that valued object. Here therefore, the ego begins to evolve those precursors that will develop into the superego, and takes a further large step in evolving object-relatedness. The cumulative effects of this conflict, hand in hand with the further development of the ego, eventually lead the child to recognize that the world is not his oyster, as Mahler likes to say, and pave the way for his next subphase of separation-individuation, the rapprochement subphase.

Practicing Subphase Conflict and Anal Phase Conflict

In her effort to further clarify the character of the child's evolving *libidinal* organization, Peller (1965) presents a formulation that is of much interest to the one advanced here: "The *sadistic-anal* phase is dominated by the drive for achieving mastery *(Bemaechtigungstrieb)*. Mouth, skeletal and ring muscles (anus, urethra) are highly charged with libido; they are the executive organs. The child strives primarily for mastery of his body, and secondarily to overcome the resistances that he encounters. He is ready to ride roughshod over anything that stands in the way of a wish. Biting into something and reducing it to a pulp; grasping something with his hands and throwing it; expelling urine or fecal matter, or holding it back—these are some of the sensations and activities he enjoys. He hears something and turns to see it; he sees something and crawls to it or reaches for it, in order to 'handle' it. . . . With the aid of this incessant motor and sensory activity, he constructs a universe that is more dependable and stable than the oral world, yet not as reliable as ours" (pp. 737–38).

Speaking further of this second *libidinal* organization, the sadistic-anal phase, Peller remarks that she sees "the ruthless drive for attaining mastery over his body and over objects animate and inanimate as the dominant drive. I am by no means the first one to do this. To Hendrick belongs the merit of having provided good evidence for the powerful 'instinct for mastery.'" On many points she agrees with him, but not on all (p. 741). One such area of disagreement is that she believes the drive for mastery to be "a pregenital sexual drive," which Hendrick does not (see chapter 2). It is also here that Peller notes that "Freud refers to *Bemaechtigungstrieb und Bewegungslust* no less frequently than to anal drives" and that "all these strivings . . . are essential parts of the second libidinal organization" (p. 742).

Peller concludes, therefore, regarding the term *anal phase,* that "if it implies the existence of a phase of development in which the anal zone, its functions, and their derivatives are as central and as dominant as the oral zone is during the oral phase, then I consider this to be incorrect. The intense *Lust* (pleasure) that young children derive from unre-strained gross muscular activity is so obvious that it cannot be over-looked. Perusal of Freud's writings (early as well as late) shows that he stressed sadistic (scil. aggressive) strivings regularly in conjunction with the anal ones" (pp. 743–74).

It seems to me that the differences in Peller's formulations from those advanced in this work may derive from the differences in our ap-proaches to this developmental period. In contrast to Peller's approach, mine is from the vantage point not of the libidinal organization, but of separation-individuation, a frame of reference chosen especially not to bias a study of aggression with the lens of the libido.

I ask now, as does Peller, what gives to the anal phase of psychosex-ual development its particular characteristics of willfulness, obstinacy, stubbornness, and indeed sadism? Certain viewpoints converge here. Mahler (1965, 1968) speaks of practicing newly developing ego appara-tuses and functions and of great narcissistic investment by the child in his own functions, his body, and the external environment. Erikson (1959) speaks of the ego's efforts to attain a sense of autonomy.

Hendrick (1942, 1943) speaks of a mastery instinct; so does Peller (1965), but she draws attention to its intensified activation during the anal phase of psychosexual development. Above all Freud speaks a number of times of sadism and mastery deriving from the same instinctual source, and repeatedly refers to the "sadistic-anal" phase at a time when the concept *sadism* (aggression) is featured prominently in his formulations of that phase.

I believe that it is this biologically determined upsurge of aggression which at this developmental period induces such large efforts at mastery and autonomy as well as the expressions of sadism associated with the anal phase. It is particularly the ego's riding the wave of aggression, along with the maturation of autonomous ego apparatuses, that leads to the efforts at mastery we see, as the ego's apparatuses and functions become progressively libidinized. This upsurge of aggression seems to account for the characteristics of obstinacy, willfulness, and sadism so identified by us as pertaining to the anal phase of psychosexual development.

Note that these conflicts appeared in our subjects before any effort to toilet-train took place; anal derivatives did not yet seem to play a part in them. Nonetheless, they had the same central characteristics of obstinacy, willfulness, and sadism ascribed to anal conflicts. On this evidence, I propose that this practicing subphase conflict which arises principally from the large upsurge of the aggressive drive is at the basis of certain features of the anal phase conflict and indeed gives to this libidinal conflict its particular character. It is here underscored that this reformulation actually adds nothing new to existing knowledge; its purpose is to formally reorder a priority taken for granted—that it is aggression which paints the anal phase of libidinal development in its well-known colors.

CONTINUING INFLUENCE OF AGGRESSION ON STRUCTURAL DEVELOPMENT

During the practicing subphase, we were impressed with the emergence of several defenses—*inhibition, prerepression, presublimation* (including *reaction-formation), internalization* of maternal dictates, and *splitting of object representations.* These were principally implemented by the ego in its efforts to cope with libidinal-object-directed hostile destructive impulses. The observations of this period show the importance of a sound and *sufficiently positive* object-cathexis to the motivation in the ego to evolve these development-enhancing part-functions, as well as to the ego's successfully dealing with the child's own destructiveness; the importance of that object-cathexis is readily discerned in the character of these defenses. In other words, the level to which these defenses evolve, and the degree as well as the manner in which they are implemented by the ego is in large part dependent on the character of the child's object cathexes (Parens 1971a, 1972a).

Inhibition of Discharge of Destructive Impulses
One can see the inhibition of object-directed destructive impulses emerge with the sufficient libidinization of the object. We found this defense already during the differentiation subphase (five to ten months) along with beginnings of the internalization of parental dictates, but it was frequently encountered in simple forms. Here is a more complex example: It was described above how Jane, at 0-10-3, exhibited the wish to get her mother's cigarettes, that she encountered mother's prohibition and frustration of this wish, which released a quickly mounted rage response directed toward the object including a very brief unleashing of hostile destructive impulses evidenced in her striking her mother once. At this time the alternation of states of calming punctured and interrupted four times by an outburst of angry crying with only the vocal-affective component led us to infer the protracted working through of Jane's object-directed destructive impulses. We could infer that the frustration of the nondestructive aggressive impulse which fueled this wish led to the rage against the frustrating mother, who was also the loved, trusted, gratifying mother. The narcissistically rein-forced destructive impulses encountered the love feelings for and the strong libidinal investment in the good mother. We are reminded of Freud's comments on remorse in 1913, and in 1926, about a later developmental period in Little Hans. One could see the manifestations of the struggle within Jane who could not be so readily comforted by her mother this time, who would not let her mother make her passive at that moment and cuddle her soothingly, but who, on the other hand, did not strike her mother more than once at the height of her outburst, and who clearly showed evidence of containing the discharge of a large load of destructiveness by her efforts at obliterating it. We felt that her rage was gratified only very little in striking her mother once, in partly

rejecting her mother's efforts to comfort her, and in the affecto-vocal discharge. The direct discharge was indeed largely *inhibited,* and aborted.

Prerepression
Turning again to Jane's cigarette episode when she was 0-10-3 of age, I focus on what in a neurophysiological frame of reference we would call the "after-discharge" of her burst of hostile destructive impulses. But I view this not at all as a physiological phenomenon, but rather as a psychological one. After her outburst of anger toward her frustrating mother, Jane gradually calmed over a period of ten minutes on her mother's lap. She then returned to her exploratory-mastery work, sober-faced. After a moment of pensive stillness, she began to cry again, bitterly, leaving little doubt in the observers' minds that the memory, only fifteen minutes old, of being frustrated by her mother was reexperienced in full force, as if it came back up from some form of repression. She calmed again, and again minutes later, a sudden outburst of crying gave evidence of the reexperiencing of the frustration and destructiveness which in actuality had occurred thirty or more minutes before. This was repeated four times over a period of one hour. It was noted above that the rage toward the frustrating mother encountered the love feelings toward the gratifying, loved mother, to speak metaphorically. The cathexis of the good mother was protected by the ego against the onslaught of hostile destructive impulses which the bad representation of that same mother aroused. In addition to being inhibited, these impulses were also pushed out of awareness.

In experiencing empathically the reemergence of frustration and rage in the child, this observer would describe it as the reemergence of a bad experience-now-in-memory which had been pushed out of awareness and remained there until the pressure of its reactive cumulative impulses could not be maintained by the young ego; then in a compromise-formation the young ego permitted a mitigated, aim-inhibited discharge to emerge. The periods of calm, sober activity between the outbursts of angry crying may be periods when the ego's efforts to cope with the instinctual conflict (intrasystemic) succeeded in keeping the destructive impulses out of awareness. It is this view that suggests that some *early form of repression* may be in effect and available to the young ego at this age.

Presublimation, or Making-a-game of a Conflict Situation

When Jane was 0-10-17, she came to an impasse with her mother, described above. Driven from within, she wanted to go out of the infant area to investigate a cleaning cart which was occasionally brought there at the early part of our sessions. Her first reactions to her mother's obstructing that investigation were rage clearly affecto-vocally directed at her mother, with total body hyperextension and moderate efforts to wiggle herself free from her mother's hold. While there was strength in the affecto-vocal component, there was no striking of her mother herself. During the course of her fifteen or so efforts that morning, the character of her effort and of her reaction to her mother's prohibition and physical restraint was very much the same, except that it smoothly, progressively decreased in intensity. This effort stopped as if spontaneously with the help of a distraction conceived and effected in a moment of tension (a transitional phenomenon) in the child-mother dyad (Winnicott 1953).

At 0-10-20 of age, she again wanted to go out the double doors, again her mother prevented her from doing so, and again Jane was angry. The tone of her anger, however, was not so harsh as three days earlier. At the fifth or sixth interaction, Mrs. K. was carrying Jane back upside down, folded on herself. Suddenly, Jane's affect changed and a smile came on her face. It is very likely, we reconstructed, that mother had intended to lighten the interaction by this maneuver. The next time around, Jane was smiling even before her mother reached her and brought her back, head hanging down, with a grin on her face. In short order, by the mutual efforts of mother and child, the conflict had become a game. The drivenness of the autonomous strivings, fueled now by amalgamated nondestructive and destructive aggression, continued for several weeks with marked intensity. Indeed, while making-a-game of the conflict with mother helped to modulate and control the destructive impulses aroused, this defense was insufficient, as were displacement and inhibition, and evidence of *splitting of the object representations* became apparent.

At age 0-11-1, Jane and Mrs. K.'s impasse proceeded as follows: Jane persisted in about twenty efforts to go out the double doors. Nearly every time her mother intervened either verbally or both verbally and physically. Each time Jane was returned with little or no gratification of the original wish to go out. Several times Jane turned back before her mother needed to intervene at all; here we considered the workings of internalizing maternal dictates. Her most frequent adaptive sequence on this day was: when her mother told Jane to not go out, Jane turned back and smiled charmingly and cleverly at her mother, as though she were playing with her. The striking feature was that no hostility was manifested on Jane's part, whereas on 0-10-20 and before, her mother's intervention had been forcible and had elicited a large rage reaction.

Our first and immediate assessment was that Jane was trying to mollify her mother into letting her have her way, and that she wanted to make her mother smile and not be angry with her. But further consideration led us to believe that the making of the game served the even more important function of helping the child master her own destructive impulses mobilized against the now-frustrating love-object.

Again, from 0-11-11 through 0-11-18, Jane carried out the routine of going to the hallway and having to have mother intervene to stop her. We noted again that she was not angry, that it had stabilized as a game. It is in the sense of Peller's (1954) classical remark "Play is a step toward sublimation" that the defensive making-a-conflict-into-play here described is suggested to be the *presublimation* work of the ego.

Internalization of Maternal Dictates and Superego-Precursors
Our observations suggest that, as was stated above, the *beginnings* of superego-precursor structuring occur during the differentiation subphase. Now during the practicing subphase, the children reliably responded to a verbal prohibition by mother with a disruption of the smooth progress of the activity which had aroused the prohibition. This behavior showed some of the earliest evidence of the internalization of parental dictates, as when the child turned to look at the mother whenever doing something which the mother had previously prohibited. Of course, at times, narcissistically supported, autonomous strivings push against both superego-precursors and actual maternal prohibition. Thus Jane, 0-10-17, went toward and/or into the hallway a number of times, disregarding the fact that her mother was telling her loudly and clearly not to go out. The sensitivity to, and denial of, parental prohibitions depends of course on the total psychic status of the child at a given moment. Thus, at one time Jane could totally deny her mother's prohibition while at another she could break into tears if her father or mother said no to one of her wishes or autonomous

strivings. This also occurred especially with Temmy, Cindy, Renée, and Bernie at this period.

In Jane, for example, the internalization of the maternal dictate to not go out the door could be followed through its progressive steps. At 0-11-1, struggling between the gratification of her wish to go out and internalizing the maternal prohibition, Jane turned back several times (out of about twenty efforts) before mother made any actual intervention at all, vocal or even visual. The evidence of the *internal* struggle in the child could be found in her sober affect, her hesitation, her bobbing her head vertically or sideways at the door—all followed by turning back and looking for her mother's acknowledgment and pleasure. At age 0-11-11, the dictate to not go out the door was assisted in its internalization by the stabilization of the defense of making-a-game of the conflict with mother's prohibition, actions, and affects.

Neutralization of Aggression

When Jane and Temmy were fourteen months of age, Candy and Cindy thirteen, and Vicki twelve, another newborn came into our group. This latter newborn brought with her a brother, Donnie, aged two and a half years. Donnie drew our attention to something which was going on under our searching eyes which we did not see. The character of his aggressive discharges alerted us to a large degree of unneutralized destructiveness in him. But it also revealed to us how much Jane, Temmy, and Candy (but not Vicki and Cindy) had achieved a degree of neutralization of destructiveness which we had not recognized.

Further observation then lead us to believe, in agreement with Spitz (1965, p. 289), that *neutralization of destructiveness begins during this last quarter of the first year of life.* One factor which contributes to neutralization is the internalization of the admonitions of the libidinal object. This factor, however, we found not to be sufficient of itself to effect the neutralization of destructiveness. As two-and-a-half-year-old Donnie showed us, parental dictates, once internalized, can act to inhibit the discharge of destructiveness *without effecting its neutralization.* I am led to conclude, as have others (Mahler 1968), that more important to achieving neutralization is the quality and positive/ negative valence of the child's investments of libido and aggression (including destructiveness) in the object of the symbiosis (Mahler's concept that the drives must have "object-passage" to come under ego control).

Our observations of these infants show that what operates to neutralize destructiveness seems to operate silently—if we may borrow another thought from Freud. This is why we did not take note at the outset of these observations of the fact that neutralization was taking place in these infants. What is visible is the character of the child's relation to the symbiotic partner which can be ascertained by the affects, by the emotional interaction of the dyadic partners, and particularly by their mutual pleasurable and unpleasurable interactions—the qualitative and quantitative manifestations of libido and aggression (destructiveness) discharged vis-a-vis the object, which reflect what is being invested in the intrapsychic representation of that developing love-object. In this regard there is strong confirmation of Freud's view (1923) that libido modulates the character of destructiveness *by fusion* with it. One must add that only a particular aspect of the libido achieves this fusion: the libido invested in the object. Hence, aggression (destructiveness) can be modulated by having "object passage."

But while this tells us that the libido by *fusion* with aggression modulates the latter, it does not take into account what leads to that *neutralization* of destructiveness which is effected directly by the ego. By virtue of the child's growing awareness of his dependence on the symbiotic partner, by his now emerging experiences of anxiety, the child begins to effect measures to protect the symbiotic partner against the child's own destructive impulses which when aroused by excessive unpleasure become directed to the much-needed symbiotic partner. No doubt the valuation of that object (the auxiliary ego, in Spitz's term) leads to the qualitative efforts of the ego to modulate and change the aim of the hostile destructive impulse directed to that object. This is the task of the ego, and is distinguishable from fusion by the libido; it is neutralization. (See chapter 14 for a fuller discussion of drive fusion and neutralization.)

Splitting and Integration of Object Representations
With the emergence of the large struggle with mother which followed on the heels of Jane's (0-10-3 on) newly differentiated autonomous locomotor strivings, we found the striking, albeit prosaic, turning of the frustrated, angry child to her mother. What we felt to be striking—since we all took for granted the frustrated child's turning to his mother—was that, first, the child was angry with that mother, i.e., hostile destructive

impulses were in a trajectory to that object and its representation; and that secondly, it was that same object which had aroused the destructive impulses and the angry affect. At 0–10–3, Jane exploded angrily at her mother and struck her once, bursting simultaneously into tears. After less than one minute, by the reciprocal effort of mother and child, Jane leaned against her mother, crying, and mother picked her up. Many times, that day and on subsequent days, when her mother would frustrate her and Jane cried, upset, Jane would turn to her mother for comforting. All the children demonstrated this innumerable times. For a time Temmy's activities seemed to be a continuous chain of events in which her mother would frustrate her with reason and Temmy would be angry, even striking mother on occasion, only to start crying and immediately turn to her mother for comforting. This pattern was more complex and unstable in Vicki who did not so readily turn to her mother for comforting; she learned to not expect such comforting (at that time) from her depressed mother.

It was our impression that this type of dynamic—which occurred many times from this period on, and especially during the rapprochement subphase—permitted us to infer the child's experiencing the same mothering object as alternately frustrating and comforting. We could infer the structuring of the good mother and the bad mother representations, their alternating cathexis in this type of event, and the child's potential ongoing experiences of both *splitting* and *integrating* these two objectal representations.

But we found more. At age 0–11–1, Jane had developed well the defense of making-a-game out of her wish to go out the double door. We also saw evidence of internalization of her mother's prohibition and the earliest superego precursors. In addition, we found that, in the course of one or two visits at this time, Jane selected one of our observers—a woman she had not befriended before—as an object to whom she smiled most charmingly, warmly, against whom she leaned affectionately, and to whom she brought toys she was using. We then found that Jane's mother was looking at this observer with displeasure. We considered the possibility that Jane was omnipotently looking for a replacement for the frustrating mother and that she was possibly directly hurting her mother by rejecting her and attaching libido to a substitute object. But these inferences seemed unsatisfactory.

At 0–11–1 we recorded the postulate that B.K. (the observer in question) had been selected rather suddenly and unexpectedly for transient displacement of the cathexis attached to the good-mother representation, while Jane directly, in vivo, worked out the problem of mitigating those hostile destructive impulses attached to the frustrating-mother representation. One might have expected that she would have displaced (externalized) the cathexis of the frustrating-mother representation; but that was not the case. We felt this formulation to be buttressed by Jane's quite optimal basic trust (Erikson 1959), in consequence of which, we inferred, she omnipotently counted on her mother to help her, as would any good auxiliary-ego, in working through those threatening hostile destructive impulses.

Whether this last postulate is right or not, we viewed these data as sufficient evidence that Jane was splitting good and bad object representations, and that she was doing so to work through some of the overload of hostile destructive impulses which, perforce, were being invested in the love-object. We found Mahler's (1968) and some of Kernberg's (1966, 1967) views on splitting of the object representation to explain very well what we found here and had found many times again. Further evidence of this particular defensive splitting of the object representation made its appearance many times at this period. I confess to having encountered Jane's splitting at ten and eleven months with particular interest, since we knew the child-mother relationship to be more than good-enough, but also since she transiently externalized the gratifying-good-mother, rather than the frustrating-bad-mother, representation. Little doubt remained for me that this defense served the young ego in coping with those troublesome hostile destructive impulses aroused by the interpersonal conflict engendered by her wishes encountering the love-object's prohibitions.

Two weeks later, at age 0-11-15, from all appearances Jane was being her now-usual charming, loving self with B.K.; suddenly, at a given moment Jane stepped hard on B.K.'s foot, as she had been doing of late with her mother. When this occurred a second time, B.K.'s quite natural reaction was to express some pain, displeasure, and say no to Jane. As if she had turned off a switch, Jane left B.K.'s side and for the next four months ignored her totally. B.K. reported repeatedly that Jane would not even look at her. During this period, Jane's relations with her mother, father, siblings, and the group mothers, children and observers remained unchanged at their usual very satisfactory developmental level.

Chapter 9

THE RAPPROCHEMENT
SUBPHASE
(about 16 to 24 months)

Anna Freud has cautioned that one should not overestimate the influence on development of a single factor in psychic life at the expense of other equally important factors. Psychic development proceeds optimally if a number of such factors exist in well-tuned balance. In the neonate, we expect that primary autonomous ego apparatuses and instinctual drives will be normal-enough where the soma is free from structural (anatomical) and functional disturbance. The anlagen of somatic and psychic organizations as well as their maturational time-tables are, first of all, dependent on the integrity of the soma for the normal-enough evolving of their interrelating apparatuses. Then from birth on, the slowly developing ego's experience of internal and external environmental events greatly influences the development of the psychic organization, a point well-developed by Escalona (1963).

With regard to psychic experience, in the first years of life (indeed for a lifetime, Parens and Saul 1971) the *libidinal object* plays a critical part in adaptation to the obtrusive psychic needs emerging from the drives and ego (Freud 1923, 1926, 1933, 1940, Spitz 1946a, 1950, 1965, Mahler, 1952, 1963, 1968, Jacobson, 1964). That part is critical from two standpoints. First, the *libidinal object* (as we mean the term in psycho-analysis, see Cobliner's discussion in Spitz 1965, and not just meaning the gratifier of physiological needs, see Provence and Lipton 1962) is important for the optimal psychic development of the infant from birth on, regardless of the child's lack of awareness of that importance. The importance of the object's function is best illustrated by what Spitz (1950, 1965) has called the child's *auxiliary ego*. Secondly, the object occupies a crucial place in the drive sphere of the developing child as well as in his unfolding ego functions and contents: it is *intrapsychically meaningful* and unique.

Psychoanalytic literature relevant to the unique part the libidinal object plays in the child's developing psychic organization and our accumulated observations from adult and child psychoanalyses, as well as from direct observational study, suggest three peaks of intrapsychic object-centeredness in early psychic life. Each of these peaks leaves its particular imprint on the life-long intrapsychic meaningfulness of the object; each has its influence on psychic development and, of course, on the predisposition to neurosis and more severe disturbance.

Our project findings indicate that the first peak, as elucidated by Spitz (1946a, 1946b, 1950, 1965) and by Mahler (1952, 1965, 1968), occurs from about three to ten months of age. From our direct observations we infer that during the *normal symbiosis* (Mahler) and the initial structuring of the *libidinal object* (Spitz), the child for the first time intrapsychically experiences the object as of central importance.

The second peak occurs during the rapprochement subphase, which in the theory of symbiosis and separation-individuation (Mahler 1965, 1968, with Pine and Bergman 1975) extends generally from about fourteen or sixteen to twenty-four months. Significantly, in her more recent work, Mahler (1972a, 1972b) and some of her coworkers (Mahler, Pine and Bergman 1975) express the belief that this phase may be more crucial to psychic development than has yet been elucidated.

The third peak in intrapsychic object-centeredness occurs from about two and a half to five and a half years of age, during the phase of the oedipus complex. Anna Freud (1963, 1965) called this phase "the object centered phallic phase of development."

From about three to ten months of age then, with the progressive intrapsychic structuring of the libidinal object, the vicissitudes of libido and aggression unavoidably become object-centered. Next, from about ten to sixteen months, during the practicing subphase, we find that the preferential investment of instinctual energy in the libidinal object seems lessened when large amounts of both libido and aggression are diverted from that object into the child's sensory-motor apparatuses and ego functioning. Nonetheless, observation reveals that during the practicing subphase the libidinal object plays a large part in arousing and drawing hostile destructive impulses to herself by her action as obstructor and resistor of the child's explorations and mastery of self and environment. At this time the object seems to act secondarily (that is, it is experiential and does not originate from within the psyche) in the vicissitudes of aggression, in spite of the fact that the part the symbiotic partner plays here is of great importance to the development of certain ego functions, such as modulation, control, delay of discharge, and neutralization of destructiveness as well as to the setting down of superego-precursors.

On the heels of the practicing subphase comes the rapprochement subphase (from about eighteen to twenty-four months) during which the child's relation to his mother seems to be the principal arena of his psychic activity. For much of his waking time we find him predominantly in interaction with objects, principally with mother, and secondly, in order of importance, with siblings, peers, and observers. (No doubt, our project suffered greatly from the fathers not participating regularly alongside the mothers.)

The increasing complexity of our observational data prompts me to present the material of the rapprochement subphase on the model of clinical presentation and formulation, rather than, as I have done up to this point, according to the categories of aggression manifestation. I have elected to detail the chronological findings on two of our children in order to illustrate some of the vicissitudes of aggression during this period. The first child shows some aspects of aggression as the drives are influenced by the rapprochement crisis. The second points up some aspects of aggression in a rapprochement subphase which is complicated and intensified by the birth of a sibling.

CANDY

From age 1-0-7 (when Candy moved away from her mother with deliberation, expanding four-fold the radius of her sphere of exploration), she exhibited what we now view as classical practicing subphase behavior (see Mahler 1968, 1972a, 1972b, with Pine and Bergman, 1975). At 1-4-24, with no discernable external precipitating event, while busily engaged in a number of activities she stayed close to her mother for the entire two-hour session. The character of her busyness drew our attention, as it had in others, to the sharp increase in differentiation of ego functions that heralds and occurs during the rapprochement subphase. As we found in the early part of that developmental subphase, in her closeness to her mother she showed the heightening and differentiation of affective experiences in her reactions of unpleasure and pleasure at separating and reuniting with mother. A blissful expression was visible when she was in contact with her mother. She engaged her mother, demanding that she share her interests, that she watch her perform and approve. We concluded here that she had entered her rapprochement subphase.

At 1-4-27 Candy was solidly self-assertive, a cardinal index of nondestructive aggression as well as one of its earliest manifestations. Candy sat in a small rocking chair. The moment Candy left it, Cindy (1-4-27) and Temmy (1-6-20) squeezed together on that rocker even though Candy was watching them with a most unpleasant look, suggesting that she intended to return to it. After a moment of watching Cindy and Temmy enjoying the chair, Candy threateningly returned to it and struck one solid blow at Temmy, toppling both Cindy and Temmy off the chair. Temmy was shocked, and Candy looked on as if to see the result of her action. The business of her aggression concluded with apparent satisfaction, Candy got back into the rocker. The discharge of destructive impulses was undertaken with a sober affect and seemed intended to remove the intruders.

As we know from everyday experience, in the normal child self-assertiveness is intensified by resistance from the animate and inanimate environments; and resistance which causes excessive unpleasure mobilizes hostile destructive impulses. Self-assertion and the reaction to environmental resistance also played a clear part in the following twice-repeated event: In a heightening of identification with mother, Candy leaned toward and wanted to kiss her twin. However, Cindy pushed Candy away. Candy pushed her back and again tried to kiss Cindy, with the same results. A little later, she handed Cindy's bottle to her, but Cindy did not reach far enough. Mrs. G. tried to help by extending Candy's effort and putting the bottle in Cindy's hands. Frustrated in her wish to act like her mother, however, Candy lightly struck at her mother's outstretched arm. Of course, the development in ego functions evident in this vignette are striking.

When Candy was 1-5-19, Mrs. G, very conflicted due to a familial event which caused her quiet rage, was manifestly depressed and irritable. Candy, too, unlike her usual calm and comfortable self, was downcast, her mood notably resembling her mother's. In what we presumed to be a response to her mother's psychic state, Candy separated from her mother a large part of the time. Also in reaction to her mother's and her own dynamic state, Candy cried when Cindy did not let her sit in the rocker. On this day self-assertiveness was weak compared to Candy's usual level. In part, I believe, this was due to Candy's coping with anger as did her mother, by turning aggression inward rather than discharging it to the outer environment.

One week later, Candy's mother's mood was lifted and so was Candy's. This day, at age 1-5-26, she held firmly and retained the toy which Jane (age 1-7-19) tried to take from her. By this and similar events, we inferred that her self-assertiveness was more stable. Again, the confluence of self-assertiveness and destructiveness was evident in the following: Cindy was sitting in the small rocker. Candy wanted to get into it. She brought Cindy a toy which Cindy accepted, and Candy, in the spirit of a trade, now wanted to sit in the chair. She squeezed into it, next to Cindy. Cindy complained and Mrs. G. intervened, pointing out that since Cindy had been sitting in the chair first, Candy had to wait her turn. Candy cried sitting on her mother's lap for about fifteen seconds, then played near her until Cindy left the rocker ten minutes later. Unexpectedly, instead of showing pleasure at being able to use the rocker now, Candy stopped in front of it, looked troubled, and slapped it several times. Vocalizing angrily, she leaned on it but never sat in it and soon left it.

Sharing the libidinal object with her twin was more difficult for Candy during the rapprochement subphase than we had seen before. At 1-6-27, Candy seemed unusually irritable. Twice, in a seemingly spontaneous move, she threw a plastic block at Mary (0-6-14). This was unusual for Candy who had already shown affectionate, mothering behavior vis-a-vis Mary. Because of this, the discharge of hostile destructiveness toward that baby was noteworthy.

One half-hour later Candy began to fuss in her mother's lap, thrashed about, cried and seemed unable to be comforted, all for no discernible reason. After about ten seconds, her mother put her down and Candy's reaction stopped. At this point Mrs. G. told us that, recently when she had left her children weekly for a couple hours, Candy had not waved "Bye" and had hit her mother when she returned.

Identification with mother as well as anger with her were prevalent at this time. When Cindy (1-6-27) fell next to Mary, Mrs. G. told Cindy to be careful. Looking angry, Candy struck Cindy hard with her hand. Because of the much more frequent anger recently exhibited by Candy, and since Mrs. G's affect in cautioning Cindy was one of protection rather than anger, we assumed that the anger came from within Candy and gave her identification with mother that affective expression. Candy's attacks on Cindy were infrequent, Candy's tolerance for frustration and impulse control being quite high. Here we felt, and later we came to know even better, that Candy was protecting her mother by displacing the discharge of hostile destructiveness onto lesser-cathected objects. However, the infrequent attacks on Cindy were evidence that having to constantly share her mother with Cindy was, at times, wearing for even so tolerant a child as Candy. Unfortunately, because it would take us too far afield, I cannot detail the fascinating and complex relation of Candy to her twin here. Suffice it to say, Candy was generally tolerant and protective of Cindy who, because of a minimal brain dysfunction, needed mother ministrations more than she.

The complex defenses available to the one and one-half-year-old—defenses erected by the ego to protect the libidinal object against the child's destructive impulses toward the same object—again impressed us. Defenses that emerged during the practicing subphase were elaborated in the rapprochement subphase. Again Candy repeated what we have so often seen: a child making a game of discharging destructive impulses against her mother. When Candy was 1-7-18, Mrs. G. offered her a pretzel. Candy pushed her mother's hand away, breaking the pretzel in the process. She then hit the pretzel breaking it further. Her mother, who had told her not to break it, lightly slapped Candy's hand. Candy began to cry and immediately leaned toward her mother to be picked up. She was comforted in seconds. Still on her mother's lap, about thirty seconds later when her mother bent down to kiss her, Candy began, with a smile, to push her head against her mother's face. Her mother made no objection and Candy pushed more aggressively and playfully. Candy then picked up pieces of the pretzel her mother had tried to give her before, and in what seemed to be a fused identification with the aggressor and the feeder—reflecting fusion of the frustrating and nurturing, the bad and good, mother representations—Candy proceeded to feed them to her mother. Her mother collaborated with her daughter's efforts to undo the destructive impulses she had unwittingly aroused. In this event, the ego and the child's love feeling toward the object joined forces to protect the object against the hostile destructive impulses mobilized, at least in part, by that object's actions.

When Candy was 1-7-21, we witnessed the poignancy of her sharply delineated rapprochement crisis (Mahler 1972c, with Pine and Bergman 1975). Candy stayed close to her mother from the beginning of the session. Cindy, Temmy, Teresa (Candy's four-year-old sister) and Donnie (just under three years) took off their shoes and went to the matted play room. Candy, who had been close to mother on the sofa much of the time, busily playing with toys, took off her shoes too, excitedly readying to join the others. However, once her shoes were off, she sobered and got back on the sofa with some help from her mother. Five seconds after she had climbed on her mother's lap, Candy began to cry and twist her body away from mother as though she were suddenly experiencing acute pain. Mrs. G. sensitively responded by putting her down. Candy dropped to the floor, crying, twisting, and kicking her legs in a mild temper tantrum—a reaction most unusual for her. Surprised, Mrs. G. tried to comfort Candy by talking and touching. Finally, through mutual accord, she picked her up. But once in her mother's arms, Candy again started to cry and twist herself away. Again her mother complied and put Candy down. Mother and daughter twice again enacted this same sequence. The ambitendent behavior (Mahler and McDevitt 1968), which occurred six times, wound down with the sixth hold-me-close! communication. Candy's pain and distress—arising out of her conflicting wishes to be close to and to be separate from her mother—were strikingly mirrored in the feelings of confusion the mother showed.

Four days later, at our next session, aggressive discharges seemed to pour out of Candy. For example, she smilingly threw the football and nearly struck Mary with it, she threw down a lollipop she had been given, and also the cup she had appropriated from her mother. At one point, Candy became suddenly irritable, cried, and twisted herself in mother's arms. As she had done four days earlier, she twisted herself out of mother's arms twice. We concluded from the sum of her recent behavior that she had thrown the football at Mary—whom she seemed to like—in displacement from her mother and that her hostile destructive impulses were aroused by and directed toward her mother, the object of her rapprochement crisis. Candy was able to protect her mother against the destructive drive discharge by a variety of ego functions: neutralization, displacement, inhibition, modulated drive discharge, and sublimation (make-a-game). The shift in affect, which reflected the interplay of the ego and drive derivatives, was notably fluid, from smiling and accepting comforting, to suddenly crying, and angrily twisting herself out of mother's arms.

At 1-7-28, the rapprochement crisis was still in evidence as manifested by a brief ambitendent spell near the end of our session: Candy stayed close to her mother the entire session, except for the brief period when mother left "their" sofa to tend to Cindy. At this point Candy stayed on "their" sofa (which especially by Candy's actions had become the family's territory) expecting that her mother would soon return there. With much pleasure, Candy engaged first her mother, then one of the observers, in a game of throwing a doll off the sofa. We thought this to be palpable evidence of ridding herself of and separating aggressively from the object. During separation, her face and actions seemed harsh. But when she brought the doll close to herself, taking possession of and caring for her, she appeared gentle and well satisfied. Her discharge of hostile destructive impulses appeared attenuated by the defense of making-a-game of it and was discharged with pleasurable affect, the anger being dissimulated.

At 1-8-2, Candy moved away from her mother several times to a radius of four to six feet for the first time since the peaking of her rapprochement crisis at 1-7-21. Still, however, she remained close to her mother for most of the session. Again, by means of discharge delay, of making-a-game, and of displacement, the ego modified hostile destructiveness successfully enough to protect the love-object against it.

During the next week renewed sharpening of the rapprochement crisis mobilized much destructiveness in Candy. However, she expressed anger toward her mother less openly. When the mother went out on Fridays for several hours, upon her return Candy now greeted her unsmilingly but less frequently struck her. Peers were now often the target of her blows, contrary to her acceptance of them with equanimity three months before. We feel this to be due largely to the displacement of destructiveness from the object of rapprochement. Two weeks later, Candy took a step further toward working through her rapprochement crisis when she engaged one of the observers pleasantly while her mother stood by readily available to her.

RESOLUTION OF CRISIS

At 1-9-13, the radius of Candy's movement away from her mother widened significantly. This day for the first time since 1-7-21 she went into the hall without her mother, autonomously separating about twenty feet. She used other objects well, asking R.H., for example, to pick her up when she became a bit anxious about separation, and to bring her back to the central infant area. She took a pull-toy she had recently invested with libido, separated from her mother, defended against Mary (0-9-0) who wanted to take it, went to a table behind "her family's" sofa, took apart the pull-toy and made its parts disappear into the drawer of that table. She opened and closed the drawer, pushing the pieces out of sight when they became visible—all with an air of working through separation, under ego control, from the libido-invested toy. After a ten-minute separation from her mother, she returned to her and the reunion reaction was mutually pleasurable.

Many times since the advent of her rapprochement crisis we had seen the acute heightening of aggression along at least two intertwining lines. First was *self-assertiveness,* deriving particularly from the wish to maintain possession of objects, toys, territory, and other object derivatives as well as from the wish to move separately and individually, unencumbered by the object. Second was *hostile destructiveness* directed toward objects, under conditions where the object threatened unpleasure-inducing separation or closeness (symbiotic fusion). Conversely, the love-object's resistance to the gratification of either the wish for separateness or the wish for closeness mobilized hostile destructiveness toward that object. Despite clear evidence of heightened ambivalence vis-a-vis mother, we found no self-directed destructiveness in Candy at this time. Aggression seemed mobilized away from conflict-free ego sphere activities to mastery of the rapprochement crisis. While self-assertiveness can follow a course parallel to that of destructiveness, each trend may also follow a divergent course. For example, self-assertiveness was observable without concomitant destructivensss. Self-assertiveness may fall by the wayside where unpleasure is excessive, while destructiveness can mount and reach the point of hate; when this happens, loss of ego control over the drive may ensue.

Further steps in the resolution of the rapprochement crisis were observable at age 1-9-27. On arrival at the project area, Candy allowed R.H. to assist in taking her out of the carriage, but, showing a shade of anxiety, as soon as her outerclothes were taken off she scurried to her mother. Later in the morning, she went to the water fountain in the hall with Cindy (her twin), Vicki (1-9-4) and Renée (1-5-5). While the others soon returned to the infant area, Candy stayed in the hall, sitting alone on the bench for about eight minutes. Poised midway between the infant area and the toddler area, she vividly illustrated her dilemma. During her practicing subphase she spent many hours in the toddler area, but she had not gone there since the onset of her acute rapprochement crisis. We also saw this midpoint station taken up by Jane, Cindy, and Temmy during the denouement of their rapprochement crisis. After about eight minutes of lone separateness, she returned to her mother who was holding Cindy. Candy lay at her mother's feet, and Mrs. G. responded to the subtle communication, bending over to pat Candy's abdomen for about two minutes. Thus, Candy showed both aspects of the pressures within her of her rapprochement crisis but was now better able to gratify her alternating wishes for separateness and for closeness.

For six weeks, during summer vacation and her mother's working outside the home, we did not see Candy. Father, laid off work, stayed home and cared for the children. Mother reported that both girls were angry with her for leaving home. Again, Candy occasionally slapped her mother upon her return from outside work. At 1-11-21, she was still in the rapprochement subphase but showed no sign of crisis. Destructiveness toward peers was expressed affecto-vocally, without any striking.

After this single visit, again we did not see Candy for four weeks due to her mother's temporary employment. She returned at age 2-0-12. During the next six weeks we found again that Candy was taking a certain pleasure in hitting her twin Cindy. Observations suggested that the displacement of anger toward her mother—partly in response to her leaving the twins transiently for work outside the home—was operating here. Candy carried out much of her object-related activity with her twin.

During this period Mrs. G. was attempting to toilet-train her twins.

At this time Candy was making the process very easy. She could let her mother know when she needed to go to the bathroom and by 2-2-14 Mrs. G. felt that Candy had nearly mastered the task. Candy responded well to compliments, and all observable indications were that there was little resistance to this task. This was in contrast to Cindy's training, where notable ambivalence was evident, along with frustration, anger, and shame. Candy's nondestructive aggression was amply evident in the good development of her cognitive, communicative, and motoric skills. Aggression was under good ego control and available when needed—for example, when she ably pushed her big sister W., who was playfully blocking her way. She moved at her with the power and no-nonsense of a small tank.

Leaving the rapprochement subphase at 2-2-17, Candy seemed to be well on the way to object constancy (Mahler 1972b). After a brief stay in the infant area, Candy went to the toddler area with her sisters W. and Cindy. When they left *en masse,* Mrs. G. waved and said "Bye" to them. Candy said "Bye" to her mother, as did W. However, Cindy refused to acknowledge separation from her mother three times this morning. Candy's casual separation reaction led us to infer the more advanced status of her separation-individuation work, a safe inference since it was made in the context of having followed these children quite closely since birth, an inference which was validated by subsequent observations. This morning, Candy was very successful in such conflict-free ego activity as coloring and cutting with scissors (which she was just learning to do), and exploring all kinds of materials. At one interval during an intimate, calm engagement with her mother in the infant area, she took the diapers off her doll, an act affirming, we inferred, that she soon would no longer need them herself.

A distinct quieting of hostile destructiveness toward the mother occurred with the quieting of the rapprochement subphase, the relation betwen child and mother remaining dominantly affectionate and quite easy going. But, as we soon found, this was only the calm before the rough seas of her castration and oedipus complexes, which soon began to emerge.

JANE

At age 1-2-7, Jane appeared low keyed, indeed mildly depressed, and stayed close to her mother. Up to now such depressive manifestations had occurred only intermittently and in direct association with the physical and hence, at this age when the child does not yet have object constancy, with the emotional absence of her mother. This day Jane stayed aloof from the other children and engaged her mother in close interaction much of the time. Since we did not yet suspect rapprōche- ment depressive affects (Mahler 1966), this mild depression first alerted us to the possibility that Jane knew that her mother was going to have another baby. The unexpected tenderness and motherliness shown toward Harold (when Jane was 1-1-19) added to this possibility.[1] Mrs. K then revealed that while visiting with Harold and his family, Mrs. K. had asked Jane playfully, "Where is your baby brother?" Jane, 1-2-5 of age, had looked at her mother's abdomen, turned and walked away. Mrs. K. and Mrs. J. were so struck by the clarity of Jane's knowledge and the affect-laden rejection of this state of affairs that they told the story many times. Thus Jane revealed that at 1-2-5 of age she knew the dwelling place of her baby-brother-to-be. (The baby turned out to be a sister, not a brother.) This information side by side with Jane's affects and behavior led us to infer that some of her low-keyedness came from the knowledge of her mother's pregnancy. On this day not only did Jane show a tender interest in Harold, but such behavior (a manner that suggested a mother gently feeding her baby) was twice directed at Cindy. Reaction-formation and identification with her mother seemed in evidence here.

During this period (thirteen to fourteen months of age) we were surprised by the fact that when Temmy wanted what Jane had, Jane often simply let her have her way. This concession was rather casual, not a giving up or backing down based on frustration or submission. During this period, on the other hand, when she so decided, Jane held onto or took toys with much assertiveness.

Separation Anxiety
At 1-2-17 Jane showed marked separation anxiety when at midsession Mrs. K. wanted to go to the bathroom. Jane had been hovering around her mother a bit low-keyed. As her mother got up, Jane stayed in close proximity to her. Mrs. K., sensing her daughter's emerging anxiety,

---

[1] We were later shown by Candy and Doris that identification with the mother of symbiosis may be operative here. Candy showed a remarkable maternal, caretaking attitude toward a doll as she turned into her second year of life; Doris was enchanted by holding a doll, hugging and rocking it at thirteen months of age. For a discussion see Parens, Pollock, Stern and Kramer (1976).

told Jane she just wanted to go to the bathroom and Jane began to pull at her mother and cry as her puzzled mother disengaged herself. Suddenly anxiety and anger—inferred from Jane's unexpected and unusual screaming-crying—mounted sharply. Angrily she permitted her mother to detach herself, but she pursued her down the hall. Her mother went into an open door and closed it. Jane saw the door into which mother had gone, but instead of trying to enter there (as a student of Piaget might draw our attention to), she went two doors further down and entered an open door, just as mother had. There she searched for her mother, all the time screaming and crying angrily. Within one minute Mrs. K, startled and concerned by Jane's reaction, came out and looked for her. Jane accepted her mother's comforting and was readily calmed. We were surprised to see no sign of angry recrimination against her mother. Thumb in mouth, she stayed close to her mother for several minutes. Then Jane ventured away into the arena with peers and for fifteen or so minutes she found outlets for her hostile destructive impulses in interaction with peers, with more grabbing and hitting than was customary for her. She seemed to displace the destructive impulses aroused by her mother's action onto less cathected objects, protecting the loved mother from her own destructive impulses. Thus she showed a frequently found relation of the ego's defenses, *displacement* and *splitting object representations.* Data of this kind, predominant during the past three weeks, led us to postulate Jane's entry into the rapprochement subphase. Neither then nor now could we be certain that the degree of Jane's depressive experiences even while her mother was physically and libidinally available to her were just the result of the work of separation-individuation (Mahler 1966, 1968, Parens, 1971a), or if these received a contribution from Jane's reaction to her mother's pregnancy. We furthermore question whether the mother's pregnancy contributed to the somewhat early emergence of Jane's rapprochement subphase. Early developmental progress was not new in Jane; she had advanced precociously along the schedule for other maturational-developmental indices—for instance, the early appearance and differentiation of her social smiling response and the structuring of her libidinal object.

At 1-2-21 Jane's mother was in the hospital for two days for benign surgery. At the onset of the session, Jane, who was brought in by her oldest sister, seemed subdued and sober. However, as the session went on, her affect lifted and her interactions with her sister, observers, and peers were quite within the usual range for her. But again we noted an increase in the discharge of destructive impulses toward peers, manifest in affecto-vocal expressions of anger, in grabbing, and in hitting.

Coping with Hostile Destructiveness Toward Mother
When Jane was 1-2-24, Mrs. K. reported that on her return from the hospital, after a forty-eight-hour absence, Jane ignored her. Jane turned her attention and warmth onto Harold (age 0-5-24) who was visiting at the time. While Mrs. K. felt that Jane kept an eye on her, she was overtly ignored. However, when mother got up to go to the kitchen (that is, on threat of separation), Jane quickly greeted her for the first time since her return. In our session, Jane was more competitive, self-assertive, pushy, and nasty with Temmy (1-2-25) than she had been since they were ten months old. Due principally to Jane's recently mobilized hostility, Temmy and she were fighting each other much of the morning, each wanting what the other had, as they had done from seven to ten months of age but not since. Hostile destructiveness was mobilized in Jane by (1) the normal conflict induced by the rapprochement task—the obligatory increased sense of separateness with the transient feelings of helplessness of the ego and loss of omnipotent control of the love-object; (2) her mother's pregnancy and her own anticipatory feelings of losing the love-object, in part induced by the mother's shift of her own libido toward herself and the baby within her; and (3) the recent forty-eight-hour separation from her mother.

In addition to these normally expectable events during her rapprochement subphase, other equally normative factors added to the arousal of destructive impulses that pertain to the category *unpleasure-related discharges of destructive impulses.* For example, at 1-2-28 Jane pulled an electrical plug from an outlet. Mrs. K. rushed to Jane, spanked her once, quite hard, more in acute anxiety than in anger. Jane cried immediately, frightened and angry. Anger seemed uppermost as the following suggests. Jane followed mother back to where mother was sitting, but she went behind mother's chair, rejecting the offered comfort. After thirty seconds, crying still, she came to the side of mother's chair and permitted the mother to pick her up. She stayed passively on her mother's lap, out in space, in a seeming dissociative state of daydreaming, while she calmed in seconds. After five minutes she got off her mother's lap, went to E.S. (observer), got onto E.S.'s lap, sat facing her mother, and stayed there for ten minutes. She had not gotten this close to anyone in our project since she abruptly terminated her closeness to B.K. (observer) at eleven months of age. She then went to Mrs. G., mother of the twins, stayed close to her, leaned against her legs for thirty seconds and returned for a while to E.S. Thus, she turned away from the spanking, hurting mother, and displaced, or externalized, the good mother representation onto E.S. temporarily, as she had done with B.K. four months before. *Splitting* the object representation in this way seemed to give Jane the time she needed to detoxify and neutralize to some degree (*have object passage,* Mahler 1968) the destructive impulses transiently invested in the representation of the mother in order to *integrate* with a more positive valence the just-activated ambivalence of the object cathexis.

At 1-3-0 Jane was mischievous. She seemed to be working on the modulation and part-discharge of destructive impulses. Smiling throughout the morning, she playfully stepped on her mother's feet. Her mother, sensitive to what was going on, tried to work out this attack on her. Once Jane pretended she was going to bite her mother on the cheek. She alternated teasing and playfully taunting her mother with long hugs, and a dreamy, dissociative, far-away look.

Thus the ego's efforts to master the hostile destructive impulses toward the loved mother employ many defenses that lie within the child's capability, a capability that enlarges as these defenses are employed for adaptive purposes. *Splitting representations, identification* and *reaction formation* (as in the development of tenderness to Harold), *making-a-game* of anxiety-producing impulses and wishes, *internalization* of maternal dictates that become structured as superego-precursors, and *displacement,* all played significant parts in Jane's dealing with, and protecting the loved mother against, her object-directed unpleasure-related destructive impulses. On this day, while with her mother Jane made-a-game of her destructive impulses, she had her most calculated, deliberate fight with Temmy to date: they faced each other, rather soberly then threateningly, and alternately struck each other mildly, ambivalently, inhibitedly—each five times. Returning quickly to her good humor, she nearly made Cindy fall (when the latter was still walking precariously), and did make herself fall to the floor. She nearly kicked Cindy but gave her mother enough time to verbally prohibit that kicking—a form of prohibition to which Jane responds well.

At 1-3-4 Jane showed that while she was close to her mother physically and emotionally and suffered from some separation anxiety and loss affects (forlorn, longing, low-keyedness, etc.), she was also pushed by strivings for autonomy which, as they had done in the practicing subphase, again lead to conflict with mother. The struggle with her mother in this regard led to many no's from her. Today Jane made-a-game of it: After several actual prohibitions by her mother to not take out all the kleenex, to not take Temmy's toy, etc., Jane began to do things she knew mother would prohibit. She *pretended* to take a cookie, to kick the mirror, to pull off tape; recognizing the game, her mother said No! each time and Jane turned, each time, to look at her with a charming smile.

Discharging destructive impulses was acutely conflictual and muted; it was influenced by defenses, by the influence of libido on aggression, by reality, and by being laden with fear of disapproval from her mother and of retaliation by peers. All the adaptive workings of the ego, so largely influenced by the love for the object and that object's dictates, led to the *neutralization* of destructive impulses. Such *neutralization,* or object-passage, of aggression, was amply manifested in this normal child's rapprochement subphase.

Nondestructive Aggression

While I have focused much on the course taken by destructive aggression during the mother's pregnancy, one cannot lose sight of aggression's nondestructive discharges which fueled so much adaptive and developmental activity. Much exploratory, sensorimotor activity characteristic of the practicing subphase evolved richly into ego functions and skills. We found in all our children, to a greater or lesser degree, that when the love affair with the world was lessened during the rapprochement subphase due to the shift in libidinal and aggressive cathexis in the relation of the self to the object, this exploratory, sensorimotor type of activity made its appearance within the relation to that object. Thus when Jane was 1-3-21 we estimate clinically (observationally) that she was spending 70 percent of her time in exploratory, mastering activity interacting with her mother; at 1-3-28 she engages her mother in 80 percent of all her explorations, spending 90 percent of our two-hour session using her mother's feet as her base of operation. Candy, who at about eighteen months went through a quite similar rapprochement peak, spent several session in complete proximity to her mother. During Candy's rapprochement crisis, however, her exploratory activity decreased sharply, with most of her energies being employed in the service of adapting to and defending against the anxiety and destructiveness elicited by that rapprochement crisis.

The constancy of Jane's exploratory, mastering activity continued to be noteworthy. Not so in Vicki, in whom depression many times obstructed the discharge of nondestructive aggressive manifestations nor in Cindy, in whom stranger anxiety and excessive stimulation (organically-determined hypersensitivity) seemed to divert such non-destructive energy from other areas of development, with resultant slowing of that development.

Nondestructive Aggression—Environmental Resistance—Hostile Destructiveness

By this phase it has become common experience in the child that the sufficient frustration of autonomous strivings leads to sufficient un-pleasure which mobilizes destructiveness. For instance, exploration and taking possession of things often leads to environmental resistance and the arousal of destructiveness. Thus, in Jane one can readily follow the sequence: There is an initial period of pressured exploring, attempts to take possession of, to assimilate and master all types of items, animate and inanimate; at some point, however, she encounters resistance, for instance, from Temmy, Candy, or her mother; one then sees the now relatively tamed expression of destructive impulses toward each which may be followed by delay of discharge, avoidance, inhibition and/ or reaction-formation. The level of aroused destructiveness is, of course, determined by the present economic and dynamic state of the child as well as by the valuation of the object of which possession is sought. Thus when Jane was 1-3-14, Temmy (1-3-15) indeed was taking possession transiently of what "belonged" to Jane by sitting on Jane's mother's lap. She had been doing this for several visits. Today Temmy appropriated Mrs. K. early in the session. Mrs. K. responded recep-tively to Temmy while she was alert to Jane's displeasure and even verbalized it. Jane soberly looked at Temmy and at her mother. She seemed arrested between striking out and turning away. Jane suddenly smiled, then by-passing Temmy on her mother's lap, picked up a toy telephone and played with her mother. The telephone game was a recent one which derived from mother's calling Jane during her recent hospitalization, when Jane would make no sound to acknowledge that she knew mother was on the line. Now Jane added a variation: she placed the phone to her ear, smiling, vocalizing for a second or two, then she threw down the receiver hard and with deliberation, smiling broadly at her mother. She repeated this six times. She again attempted and succeeded, in part, to master anger toward her mother—now activated by her mother's holding Temmy. This event became associated (as the telephone game gives evidence) to the anger engendered by her mother's being in the hospital, hence being lost to Jane. We note that she, like other children, displaced upon and enacted with toys (by throwing them harshly) the discharge of hostile destructive impulses toward objects. Her success, however, was incomplete and for the next ten minutes she managed to irritate her mother. The ego's efforts to tame destructive impulses were discernible in that the aggression came out impure, indirectly, a salutary modification of drive effected by the work of the young ego.

The vicissitudes of aggression, especially hostile destructiveness, toward the love-object are complex. Of dramatic importance, yet prosaic to be sure, was the following brief event which we saw numerous times in all our children except Vicki, dating from the time of the differentiation subphase. Still at 1-3-14, Jane obtained a magazine her mother did not want her to have lest she tear it. Mrs. K. took the magazine from Jane, and Jane grabbed it back. After two such unexpected exchanges, Mrs.K. lightly slapped Jane's hand. Jane reacted reflexively and automatically by hitting her mother back on the arm once. This we had seen only a few times with Jane and Candy, more often with Temmy, Mary, Harold, Bernie, and Renée, and most often with Cindy, and Anni. We never saw it with Vicki. (Of course more than *frequency* was relevant here.) The point to be underscored is that as soon as she had struck her mother, Jane turned to that same mother for comforting. This, too, we saw at this age with all the children except Vicki. The bad mother who frustrates often seemed blotted out, split off temporarily, and the good, comforting mother turned to with the more-or-less *confident expectation* (Benedek 1949) that she would comfort.

The many frustrations imposed on the child from the environment include, of course, hostile destructiveness from objects directed against the self. In many instances, such hostility comes from the mother, as we saw in her first year too often with Vicki; but in all cases, such aggression comes from peers (especially siblings). Thus at 1–4–2, Jane tried to ignore her older sister who wanted to make Jane play with her, the end-product of this effort being Jane's annoyance. She managed to avoid her older sister, but also tolerated much from her. Earlier we had seen Jane yield quite readily to Temmy's wish to get things for which they competed, letting go not in defeat but in a rather positive tone, seemingly altruistically. One month later Jane (1–5–2) and Candy (1–3–10) seemed to be having difficulty together. On this day they were on the point of struggling for a toy, Candy threateningly following Jane. In an effort to master this encounter Jane avoided Candy and did not respond with an affect to match Candy's. Of much importance, at one point a while later when Candy was crying because her mother had set limits on her going into the hall, Jane went to Candy, put her arm around Candy's shoulder, and comforted her for about three seconds. We found such yielding, altruistic responses to peers on the part of a number of children dating from the time of their respective practicing subphases. We believe the antecedent of this to be identification with the mother in feeding behavior particularly, as when the late-symbiotic-phase, differentiating-subphase child puts the bottle in mother's mouth and derives much pleasure from her playful participation in this game.

Not only are there early altruistic responses that in all likelihood arise from identification with the nurturing, protecting mother, there are some rather complex ways of accepting frustrations gracefully. We could ascribe the following only to early evidence of developing empathy. For example, when Jane was 1–5–16, her mother was large with her near-to-delivery baby. When Jane reached the elevator to the project area she wanted to push the button, as her older siblings did in turn. She verbalized her wish, fussing a bit. But Mrs. K., preoccupied, paid no attention. Jane's wish and demandingness just waned. Inside the elevator, I observed a fleeting movement on Jane's part to go for the elevator floor button, a brief arrest of the arm, and then a dropping of the action. Mrs. K. had not seen her daughter's fleetingly expressed wish. She did not say, of course, "I cannot lift you now." It is quite possible that she had said this many times before, but we had seen Jane many times hold vigorously to her demands in the past. I feel that empathy, rather than hopelessness that mother could gratify the wish, was at play in the dropping of this wish, which made its appearance twice. There was no manifest arousal of destructive impulses in the wake of this frustration. Possibly, the gratification of identification with protecting or taking care of her own mother played a part. During that session, she separated from her mother for much of the two-hour session, spending the time in the toddler area. She returned to her mother several times, interacted with her vocally, and with a business-like air went back to the toddler area. Perhaps we can see where some of the aggression mobilized was discharged. On this day she was particularly self-assertive with peers, as well as deliberate and in good control of her arm swinging when she struck Temmy.

AGGRESSION DURING MOTHER'S HOSPITALIZATION FOR DELIVERY

When Jane was 1-5-27, her mother entered the hospital and delivered a girl. Jane, her five-year-old sister V. and six-year-old-brother W. stayed at the home of their adult cousin N. who cared for them quite well. Even though Jane accepted going there with no fuss, during the first night she awoke screaming at 3 A.M. She cried, "Ma, Ma" repeatedly. In the morning she awoke upset and, crying, accepted being comforted by cousin N. and sister V., but asked for her mother. She was reported to be easily upset, crying at times spontaneously, with no outward cause, occasionally saying "Ma." She did not awaken during the following nights.

In observation when she was 1-5-30, Jane was notably low-keyed in mood and behavior (Mahler and McDevitt 1968). Indeed she appeared depressed. It was totally unusual for Jane that when Temmy did not want to share the pound-toy with her, Jane just burst into tears. This crying was sad, not angry; she sought comfort from cousin N. She expected comforting and gratification to come exclusively from cousin N. and sister V., rejecting offers of comforting from observers whom she knew well. Feeling powerfully the loss of mother, she seemed to restrict the number of substitutes in whom she could transiently invest libido, or more correctly, on whom she could displace the representation of the good mother.

We note two outstanding factors. (1) She was quite low-keyed in her exploratory, conflict-free-sphere mastering activity. The manifestations of her nondestructive aggression were markedly dulled, as if the energy inherently ascribed to and invested in such activity were obstructed or diverted to work elsewhere. (2) For a period of one and a half hours, even when frustrated, she showed no discharge whatever of destructive impulses toward the outside; even her crying was devoid of sounds and affects of anger and rage.

At 1-6-6, Jane was brought to the project by cousin N., although Mrs. K. had returned from the hospital and was at home with newborn sister Anni. Jane was depressed, although less than at 1-5-30 when her mother was still in the hospital. Today she smiled as the session continued. She used cousin N. very specifically, staying close to her in the rapprochement mode which had become prominent even before mother's delivery. However, she hoarded toys, putting them on N.'s lap. We had seen this type of behavior with Jane once before but only as an imitative gesture.[2] She turned to Mrs. Z. who was tickling her daughter Temmy, and expressed the wish to also be given to libidinally. However, before she touched Mrs. Z., who givingly reached out to Jane, she turned away. She also turned away from one of the observers and returned to cousin N.

She again turned to peers as objects of displacement for her currently subdued destructive impulses. An overload of destructiveness was pushing for expression. She walked low-keyed toward Temmy and Candy, who were sitting playing side by side, each with pacifier in mouth. Unexpectedly, in a subdued but painfully aggressive manner Jane pulled the pacifier from Temmy's mouth against quiet resistance. Once having pulled it out, Jane herself put it back into Temmy's mouth. She then did the same to Candy. She became more vigorous and assertive, pulling out the pacifier from each mouth again. Once she put Candy's into her own mouth briefly, then returned it. After the third time, Candy began to cry and Jane's quiet but quite aggressive activity

---

[2]When Temmy, at twelve-thirteen months of age was making large efforts to separate from her mother under the impetus of those maturational pressures that induce the practicing subphase, Temmy would fill her mother's lap with soft, stuffed animals and dolls, pretend she gave each in turn some of her bottle, and then gradually leave her mother in practicing exploratory behavior. These we felt were *proxies*, representatives of the self, employed to help her separate in an order complementary to Winnicott's *transitional object* (1953). Jane at one point imitated Temmy in this by putting a toy on Mrs. Z.'s lap. However, she did not discriminate as did Temmy, and we felt that she had failed to understand Temmy's symbolic maneuver because the toy she put on Mrs. Z.'s lap was the only *hard* toy on that lap.

was interrupted by the mothers. During this activity, Jane's depressive affect and low-keyedness slackened; she became more cheerful now, smiling occasionally.

AGGRESSION TOWARD MOTHER AND THE NEW BABY

When Jane was 1-6-10, Mrs. K. returned to the project with the new baby Anni, Jane, and her five-year-old sister V. The low-keyedness was lifted from Jane's mood and her activities. She was functioning quite normally in the discharge of nondestructive aggression through exploratory, mastering activity. Modulating, coping with the discharge of somewhat difficult-to-control destructive impulses required her mother's help. For example, Jane threw a plastic block at the knee of her mother's friend, Mrs. J. Jane looked at her mother. With some firmness, her mother told her not to do that. Jane touched Mrs. J's knee gently and looked at her mother. A moment later she accidentally hit herself on the head with the same block, turned to her mother and complainingly sought comfort, which she received. She then threw the block onto the floor where it struck no one. Her mood was much lifted, and her efforts to displace and modulate discharge of destructiveness were clear.

According to Mrs. K., Jane (at 1-6-17) was occasionally screaming at her mother during this period. For the most part, however, she was affectionate and enjoyed being with her mother. The birth of Anni created conflicts, the effects of which would be felt for a long time. Some aspects of these would be resolved well in the near future; some would not. But as analysts know, such conflicts, like all obligatory psychic conflicts, have their salutary influences as well. Under optimal conditions they lead to further developments in the ego and superego-precursors, as well as in the drives.

At 1-6-28 Jane's reaction to her newborn sister was visibly complex. She touched her gently enough, kissed her, and took hold of her hand a little roughly. Then Jane smashed toys in and out of the toy box, but without breaking them. Destructive impulses also came out vis-a-vis her mother and peers. But in all instances, the discharge of destructive impulses was mitigated by intrapsychic defenses and (inferred by the qualitative character of these discharges) by the neutralization of aggression.

A striking fact, derived from regular observation of Jane since birth, emerges. Up to now the only interferences with her strong level of performance in the conflict-free sphere of ego functioning had come from her separation from her mother. On the days that she had been brought to the project by someone other than mother, her depressive affects manifestly had interfered with her conflict-free ego activity. At other times, despite the fact that the ego was faced with large adaptive demands by the separation-individuation phase, the birth of a new sister, and efforts at toilet-training she herself initiated, her cognitive and motor skills were exercised without interruption. Thus, again at 1-7-9, Jane came to the project with her five-year-old sister. V. and her seven-year-old brother W., all having been brought by E.S. (project staff) whom Jane has known since birth. She gave much evidence of efforts at tolerating the separation from her mother, when fifteen minutes after arrival she suddenly looked up and called "Ma" three times, looking for her in the infant area. When told that "Mommy is home because she is a little sick and that Jane will see her soon," she was able to turn her attention to a toy. As the morning continued, Jane became low-keyed, restless, and less organized in her conflict-free activities. Her attention to toys was brief and scattered. At snack-time she ate little.

TRANSIENT SYMPTOM ARISING FROM A DEVELOPMENTAL CONFLICT[3]

We found a notable difference in Jane's affect and activity at the next visit. With her mother there, at 1-7-12, she was cheerful and her usual age-adequate very busy self. But we found the development of a transient neurotic symptom which shall be detailed now. Mrs. K. reported that for the past few nights Jane had been frightened at bedtime and required one of her parents or older siblings to stay with her until she fell asleep. Trusting our assessment of Jane's dynamics, I told Jane and her mother, "Jane is afraid to go to sleep, because she is afraid mother will leave her if mother knows how Jane feels. Even though Jane loves her mother very much, Jane is now very angry with mother for leaving Jane so much to take care of Anni." Even while we talked and I interpreted her symptom, Jane was cheerful and very busy. About thirty minutes into the session, Donnie (two and a half year's

[3]See Nagera 1966.

old) displacing anger onto Jane, unexpectedly slapped her rather hard three times in the face and grabbed her once by the neck. Intervention was prompt each time but came too late. Jane was shocked—as were the observers, as well as Donnie. She cried, and complaining, went to her mother. Progressively then, her mood changed to sullenness and her conflict-free activity decreased. Jane did not strike back at Donnie; and when she was angry with her mother she did not strike out at her. Characteristically during this period she threw toys down hard, thereby discharging some of the overload of her mobilized destructive impulses. In contrast to Donnie, whose aggression at this time suffered from insufficient neutralization for his age, Jane's impulses were not only significantly more neutralized but, in this period, they were constricted by defenses erected to protect her mother, Anni, and herself against their discharge and fantasied consequences. By the end of the two-hour session Jane was crying, openly irritated and angry with her mother, who told her she must return a book which Jane had taken from a shelf so that they could leave.

Mrs. K's subsequent report indicated that this entire day (1-7-12) seemed influenced by our interpretation and the event which occurred in our session. At dinner, Jane demanded that her mother stop feeding Anni, called the baby bad, and did not accept being fed or held by her father who had done both quite successfully many times before. Understanding Jane's complaint, her mother successfully accommodated both children simultaneously. That evening Jane did not cry at bedtime and went to sleep with no difficulty. From that day her bedtime fear stopped.[4] Having externalized much angry feeling toward mother and Anni by moderate behavioral and affective-vocal means and finding no disastrous consequences to this mitigated discharge of destructive impulses, Jane seemed to not require their externalization by projection and, therefore, upon separation at bedtime dreaded neither going to sleep nor separation. But the destructive impulses which had instigated Jane's current conflict were, of course, not quelled.

At 1-7-16, as if pushed to repeat a traumatic event, Donnie, driven by immediate frustration and destructiveness within him, this time lightly slapped Jane in the face. Jane screamed as if sharply hurt. When

[4]Fear of being upstairs alone before bedtime reemerged two years later at the height of Jane's oedipus complex. At nearly six years of age she still has this commonplace neurotic symptom.

Donnie then came near her again, Jane, with some trepidation, slapped him once inhibitedly on the forearm. Donnie then shook the arm with which Jane had hit him, and his mother intervened. A little later in this session, Temmy (1-7-17) tried to push Jane out of the rocker; Jane stood her ground, vocalizing angry feelings at Temmy, who retreated. Fifteen minutes later while Jane was sitting in the rocker again, Vicki squeezed herself beside Jane. Jane became very angry, got out of the chair, stamped her foot several times, cried, yelled at Vicki, and with slackening ego control made four slapping motions *at her own face,* but without touching herself. After this discharge of destructiveness she quieted and walked to her mother for comforting, rubbing her hair (as she and several of the other children have done when holding back object-directed destructiveness). For the first time we saw explicit self-flagellation in Jane. While we have subsequently not seen it again in this form, we did on two later occasions (see pp. 246–47) question if self-injury was used by Jane as a channel for the discharge of destructiveness originally destined for the love-object.

With the continuing working through of Jane's anger toward her mother for having a baby that, she felt, threatened to displace her from the quite optimal dyad with her mother, and as she conjointly continued to work through the rapprochement crisis (Mahler, Pine, and Bergman 1975), the developmental strides made by the ego and the drives were excellent. From this period on she separated with comfort from her mother to move autonomously to the toddler area for as much as an hour at a time. The assimilation into her psyche of her newly-acquired sister continued at a softer pace, aggression being better contained and discharged. When its burdensome character, however, made itself felt from time to time, the ego's defenses were mobilized effectively to deal with it. For example, at 1-8-23, after having been very "busy" with preschool activities in the toddler area, and socializing well, she returned to the infant area to be with her mother for *libidinal refueling* (Furer, according to Mahler 1965, 1968). Jane saw Mrs. K. holding a link-toy in front of her sister Anni and immediately wanted it. Her Mother told Jane that although she could not have that part of the toy, she could have the rest of it which was lying on the couch. With a broad smile, Jane gethered all the remains of the link-toy and brought all of them to Anni. Her reaction-formation was rewarded by an appreciative comment by mother. But when Cindy came and took three of the links, Jane grabbed them from her, and maternal intervention was necessary to resolve that incipient struggle. While Jane's reaction-formation, in the interest of holding onto mother's love, served Anni, it was not intended to benefit Cindy.

For the next two months, our reports show that Jane's progress continued in a steady trajectory through the rapprochement subphase toward the subphase toward-object-constancy. However, as occurs in every normal child, for taking developmental steps that are too large, Jane paid the price of anxiety. For example, at 2-1-3, when her older siblings returned to school, in imitation and identification, she too wanted to go to school. Pushed from within to separate from mother, she eagerly went to our playground with the older preschoolers. After fifteen minutes on the playground, she was pouting about the bad swings and the merry-go-round and asked to be brought back to her mother who had remained in the infant area with Anni. Once with her mother she seemed at ease. At age 2-1-14 again she asked to go to our playground and again had to be brought back subdued and pouting, the victim of her opposing wishes to separate and to be with mother.

At 2-1-21 Jane teased her mother. She had teasingly said before that her mother was bad, to which Mrs. K. had playfully asked "Am I bad, Jane?", Jane laughing and saying, "No, not bad Mommy, nice Mommy." Today she teased further, saying that she was going home with Mrs. Z. Inquiry into this wish to separate from mother led to our learning that Mrs. K. had to go to the hospital with Anni again. This meant the anticipation of another series of separations for Jane. We believe now that Jane had known this for weeks. There was also evidence that she was turning to her father. Was this turning to her father reactive to those dynamics associated with the resolution of the symbiosis (Mahler 1966b), with the rapprochement crisis, and with impending separations from mother? Was this one of the earliest expressions of an oedipal wish? Was it both? Did the first dynamic constellation activate the second?

At age 2-1-28 and 2-2-1 a bit of symptomatic behavior emerged which we concluded was related to the above material. It adds a further note relevant to the vicissitudes of aggression. While Jane (2-1-28) and Temmy (2-1-29) were playing at closing the double doors, Jane's hand was pinched and moderately hurt and she turned to her mother for comforting. She dealt with this event and the pain it induced as follows.

While on her mother's lap, she behaviorally and affectively seemed to indicate that her hand hurt. When H.P. asked "Does your hand hurt?", Jane nodded Yes, then suddenly shook her head No and dropped her Oh-my-aching-hand attitude. In other words, she denied the pain and perhaps the event which had induced it.

This event seemed innocuous until the next visit at 2–2–1, when she hurt herself three times. This cluster of self-injuries was noteworthy because it was not characteristic of Jane. We had not found a tendency to self-injury in Jane even during the practicing subphase, when toddlers tend to be unperturbed by moderate knocks and falls. Attentive to this data and in keeping with one aspect of the methodology of our project, I told Jane that something was making her hurt herself, that she was angry with her Mommy and Anni, that because she loved her Mommy and did not want to be angry with her, she was being angry with herself instead. Jane looked at me, pulled her thumb out of her mouth and pointing to Anni, quietly, unexpectedly said, "She stole my Mommy!" Then Jane smiled revealing that, while she at times felt this way, she really knew better, and perhaps also to decrease the destructive valence of her accusation.

At this time Jane had long and quietly been entering the anal phase. She was making things and bringing them to her mother for approval, washing and wiping her hands attentively, enjoying clay, putting order in her games, etc.; toilet training was slowly, casually in process.

LATTER PART OF JANE'S RAPPROCHEMENT SUBPHASE

At 2–2–5 Jane was brought to the project by Mrs. J., a project member and family friend. Jane's mother was at the hospital with Anni. Jane used Mrs. J. effectively, turning to her warmly in interactions. She was, however, particularly irritable with peers. After a separation of several hours, Jane's mother came into the project area from the hospital. Jane was casual, neither running to her mother nor ignoring her. But about one minute later, she moved to Mrs. J., thumb in mouth, slightly low-keyed. After thirty seconds there, she slowly moved closer to her mother and engaged her in interaction. Gradually, Jane interacted warmly with her. Jane's mood became cheerful, and her interest in all sorts of conflict-free, cognitive activity attained its usual level. In ten minutes she left her mother and went to the toddler area where she was very busy, with a pleasant affect and a good level of interest in her busyness. She offered tea to Dr. R.H. (a male) but refused to give tea to Drs. J.S. and B.Y. (females). Was she splitting object representations, or was she reacting to objects according to their gender? We noted, too, that Jane managed to hurt herself mildly twice on this day.

When Mrs. K. had to return to the hospital one half hour later, she went to the toddler area with her coat on. Jane looked at her mother, waiting; Mrs. K. told her she had to go back to the hospital and that Jane would go home with Mrs. J. Jane nodded her head. Jane's older sister V. kissed her mother; imitating and identifying with V. Jane also kissed her mother. Mrs. K. repeated to Jane that she would go home with Mrs. J., and Jane again nodded affirmatively, quietly. Jane then told her mother, "Bring Anni home to me!" She then turned away from her mother, set her pull-toy upright, and started back to the infant area without looking back. Her mother said "Goodbye" and Jane seemed not to hear her. Having already made her separation with a clean but evidently uncertain break, Jane just kept on moving. From then on, she simply used Mrs. J. as her mother-substitute, using her appropriately and well. But, while she functioned well, she was more easily upset than usual, sucked her thumb more, and was slightly low-keyed.

At 2-2-8 Jane was again brought to the session by Mrs. J. When Mrs. J. was obliged to leave us for ten minutes, Jane exhibited separation anxiety and, distressed, wanted to go with her. While the latter was putting on her coat, Jane surprised us by asking Mrs. J. seriously, "Is Mr. J. my Daddy?" This question was put in what seemed to be a state of confusion arising from some lability in the cathectic investment in object representations; both her separation anxiety and her question suggested a sharply displaced object cathexis—we would say at the level of her attention cathexis—from mother and father onto Mr. and Mrs. J., her neighbors. Several minutes after Mrs. J. and Jane returned, Mrs. K. came to the session from the hospital. Jane saw her mother come in but kept to her crayoning. When Jane entered the infant area she came to Mrs. J., not to her mother, and handing her her crayoned paper said, absent mindedly, "Here, Mommy." We inferred that anger toward her mother caused this absent mindedness. However, soon, as she had done before, Jane moved gradually to her mother, engaged her in interaction and devised the pleasure-filled game of mother putting Jane to bed on the floor mat, covering her with a bedspread as if with a blanket, and patting her to sleep. She repeated this a number of times, enjoying the game she had created—a game which gave child and mother (who made good use of it) an opportunity to make up for mother's not being able to put Jane to bed while she was in the hospital with Anni. This compensatory game seemed to attenuate with a good degree of success Jane's anger toward her mother.

When Jane's behavior suggested that she was entering the separation-individuation subphase toward-object-constancy, she spent most of her time in our toddler area, coming into the infant area occasionally for libidinal refueling, in which she comfortably accepted the gratification of passive yearnings. At the same time, she was very active and showed a wide range of ego development. In the conflict-free sphere for example, she crayoned, cut-tore paper with scissors, matched wooden puzzle pieces, and looked at a book. She participated well in peer activities, in hand washing, and in snack-taking. Her communications were, generally, readily understandable, and she engaged with her mother in a phrase dialogue for as long as five minutes as, for example, in caring for a doll. Her affect showed a wide range from longing and sadness, as well as clearly expressed self-assertiveness and anger, to cheerfulness and laughter. Humor was becoming another way to adapt to anxiety-inducing or frustrating experiences. For example, at age 2-3-12 Jane said unexpectedly, smilingly to her mother, "Your finger's cut and you're bleeding. You have to go to the hospital." Because her mother reacted with surprise, Jane added that it was pretend.

One stimulus for this fantasy may have come from the time at age 2-1-28, when playing with Temmy, Jane had hurt her hand in the door. (This self-injury was the first of a second series of injuries which led us to suspect a masochistic defense had been erected to protect the loved mother against Jane's hostile destructive impulses.) We felt that her mother's many trips to the hospital to take care of Anni were the source for the wish to send her mother to the hospital in a state of injury, that Jane was gratifying in fantasy a thread of her destructive impulses toward her mother. We question if here at 2-3-12 as at 2-1-28, an underlying fantasy of castration might play a part as a component of genital stirrings emerging at this time. On 2-1-28, we had also questioned if an oedipal wish were being expressed. Indeed from here on, oedipal behavior began to gradually emerge—wishing to go on a trip with father but without mother, progressively sharply felt rivalry with and nastiness toward her mother.

At 2-2-28, Mrs. K. forgot to bring a bottle for Jane, perhaps because Jane had had two bottles already before 9 A.M. Whatever the mother's motives, conscious and unconscious, Jane wanted a bottle at 10 A.M. But mother had none. Jane put her thumb in her mouth and looked moderately downcast. She went off to the toddler area. There she was busy but a bit quieter than usual. About twenty minutes later she returned to her mother, thumb in mouth, looking slightly somber, and again asked for her bottle. Mrs. K. told her she was sorry but she had forgotten to bring the bottle. Jane backed away from her mother to about five feet and stood with her thumb still in her mouth, looking sad. Mrs. K. said, "You're mad at me cause I forgot your bottle." Jane nodded once. Mother apologized again, and Jane went to the toddler area. Slightly low-keyed, she functioned otherwise at her usual level for the rest of the morning. When Jane was 2-3-12, again Mrs. K. did not bring her bottle, and Jane teased her mother with "Your finger's cut and you're bleeding, etc." Mrs. K. searchingly asked "I forgot your bottle, I'm a bad girl?" Jane hugged her mother forgivingly and said, "You're a good girl."

To paraphrase Freud, however long the infant is well fed by her good-enough mother, she feels that it is not enough. As if under pressure to resolve the tensions which create the rapprochement subphase, Jane personified Freud's observation with particular clarity at age 2-3-19: Mrs. K. brought the bottle which Jane had been asking for once she got to the project but did not ask her mother to bring along when they were still at home. She gobbled the contents rather quickly, then soon had juice and snacks, after which she playfully asked her mother again for milk from her now empty bottle.

AGGRESSION DURING THE RAPPROCHEMENT SUBPHASE

Candy's rapprochement subphase is detailed above because, occurring in a healthy child, being of good quality, well delineated, and revealing the rapprochement crisis clearly, it best shows the vicissitudes of aggression imposed by this subphase. Jane's, on the other hand, is shown to present some of the larger effects created by the frequently encountered life event, the birth of a sibling, upon the rapprochement vicissitudes of the aggressive drive in a normal, well-endowed child whose relation to parents (and siblings) is significantly better than good-enough (Winnicott 1953). Although Jane's rapprochement subphase began at about fourteen months, we could not infer entry into the object constancy subphase until she was about twenty-seven months. The rapprochement subphase, hence, was protracted. Several reasons seem to account for this long work period. First, the task of the rapprochement subphase of itself creates a large burden for the ego. Secondly, the mother's pregnancy and delivery not only helped to activate the emerging rapprochement subphase, they also increased Jane's workload by making additional demands on Jane's psychic organization. Thirdly, Anni's disturbed psychophysiological condition (based on a significant brain disorder) required several hospitalizations during this period of Jane's life. Jane was subjected, therefore, to several series of separations from her mother. In addition, Anni's serious congenital problem caused a moderate depression in both mother and father for many months, thereby withdrawing further libido from that which would otherwise have been available to Jane. Despite these difficulties, the staff agreed that Jane's psychic development was proceeding very favorably.

NONDESTRUCTIVE AGGRESSION

During the rapprochement subphase, all our children, as Jane and Candy did, showed ample sensorimotor and locomotor activity, environmental assimilation and mastery, self-assertiveness, etc., thus manifesting that a significant degree of nondestructive aggression was available to the ego. However, the demands made on that ego by the process of the rapprochement subphase, by toilet-training, and by conflicts continuing from the symbiosis and practicing subphase, diverted much energy from those activities which, in origin, pertain to the conflict-free ego sphere. Vicki best showed the effect of the more peremptory demands made by the child's libidinal needs on the ego. Her rather constant low-keyedness in affect and activities resulted in a significant lessening of the cathexis invested in such activities because her nondestructive aggressive energies, significantly mixed with chronically mobilized hostile destructive aggression, were bound by other adaptive and largely defensive functions of the ego. In Jane, too, during this subphase, we found times when such energies seemed transiently preempted by more peremptory activities, as was the case in Candy's rapprochement crisis.

During the rapprochement subphase, the specific task of separation-individuation is to effect the progressive dissolution of the symbiosis and to secure a sufficient intrapsychic separation and individuation of self from object by the internalization of that object relation (Freud 1923, Parens 1971a). This task is principally imposed by the developing ego and the libido and, of itself, draws much aggressive drive from the ego's conflict-free sphere. When the demands of this task are great, as they were during Candy's rapprochement crisis, nondestructive aggression is especially channeled to work through, resolve, and/or defend against helplessness of the ego. As a result conflict-free-sphere ego activity fluctuates depending upon the demands these dynamic and economic conditions impose upon the ego. One readily sees many instances of the ego's remarkable adaptive efforts, as when Candy was very active—working busily with a doll (of course this is not solely a conflict-free activity) or exploring the workings of some toy or piece of paper—she would sit with her back transiently glued symbiotically to her mother.

Self-assertiveness
We also found in Candy that aggression seemed especially observable along two intertwining lines: self-assertiveness and hostile destructive-ness toward the object. The history of self-assertiveness is not only that of aggression, but equally that of narcissism and libido. That is to say, that while aggression is *instrumental* (Stone 1971) in self-assertiveness (in the service of narcissistic and libidinal claims), it also seems to motivate and make a *primary,* or innate, contribution to self-assertive-ness. We saw its antecedents early, for example when fifteen-week-old Jane tried with much persistence to assimilate and master the primor-dial self and environment (Parens 1973a).

Although the course of self-assertiveness may run parallel to that of destructiveness it essentially runs its own course and is often divergent from that of destructiveness. Parallelism occurs when environmental resistance to the gratification of a wish arouses first self-assertiveness and then progressively mounting, hostile destructiveness. In such cases, self-assertiveness will continue until the expectation of gratification wanes; then under conditions of mounting unpleasure, it may give way to strong feelings of hostile destructiveness. Of course, being governed by intrapsychic dynamics, self-assertiveness will vary, as we saw in Jane's and Candy's decrease in self-assertiveness when temporarily depressed.

Of interest too are the heightened strivings *to take possession of object-derivatives* during the rapprochement subphase, with the further elaboration of what is "mine" (Bergman 1972). The aspect of aggression which fuels self-assertiveness plays a central part in this development— a development which is determined by the vicissitudes of the libido and the process of separation-individuation. We saw its influence in Candy's establishing her territory, her sofa. I would point out that the qualitative dynamics of the aggressive drive in this separation-individuation work make a large contribution toward the character not only of the individual's concept *mine* (Bergman 1972), but also of that of his home, and other related object-derivatives.

HOSTILE DESTRUCTIVENESS

The vicissitudes of hostile destructiveness during this subphase center largely around the child's actual and intrapsychic relation to the object. In Candy, during her rapprochement subphase toilet-training was nearly achieved with no manifest difficulty. Her struggle with hostile destructive impulses remained concentrated in her well-focused rapprochement crisis. Indeed we found that the peak of destructive-impulse discharge coincided with the peak of her rapprochement crisis; the waxing and waning of destructive discharge seemed directly related to the course of that crisis.

Hostile destructive impulses were mobilized by two object-related factors: (1) the mother's actual frustrations, and (2) Candy's experience of excessive unpleasure arising out of her conflicting strivings to separate from her mother versus staying symbiotically united with her. This child's intrapsychic conflictual strivings were a greater determinant of excessive unpleasure than her mother's frustrations. While the mother unavoidably created unpleasure by separating from Candy to go to work outside the home and to keep weekly dental appointments, she was otherwise determined to be libidinally available to her children and managed this task well when she was with them.

Jane also showed that the unpleasure-related destructiveness could readily be mobilized during the rapprochement subphase by the same factors reported for the earlier subphases. Prominent with her, in addition, was the rivalry with the new intruder into the symbiotic mother-child dyad who, as Jane (2–2–1) said, had "stolen her mother." This rivalry was much heightened by the nature of the task of the separation-individuation process during this subphase: to resolve the symbiosis with that object. For Jane, the hostile destructiveness mobilized by this source was intensified by the additional long hours of separation from mother imposed by her new sister's several hospitalizations. Here, we continually observed, was the sphere where Jane expended her greatest efforts to control and modulate hostile destructiveness. The degree to which Jane spared the libidinal object the discharge of what we inferred to be hostile destructiveness mobilized against that object was impressive. But even more striking was the good quality of the control and modulation of that destructiveness. Even with the optimal development of this child's ego along the lines of object relations, relation to reality (Beres 1956), neutralization of destructiveness, age-adequate sublimation, and other defenses, she came to manifest two neurotic symptoms which shall be commented on below.

The pleasure-related discharge of destructive impulses toward the mother was invariably expressed in Jane in the form of making-a-game, that is, in a defended, detoxified form. In this child, we saw very little directly expressed sadism (in the broad sense of the word) toward her mother. Overt pleasure associated with anger was, however, manifested in peer relations, as for instance in Jane's calculatedly pulling the pacifiers from the mouths of Candy and Temmy, each in turn, several times. In contrast to Jane, Donnie's and Cindy's pleasure-related discharge of destructive impulses toward the mother was quite sharper. In these two children, the ego's capability to modulate and control all trends in aggression was weaker than in Jane and Candy.

EGO ACTIVITY REACTIVE TO HOSTILE DESTRUCTIVENESS TOWARD THE
LOVE OBJECT

Jane and Candy, as well as our other children, revealed to us that significant psychic developments usher in and occur during the rapprochement subphase. Among these are developments in the drives, the ego, and superego-precursors. At this phase, the libido which is invested in the object becomes sufficiently differentiated from narcissistic-libido into object-libido. This differentiation occurs reciprocally with the stabilizing intrapsychic separation of the object representation from the self representation. Simultaneously, nondestructive aggression is invested in the object representation to the degree that reasonable efforts are required to secure sufficient physiological and drive (especially libidinal) gratification from that object. Where frustrations of these efforts reach sufficient levels of unpleasure, hostile destructive aggression is mobilized and invested in the object representation. This formulation is generally the same for earlier phases of development, as it is for this phase. By now, however, in Jane and Candy we found hostile destructiveness—which is that aspect of aggression that goes into the negative side of the ambivalence toward the libidinal object— to be already significantly controlled and modulated by the ego.

In a good-enough child-mother relationship, the ego continues to be aided by the auxiliary ego in its task of protecting the libidinal object against the child's object-directed destructive impulses well into the rapprochement subphase and beyond. Jane and Candy were at a well-advanced level in this regard, their destructiveness toward the mother being age-adequately and reliably modulated and controlled.

Excessive unpleasure at this phase, as seen already in earlier phases, has not always led to the mobilization of destructiveness toward the libidinal object. As shall be further noted below, reaction-formation here, indeed, could lead to such salutary developments as empathy and altruism. Another alternative to the mobilization of destructiveness available to the children was that where frustration, say, of libidinal supplies led to the mobilization of hostile destructiveness, that destructiveness could be transiently held in abeyance or chaneled to increase the demand for, and the extraction of, such libidinal supplies. This was observable in the game Jane devised at 2-2-8, wherein her mother would play at putting her to bed to make up for the fact that she could not be home at the actual hour of bedtime.

Our observations of these children corroborate the views emphasized by many psychoanalysts that in a normal child, the sufficient investment of libido by the parents in the child secures the inherent tendency of the (infantile) libido to attach to the object—in accord with Freud's

1920 formulation of the libido—and that this event influences the character of the aggression invested in the object, particularly the hostile destructive aspect of aggression (Parens 1972b). Whether this influence results from the attenuating powers of the libido over destructiveness, from the advantaged mixture of destructiveness with large amounts of libido, or from the neutralization of destructiveness imposed by the ego under the influence of the libidinal attachment to the object, it is effected by some form of *object passage* (Mahler 1968) of destructiveness which leads to its attenuation.

Our reports on Candy and Jane show that during the rapprochement subphase, in a well-cared-for child, the discharge of object-directed hostile destructive impulses is no longer expressed freely. Neutralization of destructiveness and defense against its discharge were widely evident. Thus, while the discharge of destructiveness toward the libidinal object was at times direct during this subphase, it was invariably sharply attenuated in Jane and Candy. The contrast between these two children, as against Donnie's occasional poorly controlled, sharp motoric outbursts against and striking of his mother, made this point clear to us. Jane's direct expressions of destructiveness occurred particularly by way of the affecto-vocal apparatus (see Jane at 1-6-10) or by rejection. At 2-1-28, when mother offered to comfort Jane, Jane declined to take that comfort and went to an adult-friend object instead; and on 1-2-24, upon the heels of a twenty-four-hour separation from her mother, Jane ignored Mrs. K.'s presence.

We recorded one direct striking of her mother by Jane, at age 1-3-14. The softness of that single blow was a beautiful example of the mitigated character of a blow fueled by significantly attenuated destructive aggression. During rapprochement we found this attenuated destructiveness in the blows of all our children except Donnie (at this time) and including those occasionally directed at their mothers by Temmy, Bernie, Harold, Mary, Doris, Cindy and Renée. Note again that this attenuation of destructiveness toward the object was observable already during the latter part of the practicing subphase.

Direct blows between peers were frequent. Except for Donnie at this period, all the children of the project showed a qualitative softening of hostile destructiveness discharged in this pathway. By contrast, the vocal apparatus (which serves the discharge of unpleasure-related destructiveness from birth) was at this subphase, as during the practicing subphase, a significantly freer vehicle for the discharge of more sharply expressed hostility among peers, a hostility more sharply discharged than that against the mother. The unworded invectives are strikingly clear in their expression of anger and hostility.

At this age, a striking array of defenses is employed by the ego to cope with destructiveness toward objects; these have already made their appearance in earlier subphases. In our field we presume that in the child's efforts to cope with hostile destructiveness toward libidinal objects and the self, the ego will employ those means available to it that are psychically most economical and self-preservative. In this regard, neutralization of aggression plays a unique role, but because the ego and its capability to neutralize emerge and develop rather slowly, a number of other defenses are brought into play.

Inhibition
We found inhibition employed quite early. Indeed, I felt that during the first part of the practicing subphase (eight-nine months) inhibition seemed especially to act as a way station for the ego's evolving capability to neutralize destructiveness. During the rapprochement subphase the other children made visible efforts to arrest a destructive discharge in-the-making. Often, they helped us to see that a dictate in the process of being *internalized* led to inhibition. When Donnie began to control aggression better he would, with arm raised to strike, arrest his motion and look up at his mother as if for renewed enforcement of dictates coming from her. As Donnie showed clearly many times, and as all analysts know, dictates governing the child's life are not solely characteristic of those that came from the mother. We saw amply the *projection* of his own hostile destructiveness into those parental dictates, as when he reacted to his mother's setting limits on his pulling an electrical cord by fearing that she would destroy him physically, although her countenance and actions did not convey such a threat. At this developmental time we also often saw a progression in the use of inhibition during the process of internalizing parental dictates, when it was no longer necessary to look at the mother or a representative object for reinforcement of the dictate. For example, when at this age Cindy

raised a hard toy in her hand to strike back at Mary, she arrested her movement, put down the hard toy with no observable cue from anyone—she had not even looked up—and rather softly hit Mary with her hand. In this complicated act, we could infer that inhibition was employed to assist the ego in its growing capacity to neutralize destructiveness—evident in the softened discharge of her blow—and that the internalizing process had advanced to the point that, in this instance, checking with and seeking reinforcement from an external object was not necessary.

Displacement

This defense was employed by Jane and the other children more frequently and more significantly than expected. While in later life displacement often appears as a defense erected to preserve the self against a more powerful adversary—as against one more powerful in the pecking order—we found displacement during rapprochement to be used principally to permit partial gratification and to protect the libidinal object against the child's own hostile destructiveness which the ego could not contain. Displacement has to be recognized as a not so salutary defense which permits gratification of hostile destructiveness, a way out in dealing with hostile destructiveness which poorly compensates for the normal weakness in the ego's capability to neutralize it at this age. Unfortunately, the normative weakness in the ego at this age sets the stage for displacement, as a prototype for such peer-directed hostile destructiveness as teasing, scapegoating, and prejudice.

Splitting Object Representations

We could also infer the splitting of the object representations from Jane's behavior, finding it at times, in association with displacement. Indeed, we wondered if splitting could be influential in the consolidation of displacement as a defense, as for instance when at age 1-2-17, Jane displaced hostile destructiveness intended for her mother onto peers. We could also infer that Jane (age 1-2-28) used splitting of the object representation as a defense that gave the ego time to detoxify and modulate the hostile destructiveness invested in the object representation. In the normal-enough development of most of these children, it seemed that splitting of the object representation during the practicing and rapprochement subphases was used as a defense that served positively adaptive function. The implementation of this defense in normal development differs qualitatively and significantly from its use in borderline and psychotic conditions (Kernberg 1966, 1967; Mahler 1968, with Pine and Bergman 1975, Ekstein 1971). This fact arises from the vastly different developmental conditions of the drives and the ego in the normal as compared to the very disturbed child. In this regard, we join others (Hartmann 1953, Stone 1972) in the viewpoint that the ego's inability to sufficiently neutralize the destructive drive is a central factor in the development of severe pathology, as it is in the development of defensive splitting which is pathological to the degree described by Kernberg and Ekstein.

Reaction-Formation and *Identification*
When Jane, age 1-2-7, showed tenderness and a "motherly" attitude toward baby Harold, we concluded that *reaction-formation* and defensive *identification* were used to protect the object against hostile destructiveness arising from the self. That the tenderness Jane exhibited to this boy came at a time when she had discovered her mother to be pregnant led us to postulate the identification to be defensive. On the other hand, in the behavior shown by Candy, Mary, and Doris toward dolls at about this same age (fourteen months), we could not detect evidence that the identification was defensive, although in the case of Candy we could not rule out this possibility in light of the fact that her twin was a constant rival for her mother's ministrations.

Often Jane would bring small toys to her sister Anni. That *reaction-formation* played a part in this behavior was evident from its somewhat obsessive character: for example, she would bring Anni eight to ten toys, one after the other, in an overt conciliatory tone; at the same time her mother gave Anni one or two toys only. The way this *reaction-formation* and *identification* developed observably at age 1-8-23 made clear Jane's underlying rivalry and anger: Jane wanted the toy her mother had given to Anni; her mother said she could have another part of the toy, not Anni's; then Jane, her affect saccharine albeit pleasant and conciliatory, gave it all over to Anni. However, when Cindy took a part of the toy, Jane's hostile impulse derivatives promptly made their appearance. Under the conditions imposed by these current dynamics, Jane's reaction-formation and identification with her mother were not intended to benefit Cindy. We could also infer in this event that the object cathexis caused the reaction-formation and that identification with her mother helped to determine the character of this reaction-formation.

Presublimation

"*Making-a-game,*" or *pretending,* is a *presublimation* (Peller 1965) defense which Jane employed extensively to cope with hostile destructive impulses toward her mother and Anni. At 1-3-0, making-a-game of it, she attacked her mother by stepping on her feet and pretending to bite her. As I detailed in the narrative of her rapprochement subphase, at 1-3-4, Jane made a game of her reaction to all the No's with which she seemed to feel her mother plagued her. In this regard too we found, with particular interest, Jane's experimentation with destructive impulses when at age 1-3-4 she deliberately struck Candy, watched to see what would happen, and indeed watched how both Candy and her own mother observed her experiment. This presublimation defense, in its forms of making-a-game, pretending, and experimentation, is of particular interest in that here the ego is dealing with the hostile destructive trend in aggression in an active rather than a passive mode. Therefore, the ego's mastery is of a different order here than it is in the implementation of those defenses that are effected at a more unconscious and conflictual level.

NEUROTIC SYMPTOM-FORMATION

We found two additional defenses: *projection* and *reactive masochism.* Because these defenses led to transient symptom formation in Jane, they are of particular interest.

Projection

As reported above, Jane suffered from a transient neurotic symptom, fear of falling asleep. While the frustration of the libidinal wish to solely possess the object, so crucial a factor in the rapprochement subphase, was the motivating force which led to symptom formation, it was the unexpressible hostile destructiveness mobilized by that frustration which directly caused the conflict and symptom. Because of Jane's projection of her hostile destructive wishes upon her mother, she dreaded that her mother would abandon her. Dread of abandonment by her mother, and of loss of her mother's love, the sources of anxiety experienced by the ego, led to efforts at ridding the self of the destructive impulses arising out of the id. Interestingly, however, the implementation of *projection* resulted in the emergence of exactly the threats of abandonment and loss of love that she dreaded. This miscarried defensive operation led to the emergence of anxiety at bedtime expressed in fear of going to sleep. While we cannot be certain what role Donnie's aggressive outbursts toward her played in the resolution of Jane's symptom, we have ascribed only a loosening, an activating function to them. I felt that it was my interpretation[5] that led to Jane's direct, controlled expression of anger toward her mother and her demand that her mother feed her as she did Anni, and as she used to feed Jane. This symptom vanished at this time, to recur at the height of her oedipal phase.

Masochism

Jane's episode of near self-flagellation (when, at 1–7–16, angered in turn by Donnie, Temmy, and Vicki, she made four slapping motions at her own face) is just another demonstration that even in a well-cared-for, well-endowed child, hostile destructiveness can mount to the point that the ego cannot contain its discharge. In this instance, however, the self became the object for that discharge. We are too well acquainted with masochism to be impressed with this behavior. However, for those of us who reject the concept of a death instinct and who, consequently, must doubt the concept of *primary masochism,* Jane's act requires explanation. Pressured from within to protect the love-object against her own hostile destructive impulses, at a time when the currently heavily burdened ego had newly effected some structuralization, Jane seemed suddenly overwhelmed by the cumulative attack and intrusions made on her in turn by Donnie, Temmy, and Vicki. As a result, she momentarily lost partial control over her hostile discharge and by displacement

---

[5] Just one datum from a number of such data will help to allay doubts on the part of the reader that the reported interpretation (from an analyst engaged in a participant observer relationship which is calculatedly and unavoidably a relationship which bears some resemblance to that of the therapeutic analytic relationship) had the influence here suggested. About ten months later, when Jane was beginning to show ample and clear evidence of oedipal angry feelings toward her mother, and Mrs. K. pressed some limits on a symbolic transgression, Jane said to her mother: "Me hates you, me tell EPPI!"—EPPI being the acronym of the Institute where this work is done and the name by which Jane identified the project and myself.

nearly struck herself. At this time, the direction of Jane's inhibited attack was decided by the large trend of this subphase to protect the love-object against the child's own destructiveness. Perhaps, too, some momentary regression led to a fusion of Donnie, Temmy and Vicki·as extensions of the object so that Jane, therefore, directed her inhibited discharge against the self.

Further confirmation of these dynamics were manifested at 2-2-1 when a more extensive and symptomatic (defensive) *masochism* gave way to an interpretation. Recently Jane had been getting hurt physically, which was very unusual for her. Interpretation of her defense and the underlying conflict arising out of her ambivalence toward her mother (and sister) led Jane to candidly reveal one of her fantasies. Speaking of Anni, she said, "She stole my Mommy!" She did not deny her anger; she told us one of its causes. Sibling rivalry became mixed with, and took some of the blame for, the unavoidable angry and hostile destructive reactions aroused in Jane by the obligatory separation-individuation work required by those developmental forces that lead to the rapprochement subphase. Jane gave ample evidence that her hostile destructive feelings toward her mother were mobilized by the too painful frustration of her wish to solely possess her mother at a time when she was working to intrapsychically separate self and libidinal object out of the symbiotic self-object representation. The length of her rapprochement subphase, thirteen to fourteen months, attests to the burden of work imposed on her psyche at this time.

SOME SALUTARY DEVELOPMENTS

The Ego's Control of Aggression

Defenses of the ego in acting upon object-directed hostile destructiveness can lead to symptom formation. But even more important is the fact that these intrapsychic interactions—the mutual relations of the ego, libido, and the destructive drive—also lead to salutary developments within psychic structure. The nondestructive current of aggression is available to the ego without necessary transformation or defense, and has a large influence in developing the conflict-free sphere of the ego. Hence, both nondestructive aggression and destructiveness play a large part in psychic development by the demands they make on the ego.

Nondestructive aggression, for example, by the expression of its *aim*—to control, master and assimilate—makes demands on the ego which the normal ego is innately equipped to progressively fulfill. Destructiveness makes demands on the ego to control and modulate it which bring a number of defenses into play. Nondestructive aggression too, of course, must come under ego control for optimal psychic functioning. The implementations of the ego to achieve this control over both currents of aggression, as well as the characteristics of the drive itself, make a significant contribution to character formation.

At a less global level of formulation, we found during the rapprochement subphase that the defenses of the ego (detailed above) against hostile destructiveness directed to the object yield significant salutary developments. These developments are dependent upon the quality of the child's object cathexis and the child's anaclitic relations to the object (Freud 1923, Parens and Saul 1971). Especially important is the fact that the character of the child's object cathexes during this subphase is a most significant determinant of the degree to which the hostile destructiveness mobilized by the threat of loss of the symbiotic partner is rendered benign. This is of course a critical determinant of *the way* the child will give up that symbiotic partner and attain libidinal-object constancy. In this regard, few developments in the ego are of more practical concern than its function of neutralization of destructiveness.

Altruism

Jane's dealing with her hostile destructiveness against her mother by reaction-formation and identification also, in many instances, yielded altruistic conduct on Jane's part. Thus at age 1-2-7 she could be tender, cautious, indeed "maternal," with infant Harold in association with, and we believe in reaction to, learning that her mother was in the process of having a baby. At 1-8-23 she imposed on herself, by giving up a toy to that new baby, a reaction-formation that was labored but which nonetheless already had the stamp of *altruism* on it. In such a reaction-formation and in identification, she could also comfort the shamed Candy who had struck her just moments before.

Humor

At this phase too, both Candy and Jane showed the beginnings of humor. Especially in making-a-game of these impulse-discharges toward mother and in pretending, we found humor. Of course, the ego's efforts to deal with sexuality also plays a part in this development, as Freud suggested in 1905 and 1927 (see also Wolfenstein 1951). Freud (1927) observed that "humor [is effected] through the agency of the superego" (p. 165). Indeed, we found humor to emerge under the influence of superego-precursors, prior to the resolution of the oedipus complex, and to arise from the ego's efforts to protect the beloved object against the self's hostile destructiveness.

Toward Superego Development
Many reactions occur in the child during the rapprochement subphase that give further evidence of the development of the superego-precursors reactive to the vicissitudes of the destructive drive. It is insufficiently noted that much superego development is already underway prior to the resolution of the oedipus complex. There is little doubt that these preoedipal reactions which lead to the development of the superego derive, as Freud observed in 1923 (p. 35, see also Parens and Saul 1971), from the lengthy duration in humans of their childhood helplessness and dependence on objects. As Jacobson (1964) and others have amply emphasized, early superego reactions of shame derive from experiences in the second and third years of life. We were impressed with the significant shame reactions we found in these children during the rapprochement and toward-object-constancy subphases.

Part III

TOWARD AN EPIGENESIS OF AGGRESSION IN EARLY CHILDHOOD

Chapter 10

EARLIEST
MANIFESTATIONS OF
THE AGGRESSIVE DRIVE

It is understood that our formulations derive from inferences in turn based on what we have taken to be manifestations of aggression. The psychoanalyst observing children or adults, be it in direct child observation study or in analysis or therapy, is secure only to a limited degree in the inferences of psychic activity which he draws and from which he proposes metapsychological formulations. There is no gift of direct evidence for him; like the physicist and many other scientists who work at equivalent levels of conceptualization (Lustman 1963, 1969), he can only infer the existence of an instinctual aggressive drive by its manifestations in behavior (Loewenstein 1940). This process is of course uncertain, and the investigator is both free and helpless to come to whatever conclusion he does. We cannot be surprised then that the range of disagreement between investigators can be so wide, especially on inference-based formulations. For psychoanalysts, this is nowhere better demonstrated than in the question of aggression.

My observation of children from birth on, in a manner derived from that of the child psychoanalyst in the office, led me to group the manifestation of aggression into four categories. Daily encounter with the data of observation, and the research discussions these engendered, led to this categorization. It proved a useful methodological effort, since it permitted an ordering of an ever-growing body of data which had a rather amorphous character. I came to feel that such a categorization might be helpful since data which we considered to be manifestations of aggression seemed to have distinctively different characteristics.

The material in part 3 will show the course taken by the aggressive drive in its evolving, epigenetic development and detail any differentiation we found. Hence, epigenetically, the first clearly observable evidence of aggression is the rage reaction of infancy. From such data I eventually suggested the category of the *unpleasure-related discharge of destructive impulses*. This category is distinguished from others by the constant presence of two manifest interrelated features: *destructiveness* and the attendant affect of *unpleasure*. As I have noted above, observation suggested that in this category of data, unpleasure is a decisive factor in the mobilization of destructive impulses.

Within hours of birth, alongside this category we found that of the *nonaffective discharge of destructive impulses*. The prototype for this group of data, following a suggestion by Eissler (1971), is the *nonaffective destruction* which occurs in sucking and eating—acts in which animate structure, animal or plant, is thoroughly broken down and hence, destroyed. This category is distinguished from the others by the *nonaffective* quality and character of the *destructiveness*. The prototype for this category, sucking and eating, by its anaclitic relation to physiologic need (hunger) can readily be assumed to be cyclically and *spontaneously* activated within the somatopsychic continuum. The drive characteristic of *spontaneity* is more clearly assured for this category than it is for that of the *unpleasure-related discharges of destructive impulses* (a point developed extensively in chapter 3). If we assume that the drive component of sucking which pertains to aggression may be representative for this category, then the two categories of drive manifestation mentioned so far are discernable at the latest within hours from birth.

The third category, the discharge of *nondestructive aggressive impulses* is observable within several weeks from birth, its manifestations being discernable during states of alert wakefulness. Here, the earliest evidence of self-assertive, controlling behavior may be inferred. Within three or so months from birth, during the first part of the normal symbiotic phase, manifestations of this category become amply observable. This category is distinguishable from the others by virtue of its *not having an inherent destructive quality*, while it is recognizable by its characteristics to pertain to aggression. For example, the earliest representatives of this type of data are the constant explorations of the self and environs, at first visual, but as soon as maturation of the musculomotor apparatus permits, prehensile and locomotoric. Some of the children impressively demonstrated during states of alert wakefulness as early as three months of age, the compellingness, constancy (persistency), and inner-drivenness of this activity. While libido plays its part in this activity, I infer from it here the tendency in the child to assert himself upon, control, assimilate and ultimately master both himself and the environment. In chapter 1, I detailed with data the developmental line of this aspect of the aggressive drive. It was presented at that point to document and support the hypothesis that there is a trend in the aggressive drive that is inherently nondestructive and which is tracable in its origin to the period of id-ego undifferentiation (Hartmann, 1939). In chapter 2, I explained why I view this trend in psychic life to pertain to aggression rather than to noninstinctual neutral ego energy as advanced by Hartmann.

We found such looking-exploring activity during the normal autistic phase, as when twelve-day-old Bernie looked at his mother's face for minutes on end with striking persistence. However, it was especially during the first part of the normal symbiotic phase that this activity made its appearance with impressiveness. In assessing this type of activity for its drive components, (even at this early age), we were impressed with the complexity and multiplicity of intertwining autonomous ego functions and drive discharges. Thus we found: (a) nondestructive aggressive strivings in the looking-exploring activity, these drive derivatives subserving autonomous sensorimotor ego apparatuses; (b) oral libidinal excitation with exploratory and erotic sucking; (c) socialization, with looking-exploring (not only libidinal but also nondestructive aggressive strivings) applied to libidinal object relations; and (d) large efforts and long periods of skill (ego) developing activity, as in gaining control of the motor apparatus.

The last category to emerge epigenetically, the *pleasure-related discharge of destructive impulses,* becomes discernible during the early part of the separation-individuation phase. This category is distinguished from the others by the constant presence of two interrelated features: *destructiveness* and *pleasure-affect.* We found that this category of drive discharge evolved later than the others, making its appearance from the last quarter of the first year of life on. Partly because of its late emergence as a trend in the aggressive drive, it has been a troublesome category to dissect as to origin and inherent character. As I detailed in part 1, these categories of aggression-manifestation yielded the theoretical assumption that each represents a distinguishable trend in the aggressive drive.

NEONATAL DIFFERENTIATION OF AGGRESSION AND LIBIDO

The fact that within hours from birth two trends of the aggressive drive are discernable, supports the contention that the libido and the aggressive drive emerge as separate instinctual drives with independent roots, as Freud held in 1905 and 1915. In this sense, the libido and aggressive drive are differentiated from one another at birth and the possibility of a single source or type of psychic energy is in doubt. The assertions of Jacobson (1964) and Spitz (1965) that the drives are not differentiated at birth, requires a word of clarification. If by this they mean that no distinction can be made between manifestations of libido as opposed to aggression, the evidence rejects this assumption. If they mean that the drives exist then in an archaic, immature form, this the data supports fully. *Absolute* and *relative* undifferentiation (Hartmann 1939) or nondifferentiation (Spitz 1965) must be distinguished. Assumptions of an undifferentiated id-ego (Freud 1937, Hartmann 1939, 1950b, 1952) or nondifferentiation (Spitz 1965) of psychic structure, or of instinctual drives (Spitz 1953, 1965, Jacobson 1964), cannot refer to *absolute undifferentiation,* but must rather refer to *relative undifferentiation.* No doubt it is in the sense of not being differentiated *into agencies* that Hartmann, after 1939, spoke of an undifferentiated id-ego. This applies equally to the term Spitz (1965) used , nondifferentiation, a term he used in reference to developments not only of id and ego as agencies, but also of *self* and *object,* of *inner* and *outer,* etc. But just as Hartmann (1939) proposed that there are structural elements present at birth (primary autonomous ego apparatuses), so too, as Schur (1966) suggests for the id, are there elements of drives present at birth, the manifestations of which permit us to distinguish libido and aggression from one another. Thus the concept of drive nondifferentiation at birth, as advanced by Spitz and Jacobson, must mean relative nondifferentiation (Parens and Saul 1971, Parens 1973a).

In insisting that the drives at birth are only *relatively* undifferentiated, I point to the rage reactions of the neonate. It is as certain that these are sharply inferrable as manifestations of aggression as it is that well-known nonnutritive (erotic) sucking which occurs in the newborn, and even in the fetus, represents libidinal trends. Doubtless there is no *diacritic* psychic content (Spitz 1945b, 1965) in these earliest libidinal and aggressive discharges. This, however, hardly suffices to sustain the view that drives are totally undifferentiated, or that such discharges have *no* psychic content. Perhaps it is plausible to suggest that, since the instinctual drives are phenomena in the borderland between the psyche and the soma (Freud 1905b, 1915), they have substrates conjointly in both realms and hence any somatic manifestation of such drive activity may suffice to infer the possibility of psychic content as well, not diacritically experienced, but at least experienced coenesthetically.

REGARDING NEONATAL SELF-DIRECTED DESTRUCTIVENESS

In accord with Freud's postulates on the nature of the destructive drive, we must look, during the normal autistic phase, for the directedness of the impulse. That is we must look for its *object,* in this case for possible evidence of self-directed destructiveness. I have emphasized the *relativeness* of id-ego undifferentiation and of drive nondifferentiation. But now it seems as justifiable to hold to the *absolute* nondifferentiation of self-object and of inside-outside (internal-external) in the newborn, with a slowly progressing differentiation of these only to a degree that is "not so absolute" by the end of the normal autistic phase (Mahler 1968, Spitz 1965). That is to say, we cannot speak of a destructive impulse being directed against the self nor against the object, nor toward the inside nor toward the outside until some differentiation of self and object, inside and outside, begins. It is indeed likely that the experience of a destructive impulse plays a part in the differentiation of these two lines of psychic development. More correctly perhaps, it is the experience of affective pleasure (good feelings) and unpleasure (painful, bad feeling) that plays this part. The anaclitic relations of the development of the drives, the ego, and the object are well documented.

I would ascribe to two sources Freud's postulation that the destructive drive is inherently self-directed. First, to postulate that the destructive drive derives from and is the psychic representative of the death instinct requires that the destructive drive is directed against the self. Second, the theory of *narcissism* holds that during the neonatal period of *primary narcissism* all experience emanates from and is directed toward the archaic self since only that self exists psychically, coenesthetically. In the further study of the earliest developments of the infant, the concept of an undifferentiated phase has helped to better assess the developmental status of psychic organization. The *self* of the period of *absolute* primary narcissim is a vastly different psychic organism from the *self* of the later separation-individuation period. Indeed the self of the absolute-narcissism period is not a delineated, self-contained, reality-oriented organism but rather an amorphous, nonoriented, pretransitional phenomenal (Winnicott 1953) organism (Spitz 1965, Mahler 1968, Jacobson 1964, Loewald 1952, Parens, 1971a). Thus, for example, scratching the self in the early normal autistic phase makes no contribution to a confirmation that the destructive drive is self-directed at birth.

We emerge then from the study of our data for the first six months of life with the assumption that one can discern with some confidence three trends in the aggressive drive, the fourth emerging near the end of the first year. The first three trends pertain to *the unpleasure-related discharge of destructive impulses, the nonaffective discharge of destructive impulses,* and *the discharge of nondestructive aggressive impulses,* the fourth to *the pleasure-related discharge of destructive impulses.*

While the first events to be associated with the unpleasure-related discharge of destructive impulses are physiologically painful events, which we presume are experienced coenesthetically in the psyche, a number of other events become capable of arousing unpleasure-related discharges during the period from two to six months of life. As I noted in detailing our observations (part 2), in addition to physiologically painful events, there are the undue restriction or interruption of sucking or of contact needs, traumatizing handling and traumatizing object-relatedness, undue precocious stranger anxiety, and the frustration of nondestructive aggressive strivings. This is not intended to be a complete listing but rather to show that *unpleasure-related discharges of destructive impulses multiply rapidly.* As already noted, it is particularly during the symbiosis that one gets a clear picture of the nondestructive discharges of aggression, a trend in the aggressive drive which is only weakly manifest during the first two months of life. As one approaches the six-month period, teething brings a new and important characteristic to the nonaffective spontaneous discharge of destructive impulses, for biting and chewing are added to sucking as part of food ingestion. Here, in addition, in all cases the painful emergence of teeth draws this trend in the aggressive drive closer to that of unpleasure-related destructiveness. No doubt, fusion of these two trends may occur where teething is particularly painful and protracted, and this painful event may serve as the model for biting as a mode of hostile destructive discharge.

A most important feature of these data and the inferences deduced from them is that we may see here *the characteristics of the aggressive drive prior to any organized influence upon them by the ego,* since the ego does not yet exist as agency. I assume from this that little if any ego defense, certainly not neutralization, has as yet played a part in influencing the character of the drives. Hartmann (1955) eventually came to suggest that perhaps neutralization of aggression may occur even before structuralization of the ego, an assumption, it seems to me, given impetus by Hartmann's view that a *primary* antagonism may exist between id and ego. Question is raised with both these assumptions in a discussion of Hartmann's evolving views regarding ego energies (see chapter 2), but suffice it to say that unless one postulates a function of primary neutralization—which Hartmann did not suggest—one is more secure in proposing that neutralization of drive must await sufficient ego structuralization. Such ego structuralization seems to begin with the structuring of the libidinal object; thus neutralization can be inferred to emerge as a function, as shall be detailed below, during the fourth quarter of the first year of life.

From the beginnings of the normal symbiosis, generally from the second month onward, progressive differentiation of the primary autonomous ego apparatuses and the drives can readily be discerned particularly as absolute primary narcissism differentiates to "not so absolute" primary narcissism (Mahler 1968). During this period, one can also follow, in the child's manifest selective attachment to his particular mother, the evolving structuring of the libidinal object. This course is accompanied by the beginnning development of the ego as agency. The structuring of the libidinal object, the child's first valuation of his particular mother, brings with it a number of findings regarding the aggressive drive.

The confluence of the maturation and development of the ego and the drives with the structuring of the libidinal object leads to developments of enormous significance during the second half of the first year of life (Spitz 1965). The complex differentiations of that period are highlighted by the fact that it is then that we find, not only the second part of the oral phase (Abraham 1924, Freud, 1933)—indeed the oral sadistic phase of psychosexual development—but also the second part of the normal symbiosis and the first part of the separation-individuation phase, the differentiation and practicing subphases (Mahler 1972a, 1972b, Mahler, Pine and Bergman 1975).

It is my impression that two major developmental events occur at this important crossroad. The first temporally is the structuring of the libidinal object. I mean this in exactly the sense Spitz (1950, 1965) and Mahler (1965, 1968) have formulated it. The second is a marked upsurge in the aggressive drive, which is, it seems to me, of biological origin. While, on the average, the libidinal object begins to be structured at about six months of life, the upsurge in the aggressive drive of this period occurs at about nine-to-ten months. Of course such age figures vary from child to child. In our children we found the sequence to be in the order noted, but since these developmental events pertain to different lines of development (A. Freud 1963)—the first being a complex psychic *development,* the second a drive *maturation* (as Hartmann defined them)—it is not necessary to assume that they must follow, in every child, the sequence we found.

Chapter 11

EARLIEST INFLUENCE OF LIBIDINAL OBJECT STRUCTURING ON THE AGGRESSIVE DRIVE

When the mothering person becomes sufficiently structured as libidinal object, she begins to play a unique role in the vicissitudes of the infant's aggressive drive. From the vantage point of Mahler's theory of human symbiosis and individuation, this is when the symbiotic partner *begins* to be recognized as separate, and to be differentiated, from the self. Whatever its first degree of representation in the psyche, and whatever the first character of that representation—recognitive memory and not object-permanence (Piaget 1937, Spitz 1950, 1965, Mahler 1968, Fraiberg 1969)— the object here attains its first valuation qua object, a valuation that will never be surpassed for its need-satisfying, dependence, and anaclitic valence.

Useful indices for sufficient structuring of the libidinal object are, first of all, the presence of a specific smiling response, indeed a global affective responsiveness to a specific object—one which is distinguishable from affective responses to others. We find the emergence on the one hand of gratifying, pleasurable, affect-laden reunion reactions with the specific object, and on the other, that of frustrating, unpleasurable, affect-laden separation reactions, in particular, separation anxiety. In conjunction with these, one also finds stranger reactions, and in most children, some mild degree of stranger anxiety. Some normal children show no evidence of stranger anxiety per se, but a mild degree of such anxiety would not be distressing clinically. Sharp persisting stranger anxiety, however, as we found in Temmy from seventeen weeks of age on, will leave its mark in the child's psyche and become manifest in the personality—indeed as it did in that child.

This concomitant valuation of the object and the beginning structuring of the ego as agency are the first great tamers of the destructive drive in the infant. Of course, the influence of the object on the vicissitudes of the infant's destructive drive has a history that antedates the infant's valuation of that object qua object. Prior to that valuation, the mother has already played her important part as the sufficient gratifyer of needs (drive and physiologic derivatives). She has protected her infant against protracted periods of excessive unpleasure and the undue mobilization of primitive hostile destructive impulses. By her interventions, long before she becomes valued, the mother will influence positively or negatively the vicissitudes of the destructive drive in her infant and will thereby impose a more or less optimal task with which the infantile pre-ego will have to cope.

With the valuation of the object as object, and the concomitant earliest structuring of the ego as agency, we found several progressively evolving, most significant developments pertaining to the aggressive drive.

With the instigation of anxiety in the six-month-old, unpleasure is experienced. If anxiety and unpleasure are protracted, under the aegis of primary narcissism, hostile destructive impulses are mobilized (see part I). A cardinal illustrative event is the one described by Freud (1926) which pertains to the first psychically perceived danger situation—a perception which induces separation anxiety, dread of object-loss. Often separation anxiety in the six-to-eight-month-old infant can clearly be seen to induce first anxiety and then marked unpleasure affects, followed in many cases by rage. Observation leaves little doubt that separation-induced rage is at this point directed for the first time against the object qua object. Rage-discharge here, however, begins to become complicated, and a comment on this is in order.

Prior to the structuring of the libidinal object, the discharge of rage in the infant follows a rather simple, observable pattern: as excessive unpleasure gradually mounts, concomitant affects appear which culminate in rage if the unpleasure is not undone by the auxiliary ego, or nurturing object. The three-month-old infant has little power to arrest certain painful stimuli autonomously except by the mechanism of hallucinatory wish fulfillment, described long ago in psychoanalysis. As that mechanism fails to achieve the necessary alleviation of un-pleasure, unpleasure mounts further and eventually induces rage. At the height of the rage, only action by the nurturing, not yet differentiated, libidinal object can stop the rage reaction. If the object does not intervene, the rage reaction will essentially run its course to exhaustion. If repeated too many times, withdrawal will occur and hospitalism-like phenomenology will follow (Spitz, 1945b). We presume this withdrawal, along with hallucinatory wish fulfillment, to be a most archaic and global organismic defense (Engel 1962) which has spore-formation as its model. Destructiveness is then turned upon the archaic self as Spitz (1946a) has suggested.

Now, with the structuring of the libidinal object, the reaction to unpleasure and the vicissitudes of destructiveness become more complex. As unpleasure intensifies, the infant turns to the specific object with the expectancy (*basic trust,* Erikson; *confident expectation,* Benedek) that the object, the symbiotic partner, can rid the infant-self of pain. In instances where the arrest of unpleasure is prompt, little more can be seen of the child's reaction of destructiveness, and there is ample evidence that the destructive impulses no longer press for discharge. Where unpleasure is protracted, however, one sees much evidence that the libidinal object becomes blamed—in a primitive sense—for excessive sources of unpleasure, and destructiveness becomes directed toward that object. For example painful teething, one may assume, leads to the infant biting the object, presumably because the object, by virtue of the omnipotent powers with which he or she is endowed by the narcissistic, omnipotent infant, is found slack in the expected functions of comforting and protecting against unpleasure.

Separation anxiety, however, is a more complex source of unpleasure and the mobilization of destructiveness. By virtue of its valuation by the six-month-old child, the object here becomes the *causative factor* in instigating the child's unpleasure. It is the experienced threat of loss of the valued object, of the auxiliary part of the ego which comforts and protects against unpleasure, which by its action of leaving the self instigates unpleasure. The valued, good object here becomes the instigator of unpleasure, and hence of pain and hostile destructiveness.

In a similar vein, with a child seven, eight, or nine months of age, the object instigates the infant's unpleasure when it imposes prohibitions against various forms of gratification. For example, prohibitions against taking a toy from another child, or touching certain items that are breakable, also make the object the instigator of unpleasure and hence of hostile destructiveness which becomes attached to the object cathexis and representation. It is by these *unavoidable* unpleasure experiences that, attached to the powerfully positive cathexis of that symbiotic partner, *the libidinal object also becomes the first object qua object of the infant's destructive impulses.*

At about five months, when the mothering person has become sufficiently specific (emotionally distinguishable from others), there is still indefiniteness in the directedness of aggressive drive discharge because the lines between self and object, inside and outside, are not yet well delineated. Nevertheless there is some evidence to show that the destructiveness's becoming directed toward this newly structured libidinal object makes significant demands on the psyche, particularly on the budding ego, and seems to activate certain processes and defenses specifically erected to protect the object against destruction by the infantile self.

After observations of our infants at this age, one comes away with the impression that the destructiveness mobilized by excessive unpleasure no longer finds so straight a line for expression as it did prior to the structuring of the libidinal object. Several sets of data point to this inference. First, we observed notable persistence, greater ease, and more neutral attitude in the discharge of destructiveness toward objects other than the libidinal object. This was particularly so with peers. Gestures of threatening and striking and aggressions against an object were more explicit when directed toward an object other than the libidinal object. Second, the behaviors that led to prohibitions by the libidinal object in turn led, from about nine months of age on, to observable activity from which one could infer compliance with maternal dictates and indeed the earliest internalization of such dictates. Third, from this one could already see a modification in aggressive behavior which may be presumed to derive from the influence upon it of the libido (fusion), and one might infer the early influence of the ego (neutralization). Some elaboration is warranted.

As I noted in part 2, a striking and puzzling phenomenon occurred from about six months of age on—one which has significant consequences regarding the aggressive drive, object relations, and structural development. It must be noted that our project, being an experience in group living so to speak, of an order quite different from the family unit, may have caused an artifact relevant to the phenomenon under consideration: By a dynamic difficult to ascertain with confidence, Jane, for example, from time to time would want and make marked efforts to get hold of whatever toy or thing Temmy was presently in possession of. Or, Cindy, having exactly the same toy as did Candy, would nonetheless seem compelled from within to take the toy Candy held. As I noted earlier, this taking-what-the-peer-has was compelled by several interdigitating, evolving psychic elements. (1) Developing *ego functions,* particularly sufficient cognitive function and control of the motor apparatus, make this event possible. (2) An underlying tendency to imitate the object, here a peer, also, I assume, contributes to ego functioning. This tendency might well derive from a mechanism on the order of an innate releasing mechanism (Lorenz 1935, 1953)—*an IRM which*—(as Spitz 1965 proposes for the smiling response) *underlies the tendency to identify with the object.* It is plausible to propose such a mechanism, an *imitation IRM,* in the domain of the ego (Hartmann 1939), which would represent a phylogenetic residual and would play an all-important part in the processes of internalization and identification in the development of the human psyche. (3) The current *structuring of the libidinal object,* under the aegis of the libido and narcissism, intensifies and may even simply dictate the wish to possess anything which receives a sufficient attention cathexis. (4) A contribution to such advance on the thing held by another object comes from the *aggressive drive.* From the nondestructive current comes the exploration directed at the thing which has received the scanning attention cathexis, as does the impulse to control that thing, to assert oneself over it. As external resistance against the self taking possession occurs, a greater investment of aggression is instigated; and if sufficient resistance persists, unpleasure will mount and hostile destructive impulses will be mobilized.

In the social situation of our project, this type of event became a frequent source of maternal prohibition for the child from the age of about six months on. It served well to show the child's reaction to, and comprehension (at an archaic level), of maternal prohibition and dictate. Narcissism, aggression, libido, and ego functions interdigitated to instigate action against the peer, of which the libidinal object disapproved and in which that latter object interceded. We found that while resistance by the peer, a nonlibidinal object, often led to a greater aggressive effort by the budding ego and self, intervention by the libidinal object caused a different order of unpleasure which seemed more painful. It is to be expected that any adult object by virtue of greater size and mass can subdue the aggressive strivings of the infant. But observation gives much reason to believe that the part played by the libido invested in the libidinal object (symbiotic partner) is what leads to behavior from which one can infer a different compliance reaction when the *libidinal* object intercedes. Observation suggests that when the libidinal object intercedes, compliance comes in most instances from the wish to please and to arrest mother's anger toward the self, to hold to her loving affects; in other instances, however, compliance can be inferred to come from the fear of the object's anger and the threat of hateful affects. In the first instance, one can presume the quieting influence of positive affects (libido) on aggression, and of the change and slackening within the child of the aggression-determined affects—overassertiveness, stubborness, and anger. By contrast, at this age, this fear of the object's hateful affects, while arresting the child's active aggression, may not modify the aggression-derived affects themselves but merely inhibit them; it may arrest their discharge without reducing their inherent compelling character. In these instances, there is no softening of the child's unpleasure-derived impulses and associated affects; there is only the inhibition of their libidinal-object-directed discharge.

From the characteristics of the nine-month-old's compliance reactions to maternal prohibition as compared to that to prohibitions by nonlibidinal objects (peer and adult), one can readily infer the part played by libidinal attachment in the modification of varying levels of aggression, from assertiveness to anger. The more the aggressive thrust has gathered momentum, the greater must the influence of the libido be to effect compliance with the object's prohibition. At this age, the beginnings of compliance in simple events (not touching certain items, not taking a toy from another), while already observable, often cannot be carried out by the infantile self and require the assistance of the auxiliary ego. There is, however, ample evidence at this period to show that such modifications of unpleasure-derived destructive impulses (attenuation, decrease in compellingness, arrest of a movement in the course of its trajectory) are due to the influence upon these of the libido invested in the libidinal object.

We found additional data from which we had to infer already at this age another parameter at play in modifying unpleasure-derived destructiveness. Mrs. K. scolding 0–8–4–old Jane led to Jane's arresting her threat to strike Temmy. Soon, thereafter, when Jane would be about to strike Temmy, inhibition many times already seemed built-in. While Jane did not seem to invest her peer with sufficient libido to influence aggression toward that peer, the libido toward the libidinal object played a part here nonetheless. By the influence on destructiveness of the libidinal object cathexis, the destructiveness toward the peer became modified, even though the libido attached to the representation of the peer could not carry sufficient weight to lessen (in and of itself) the compellingness of Jane's destructive impulses. Confirmation of this phenomenon is amply observable in the frequent turning by the infant to the object for renewed enforcement of the inhibition of the aggression in question. Here then, we assume that the ego must play a part, since the libido invested in the object of the aggressive impulses (the peer) is of itself too weak to effect inhibition of that aggression. Here, we infer that by its relation to a *sufficiently positive libidinal cathexis,* by virtue of the destructive impulse's passing through the libidinal object which can modify it in the sense of Mahler's 1968 conceptualization of *object passage* of the aggressive drive, the destructiveness instigated by unpleasure, now *under the influence of the ego,* begins to become neutralized.

It is in this sense that, with the earliest structuring of the libidinal object qua object, unpleasure-related destructive impulses no longer find so straight a line for outer-directed discharge. From about nine months we find differences in the discharge of destructive impulses toward objects—differences which derive not just from the intensity of unpleasure or drive mobilization but, we believe, from the variable quantitative and qualitative investment of libido in objects. We infer from these observations in turn the earliest influences of the libido on unpleasure-derived destructive impulses, evidence in support of the concepts of fusion of libido and aggression and object passage of aggression, and the earliest suggestions of the ego's use of neutralization. (See chapter 14 for a discussion of the earliest evidence of neutralization of destructiveness.)

Chapter 12

BIOLOGICAL UPSURGE
OF THE AGGRESSIVE
DRIVE

We came to observe evidence of a striking upsurge in manifestations of the aggressive drive in most of our subjects at about nine months of age. This upsurge pertained to all aspects of aggression (see chapter 7).

It is long established in psychoanalysis that the epigenesis of psycho-sexual development—which is based on differentiations in the libido—consists of a sequential evolution from the oral to the anal and then to the genital phases. There are indications that the epigenesis of the aggressive drive, other than for those elements that are anaclitic concomitants of the libido, does not have phases as clear as those found for the libido. This may be due to the fact that the somatic substrate of the aggressive drive does not have the zonal characteristic of the libido (oral, anal, genital) which determines the characteristic of its drive differentiation. Nor does it have the all-important drive differentiation from primary narcissistic libido to heterosexual-object libido which derives from the evolving congenitally programed somatic substrate of the libido. Rather, the somatic substrate of the aggressive drive (Parens 1973a)—the sensori-receptor-musculomotor organization—is more fluid in its maturation and development. However, some peaks of excitation and dominance (in Erikson's 1959 use of the term) are discernable. We assume that the differentiation of the sensorimotor organization begins in utero where the first expressions of the aggressive drive in motor-muscular activity are detectable. It is my impression that, out of utero, the single, largest peak of the primary differentiation (maturation) of the aggressive drive occurs during the second half of the first year of life, and that it occurs concomitantly with the maturation of the central nervous system and the musculomotor organization. In the first three years of life, the other peaks in aggressive drive excitation seem to be anaclitic (that is, to follow upon, rather than to lead to, change), being determined by the vicissitudes of the libido and the development of the ego, as I shall note below.

The biological upsurge of aggression is manifest in all trends of the drive. In the nondestructive current it is amply demonstrated in the increased exploratory-mastery type of activity which pertains to the locomotor apparatus—indeed, in the activity by which that subphase of separation-individuation is identified, the practicing subphase. In the nonaffective destructive current it is represented by the marked ingestive activity associated with the change in food intake which now begins to include solids. This occurs under the maturational influence of the CNS and the masticatory apparatus of the mouth—the eruption of teeth and concomitant increased activation of the masseters (as compared to the orbicular muscle of the mouth, which acts preponderently in sucking). The unpleasure-related destructive current of the aggressive drive is amply exercised by the conflict of ambivalence described just below.

An important distinction between the currents of aggression has to be made with respect to the mutual influence of the ego and aggression. The theoretical assumptions regarding aggression advanced in this work hold that the nondestructive current of aggression, by the dynamics of its discharges, does not create a conflict in the ego and, in the first order of things, enters the conflict-free-sphere ego activities. By contrast, the unpleasure-related mobilization of destructiveness pertains eventually to the conflict sphere of the id and ego.

Dissection of the dynamic conflict under consideration in this section will help to highlight the distinction of these currents in aggression. In essence, the upsurge in the nondestructive trend in the aggressive drive seems to be the motivating force of the practicing behavior characteristics of this period of development (from nine to sixteen or so months). Unavoidably, the pressure of exploration, of asserting oneself upon, and of mastering the environment and the self, leads to prohibitive interventions by the mother. This aspect of the aggressive drive leads to a conflict between self and reality; it does not in and of itself pertain to an intrapsychic conflict. Many times there is no need for the ego to do any more than to redirect this aggression and gain control over it. However, once unpleasure mounts sufficiently, due to the mother's intervention, the aggression that is mobilized is of a different order. It is hostile-destructive and becomes part and parcel of a conflict of ambivalence within the psyche. Indeed it is activated by the interpersonal conflict which has just made its appearance. Here the ego must do more than just redirect or gain control over the aggression. The conflict of ambivalence is created by the hostile destructive trend in aggression, not by the nondestructive trend. The ego finds the destructive trend to be directed to the object which has been invested with libido, and this destructiveness is experienced as alien to that paramount libidinal cathexis which the ego experiences as an extension of itself, the auxiliary ego (Spitz 1950, 1965). It is against this trend of the drive that the ego has to erect defenses, which I shall discuss in some detail below.

FIRST CONFLICT OF AMBIVALENCE

This biological upsurge in the aggressive drive, as I just indicated, seems in large part to be responsible for the development of a conflict which we found characteristic for this period of development, the first part of the separation-individuation phase. Some of the children showed a most impressive mounting of strivings toward autonomy: assertiveness, efforts to gratify compelling omnipotent strivings, and efforts to control and master the environment. At times of pleasure, these strivings give the impression so aptly described by Greenacre's "love affair with the world" (1960) and by Mahler's concept of *practicing*. But when these autonomous strivings are thwarted, mounting unpleasure is experienced and, often as not, where resistance is protracted, an enormous upsurge of hostile destructiveness makes itself felt. Since the mother, the libidinal object, in the service of protecting the child or breakable things is the most frequent obstacle to the gratification of these autonomous strivings, the destructiveness mobilized in the child is directed toward that same libidinal object. The *interpersonal conflict* which now results takes on the character of a battle of wills between child and mother. As I showed in part 2 with regard to Jane and Mary, and as was the case with our other subjects where the pressure of the aggression was especially sharp, this conflict may create an acutely difficult situation for the self and the object.

Observations of this period compel us to assume that often when the pressure of these autonomous strivings of the aggressive drive, sustained by infantile narcissism and omnipotence, is excessively frustrated, this leads to significant unpleasure and hence to the emergence of hostile destructiveness toward the source of resistance, the object (Freud 1915, pp. 120–21; Spitz 1965, p. 137; Winnicott 1950x). Under these conditions, we found, to no one's surprise to be sure, a notable automatic responsiveness in our infants to environmental resistance. The pressure from within seemed more often than not to propel the child in exactly the direction prohibited by the object. There the infant would usually again encounter persisting resistance from the object which would in turn, by way of mounting unpleasure, mobilize further hostile destructive impulses directed toward the libidinal object. Again and again, one could see evidence of the *intrapsychic* reverberations of the emerging interpersonal conflict between self and libidinal object.

Observing the ten-to-fourteen-month-old junior toddler engendered the inference that the conflict between child and mother led to the emergence of an *intrapsychic conflict* within the child: an intrasystemic conflict of ambivalence. This intrapsychic conflict, which arises out of the upsurge in the aggressive drive, occurs in part because of the libidinization of the object. It is the sharp upsurge in the autonomous strivings of the aggressive drive, derivatives of the nondestructive current of aggression, which creates the conditions for the conflict under discussion. Then it is the object's interfering with drive gratification which by arousing unpleasure mobilizes hostile destructive impulses that are directed against that object. Hence, the object's action makes its contribution to the interpersonal conflict. It is, however, in consequence of the *valuation of the object* (object cathexis) that this interpersonal conflict creates the necessary conditions for the development of an *intrapsychic conflict*.

First, by its causing unpleasure, the libidinal object (symbiotic partner) becomes, par excellence, the object of the child's hostile destructive impulses, and thus the conflict of ambivalence is set up within the infantile psyche. Again and again one sees clear manifestations of the child's ambivalence. Frequently, as we have seen, at this age (and later too), the experience of excessive unpleasure leads magnetically to seeking comfort and the cessation of unpleasure, via the libidinal object (auxiliary ego). Where the libidinal object is invested with a strong positive cathexis, at such times of excessive unpleasure, and just when destructiveness is directed to that object, the one-year-old will invariably turn for such comforting to the libidinal object, *even when the excessive unpleasure is instigated by that same object.* During this conflict of ambivalence, it is important to recognize that a sufficiently positive valuation (cathexis) of the object activates two processes: (1) the overbalance of the hostile destructive cathexis by the positive libidinal cathexis (that is, by the influence of the libido on the destructive impulses), and (2) the demands made upon the ego by the positive libidinal cathexis of the object and by the state of helplessness engendered by the ambivalence. By contrast, an insufficient positive libidinal investment in the object may insufficiently mitigate the harshness of the destructive cathexis, as we could infer in Vicki. And, such an insufficiently positive libidinal cathexis makes somewhat different demands upon the ego. The conflict of ambivalence, particularly highlighted at this time, leads to most salutary developments where the influence of the libido on aggression and the demands it makes upon the ego are optimal. It is easy to see that in the normal child, one factor here plays a most important part: the sufficiently positive cathexis of the object.

In this conflict, the average child encounters the good-enough object's first strong prohibitions. It is here that the child first experiences, that his ego first registers, the condition of ambivalence, where strong destructive impulses are directed toward the omnipotent and omnipotently positively cathected object. And it is here that the child's ego takes its first stand in a conflict between the drives on the one hand and the highly cathected libidinal object on the other. This is where the ego's work to tame hostile destructiveness begins. The young ego, rendered anxious by the attitude of the self and the object, sets itself the great task of mediating between the drives and reality and begins to internalize dictates from the libidinal object, and activates neutralization of destructiveness toward it.

THE AGGRESSIVE UPSURGE, THE FIRST CONFLICT OF AMBIVALENCE, AND THE ANAL PHASE CONFLICT

In part 2, I detailed Peller's efforts to redefine the second phase of the libidinal organization (1965, p. 742) wherein she recognizes the part played by the drive activity here considered to pertain to the aggressive drive. She noted that Freud stressed aggressive strivings "regularly" in conjunction with the anal (libidinal) ones (pp. 743–44). I there suggested that perhaps the differences in Peller's formulations in this regard from my own might derive from the differences in our approaches to this material of observation. In contrast to Peller's, our approach is from the vantage point not of the libidinal organization, but of separation-individuation, a vantage point chosen especially not to bias a study of aggression with the lens of the libido.

What gives to the anal phase of psychosexual development its particular characteristics of willfulness, obstinacy, stubborness, and sadism? Certain viewpoints converge: Mahler (1965, 1968) speaks of *practicing* newly developing ego apparatuses and functions, of great narcissistic investment by the child in his own functions, his body, and the external environment. Erikson (1959) speaks of the ego's efforts to attain a sense of autonomy. Hendrick (1942, 1943a, 1943b) spoke of a mastery instinct, as did Peller (1965). Peller, considering a mastery instinct in the context of the anal phase of psychosexual development, believed it to be "a pregenital sexual drive" (p. 742). And above all, Freud spoke a number of times of sadism and mastery as deriving from the same instinctual source (unlike Peller), and repeatedly referred to the sadistic-anal phase of development, where sadism was the representative of aggression.

I suggest that it is this biologically determined upsurge of aggression which at this developmental period induces such large efforts at mastery and autonomy and makes possible the expressions of sadism associated with the anal phase. It is this upsurge of aggression which accounts for the characteristics of obstinacy, willfulness, and sadism that have been identified by us as pertaining to the anal phase of psychosexual development, a development representative of the libidinal organization.

It is emphasized that the practicing subphase conflict here described appeared before any effort to toilet train took place and that anal derivatives per se did not yet seem to play a part. Still, it has the central characteristics of obstinacy, willfulness, and sadism ascribed to anal conflicts. I am prepared, therefore, to suggest that the practicing subphase conflict, which is common and may be more or less obligatory, arises principally from the large upsurge of the aggressive drive, is at the basis of certain features of the anal phase conflict, and indeed gives to this libidinal conflict its particular character. As I noted above, this formulation actually adds nothing new to existing knowledge; it is essentially a *re*formulation, a reordering of priorities too long taken for granted.

Chapter 13

THE EGO'S REACTIONS
TO THE FIRST CONFLICT
OF AMBIVALENCE

The conflict of ambivalence which occurs during this period of the biological upsurge in the aggressive drive results from the mobilization of a marked cathexis of destructiveness toward the positively cathected object. It was already noted above that, in accord with Freud's 1923 postulate, by virtue of the nature of id cathexes, the positive cathexis mitigates the destructive cathexis by the influence of the libido on the destructive impulses. It is difficult to ascertain whether the mitigation of destructiveness toward the libidinal object derives from the valuation of the need-satisfying object (A. Freud, 1946, 1954, 1963) or from the inherent nature of the libido—which imposes the need for an object relation by its tendency to bind organisms together, particularly as is reflected in the object-anaclitic character of sexual gratification and bisexual reproduction. Possibly it is both. Whatever its nature, observation suggests that in this conflict of ambivalence, at this time in the course of the protracted and intense dependence of the child, the balance of forces in the psyche heavily favors the libidinal cathexis. However, even with heavy odds in favor of the libidinal cathexis, too great a cumulative hostile destructive cathexis may not yield to the influence of libido which is not stably attached to the gradually structuring object representation. Too strong a destructive cathexis may cause too great anxiety and hence effect ego activity that would interfere with the "object passage" of destructiveness and would interfere with its mitigation by an admixture with libido (as occurs in pathological splitting of object representations).

This condition of ambivalence, as Mary showed so well, leads to anxiety. Already at this time the infantile ego is surprisingly able to deal with its condition of helplessness. I have illustrated and discussed the defenses observably employed by the child to protect the libidinal object against the destructiveness which emerges at this period.

A brief comment is warranted. It is of interest that *in the normal, well-cared-for child* comparatively little effort seems exerted by the ego to protect the self against destructive impulses emanating from the self. It seems that the archaic, cohesive and integrative influence of primary narcissism tends to protect against self-destructiveness by the externalization of such impulses, a pattern that emerges well before the ego becomes structured as agency. The principal observable efforts of the ego's work with regard to troublesome aggression seems to be in the arena of object-directed destructiveness.

Although the libido influences destructiveness, the ego also functions autonomously in coping with object-directed destructiveness. In this, observation suggests that a number of well-known functions (defenses) begin to evolve in the healthy ego of the about-to-be-one-year-old. From the age of about nine to eighteen months, behavior from which we can infer *inhibition* of impulse discharge begins to be observed. We also find a repression type of mechanism which cannot be inferred to be the same as that characteristic for the oedipal period of development but which by its manifestations can be construed to be a *precursor of repression* (hence I suggested it to be *prerepression).* Similarly, we find early efforts that eventuate later in sublimation and hence suggest precursor mechanisms of *presublimation,* which includes *reaction-formation. Splitting of object representations* can be inferred to derive from the first conflict of ambivalence, and we can find in it the mechanism (proposed by Kernberg 1966, 1967) to protect the good object from the destructive cathexis invested in the bad object representation. Most significant too, we find here the earliest signs of beginning *internalization* of maternal dictates and of course with this, the earliest *precursors of superego formation.*

INHIBITION OF DESTRUCTIVE IMPULSE DISCHARGE

As we have noted, under the influence of the libidinization of the object and that object's prohibition, already during the latter part of the normal symbiosis (five to ten months of age), one can observe simple forms of impulse-discharge inhibition. These emerge in compliance with dictates (usually maternal) antagonistic to the discharge that is in progress or just impending. It seems particularly under the impetus of the biological upsurge in the aggressive drive and the concomitant maturation in sensorimotor ego apparatuses that events call upon the ego to inhibit that discharge of hostile destructiveness which becomes particularly directed against the libidinal object. The inhibition of nondestructive aggression on the other hand, which is often required at this time too, does not create as difficult a problem for the child and does not require the efforts exerted by the ego with regard to libidinal-object-directed destructiveness. Nondestructive aggression by virtue of its inherent conflict-free derivation and characteristics is more easily redirected and deflected by the ego or the object than is unpleasure-derived destructive aggression.

The remarkable factor for the vicissitudes of the mutual relation of aggression and the ego is that the currently greater pressures from aggression on the maturing ego apparatuses make greater demands on the ego in both conflict and conflict-free spheres of function. By these greater demands, *inhibition* of destructiveness becomes insufficient and more vigorous defensive steps are taken which are themselves evidence of the ego growth effected and indeed energized by aggression itself (Hartmann, Kris and Loewenstein 1949).

While inhibition is one of the earliest defenses erected against the discharge of destructive (as well as nondestructive) aggression, it is also among the first to become associated with the *internalization* of maternal dictates. Its part then is significant in the all-important process of superego formation. At this time too, it can be seen to become associated with, and often lead to, *displacement* of destructive cathexes, a defense which can become costly in peer relations and object relations in general—for example, later in development, by fueling prejudice. Inhibition also often becomes associated with, and seems to lead to, *reaction-formation*. In fact it seems to be necessary for the earliest efforts at reaction-formation; it gives to the ego the time necessary for these earliest efforts and provides the delay required for the defensive turning about of affects and impulse impetus. On the other hand, reaction-formation provides a way out for the impulse discharge that is suspended, hanging in midair so to speak, by inhibition. Simple inhibition of impulse discharge can no longer meet the demands made on the ego by the much more powerful aggressive drive discharge of the about-to-be one-year-old.

DENIAL

Denial does not seem to be among the very first defenses to appear vis-a-vis the discharge of aggression. We did, however, find it among the first defenses *against being the object of an aggression discharge,* against the suffering of unpleasure of whatever origin. We found that nine-month-old Temmy denied that Jane was aggressing against her, that Jane was taking the pacifier from her mouth despite her own resistance and overt unpleasure and that of both mothers. Denial of unpleasure, of the passive experience of aggression, was found in Temmy at that age, who, as we can show on film, seemed momentarily in a dissociative state. The denial of *being the aggressor,* however, seems to await sufficient internalization of specific maternal prohibition which comes with the cognition that mother does not approve of certain types of direct aggression discharge.

SPLITTING OBJECT REPRESENTATIONS

I have reported in part 2 the clustering of events at this time from which one could infer the splitting of object representations, as described by Kernberg (1966, 1967) and Mahler (1968) along lines of the good (gratifying) and bad (frustrating, hurtful) object-related experiences. As was noted above, the omnipotent libidinal-object becomes the first to be invested with a hostile-destructive cathexis but is, on the other hand, the foremost object protected against that destructive cathexis. Our findings suggest that such splitting is temporarily employed at this time by the normal child, due to the child's frequent experiencing of the same mothering object as alternately comforting and frustrating. We could infer from observation the structuring of the good and bad mother representations and their alternating cathexis with positive and negative drive derivatives as well as the child's ongoing experiences of *integrating* these object representations.

It is just in this area of integrating split object-related experiences and representations that we found a mistake too frequently made by some of the mothers. We found splitting to be a problem not only for the child but for the mother as well, and found that it created confusion not only in the mind of the child but also in that of the mother. When the mother obstructs the nondestructive aggressive thrust of her practicing-sub-phase child, the child often reacts with unpleasure and the mobilization of hostile destructive impulses. These are directed to the mother who by her action instigated them. Frequently, under such conditions, the child finds himself angry with the frustrating bad mother; but by virtue of the unpleasure experienced by this state of affairs, the child turns to the same object (auxiliary ego), the comforting good mother, for the relief of this unpleasure.

Many a mother rejects her child at that moment because she does not want her child to be spoiled. By her action she withholds the good mother from comforting and further enhances the valence of the bad mother and the child's destructive cathexis of her. Thus she compounds the bad experience, and enhances the use of negatively valenced defenses all in the belief that she is insuring the child's growth. Unwittingly she takes from the child the greatest source for the integration of good and bad object-related experiences: The influence of the positive-enough libidinal object cathexis on the efforts of the ego to integrate these two representations into one stable object representation. Again I note that the great anaclitic needs of the infant favor the libidinal cathexis, but much harm can be done to this process by the excessive mobilization of destructive cathexes.

Caution is warranted in assuming that a destructive cathexis, by interfering with the ultimate attainment of libidinal object constancy (as Mahler 1968, with Pine and Bergman, 1975, conceptualizes the term), does not attain a form of constancy of itself, in the sense of an immutable stability. As Ekstein (1971) has shown well, and as I noted earlier (Parens, 1972a) in accord with Freud's (1940) view on the indelibility of the earliest cathexes, a sufficiently reinforced destructive object cathexis can become indelible, it can attain more or less constancy (immutability) and influence object relations for years to follow. It is in this spirit that the concept of libidinal object constancy (which begins to stabilize at the end of the separation-individuation phase proper), the governor of successful object relations, holds within it a *sufficiently positive* libidinal object cathexis.

PRECURSORS OF SUBLIMATION—PRESUBLIMATION

In considering Jane's behavior, we came to believe that in order to cope with destructiveness directed toward her beloved mother, she split the affect-laden object representations and temporarily assigned the good representation to a neutral (other than mother) object—perhaps to hold it in safe-keeping on neutral grounds, her basic trust in objects having been realistically as well as omnipotently self-secured. Jane then proceeded to actively, directly work through the destructive cathexis of the libidinal object with her actual mother. The work of the ego was readily discernable when Jane made a game of the conflict with her mother.

As was noted in chapter eight, we saw the ingeniousness and resourcefulness of the infantile ego. At less than eleven months of age, from all appearances, Jane made a game of the conflict that had developed between herself and her mother. It must be emphasized that while it is correct to assume that the ego worked to allay the conflict between the self and the object, the ego had a greater task at hand: to resolve the intrapsychic conflict of ambivalence which was evolving in consequence of the interpersonal conflict. The least that can be said is that the ego dealt with both interpersonal and intrapsychic conflicts at once.

The defensive nature of the game that emerged in the child-mother dyad was clear, its conflict solving capacity most effective. The child's ego here clustered several defenses, including inhibition and reaction-formation, to effect a sublimatory type of activity which may be viewed as a *precursor of sublimation,* hence as *presublimation.* How well we saw, as Peller (1954) described it, that play is not only an attempt to compensate for anxieties, but that it is also a step toward sublimation (p. 180).

A PRECURSOR OF REPRESSION—PREREPRESSION

In chapter 8, I also detailed evidence of some form of repression. This manifestation may represent the earliest efforts by the ego as agency to effect repression. It seems distinguishable from the earlier *hallucinatory wish fulfilment,* well known to psychoanalysis, which occurs from the earliest months of life on, a mechanism activated by and aimed to allay the accumulation of painful stimuli. The principle mechanisms involved in hallucinatory wish fulfilment are *denial* and *omnipotent wish fulfilment* (hallucinated gratification). Up to a point, denial and hallucinated gratification hold in abeyance unpleasure deriving from an organic source of painful stimuli.

Acknowledging that I cannot see as clearly here as I would wish, it seems to me that a different process was at work in Jane's intermittent, serial reemerging rage toward her mother in the episode I described earlier. It appeared as if the bad experience which was just recorded in memory was actively kept out of awareness by a force that would yield intermittently to the cumulative pressure of the impulses aroused by that recorded bad experience. The periods of calm, sober activity between the outbursts of angry crying seemed to be periods when the ego's efforts succeeded in keeping the object-directed destructive impulses under control by keeping them out of awareness. The actual interpersonal conflict was no longer enacted once Jane started to cry. The pressure from within Jane to do what she wanted to do yielded to a pressure of greater momentary import—that deriving from the intrapsychic conflict of ambivalence, most specifically the pressure from the object-directed destructive impulses. What seemed active to me were the memory of the event, the mobilization of destructive impulses it engendered, and the protracted afterdischarge of these. Both the strongly cathected memory and the momentum (impetus) of impulse discharge created the long afterdischarge observed. It seemed that the memory (with its impulse derivatives) was actively being put out of the conscious mind (in the topographic sense), but that when the force of these associated impulse derivatives intermittently waxed too large to be held in the unconscious, it then broke through the defensive efforts of the ego into consciousness. It is this reasoning which leads me to suggest that some early form of repression, other than denial, is available to the ego of the ten-to-twelve-month-old child.

I would ask if it is here, when repression as an *active* process may begin, that the conceptualizable remberable emerges, in the sense of, and as the counterpart of, Frank's important views (1969) on the unrememberable and the unforgettable of the primary passive repression and pre-concept-formation era. What the ego *actively* works to repress must not only be recorded but indeed be conceptually rememberable. I would note here that much observable evidence suggests that there is a long period *during the preverbal era* in which the ego's capacity to conceptualize—both in the child's understanding maternal communications and in his nonverbal communications to her—is sufficiently developed to record in memory and hence to remember in conceptual form, albeit at a simple age-adequate cognitive level. This assumption recommends the view that what is actively repressed at this time may be rememberable already in conceptual form.

INTERNALIZATION OF MATERNAL DICTATES

Our findings lend support to Freud's postulate (1930) that guilt derives particularly from the superego's reaction to (object-directed) hostile destructiveness (see Piers and Singer 1953). I have detailed before Freud's view, so importantly formulated already in *Totem and Taboo* (1913), that conscience "arose on a basis of emotional ambivalence, from . . . specific human relations" (p. 68). In speaking of the primal horde, Freud observed that the tumultuous mob of brothers hated their father, but they also loved and admired him. "After they had got rid of him, had satisfied their hatred. . ., the affection which had all this time been pushed under was bound to make itself felt. It did so in the form of remorse. A sense of guilt made its appearance" (p. 143). There is a prehistory to that development, indeed a prehistory to the "emotional ambivalence in specific human relations" of the oedipus complex to which Freud referred in 1913.

That prehistory begins in the arena of the earliest object-related destructiveness, when, during the first conflict of ambivalence, the newly structured libidinal object by frustrating drive derivatives mobilizes hostile destructiveness toward it. I have detailed how even before that conflict emerges, the earliest socialized infantile responses to maternal prohibition emerge soon after the structuring of the specific libidinal object (just beyond the peak of the normal symbiosis and the beginnings of the separation-individuation phase). There, the seven-month-old encounters the mother's first prohibitions and responds variably to this challenge of his omnipotence from the most valued object itself. We found at this stage, during the latter part of the first year of life, that the prohibition by the libidinal object begins to be internalized and by its qualitative manifestations already takes on that character which in psychoanalysis we ascribe to the superego and its precursors. In reporting observations for the practicing subphase, I detailed some examples from which we infer identification with maternal prohibition, as in the first instances when the child exhibits behavioral responses to a dictate which at the given moment does not come from the actual object, but rather from a source within the child himself: The child's turning to look at mother while on the point of doing something which she has prohibited earlier, the actual doing and its interruption, its *undoing,* so to speak, the child's readying to do something and stopping himself with a visible prohibition, such as the identification-derived head-shaking—all of these, repeated many times, suggest that internalization of maternal dictates has *begun,* that such maternal prohibitions are taken over by the ego, and that they *begin* to exercise some influence, however weak, over the child's actions. In this instance, as in many others, our findings support those of Spitz (1953, 1957, 1965).

These infant observations support the assumption, derived from clinical psychoanalyses, that the vicissitudes of aggression—particularly, object-directed hostile destructiveness—pertain quite specifically to superego formation. The point I want to emphasize here is: our observations suggest that in many instances the internalization of maternal dictates—which are but the start of the long process of civilizing the child (Freud, 1940)—clearly begin under the influence of the first conflict of ambivalence. During this most anaclitic life period, the anxiety aroused by destructiveness being directed to the libidinal object leads to identification with the prohibiting object as a defense instituted by the ego. We find here the emergence of superego precursors.

Chapter 14

BEGINNINGS OF NEUTRALIZATION OF AGGRESSION

Our attention was sharply turned to the question of the neutralization of aggression when newborn Mary entered our project, accompanied by her two-and-a-half-year-old brother, Donnie, as a research-subject sibling. Donnie, an apparently healthy and attractive toddler, tended to suddenly lash out when frustrated, in a manner that alarmed the mothers. Indeed, unexpected large knocks by Donnie against Candy, Cindy and Jane upset the mother of the twins (Candy and Cindy) and led her to consider leaving the project.

I shall not discuss here what we did, which (by work with the mother, limit setting, and therapy-type verbalizations) resulted eventually in a gratifying change in the direction of Donnie's neutralization of destructiveness. More relevant here is the fact highlighted by Donnie's un-neutralized aggressive drive discharges—the fact that except in the case of Cindy, who suffered from a minimal brain dysfunction, such harsh, hostile destructive drive discharges were absent in our then less-than-eighteen-month-old project toddlers. We came to feel that an active process was at work which had led to the already much more tame aggressive drive discharges in these research subjects.

We were satisfied that we were not observing children with a low level of aggressive drive endowment, certainly not when we considered Jane, Mary, Vicki, Bernie and Harold. Some *active process* had to account for the differences in destructive drive discharge, an active process which up to the time of our observation of Donnie had escaped our detailed and continuous observations. Our clinico-observational impression was that Donnie exhibited a high level of unneutralized hostile destructiveness, whereas our toddler subjects by the turn into their second year of life exhibited aggressive drive discharges in which destructiveness seemed already quite tame and under some primitive ego control.

OBSERVATION

Shortly after his arrival into our project (as a research subject sibling) two-and-a-half-year-old Donnie was in interaction with several of our research subjects who were then from thirteen to sixteen months of age. Before anyone knew what had happened, Donnie had swung his arm widely and forcefully struck fourteen-month-old Candy in the head. Candy was not the only one stunned by such a blow. Several minutes later, after some alarm and sharp admonitions by his mother, Donnie struck Cindy, again harshly. The group reaction—particularly that of the mothers and participant observers—revealed a notable degree of uneasiness. Several weeks later, during the course of one session, Donnie harshly struck Jane (then sixteen months old) at three different times. This created another sharp wave of uneasiness in the project group and led to some staff intervention with both mother and child. The qualitative features of Donnie's destructive discharges gave the clinical impression of a harshness and lack of control over impulse which led us to assume that these destructive impulses were unneutralized. This did not surprise us clinically, but it did highlight, as I have already indicated, the fact that our thirteen-to-sixteen-month-old subjects in their destructive drive discharges already showed an absence of the harshness and impulsivity now found in Donnie, which we could have expected to find in them had their infant rage reactions followed a straight developmental line.

The sufficient clinical impression that qualitative differences existed between two-and-a-half-year-old Donnie's discharges and those of our twelve-to-sixteen-month-old subjects faced us with several issues: (1) What were some of these qualitative differences? And, (2) What implications did we draw from them?

TOWARD A QUALITATIVE EXAMINATION OF
UNNEUTRALIZED AND NEUTRALIZED
DESTRUCTIVENESS

I can answer the second question more briefly than the first. I inferred from this finding that an active neutralization process had already begun; indeed by the beginning of the second year of life it was already successfully playing a significant and age-adequate part in the ego's work to control and modify destructiveness. We began to look for the beginnings of this process by considering that they might be found in the second part of the first year of life. Before I detail this consideration it must be clear what the evident differences in behavior were from which we inferred unneutralized as compared to neutralized destructiveness.

First of all, I am not speaking of an all-or-none phenomenon but of an evolving capability of the ego vis-a-vis troublesome aggression. Thus neither did Donnie's destructive drive discharges always exhibit a harshness from which we could infer unneutralized destructiveness, nor did some of our one-year-olds never show discharges which had features from which we could infer unneutralized destructiveness. Our observations made particular note of differences in (a) the behavior characteristics of the impulse discharge, (b) the child's reaction to his own discharge, and (c) the child's relation to the object in reaction to his own drive discharge.

Behavior Characteristics of the Impulse Discharge
Donnie's discharges, at the time of these observations, were especially startling because of their unexpectedness, suddenness, peremptoriness, and impulsiveness. By contrast, those of Jane (sixteen months) and Candy (fourteen months) did not show such a degree of impulsiveness; for them a delay—a forewarning followed by a more-or-less long lag period—was already typical, as were threat and warning gestures with and without a follow-through of the actual motor discharge. Characteristics equally as important as impulsiveness versus delay of discharge are its momentum, rate and weight. Donnie's discharge actions were strong, sharp, rapid , and rather unimpeded. Once he had unleashed the action, it seemed he could not arrest it in its trajectory. His entire arm, indeed his entire torso, was involved as a weapon. Once he put his hands around Jane's neck and shook her harshly. Again, although there are dynamic explanations for these actions, I want only to describe what we considered to reflect neutralized as compared to unneutralized destructive discharges.

Candy, Jane, Mary, Harold, Renée, Doris, and Vicki, whom we studied in much detail from birth for over five years, at no time showed such aggressive drive discharges. Cindy, Temmy, and Bernie did at various times, to varying, but lesser degrees. While Donnie's destructive discharges were strong, sharp, rapid, and often unimpeded, those of Candy, Jane, Harold, and Mary already tended to be comparatively soft, slow, rather short in trajectory, and held-back. The quality of their destructive discharges never shocked, alarmed, nor made project members or observers uneasy. I am of course not describing all features by which neutralization or its lack may be assessed; that would be a large work in itself.

The Child's Reaction to His/Her Own Discharge of Destructiveness
Donnie seemed as startled by his actions in these instances as were the project participants and the observers. At the risk of anthropomorphizing, Donnie presented the picture of a child whose ego is startled by what the id has done. This is to be distinguished from such reactions as shame and the fear of love loss which also played their part in two-and-a-half-year-old Donnie's dynamics. By contrast the startled-ego reactions were not featured in the discharges of Jane and Candy, who during the rapprochement subphase began to exhibit shame reactions and fear of love loss.

The Child's Relation to the Object
Donnie had no time to check with the object before his blow was unleashed. By contrast, checking with mother *before* striking her, striking a peer, or taking a toy from another was frequently observable in our subjects by twelve or so months of age. Such checking, of course, derives from the ability to delay discharge. After the discharge, Donnie's communications with his mother clearly gave the impression of helplessness and fear of maternal displeasure. In contrast, with Jane and Candy, postdischarge communication with the mother did not show such helplessness.

FORMULATION

Using clinico-investigative tools and assessments, we found that qualitative distinctions are observable among manifestations of aggression and that from these distinctions inferences can be made that neutralization of destructiveness is already active in the child by his turn into the second year of life. The question posed by Hartmann (1955) is raised: whether there is a *primary* tendency to neutralize destructiveness which is active even before the structuring of the ego as agency. It seems to me that if we do not base destructiveness on the death instinct (Freud 1920) and if we doubt the view that a primary antagonism exists between the drives and the ego, then there is no necessary innate, that is, primary, pressure to neutralize destructiveness. The pleasure principle demands that drives be gratified, not neutralized. The reality principle, on the other hand, which more-or-less compels the neutralization of destructiveness, is effected by the ego and, therefore, must await the structuring of the ego before it operates. In this light, like such other nonprimary ego functions as intentionality (Hartmann 1952, p. 43), the capability to neutralize destructiveness must await sufficient structuring of the ego as agency. Spitz, (1965, p. 289) who also feels that neutralization must await such ego development and the structuring of the libidinal object, dates the beginnings of neutralization of destructiveness to the last quarter of the first year of life.

The questions for us here are: What seem to be the conditions for the elaboration of neutralization? How does neutralization come about? And what relations does it bear to the libido and to the *fusion* of libido and aggression? It seems that while direct prohibitions and dictates from the libidinal object play some part in the taming of destructiveness, the major influence on neutralization evolution does not come from this source as many failures of law enforcement agencies and clinical practice well document. Two-and-a-half-year-old Donnie readily responded to direct prohibitions unless the discharge had already gone too far in its trajectory, and he then seemed neither able to stop nor deflect it from its target. At this point an auxiliary ego (mother or other adult) had to help him, to act for his too helpless ego. Such dictates, it seems, lead to inhibition, to blocking of aggression. This, however, does not change the quality of destructiveness, but acts mechanistically, so to speak, to hold back its outward discharge. While the inhibition of destructive discharge assists in its neutralization, it is not sufficient to effect neutralization.

Apparently, neutralization has its beginnings in the first conflict of ambivalence, during which the upsurge of hostile destructiveness is directed to the newly structured libidinal object. The essential condition of this intrapsychic conflict is the same as that which will later lead to the formation of the superego proper (Hammerman 1965): destructiveness is directed toward the beloved object. The libido by its attachment to the object invades the same territory as does the destructiveness (to use the now archaic but useful topographic image of the pre–1940 era). Where that libido is preponderent it mixes and fuses with aggression, more-or-less diluting it. But the libido also does more.

The immaturity and helplessness of the infantile self and ego, and the large underlying positive libidinal cathexis of the object, require of the ego activity which under appropriate conditions will lead not only to inhibition or displacement of drive discharge but also to an actual *deinstinctualization* of the powerful, threatening, hostile destructive impulses. Clinical experience overwhelmingly teaches us that hating a beloved object leads to ego activity of such significance that it can alter the ego itself, in the beginning formation of the superego (Freud 1913, 1923, 1930).

We may assume that, during the first conflict of ambivalence, the infantile ego, which has now psychically come to perceive its helplessness and object-anaclitic condition, when pressed by hostility to destroy the libidinal object, experiences anxiety due to the dread of libidinal object loss (Freud 1926, 1933). It is here suggested that due to both the libidinal cathexis of the object and the object-anaclitic condition of the infantile ego, that ego attempts to protect the object against the destructive impulses which emanate from within the self. Here then the nearly-one-year-old's ego bears upon the hostile destructive impulse to effect its modification, to weaken its impetus and its peremptoriness, but also to detoxify it, to take out its hostile quality. Doing so neutralizes the destructive impulse, making its energy available to the ego. By this modification, the *impetus* and *aim* of the impulse (Freud 1915) are changed, and, in this sense, the destructive impulse is deinstinctualized. The object-libidinal cathexis and the object-anaclitic relations of the ego have influenced the child's civilizing his libidinal-object-directed hostile destructive impulses. The hostile destructive impulse has had *object passage* (Mahler 1968).

The formulations on aggression advanced in this work require the statement that *deinstinctualization* means not just that unpleasure-derived hostile destructiveness loses its peremptoriness, and that this aggressive energy now becomes stored in the reservoir of ego energies

(Hartmann 1955, Kris 1955). It also means that the qualitative aim in the activated hostile destructive impulse is taken out of that impulse. I would add here too, that in time, with the sufficient institution of neutralization of hostile destructiveness, such neutralization can influence all future conditions of unpleasure which might lead to the mobilization of hostile destructiveness. Thus the early and sufficient acquisition in the ego of the neutralization function leads to its continued use in the self's relations to objects, animate and, by extension, inanimate.

FUSION AND NEUTRALIZATION

Some dissatisfaction has been expressed with the concept of neutralization; some colleagues hold the view that it is essentially only the fusion of aggression with libido that leads to the taming of destructiveness. But it seems plausible, as I will try to show, that the ego has an influence in transforming destructiveness into nondestructive aggression.

Fusion of aggression with libido seems essentially effected by the coexistence of hostile destructive feelings and love feelings toward the same object.[1] Metaphorically speaking, it is like the mixture of an acid and a base within the same container, each directly modifies the other. The pH of the resultant solution will be determined by the relative strength of each, taking on the character of the more concentrated and/ or voluminous component. Fusion, in this view, is a rather passive id phenomenon. It may be that the ego plays a part in effecting fusion of aggression and libido by acting like a catalyst.

Furthermore, one gains the impression that in the first year of life, it is a particular aspect of the libido which engenders and achieves fusion with aggression: the libido invested in the libidinal object. In the tendency to rid the self of unpleasurable feelings, which is governed by

---

1. Although the splitting of *gratification-frustration experiences* and their affective components occurs in compliance with the pleasure principle and the activity of the pleasure-ego, the splitting of *object- and self-representations* awaits at least the structuring of the libidinal object. Evidence suggests, however, that coexisting love and rage toward the same object are not split off until the necessity for such splitting emerges—that is, the protection of the love-object against destruction. In this view, the splitting of representations is a defense and not just a continuing activity of the pleasure-ego.

primary narcissism, the discharge of destructive impulses is presumed to be to the outside. This may occur even while inside and outside, self and object, are not yet diacritically (cognitively) perceived, the discharge of unpleasure-related impulses being effected by the tendency of an organism to rid itself of noxious stimuli. According to this view, libido directed to the self does not serve to neutralize destructiveness since the aggression can simply be turned to the outside. With the centrality that the part-object occupies in the symbiotic-phase infant's life, it is generally toward that part-object, before mechanisms of displacement come into play, that destructiveness will be turned. In line with these considerations, if the part-object is sufficiently invested with pleasurable, good feelings, we presume that positively valenced libido will fuse with whatever destructiveness may be invested in the evolving object-cathexis. Where unpleasure and bad feelings predominate, the positive influence of the libido will be weak, its investment in the part-object being insufficient to outweigh by admixture the aggression invested in the part-object cathexis.

Neutralization of hostile destructiveness, on the other hand, is an ego function developed out of a need to preserve both the libidinal object and the auxiliary ego against destruction by the self. In this, it originates later than fusion and cannot, in fact, emerge prior to the structuring of the libidinal object and of the ego as agency. It seems to emerge, as does splitting of object- and self-representations, with the advent of the first conflict of ambivalence, during the first part of the separation-individuation phase. Destructiveness invested in the object which holds a large positive libidinal cathexis, as Jane, Candy and others showed, creates a condition of ambivalence which the one-year-old child experiences more-or-less with a feeling of helplessness, that is, of anxiety. The ego does not play a passive part in this conflict of ambivalence, and we can infer from observable defensive activity and from qualitative assessments of drive discharge that it undertakes the task of neutralizing object-directed destructiveness.

On the other hand, as Vicki, Cindy, and Temmy showed, and as clinical experience documents overwhelmingly, a troubled or insufficiently positive libidinal cathexis of the object does not compel the ego to act as vigorously or as effectively in the process of neutralization. When the cathexis of the object is not sufficiently positive or is laden with hostile-destructive impulses, the ego will be compelled to yield to the demands from that overriding destructive drive source. Under these conditions, the infantile object-libidinal and object-anaclitic ego needs press only too weakly for neutralization of large and intense doses of destructiveness. But due especially to its object-anaclitical condition, the ego will fall to more global and drastic means of protecting even the incompetent need-satisfying object—means such as splitting, inhibition, and denial. As innumerable of our observations have shown, where the relation to the object is positive-enough (good-enough in Winnicott's sense), the conflicted, angry child turns to the libidinal object for comforting, even when that same object has been the source of unpleasure and the arousal of destructiveness. Where the relationship is too depriving (as it was for some time with Vicki), the child eventually no longer turns to that object. Under these conditions, the infantile ego has neither the pressure from a powerful positive libidinal cathexis nor the help of the auxiliary ego to assist in its efforts to cope with the destructive side of the first conflict of ambivalence.

Here then, due to the emergence of the first conflict of ambivalence, neutralization of destructiveness *begins.* Our observations suggest that it is the libido as well as the long period of childhood helplessness and dependence (Freud 1923, 1930) which compel the infantile ego to neutralize unpleasure-derived destructiveness, doing so especially at its fountainhead, its earliest object cathexes. The danger of losing the newly structured libidinal object leads not just to activity of the libido, but particularly to adaptive (defensive) activity on the part of the ego. The libidinal activity is *fusion,* the ego activity is *neutralization,* and in this sense the distinction of these two related psychic activities vis-a-vis aggression is useful.

One more note is warranted here on this question. In the earliest efforts by the ego to control aggression, one can distinguish, by their manifestations in behavior, those ego efforts which pertain to the neutralization of hostile destructiveness from those which pertain to aggression that is in essence nondestructive. The task for the ego is very different in each instance. The exploratory tearing of a piece of paper or the wide swinging of a pull-toy which may strike an object represent not only pleasure-in-function but also efforts to assert oneself over, control, and master these inanimate objects. Here the ego's task is to learn the limits and characteristics of the self and the environment and to learn to control and use efficiently developing motor apparatuses and benign aggressive trends. It is a very different, but equally important, task from that of effecting neutralization of unpleasure-derived anger, hostile destructiveness, and hate.

Chapter 15

AGGRESSION DURING
THE RAPPROCHEMENT
SUBPHASE

Marked developments in psychic function occur upon entry into, and during, the rapprochement subphase. The cognitive aspects of ego function have now evolved to the capacity for object permanence (Piaget 1937, 1954, Gouin-Decarie 1965, Bell 1969); with this capacity, the child's relation to reality enlarges significantly. Self and object differentiate apace (Mahler 1968, with Pine and Bergman 1975, Jacobson 1964) with the differentiation of inside and outside of self (Loewald 1952, Parens, 1971a).

Entering into the rapprochement subphase, the ego achieves a first degree of control over, and modulation of, the instinctual drives. Thus, we have come to believe that, due to a large endowment of aggression, Mary experienced a prolonged practicing subphase, extending from seven-and-a-half to twenty-one months, and did not enter her rapprochement subphase until that aggressive drive had come under sufficient ego control. While such ego control over the biologic upsurge of aggression is not obligatory before entry into the rapprochement subphase, such a condition greatly facilitates progression into the phases which follow.

Equally dramatic at the point of entry into, and during, the rapprochement subphase is the widening capability of the ego to register and express affects. The details of pleasure and depressive affect (see Mahler 1966) increase and become more varied in expression. For example, humor and shame reactions become observable now, manifesting a remarkable enrichment and development in the psyche.

Now due to the cumulative work of a number of investigators, we can measure developments in object relatedness which, in turn, lead to developments in the ego and the drives. We now have landmarks for the beginnings of object-relatedness: the nonspecific smiling response of the six-to-twelve-week-old is followed by the gradually evolving specific smiling response, coinciding with the stranger, separation, and reunion reactions of the five-to-eight-month-old, all of which can, in effect, be qualified and quantified. Now at the rapprochement subphase, as Mahler has formulated in detail and our findings amply document, object-relatedness receives a further major developmental thrust. It was exactly the temporary, self-imposed limiting of the child's activities within a narrow radius near the mother following upon many distant practicing excursions away from her which led Mahler to label this subphase rapprochement (to bring oneself close to, to come together, to reapproach).

Concurrent with these changes in the ego and object-relatedness, changes also occur in the id (Schur 1966). Some colleagues doubt that the basic elements in the id, the drives, are subject to ontogeny, to epigenetic change, that is to say that they *differentiate* in the embryologic sense (Erikson 1959). Yet, it seems that changes in the drives, and hence in libidinal and aggressive energy, are a basic assumption of psychoanalytic drive theory. The classical epigenetic changes in the libido pertain first to orality, then anality, and then genitality, which further includes a phallic phase, then an oedipal phase, and finally at puberty a second, genitality-proper phase, the earliest period of adult genitality. Equally important are those changes in the libido which pertain to the differentiation of, and from, narcissism to object libido and hence to heterosexual-object libido. Qualitative aspects of behavior seem to indicate that these changes do not occur solely as the result of evolving ego functions and contents. Rather, the drives themselves *inherently* evolve, which brings with them changes in drive energy itself. In this regard, two points must be made: (1) The aggressive drive seems less inherently changeable than does the libido; as I noted above, it does not seem to have the congenitally programed diversity which resides in the somatic substrate for the libido. (2) The developments in the ego are essential to the assimilation of these inherent drive changes during the progressive developments of the psychic organization. Thus for example, the integration in the psychic organization of the change from narcissistic to heterosexual-object libido no doubt depends upon specific-object related developments in the ego. But at the same time, there is rich evidence (Parens et al. 1976) which suggests that a primary heterosexual differentiation occurs in the libido at about two-and-a-half-years of age and that this reflects a change in the libido of the type presumed by Freud (1905, 1923) to be congenitally, biologically programed.

The phasic course of the drives, as it pertains to the vicissitudes of aggression, is relevant here. Developmental phases formulated by Freud and Abraham (regarding psychosexual development particularly), by Erikson (regarding ego identity), by Mahler (regarding the symbiosis and separation-individuation process), and by Spitz (regarding the structuring of the libidinal object) are based on developments propelled by differentiations of both the drives and the ego. Regarding symbiosis and separation-individuation, the normal autistic phase is governed by primary narcissism wherein the libido flows out from, and is directed toward, the self, while the very limited ego's autonomous functions pertaining to cognition (coenesthetic function here) allow for experiencing the environment as part of the limitless self-object. I find it useful to consider this as the period of the primordial self. The symbiotic phase seems dominated by the ego's growing awareness of the self's dependence on the object, a condition again secured by the libido which here insures object attachment and makes up for the helplessness of the human infant (Freud 1926, Mahler 1952, 1968, with Pine and Bergman 1975, Parens and Saul 1971).

Developments in the ego particularly effect the sequential phases of separation-individuation, but again, the drives play a most important part. I have difficulty discerning the primary drive elements that lead to the differentiation subphase. Nondestructive aggression and strivings for autonomy play a large part. Yet, as I have suggested elsewhere (Parens 1973a), it is difficult to sustain the hypothesis that the aggressive drive thrusts the infant to separate from the object. While the hypothesis that libido brings together and binds (Freud 1920) and aggression separates, push-pulls apart, (derived from a restricted application of Freud's 1920 death instinct-aggression theory) is attractive, it cannot be simply or directly supported by our observations. This, because observations also reveal that aggression is at least instrumental in bringing the object close under certain conditions of anxiety and does not effect separateness alone.

On the other hand, as I have described and formulated in this work, the practicing subphase seems largely to be determined by the biological upsurge in the aggressive drive, with a secondary, consonant heightened investment of libido in sensorimotor apparatuses and a seemingly lessened claim of object-directed libido. Observations suggest that coinciding with the ego's gradually attaining sufficient mastery over the practicing subphase upsurge in the aggressive drive, a new and primary upsurge and differentiation of the libido occurs which propels the fourteen-to-eighteen-month-old into the rapprochement subphase—a differentiation from the narcissism of the symbiosis toward a dichotomy of self *and* object libido. This assumption holds that a new ego awareness is created not only by those evolving ego functions enumerated above, but equally by an upsurge in newly evolving object libido.[1] This change in the drives hand-in-hand with given ego maturations leads to the emergence of the rapprochement subphase.

TRENDS IN THE AGGRESSIVE DRIVE

We are now prepared to turn to the various trends in the aggressive drive. During the rapprochement subphase, the vicissitudes of aggression are significantly determined by the primary maturational changes in the libido and the ego. No such primary maturational change seems to occur in aggression itself at this time.

While the powerful impetus of the practicing subphase upsurge in aggression seems somewhat slackened, within even a few feet of the mother, the toddler's conflict-free exploratory, manipulative, locomotor, and other nondestructive-aggression-fueled ego functions continue to be practiced extensively. So too, we see cyclic, rhythmic manifestations of nonaffective destructiveness. Both nondestructive and non-

---

1. Two points are relevant here: (1) Freud, even up until 1939, held the view that the instinctual drives "are the ultimate cause of all activity" (1940, p. 148); they are the primary and lifelong reservoir of psychic motivation. And (2) A strong conviction has been voiced in psychoanalysis as well as in ethology (if one allows a significant permutation) (Lorenz 1935, 1953, Hess 1958, Bowlby 1958, Parens and Saul, 1971) that the libido in the newborn is inherently directed to eventually attach to an object, ultimately for the purpose of reproduction and the preservation of the species (Freud 1915, 1920, Fairbairn 1954, Guntrip 1961, Balint, 1953, Parens and Saul 1971). Of course we do not ignore the secondary aspects of the libido's attachment to the object on a need-satisfying basis (A. Freud 1946, p. 124; 1954, p. 12; 1965).

affective destructive trends in aggression may become involved secondarily in conflict. Regarding nonaffective destructiveness, for example, weaning from the bottle may become more-or-less conflicted experience. In Candy and Jane, as well as in the other children, we found a dampening of exploratory, conflict-free ego activity at times when the child seemed preoccupied with mastery of the rapprochement task, such as dealing with conflicted feelings toward mother.

The hostile destructive, including pleasurably destructive, trends in aggression, on the other hand, have a direct involvement in the vicissitudes of the rapprochement subphase. In considering the arousal of unpleasure-derived hostile destructive discharges, we felt two factors to be particularly influential: (1) the major task of the rapprochement subphase of itself will mobilize hostile destructiveness, and (2) a greater or lesser degree of hostile destructiveness will be carried into this subphase from the preexisting residual conflict of ambivalence.

As already remarked, the task of the rapprochement subphase holds an obligatory intrapsychic crisis (Mahler 1965, 1968, 1972a, 1972b, with Pine and Bergman 1975). The ego must mediate and resolve the pull of ambitendent wishes: those to be separate from the object, to individuate, to experience the self and the object as related but separate organisms; and pulling against them, wishes to remain symbiotically fused with the libidinal object.[2] These wishes lead to a normal crisis in which they more-or-less acutely coexist or are experienced in rapid alteration whereby they exert an ambitendent pull within the psyche. I have described the manifestations in behavior of such a rapprochement crisis in Candy. It must be emphasized that, strictly speaking, this intrapsychic conflict created by the pull of ambitendent wishes is not a neurotic conflict and does not originate in feelings of ambivalence, that is, it does not arise out of coexisting love and hate feelings toward the libidinal object.

Where a marked conflict of ambivalence exists, arising out of the practicing subphase or out of the symbiosis, the valence of hostile destructiveness will be greater in the psyche and the ambitendent crisis of the rapprochement will be more disposed to the production of further hostility and ambivalence. However, while a strong preexisting

2. Presented by Margaret Mahler to the May 19, 1974 Meeting of the Study Group in Child Analysis, Philadelphia Psychoanalytic Institute, chaired by Drs. Selma Kramer, Robert C. Prall, and Henri Parens; Dr. David Ellis, reporter.

practicing subphase conflict may intensify during the rapprochement subphase, in some cases, as we found in Louis (a more recent subject), the practicing subphase conflict and ambivalence may be notably ameliorated by the work of the rapprochement task.

THE TWO BASIC CONFLICTS OF AMBIVALENCE

Everyone agrees that hostile destructiveness plays a key part in ambivalence. As I use the concept *ambivalence* here, I restrict it to mean that the self experiences coexisting and mingled love and hate feelings toward the same libidinal object. The experience by the ego of such coexisting antagonistic feelings toward the object leads to a conflict of ambivalence. In observing children, one can often infer the acute discomfort and struggle such an intrasystemic (id) conflict engenders in the ego. The ego can protect, of course, against too intense helplessness (anxiety) in the face of such opposing feelings (their underlying opposing instinctual impulses) by such defenses as denial, splitting object representations, and repression.

As we consider the vicissitudes of destructiveness during rapprochement, two factors recommend that we look at ambivalence developmentally which in turn leads me to propose that two basic conflicts of ambivalence evolve in early childhood. The factors are: (1) that much greater complexity exists in the second conflict of ambivalence than in the first, and (2) that an important distinction occurs in the attachment of ambivalent cathexes in girls as compared to boys.

The *first* conflict of ambivalence is the progressively emerging and stabilizing balance of love and hate feelings toward the libidinal object during the preoedipal period of development. It is ambivalence in *dyadic* object-relations. The *second* conflict of ambivalence which essentially pertains to the oedipus complex arises in and from specific *triadic* object-relations.

At this point I shall focus on the first conflict, sketching its course into and through the rapprochement subphase. In the next chapter, I shall elaborate on the second conflict, highlighting especially the differing object-relatedness of these conflicts in boys and girls, and shall point to the potential influence of this second conflict in the psyche on subsequent object relations.

THE FIRST CONFLICT OF AMBIVALENCE

The first conflict of ambivalence has roots in the symbiosis, emerges during the differentiation-practicing subphases, and undergoes change during the rapprochement subphase when it may intensify or ameliorate.

Symbiosis

Primitive feelings of love as well as rage may coexist and vie, so to speak, for dominance in the infantile psyche and object relations. Taking the views of Mahler (1965, 1968) as a working model I have suggested (Parens 1971a) that during this phase the dyad of self and object is in process of differentiating from the fused self-object (I—not-I) of the symbiosis to the structuring of separate libidinal object and self (Mahler, Pine and Bergman 1975). While representation of good and bad self-object experiences may evolve separately (we are following here Freud's view that in the infantile psyche what is good is retained to the self and what is bad is ejected), observation suggests that once the libidinal object is structured, a degree of unification of good and bad object representation exists (see discussion above on the emergence of splitting object representations as a defense). More specifically, as an outgrowth of maturation, sufficient recognitive memory exists when the libidinal object becomes structured (at about five to six months on the average) so that this object seems to be recognized as the source of both gratification and frustration. On this basis, it becomes a complex matter to decide whether coexisting love and hate feelings toward the evolving libidinal object may or may not induce in the seven-month-old ego the experience of ambivalence. Observation strongly suggests that if ambivalence does not exist before, it does exist with entry into the practicing subphase, and that by way of anxiety, it induces the ego to develop defenses to cope with it. It remains that even if we cannot ascertain that ambivalence per se exists during the symbiosis, coexisting feelings of primitive love and rage (which with the structuring of the libidinal object evolves into hate) do exist and become embedded in the psyche by virtue of their connection with the drives and affects; they thus become roots that in soon to follow development will yield ambivalence.

Differentiation and Practicing Subphases
During these overlapping subphases we have found a notable precipita-
tion (in the chemical sense) of the first conflict of ambivalence. I have
extensively described how the biological upsurge of aggression propels
powerful strivings for autonomy (expressing both differentiation and
practicing activity) which invariably lead to an *interpersonal* conflict
between child and mother when the mother must restrict or obstruct
gratification of these omnipotent autonomous strivings. The interpersonal conflict and resultant hostile destructiveness lead to the development of a more-or-less strong *intrapsychic* conflict within the child.
Taking root in whatever ambivalence potential may reside in the psyche
from the symbiosis, a greater or lesser first conflict of ambivalence
emerges during the practicing subphase.

Rapprochement Subphase
At this time two factors especially play a part in the mobilization of
hostile destructive impulses in the child: (1) continuation, albeit with
modification, of the practicing subphase conflict and (2) the rapprochement crisis itself. Both factors further elaborate, either enlarging or
lessening, the first conflict of ambivalence.

    During the practicing subphase, the toddler remains oblivious to the
mother's wishes until such time as she unyieldingly imposes them,
thwarting and restricting the child's exuberant sensorimotor activities.
Because the limit-setting object is also the libidinal object, the child
develops an intrapsychic conflict and erects defenses to dispose of the
rage side of the ambivalence he now experiences toward that love-
object. During the rapprochement subphase new developments modify
that conflict importantly. Strivings for autonomy, which do not abate
significantly, nevertheless are now robbed of the elation they induced
during the practicing subphase by two phenomena: (1) lessening of the
omnipotence and excitement associated with the upsurge of aggression
and the developmental spurt of the sensorimotor organization of the
ego, and (2) the newly aroused libidinal need for the object's love
induced by the maturation and development of the ego and libido. In
well-developing children like Candy and Jane, the dampening of
omnipotence and the new and acute awareness of the need for the
object's love now decrease the intensity and frequency of the struggles
for autonomy. In children of the same general quality of maturation as

these, we found that such struggles are now avoided by a more developed relation to reality, by better adaptive reactions to the demands of the environment, and by finding ways of gratifying these strivings within permitted ranges of movement (locomotion) and activity.

This quality of adaptation was not achieved by Louis (a child not included in our first series of research subjects) nor with Cindy, Mary, or Bernie. In these children, the practicing subphase conflict of ambivalence seemed to continue unabated into the rapprochement subphase, which it complicated. In these children, this latter subphase was more laden with ambivalence than it was in Candy, Jane, Doris, and Harold.

During the practicing subphase, the need for the object and the object's love and approval already plays a part sufficient both to create the first conflict of ambivalence and to stimulate the ego to erect defenses to protect the love-object against the child's own hostile destructiveness toward it. However, under good-enough conditions of practicing sub-phase development, the ego's interests seem inclined in the largest part, not to the object, but to the child's mastery of himself and his rapidly expanding environment. Then, during rapprochement, the ego's priorities (interests) shift again, now focusing sharply on the relation of the self to the symbiotic partner, as the child, propelled by maturation and development (Hartmann), attempts to resolve that symbiosis. This process, leading to a more acute awareness of the need for the object's love and approval, takes priority over those strivings for autonomy which emerge and feature so sharply during the differentiation-practicing period. Hence, the conflict of ambivalence induced by the obstruction of such autonomy strivings during the rapprochement subphase may be more-or-less attenuated by the child's need for object-love.

Where the mother-child relation was least laden with prerapprochement ambivalence in our project children, strivings-for-autonomy struggles seemed to lessen notably during rapprochement. By contrast, where the prerapprochement relation to the object was especially negatively laden with ambivalence (from the symbiosis as in Vicki, or from practicing as in Louis and Bernie), such strivings-for-autonomy struggles continued into the rapprochement subphase and, becoming part of it, made more difficult the task of that subphase.

Ambivalence from the Rapprochement Crisis

Whatever its antecedents, however, the rapprochement task—resolving ambitendent wishes to regress and remain fused with the symbiotic partner versus separating and individuating from her—creates its own component of ambivalence in the child. As Candy showed, the ambitendent wishes in the child lead to a state of ego helplessness, that is, to anxiety, which indeed creates an intrapsychic crisis as McDevitt, Bergman, and Mahler have reported. Where sufficient anxiety mounts, by virtue of its unpleasure, further hostile destructive impulses become mobilized and directed toward the self and the love-object. Observation amply documents the fact that the object (auxiliary ego), by her reactions, plays a significant part in allaying or intensifying anxiety in the child, thereby reducing or increasing the mobilization of hostile destructiveness and the potential development of ambivalence. But equally important in this regard is the fact that in some children (Candy, for example), the pattern of the rapprochement crisis, the quality, intensity and frequency of intrapsychic tension created by the ambitendent wishes, may be the principal factor which determines the degree to which the rapprochement crisis mobilizes hostile destructiveness. A more gradual working-through of the rapprochement task is less likely to produce intense periods of anxiety, pain, and ambivalence than is an acutely telescoped, condensed crisis, as we saw in Candy.

EGO REACTIONS TO HEIGHTENING AMBIVALENCE

The magnificent maturational change of a large segment of narcissistic libido into object libido[3] dramatically influences the destructive trends of the aggressive drive. Without this differentiation in libido, civilizing the child would not proceed, at least, not as we know it. This

---

3. Kohut (1971), whose contributions recently have had a striking impact in psychoanalytic theory and practice, rightly emphasized and enlarged upon Freud's view (1914) of the unending contribution of (healthy) narcissistic libido in the economy of self-esteem, and hence in the energic economy of the self. Much primary narcissism remains indelibly attached to the self-representation, since it is after all the source as well as the earliest and most adherent of all cathexes; however, much libido as well has become over time attached to that part of the self which evolves into the object. It becomes changed into object libido much later, it would seem, than Balint (1953), Fairbairn (1954), and Guntrip (1961) have suggested. In the view advanced in this study, this change to object-libido is biologically predetermined to emerge generally during the second year of life.

modification into object-libido makes great demands on the ego to neutralize, control, and selectively dispose of object-directed hostile destructiveness. Now by virtue of its greater functional capability, the ego, in addition to neutralization of aggression, effects further changes in the psyche of remarkable character, as in the broadening of shame reactions and the beginnings of humor. Consequent, too, upon these developmental changes in the libido and ego, a further stage in superego formation is now inferrable from observation, particularly with respect to the nodal part played by the danger-situation current for this subphase, the fear of loss of love from the object, and its shame-related phenomenology. It also seems warranted, in the sense of Freud's 1913 formulation of the dynamics of remorse (guilt), to expect the current change in libidinal cathexis of the object to play a part in the beginning development of guilt, thereby furthering as well superego-precursor formation. Regrettably, I cannot now look more closely at this latter phenomenology.

Also related to these current vicissitudes of both libido and aggression, we find changes in the ego of most salutary consequence: emerging *empathy* and *altruism*. Not all of the ego's efforts, however, are salutary. For example, displacement of destructiveness from the ambivalently-beloved object onto weakly valued objects, such as peers, may become the basis for the later emergence of prejudice and scapegoating. Similarly, some instances of reaction-formation take a turn that leads to serious problems for the self and society, as in the pleasureful expression of hostile destructiveness (*sadism* in the broad sense) in place of the original rage and hate.

While one observes evidence of the pleasure-related discharge of hostile destructiveness from about the end of the first year of life, the developments in the ego and the libido of the rapprochement period provide a more complex capability to delay the discharge of destructiveness mobilized at times of heightened unpleasure. This new capability in the ego results in more controlled, deliberate, and elaborate discharges of stored unpleasure-derived hostile destructive impulses. This occurs often, but not necessarily, under conditions of pleasurable affect. Here we are, I believe, speaking of *sadism* in the broad sense. Especially during the rapprochement subphase, when humor begins to emerge in some children (Jane, Cindy, Candy, Harold), the pleasurable discharge of hostile destructiveness emerges too—for example, Jane's teasing, by biting rather hard with a smiling affect, or Cindy's and Jane's seemingly prethought hitting of Candy. These discharges, we found, became more elaborate with peers particularly in relation to sibling rivalry and object-related jealousies. Later, when the rivalries of the oedipal phase emerged, pleasure-related destructiveness became further elaborated. Fortunately, this tendency in the normal child is offset by the further capability of the developing ego to neutralize destructiveness.

In consequence of the developments noted in this chapter—the increased demands of the ego for neutralization of destructiveness, the further development of superego precursors leading to shame and the beginnings of guilt, the emergence of humor, empathy and altruism, as well as the further elaboration of sadism and possibly of those mechanisms that effect prejudice—the changes in the ego and the libido which lead to the dynamics of the rapprochement subphase would seem to be the prime effectors of the vicissitudes of the aggressive drive during this subphase.

Chapter 16

A NOTE ON AGGRESSION DURING THE SUBPHASE TOWARD-OBJECT-CONSTANCY AND UPON ENTRY INTO THE OEDIPUS COMPLEX

In the course of these investigations, I have been especially interested in examining, *in situ,* the manifestations of the aggressive drive prior to the rather stable development of the ego, competence in verbal language, and the emergence in the child of the oedipus complex. As we proceeded, I have found ample support for the view that understanding of aggression from about thirty to thirty-six months on can best be attained by the psychoanalysis of children and adults. Defensive operations of the child's ego now begin to cloud direct observation to a marked degree. This does not mean that benefit may not derive from direct observation beyond the first two years of life, quite the contrary, as our project on early gender formation shows.[1] The meaningful interpenetration of reconstruction and direct observational materials, of which Kris and Hartmann have spoken, can apply not only to preverbal but to postverbal phases too. There is no doubt, however, that from here on, one can see much less *directly* than one could in earlier stages of development.

In terms of the areas of aggression under scrutiny in this work, I have found that the formulations advanced here, which derive from direct infant observation, apply readily to material derived from clinical psychoanalysis. Indeed, from the start of this study to the present,

1. One major aspect of our project on early gender formation addresses itself to direct observational data pertaining to the girl's entry into the oedipus complex (see Parens, Pollock, Stern, and Kramer 1976).

direct observational findings have been superimposed on past and on current, ongoing *clinical* observation, and I have found no difficulty in subsuming the findings from both into the formulations proposed here. With caution, but also with conviction, I find that what we have learned of aggression during the oedipus complex from its manifestations in the psychoanalyses of children and adults can in every way be explained by the formulations of aggression advanced in this work.

TOWARD-OBJECT-CONSTANCY

Before closing this work, I want to touch on those childhood phases of development which follow the rapprochement subphase. From our observations, the rapprochement subphase tensions slacken into the phase which Mahler (1972a, with Pine and Bergman 1975) tells us leads to a significant, albeit incomplete, attainment of object-, self-, and reality-constancy (Frosch, 1966). This last part of the separation-individuation phase, the subphase toward-object-constancy, which emerges at about two years of age, tends to be identifiable in direct observation by a more-or-less progressive decrease in the physical closeness of the child to the mother—the hallmark of the rapprochement subphase. One can deduce from this comfortable-enough slackening of physical (and intrapsychic representational) closeness that the child's rapprochement crisis is resolving to a sufficient degree and that during the subphase toward-object-constancy, the ambitendent rapprochement task continues to be further mastered in graduated doses. In a manner of speaking, this subphase seems to be a period for the working through of the crisis and for consolidating the achievements created by the important task of rapprochement. In regard to the separation-individuation process, toward-object-constancy seems to be a subphase in which no new demands are made on the psyche by a differentiation in the drives.

EMERGENCE OF THE OEDIPUS COMPLEX

The quiet of the consolidating subphase toward-object-constancy was soon disrupted in the children of our project by manifestations of one or more basic behavioral elements of the oedipus complex: the classical castration complex,[2] observably heterosexual and rival attitudes toward objects according to their gender, as well as other gender-specific patterns of drive discharge and ego functioning as the girl's wish to have a baby (Parens et al. 1976). In those of our children whose behavior showed clear evidence of oedipal activity, it emerged from about two-and-a-quarter to two-and-a-half-years of age on, early during the subphase toward-object-constancy.

The quality of these behavioral events leads me to infer that again this emergence of newly-directed psychic activity is instigated by a change in the drives and the ego. As regards the drives, the inherent change is in the libido, and changes in aggression seem to follow from it. Elsewhere (Parens 1973b, Parens et al. 1976), we reported that data from our project on aspects of early gender formation support Freud's assumption (1905b) that heterosexuality has a primary biological root which is expressed in the libido. Our data also recommends the hypothesis that primary heterosexuality makes itself evident for the first time at about two-and-a-half years of age. I have for some time now adopted the position that a primary (congenitally predetermined, as Freud held) change in the libido and the ego (due to which heterosexuality emerges at this age) creates, in an average expectable environment (Hartmann), the conditions for the emergence of the oedipus complex in both boys and girls equivalently (Parens et al. 1976). Suffice it to say, the assumption here is that an inherent, biologically determined differentiation in the libido and the ego leads from psychic gender-nondifferentiation to the emergence of heterosexuality (manifest in behavior) from about two-and-a-half years of age on. Entry into the oedipus complex may be assumed to be activated by this primary differentiation in the psychic

2. In our observational studies so far we have not encountered the finding described by A. Freud (1951, pp. 27-28), Mahler (personal communication, 1972b, with Pine and Bergman 1975) and Roiphe and Galenson that some children between the age of eighteen to twenty-four months show evidence of a castration complex. This is considered by them a preoedipal form of the castration complex. To date, we have found a *curiosity* and *interest* in genitals in children of that age; but in no instance so far have we seen evidence of *undue concern*, the expression of *unpleasure affects,* or anxiety in association with the discovery, for example, by the girls of the boys' penises. This is in marked contrast to clear evidence of a castration complex that we have found in them from age two-and-a-quarter to two-and-a-half-years on. Perhaps this difference results from methodological variations in investigation. Assessment of the above authors' reports, however, suggest that variations in individual children's dynamics, including especially significant developmental stresses due to deprivation or overstimulation and consequent precocity (Greenacre 1950), may account for this difference in data.

apparatus, and, as we know well from psychoanalyses and from direct observations, it influences strongly the vicissitudes of aggression.

PHALLIC AGGRESSION

While I suggest that during entry into the oedipus complex the vicissitudes of aggression are determined by a primary change in the ego and the libido, one aspect of these vicissitudes may derive from a primary differentiation and upsurge in the aggressive drive itself—that which is clinically identified, and easily observable, as *phallic aggressiveness*. In our subjects we found that the girls do not exhibit as distinctly phallic-aggressive behavior as do the boys. But our sample is very small and this consideration requires specific and extended study. Until that is done, I report that from these and other clinical observations, at this developmental period, we find more boys begin to discharge aggression in larger muscle mass, more heavily, more vigorously than girls. We find boys to be more rammy, more compelled to push and pull things with their whole body, to crash toys together, or indeed to crash their body into something or someone, more frequently than the girls. Differences in body posturing, stance, and locomotor characteristics begin to be discerned. For the first time, we see behavior which can be identified as boyish and girlish. While some individual children may show such gender-specific features earlier, our impression is that, as a general phenomenon, distinctively boyish or girlish behaviors begin at this developmental period.

Our girls' behavior with regard to babies became notably distinctive at this developmental period when compared to that of the boys. The differences were sufficiently striking to raise into question whether the term *phallic phase* is appropriately descriptive for the girl's first genital phase. Elsewhere (Parens et al. 1976) this thesis is developed in detail. Let it be said here that our studies make it difficult to hold to the notion of an obligatory phallic phase in girls. This term does not take into account the uniquely female features of the little girl's so-called phallic phase. It is, therefore, suggested that the term *phallic phase* be changed to the *first genital phase* of psychosexual development to account for the unique male and female behaviors which become amply observable during the third year of life.

My impression to date is that these gender-specific characteristics are observable in the discharge of both libido and aggression. Are three-year-old boys more aggressive than girls? While this is a subject of inquiry in and of itself (I plan to report our findings on this issue in a separate work), for our present purposes, it is sufficient to say they are not. Rather, the distinguishing characteristics seem to lie especially in the qualitative differences of their aggression-discharge patterns. To this difference, what we call phallic aggression makes an important contribution. The little boy's frequent collisions into objects and things, his king-of-the-mountain or King-Kong stance on an uprighted toy-cart are evidence of this. Perhaps more to the point, the boy's playful wielding of a hard toy while chasing a squealing three-year-old girl who smilingly, anxiously runs to her mother saying "Save me, save me," are features that give the boy's aggression a libido-related characteristic which is distinctive from that of our girl subjects. In our girls, all of whom were as aggressive, as self-assertive, as demanding as the boys, we did not find a dominant phallic quality to their aggression-discharge patterns.

At this time there is also, as is amply documented in psychoanalysis, a marked upsurge of anger and hostility on the part of the little boy toward his father and the little girl toward her mother. In terms of gender-specific characteristics, Jane's then-current aggressiveness toward her mother had a unique feature: it was a particular brand of nastiness, usually called *bitchiness,* in a girl who heretofore had and continued to have a warm and most positive relationship with her mother. We find this quality of hostility typical in many little girls of this age. Such an upsurge of hostile destructiveness, however, is of a very different order than phallic aggression. Evidence shows that this upsurge of the girl's hostility toward her mother, as well as that of the little boy toward his father, is a *reactive* derivative from the oedipus complex. It is not endogenous. This reactive aggression, in both girls and boys, is an experience-determined upsurge in aggression which invariably expresses itself even in well-cared-for children for the first time in association with this complex.

In contrast, the upsurge of phallic aggression is not reactive. Rather, it seems to be a biologically predetermined differentiation within aggression that serves the libido—a differentiation which is not inherently destructive. An alternative explanation is that this aggression may simply be given its phallic quality by the then-current influence of the libido upon it. Behaviorally, this differentiation goes far to provide the male image of king-of-the-mountain aggression, narcissistic bicep comparison among four-year-old boys, bullishness, gorilla-like posturing, and gestures of penetration-proneness.

When we speak of phallic aggression, we do not mean assertiveness. While many a three-year-old like Harold and Bernie uses phallic-aggressive attitudes to achieve such ends as being self-assertive, these elements of aggression are distinguishable. When we speak of phallic aggression, we refer to a form, pattern, or mode (Erikson 1959) of aggression discharge, just as *oral* and *anal* are forms of aggression discharge. One can be self-assertive using any of these forms or modes of aggression discharge. Self-assertiveness, on the other hand, is an inherent tendency in aggression; it is part of its *aim,* in the sense of instinctual drive theory (Freud 1915). Self-assertiveness is found equally in girls and boys; it is essentially neither masculine nor feminine. But it may be expressed quite differently according to both gender and individual variation.

We were struck, for instance, by Mary, who during her practicing subphase, learned to locomote on all fours in a manner that made her look like a football tackle. But when she entered her first genital phase (Parens et al. 1976) that heaviness and tank-like approach to things changed dramatically. She became much lighter in locomotive appearance and no longer at all like a football player. However, she became no less insistant or self-assertive. Now close to six years of age, one finds no trace of that pregenital locomotor heaviness and bulk-muscularity. A similar phenomenon was found in Candy.

The change in pattern of aggression discharge occuring especially in boys at this developmental period, which we clinically identify as phallic aggression, seems to be either a primary differentiation in aggression itself or one secondarily determined by the first genital phase change in the libido and ego. Whether it is a primary or secondary differentiation in aggression, it seems to be determined by those congenital dispositions predetermined, as Freud believed, to differentiate at this time, which in an *average expectable environment* (Hartmann) lead the child into the first genital phase. It is not clear whether an actual upsurge or increment in aggression occurs in association with this change in discharge pattern.

In our small subject sample we did not find the girls to show a convincing patterning of aggression discharge into phallic aggression. We gained the impression that this is one of the spheres where our subjects showed a gender-related distinction.

THE SECOND CONFLICT OF AMBIVALENCE

The markedly hostile destructiveness toward the rival love-object characteristic of this developmental period reflects both an upsurge of aggression and a further gender-related distinction between boys and girls. After several months of increasingly more troublesome interaction in two-and-a-half-year-old Jane's relationship with her mother, a relationship heretofore significantly positive and affectionate, this experienced mother complained that her daughter was becoming very difficult to handle. One morning Jane's mother asked with a half-smile: "Anyone want her for a year?" We had already recorded from the upsurge of hostile, rivalrous behavior toward her mother that Jane had entered her oedipus complex.

Observation of mother-child dyads made us strongly aware of the fact that normal-enough girls like Jane and Candy, after experiencing first their practicing subphase conflict and then the rapprochement crisis with their mothers, experience a further intense conflict of ambivalence, due to their oedipus complex experience, again with their mothers. The normal-enough boy, on the other hand, who also experiences his practicing subphase conflict and rapprochement crisis with his mother, experiences his basic oedipal conflict of ambivalence with his father, not his mother. The upsurge of hostile destructiveness—and with it a further conflict of ambivalence—which emerges in the course of the oedipus complex makes for an important distinction in the psychic life of boys and girls. The thesis of a first, dyadic conflict of ambivalence which develops during the preoedipal period of life and a second triadic conflict of ambivalence which emerges during the first part of the oedipus complex highlights the important fact that girls have both first and second conflicts of ambivalence with their mothers, while boys have the first with their mothers and the second with their fathers. While the resultant ambivalence varies widely, depending especially on the quality of intrapsychic development and pressures as well as on the quality of object relations, the girl's ambivalence toward other females tends to be more intense than is her ambivalence toward males. In the boy, ambivalence toward male and female tends to be less biased by the distribution of ambivalence conflicts. Emphasis, however, must be placed on the fact that ambivalence is not predetermined, but rather is the result of experience, being determined by the vicissitudes of instinctual drives and ego functioning in the child in reciprocity with the quality of his object relations. In other words, the schema of conflicts of ambivalence proposed here, and the resultant distribution of ambivalence in object relations suggested by it, is a simplification. Nonetheless, it is often encountered even within a maze of dynamic complexity.

In attempting to delineate these two conflicts of ambivalence, I have noted that the first occurs in the context of dyadic object relations, while the second occurs later in that of triadic object relations. The second conflict, as a result, is quite more complex than the first. Upon entry into the oedipus complex, the little girl loves her father while she also loves and hates her mother who is now more-or-less acutely experienced as the rival for her father. The complement is experienced by the three-year-old boy. During the first part of the oedipus complex the second conflict of ambivalence in both the boy and girl is experienced toward the rival but beloved parent of the same sex, while, in parallel, the heterosexual oedipal relation is highly invested with a powerful positive emotional (cathectic) valence. Further developments in the ego add significantly to the greater complexity of the oedipal conflict of ambivalence. They do so especially through the production of intense feelings of guilt vis-a-vis the hated love object and through the structuring of the superego.

While the findings from our project and from clinical analyses show these triadic dynamics of ambivalence, they also show a further complication which sets in during the latter part of the oedipal phase. Both the oedipal girl and boy come to realize that the heterosexual oedipal love-object does not gratify oedipal wishes but, by his or her own action, frustrates them intensely. In the course of clinical psychoanalyses, one often encounters feelings of rage toward that frustrating love-object which date from the latter part of and beyond the oedipal phase. From this time too, then, of course, one encounters a greater or lesser degree of ambivalence toward the heterosexual love object.

Therefore, we find a second factor which contributes an opposing pull within the second conflict of ambivalence. Clinical findings suggest that this second factor, however, is generally less constant and not as intense as the first one—that which arises out of the rivalry with the parent of the same sex. We find that when the little boy experiences painfully the frustration imposed by his mother's benevolent refusal to gratify his oedipal-sexual wishes, he often blames his father. Often, too, the little girl now blames her mother for the frustrations she sustains at the hands of her father. While ambivalent feelings are experienced toward both love-objects during the course of the oedipus complex, those which emerge toward the rival for the heterosexual love-object remain by far the most powerful and conflict-inducing.

From Freud's formulations of 1913 *(Totem and Taboo)* and 1923 *(The Ego and the Id)* and from our own subsequent psychoanalyses of adults and children, we know that the destructiveness mobilized by the child's oedipal wishes is the large determiner of the development of the superego. To paraphrase Freud (1913), the threat of consummation of the destructiveness toward the oedipal rival makes the love feelings toward that rival felt even more intensely, precipitating then an often intense feeling of remorse. At this time, the superego becomes structured as agency. All this requires no elaboration here. The role of aggression is central in the structuring and the character of the superego, as well as that of the ego's defenses.

Chapter 17

IMPLICATIONS FOR PRIMARY PREVENTION

Recently, Aring (1973) made an eloquent plea that we aim in our work less at further research in aggression and rather expend more energy on developing interventional and preventive measures against the development of untoward hostility and destructiveness. In concurrence with Aring's plea, we want to put forward the following recommendations for such preventive and interventional efforts.

EXCESSIVE UNPLEASURE MOBILIZES HOSTILE DESTRUCTIVENESS

Our findings support the widely accepted view that human patterns of hostile destructive behavior are determined by our earliest life experiences (see Saul 1976). This applies to both the mobilization within the psyche of hostility toward objects and its discharge upon them. Observation persuades me that the human infant is not born with a certain quantity of hostility or hostile destructiveness which he must discharge. Rather such hostile destructiveness is mobilized within him by the experience of excessive unpleasure which seems felt by the infant as too painful. As the protoplasm responds with irritability to noxious stimuli, so too there are mechanisms within the neonate psyche which respond with irritability to stimuli noxious to it. At a psychophysiological level this latter irritability, when sufficiently intense, becomes the rage reaction one readily finds in the normal neonate.

On this basis one might be tempted to appeal for the elimination of unpleasure experiences in our infants and children. But there are, of course, obstacles and dangers in that appeal. First of all, unpleasure is an integral part of human psychic functioning. For example, it functions in even the most basic physiological reactions that ensure survival, such as in the unpleasure involved in even the first pangs of hunger, of gastrointestinal and bladder distention leading to elimination, and of responses to harsh noises, lights and brusque body movements. Secondly, the elimination of unpleasure, were it at all possible, would rob the infantile psyche of the development within it of remarkable adaptive ego capabilities as well as of the magnificent development of the superego. Without unpleasure experiences our constructive and creative humanness would be in jeopardy.

A mildly noxious stimulus causes a benign degree of irritability in the cell which leads to a defensive, adaptive change within it. Such experiences, repeated in doses so graduated that the cell is not overwhelmed by them, leads to the development within it of stable adaptive mechanisms which insure not only protection for the present and future but, indeed, propel growth. Toxic stimuli, on the other hand, create conditions which overwhelm the protoplasm, so to speak; they lead to a state of too great tension and excessive irritability; they activate ejection mechanisms, and where these fail, they lead to damage if not death of parts or the entire cell. So too, at a higher organizational level, in the psyche, benign experiences of unpleasure lead to adaptation and growth. As I have emphasized throughout this work, it is when unpleasure is felt as *excessive,* is experienced as *too painful,* that it may wreak havoc in the psyche. Excessive unpleasure causes an affective experience which modifies aggression into hostile destructiveness in order to destroy and eliminate the source of unpleasure. It is not yet clear how excessive unpleasure which causes a negatively-valenced affective psychic state transforms aggression into hostility. For the present, we can only recognize that the affective state is instrumental in modifying the aggressive impulse. This also means, of course, that excessive unpleasure, which is experienced as noxious to the psyche, is the precondition to the mobilization of hostile destructiveness in the self. By *mobilization,* I do not mean that the psyche contains innately-present hostile impulses which can be marshaled to serve the psyche when needed, but rather that, as in the military, there is a governing force (some aspect of the pleasure principle) capable of transforming supposedly nondestructive civilians (aggression) into soldiers ready for battle (hostile destructiveness).

CHILDREN MUST BE PROTECTED AGAINST TOO
FREQUENT EXCESSIVE UNPLEASURE

It is essential that in the first years of life, the infant be protected against too frequent experiences of excessive unpleasure. Because of the long period of childhood psychic immaturity, hence helplessness and dependence, the child's parenting objects (mothering object in particular) serve as his *auxiliary ego*. In other words, in the young child the agency which reacts adaptively to unpleasure is the ego—auxiliary-ego. Variation in the child's *basic core* (Weil, 1970), in his own psychic adaptive capabilities, makes for a complementary variation in necessary adaptive reactivity on the part of the auxiliary ego. Some infants need more help from the auxiliary ego than others, some need help more quickly (as Cindy did in contrast to Candy). The better that auxiliary ego is attuned to, and functions complementarily to the infantile ego, the less will excessive unpleasure be experienced in the infant's psyche.

The child is subjected to multiple internal and external sources of excessive unpleasure, some of which are more easily eliminated than others. For example, hunger is more easily dealt with by the mother than is painful teething or constipation. Dynamic factors in the mother, of course, will make her less able to deal with one source of unpleasure in the child than another. One mother, for instance, will unconsciously induce excessive unpleasure in nursing while another may do so in toilet training.

Our project findings, as well as those from clinical practice, support the view expressed by Hartmann (1950b) that optimal development occurs where there is an age-adequate optimal balance of gratification and frustration of needs. Each child will, however, by the reactivity of his psychic apparatus, require a different equation of gratification and frustration to secure his optimal development. Children vary widely in how they tolerate unpleasure. But in all instances in the earliest years, a sufficiently identifiable fundamental phenomenon occurs which it behooves every parent to learn: the means by which that parent's particular child expresses the experience of feeling too much pain. The parent must feel what is too painful for the child, must see and hear his or her vocal and affective expression of excessive unpleasure.

Many mothers and fathers, feeling when their child is in pain, can intervene quickly enough most of the time. Unfortunately, for a variety of reasons, too many parents cannot and do not empathize with their child's experiences of excessive unpleasure. Emotional disturbance in the parents plays a large part in this. Foremost, however, is the fact that too many parents are remarkably ignorant of children's basic needs for healthy psychic development and of child rearing methods and skills that optimize psychic growth. For this reason, during the past several years we have emphasized the need for, and are developing programs toward, parent education (Parens, Pollock, and Prall 1974, Parens 1976). We have found that many parents are receptive to instruction by mental health professionals regarding the needs of their children, the meaning of their children's behavior, and modes of facilitating their emotional growth.

By optimizing early development, a path must be found in child rearing between too frequent or protracted excessive unpleasure experiences on the one hand and too protected experiences which rob the infantile psyche of growth-promoting levels of unpleasure on the other.

INTRAPSYCHIC MODIFICATION OF HOSTILE DESTRUCTIVENESS

I have tried to indicate that the nurturing environment can create conditions in the child's life whereby the mobilization of hostile destructiveness can be markedly reduced, even, minimized. But even in optimal nurturing circumstances it is not possible to totally prevent the mobilization of hostile destructiveness in the human child. Fortunately, in the context of his epigenetic development, there is *within the child* a far-reaching potential capability to lessen the amount and to mitigate the intensity of hostile destructiveness mobilized within him. This evolving capability in his own psyche to modify or detoxify hostile destructiveness is carried out by two intertwining intrapsychic processes: (1) The *fusion* of libido with aggression to which Freud referred many times from 1923 *(The Ego and the Id)* on, and (2) the *neutralization of destructiveness* as described by Hartmann and his colleagues (Hartmann, Kris and Loewenstein 1949, Hartmann 1950b, 1952, 1955).

Fusion of aggression and libido probably begins even prior to the structuring of the libidinal object and of the ego as agency. We may assume, however, that once the structuring of libidinal object and ego as agency is sufficiently under way, from about six or so months of age on, fusion becomes a catalyzed and more stable activity. These two intrapsychic structurings also begin to effect the even more far-reaching capability to neutralize destructiveness. Unlike the tendency for fusion, *neutralization* is not built-in in the psyche; it must be developed. The factor which propels its development is the wish to protect the love-object from the child's own hostile destructive impulses mobilized against that object.

In our children we found that the earliest evidence of this wish to protect the beloved mother against the child's own hostile destructive-ness occurred in reaction to mother's repeatedly thwarting the gratifica-tion of the child's powerful strivings for autonomy characteristic of the differentiation and practicing subphases of separation-individuation. Here a crucial phenomenon occurs. The nearly-one-year-old child whose valuation of the mother is sufficiently positive[1] experiences an acute conflict within his psyche due to the sharp upsurge of hostile destructiveness toward that mother. By the force of these impulses he feels compelled to destroy his symbiotic partner, his auxiliary ego, and his first love-object all in one blow. The more he values the object, the more optimal will be his reaction to protect her against his omnipotent rage. The more he is already pained by that object, the more his valuation (cathexis) of her is already laden with rage, then the less constructive and effective his reaction to protect her against destruc-tion. At this age the ego will begin to *neutralize* the hostile destructive impulses according to the qualitative valuation of the love-object. I have gained the impression that the less the ambivalence toward the libidinal object the greater the ego's developing capability to neutralize hostile destructiveness.

The stabilization of fusion and the capability of the child to neutral-ize destructiveness accrues as he goes from one conflict of ambivalence toward love-objects to another, from those of the practicing, and rapprochement subphases, through that of the oedipus complex and beyond. Somewhat as Freud stated about the developments of the ego and superego (1923), in our view the degree to which the intrapsychic modification of hostile destructiveness develops is the history of the

---

1. The quality of the child's attachment and valuation of his mother is, of course, discernable in his behavior toward her and other objects, in the quality of his well-being and affects, especially in reactions of anxiety, low-keyedness, and depression, and in the quality of his practicing activity.

child's object relations. Of course, we speak here of the somato-psychically normal-enough child. In a very small percentage of children, as in some autistic children, there is reason to believe that some organic processes interfere or prevent the attachment of an object cathexis as well as the development of neutralization of destructiveness.

SECURE SUFFICIENTLY POSITIVE VALUATION OF THE OBJECT

Since the evolving of both fusion and neutralization of aggression in the child depends on a sufficiently positive attachment to the object, it is imperative that he or she is helped to secure such a qualitative attachment. Ethologists, Lorenz (1935, 1953) in particular, have documented and described the phenomenon of imprinting, a primary object attachment which occurs in many animal species—a phenomenon, no doubt, imposed by evolution to insure the preservation of the species. The corollary of imprinting in humans, as explained by psychoanalysts (Bowlby 1958, Spitz 1965, Mahler 1952, with Pine and Bergman 1975, Jacobson 1964, Parens and Saul 1971), emphasizes another important consideration. Briefly, whereas certain animal species imprint (that is, attach to any object with specific, but not species-exclusive, characteristics which are present during the neonatal critical period for imprinting), humans, due to their immaturity at birth (altriciality), are not capable of imprinting (Parens and Saul 1971). The normal child, however, is primed psychobiologically to attach emotionally to a parenting object, but it is necessary for the parent, especially the mothering object, to sufficiently value the child emotionally for that attachment to materialize and to grow. In our view, even at the earliest level of object attachment, during the first six months of life, the mother, and the father, must sufficiently invest emotionally in the child, and must, as Mahler says, be sufficiently *emotionally available* to him to enable the child to begin to form a sufficiently meaningful and positive object attachment.

Emphasis is placed here on the importance of the quality of the valuation by the parents of their child, which reciprocally is vital to the quality of the child's emotional investment in the parents and, hence, to the evolving of fusion of hostile destructiveness as well as to the ego's developing the capability to neutralize it. Therefore, our second recommendation to parents is to provide as optimal as possible a relationship—loving, respecting, age-adequately nurturing, supporting and protecting—to their child. In order for the mother (and father) to do this well, the mother's long-standing needs for optimal self-realization must be considered side by side with the needs of her child. In average circumstances, this *dual and complementary* consideration will lead toward securing an optimal child-mother relationship. From such an optimal child-mother relation, child-parents' relations will follow not only a sufficient degree and quality of fusion and neutralization of destructiveness, but also an optimal development of psychic structure (ego and superego).

Because the development of the individual occurs epigenetically, that is, develops from an undifferentiated psychic matrix progressively into more and more complex structures, efforts to optimize that development must begin from birth. The integrity of the edifice of individuality depends on the foundation on which it is erected. That this foundation is established during the first five to six years of life is widely accepted, as is the view that, in essence, the younger the child, the greater the impact of experience upon his psychic development. For this reason, it is to the child's advantage that his relation to his mothering parent be optimal from birth, indeed, from before his birth. Against this backdrop, it is well to underscore that destructiveness in the adult's object relations results in largest part from the quality of his or her object relations in early childhood, that is, from the way hostile destructiveness was mobilized and coped with during those early years.

A PLEA FOR PARENT EDUCATION

Because of a lack of formal and technical training for parenthood, parents too often do not optimally foster their child's attachment to them and too often fail to understand their child's needs and behavior. As a result, parents frequently cannot evaluate what is a normal demand in their child, or which demand ought to be gratified and which benevolently frustrated. They often do not know how to minimize or help the child cope with excessive or benign unpleasure. Similarly, they too often cannot choose the best alternative for handling problematical behavior. In fact, many times parents interfere with behavior which is not only reasonable but growth-promoting.

Of course, many parents have an excellent intuitive feel for the needs of their children, how to protect them and help them cope. Particularly capable are those parents who feel within themselves the residua of their own childhood yearnings, as well as their own past growth-promoting and growth-inhibiting experiences.

We deduce from our work that, while it is the *sine qua non* of good-enough parenting, parental love alone does not secure a sufficiently positive relationship on the part of the child toward the mothering parent. Not only does securing such a relationship require stable object-love, it also requires a working knowledge and acceptance of the child's changing physical and emotional needs and of his developmental psychodynamic functioning. In addition, it requires sufficient skill in child-rearing based on such an understanding of psychic development and on the ability to determine what is growth-promoting and growth-inhibiting. We can go beyond intuition to ensure improved knowledge and skills in parenting. To a significant degree, the latter can be taught.

Therefore, I want to add two recommendations I have made elsewhere (Parens 1976): (1) For the present generation of parents who had no formal or technical education in parenthood, psychiatrists, psychologists, and social workers trained in child development (based especially, I believe, on psychoanalytic child development theory) should provide them with a parent education service, not in the context of psychotherapy, but in that of education. (2) For our children who will otherwise also achieve parenthood without formal or technical preparation for it, it is imperative that we develop appropriate curricula for the earliest elementary school level on. In this regard, we envision a curriculum[2] that will give children the opportunity to learn, in a formal school setting, about (a) *parenting functions,* that is parenting work, roles, and child rearing issues and techniques, (b) *human development,* focussing on id-ego-superego concepts, psychosexual development, aggression, dependence in the life cycle, the emergence of individuality, and the process of separation-individuation, (c) *object relations,* dyadic, triadic, familial and societal. Sex education courses, a most

2. From our Early Child Development Program, EPPI-MCP, Project #5: The Development of Curricula for Education for Parenthood from Elementary Through High School.

welcome, albeit not easily digested, addition to our children's school diet, should be expanded to cover other equally important aspects of human functioning and development, not the least of which is the ubiquitous function of parenting.

OUTLINE DEVELOPMENT PROFILES OF THE SUBJECTS

The author empathizes with the reader who feels that any effort to draw a brief development profile of psychic development is almost futile. The enormity of detailing psychic development is well illustrated by the extensive profile developed by Anna Freud (1963, 1965) and the efforts of those who have applied it variously. Even while I try to develop these developmental outlines, I find them very inadequate. They are nonetheless prepared to give the reader a bird's-eye view of each child's development of the aggressive drive.

NEONATAL STATUS OF DRIVES AND EGO APPARATUSES

An effort is made to state succinctly the character of neonatal givens (embryonic, natal, and neonatal) regarding drive activity and the functioning of primary autonomous ego apparatuses. While these are evaluated within days from birth, later on-going observation during the autistic and symbiotic phases helps to confirm or reject the neonatal assessment. While in most instances this could be done with a reasonable degree of success, Mary, for example, showed between years one and three greater endowment of libidinal and aggressive drives than we had initially estimated.

PSYCHIC STRUCTURE

Early structural development is stated in terms of drives and ego development, including that of superego-precursors. Because aggression is detailed separately in the profiles, here only libidinal development is addressed; psychosexual development is sketched, especially as it influences and is influenced by the vicissitudes of aggression. In addressing ego development attention is especially paid to the ego's efforts to cope with aggression. The central part the libidinal object plays in this development, as well as the object's role in the development of superego-precursors, has been emphasized in the text.

OBJECT RELATIONS

The child's relation to the mother is outlined separately from the child's other relationships because of the former's paramount influence on aggression and psychic development. Object relations with siblings, other peers, and staff members are also sketched because, while their role is secondary to that of the mother, these nonetheless have a large input into the child's development. The fathers are not accounted for because we want to present only data coming directly from our observations.

SYMBIOSIS AND SEPARATION-INDIVIDUATION

The few words describing the children's progression through their respective symbiosis and separation-individuation phase reveal that not all the children showed clearly delineated phasic progression. In most instances, those children who developed without large developmental strains showed clearer progression from one phase to the next. In the others, especially those who experienced deeply painful developmental strains as protracted depression or intense recurring anxiety, phasic progression was less discernible, often prototypic behavior of several phases coexisting. For example, Temmy at one year showed more than some symbiotic phase activity and practicing activity to alternately dominate the psyche due to harsh, recurring stranger and separation anxiety reaction arising out of the symbiosis.

SIGNS OF DEVELOPMENTAL STRAIN

Symptoms and symptomatic behavior, revealing some developmental strain, interestingly, were found in all our subjects, including those whose development we felt progressed very well, as for instance in Jane, Candy, Mary, Harold, Doris. Also of interest, in these subjects we found symptoms to arise from developmental neurotic conflicts

(Nagera 1966) and, or, the more structured neurotic conflicts of the oedipal phase, rather than from more serious disturbance.

MANIFESTATIONS OF AGGRESSION

As was detailed in the text, categorizing manifestations of aggression is useful but replete with difficulties. Some aggression manifestations are exemplary for, and dictated, the categories we developed, for example, pressured exploration and self-assertiveness suggesting aggression that is nondestructive in its aim. Similarly, rage reactions suggested unpleasure-related destructiveness. Other manifestations are phenomenologically difficult to assess and defy categorization, such as seven-month-old Mary's pleasurable floor and toy poundings. Lines between categories are broken to convey their overlapping in psychic activity. Overlapping occurs not only between the categories as shown on the chart, but between each other in a number of forms and permutations. Simplification was intentional in categorizing these aggression manifestations, in the hope that they might help to sort out the enormous amount of data we found, as well as clarify the nature of aggression.

Early in life, the *unpleasure-related discharge of destructiveness* was found especially in association with painful somatic stimuli (1), traumatizing object relations (2), separation and stranger reactions (3), frustration of autonomous strivings (4), and other states of ego helplessness.

Nonaffective discharges of destructiveness, being induced by neither unpleasure nor pleasure in the affective sense, are best represented by (1) oral nutritive activity, in sucking, biting and chewing. Vigor in sucking is of notable concern especially where it is too weak, as it was in Anni, and at times when it is too vigorous (see Solnit 1972). I doubted that the adventitious scratching by an infant of his own face represented instinctual drive activity. Similarly, occasional hair pulling did not represent a convincing manifestation of nonaffective destructiveness, since in the instances we saw it, we found it associated with unpleasure experience.

Of course, a large category of aggression manifestations, according to our view of it, is that of *nondestructive aggressive discharges.* The character of exploratory activity (1), especially locomotoric, but also visual and oral, convinced us that aggression has an inherently non-destructive trend. So too, we found strivings for autonomy (2), especially as associated with the practicing subphase but even before, as in fifteen-week-old Jane's repeated efforts to feed herself, convincingly pushed by aggressive drive activity. Where it was not thwarted, as it was for example in Vicki during her first year, self-assertiveness (3) was readily manifest where the less than one year old encountered resistance from the object he/she attempted to get hold of. Efforts to control and master (4), inherently serving adaptation to the self and the environment are amply manifest (see Hendrick 1942, 1943a, 1943b) from within the first year of life, and convincingly manifest a pressure and motivational force of a nondestructive aggressive kind.

We found *pleasure-related destructive discharges* in teasing (1), more sadistic taunting (2), and even calculated physical attack (3), especially from the latter part of the first and the second year of life on. By the middle of the second year, during the rapprochement subphase, all of these are evident in the relation to the mother but also in peer relations. Whether poundings against things with excitement, as was the case with seven-month-old Mary, represent a destructive trend is, as I described in the text, highly doubtful.

OUTLINE
PROFILES

OUTLINE-PROFILE OF DEVELOPMENT:
Anni (age at date of tabulation: 4-0-7)

Neonatal status of drives: very poor endowment,
with pathologically low pressure
Neonatal status of ego apparatuses: seriously defective due to
moderate-severe organic brain damage, high arousal threshold

Phase progression of *	Normal autistic phase 0 to about 6 months	Normal symbiotic phase 6 to about 18+ months
a. libido (psychosexual) b. ego	a. very weak orality; gradually increasing pressure b. totally dependent on auxiliary virtually nonfunctional at first	a. progressive attachment, structured libidinal object b. progressively developing ego, still very dependent on mother
a. object relation: mother b. object relation: other	a. deep autism; mother labored to bring her to consciousness and to libidinal responsiveness b. (father &) siblings helped	a. large continual effort by . mother to match-in with Anni ⟶ to become libidinal object b. (father &) siblings helped
separation-individuation	not normal autism	symbiotic tie good, weak good libidinal gratification
signs of strain	seemed an effort to be alert, awake	———
manifestations of aggression a. unpleasure-related destructiveness 　1. painful somatic stimuli 　2. traumatic object relations 　3. separation & stranger responses 　4. frustration of autonomous strivings	1. almost nonresponsive; no rages 2. none 3. ——— 4. none	1. slowly increased responsiveness, still weak; no rage 2. none 3. none seen 4. none
b. nonaffective destructiveness 　1. oral nutritive activity	1. very weak and short periods of sucking	1. slowly increasing pressure
c. nondestructive aggression 　1. exploratory activity 　2. autonomous strivings 　3. self assertiveness 　4. control & mastery	1. none at first, little by little explored visually 2.⎫ none at first, 3.⎬ then very weak 4.⎭	1. visual and motoric, weak busyness 2.⎫ pressure and 3.⎬ effort mounting, 4.⎭ still weak
d. pleasure-related destructiveness 　1. teasing 　2. taunting 　3. attack	1. ——— 2. ——— 3. ———	1. ——— 2. ——— 3. ———

*Associated with her organically-based mental retardation, in Anni, phase progression occurred much more slowly (i.e., developmental retardation) than with our other subjects.

NAME: ANNI

Differentiation subphase from about 14 months on	Practicing subphase 18 to about 36 months	Rapprochement subphase 40 months on
a. pressure increasing, orality, biting objects b. neuromuscular coordination slowly emerging; poor control	a. increasing pressure oral and early anal b. long, slowly evolving defenses, superego precursors, locomotor skills	a. rapprochement clear b. weakness in evolving defenses, skills, and superego precursors
a. despite neuromuscular pathology, with mother's support, slowly progressed b. responsive also to siblings	a. separated and refueled well; long, repeated struggles with mother over limits b. sought others to help her walk	a. cried when separated from mother b. much relatedness to family members
seemed satisfactory	vigorous practicing with limited achievement; much excitement	rapprochement evident
struggle to activate and control sensorimotor apparatuses begins	heroic efforts to learn to walk, demanded that people help her	strenuous efforts for ego control over sensorimotor apparatuses

1. response to pain quicker, clearer 2. none 3. none 4. by own poor ego control emerging	1. same 2. none 3. none 4. by own poor ego control †††; due to mother's limits ††	1. same 2. none 3. separation anxiety † 4. lessens some as better ego control, but both continue

1. further pressure increase (biting mother often)	1. same	1. same (biting mother stops)

1. increases 2.⎫ pressure 3.⎬ and effort 4.⎭ increasing	1. marked increase 2.⎱ large increase 3.⎰ 4. effort heroic, of long duration at times till exhausted	1. lessens some 2. quite strong 3. quite stubborn 4. enormous efforts continue for control of self & environment

1. ——— 2. ——— 3. ———	1. teases mother; takes other's toys 2. ——— 3. attacked mother with spitting and biting	1. teases mother; takes other's things 2. taunts mother 3. if any, attacks not seen

†Here and elsewhere in the profiles daggers indicate levels of intensity above the average for the phase in question; inverted daggers indicate levels of intensity below that average.

OUTLINE-PROFILE OF DEVELOPMENT:
Bernie (age at date of tabulation: 3-7-22)

Neonatal status of drives: well-endowed; with moderate pressure
Neonatal status of ego apparatuses: very good

Phase progression of	Normal autistic phase	Normal symbiotic phase
a. libido (psychosexual) b. ego	a. very good; oral b. very good	a. very good b. very good
a. object relation: mother b. object relation: other	a. good maternal responsiveness b. ———	a. very good structuring of libidinal object; good dyad b. ———
separation-individuation	very good	very good quality and gratifying
signs of strain	none	none

manifestations of aggression		
a. unpleasure-related destructiveness 　1. painful somatic stimuli 　2. traumatic object relations 　3. separation & stranger responses 　4. frustration of autonomous strivings	1. prompt, few rages 2. none 3. ——— 4. none	1. cries quickly, angrily 2. none 3. few, moderate reactions 4. emerging, moderate
b. nonaffective destructiveness 　1. oral nutritive activity	1. good moderate vigor in sucking	1. same, eating well
c. nondestructive aggression 　1. exploratory activity 　2. autonomous strivings 　3. self assertiveness 　4. control & mastery	1. visual, quite alert 2. little 3. clear cry, demand, firm 4. some effort	1. visual and motoric, busy 2. increasing 3. increasing 4. increasing
d. pleasure-related destructiveness 　1. teasing 　2. taunting 　3. attack	1. ——— 2. ——— 3. ———	1. ——— 2. ——— 3. ———

NAME: BERNIE

Differentiation subphase	Practicing subphase	Rapprochement subphase & Toward-object-constancy subphase
a. very good b. very good; superego precursors	a. very good; early anal b. good skills; obsessional defenses too harsh; superego precursors harsh	a. good; anal, early first genital (phallic) b. same, age-adequate
a. good b. good	a. good; but harsh limits imposed by mother b. morose with peers	a. clear rapprochement, affectionate b. morose with peers
clear, good	marked motor activity †; excitement, pleasure high at first, then sobers	good; but conflict from practicing continues and dampens mood
none	obsessional hand-inhibiting rituals when wants to touch things he should not	morose in extra-familial relations

1. same 2. none known 3. same 4. moderate	1. sharp but quiet response 2. limits harsh, reaction suppressed 3. none 4. sometimes intense but suppressed	1. same 2. same 3. separation reactions † 4. same
1. same	1. same	1. same
1. } busy 2. } successful 3. } efforts 4. }	1. marked upsurge 2. marked upsurge 3. inhibited 4. inhibition, massive control	1. busyness lessens 2. active 3. some inhibition 4. same
1. ? taking from others 2. 3.	1. takes from others at first; decreases 2. — — — 3. none	1. little teasing 2. none 3. none with mother; scowling, grimacing, gestures threat

OUTLINE-PROFILE OF DEVELOPMENT:
Candy (age at date of tabulation: 5-4-10)

Neonatal status of drives: well-endowed, with moderate-low pressure
Neonatal status of ego apparatuses: very good

Phase progression of	Normal autistic phase	Normal symbiotic phase
a. libido (psychosexual) b. ego	a. good; oral b. very good	a. very good b. very good
a. object relation: mother b. object relation: other	a. good maternal responsiveness b. ? twin, tolerant of twin's presence	a. very good structuring of libidinal object; good match b. tolerant of twin's needs being met before hers.
separation-individuation	very good	good quality and gratifying
signs of strain	none	none

manifestations of aggression
a. unpleasure-related destructiveness
  1. painful somatic stimuli
  2. traumatic object relations
  3. separation & stranger responses
  4. frustration of autonomous strivings
	1. slow; no rages
	2. none
	3. — — —
	4. none
		1. same
		2. none
		3. few, moderate
		4. emerging, placid

b. nonaffective destructiveness 1. oral nutritive activity	1. good, calm, strong sucking	1. same. Pacifier in mouth often

c. nondestructive aggression
  1. exploratory activity
  2. autonomous strivings
  3. self-assertiveness
  4. control & mastery
	1. visual, alert
	2. little
	3. soft
	4. soft
		1. visual, especially †; sessile
		2. active, moderate, firm
		3. active, moderate, firm
		4. active

d. pleasure-related destructiveness
  1. teasing
  2. taunting
  3. attack
	1. — — —
	2. — — —
	3. — — —
		1. — — —
		2. — — —
		3. — — —

NAME: CANDY

Differentiation subphase	Practicing subphase	Rapprochement subphase & Toward-object-constancy subphase
a. very good b. very good; superego precursors	a. very good; early anal b. good defenses, superego precursors, and skills	a. very good; anal; early first genital b. good defenses, superego precursors, and skills
a. good b. good with siblings and peers	a. good practicing; mild struggle with mother b. active with siblings and peers	a. strong rapprochement b. good activity with siblings and peers
good	very good, although tends to move less than others	very good; clear rapprochement crisis
transient fear of going into hall without mother (separation anxiety)	none	several mild phobias; enuresis post-rapprochement (first genital phase)
1. same 2. none 3. moderate but with anxiety 4. mounting	1. same 2. none 3. none 4. object directed hostility mild	1. same 2. none 3. separation anxiety † 4. object directed hostility ††
1. same (including pacifier)	1. same (including pacifier)	1. same. Pacifier given up
1. busy in all. 2. visual apparatus 3. especially used. Success 4. in efforts is good	1. very busy † 2. very active † 3. firm, but malleable 4. good quality	1. very busy 2. very active 3. firm 4. strong efforts
1. ? taking things from others 2. — — — 3. — — —	1. takes from peers 2. — — — 3. pushes peers	1. teases mother and peers 2. taunts peers 3. attacks peers, mother only in play

OUTLINE-PROFILE OF DEVELOPMENT:
Cindy (age at date of tabulation: 5-4-10)

Neonatal status of drives: well-endowed, moderate pressure
Neonatal status of ego apparatuses: low stimuli thresholds,
low frustration tolerance, later found slight motor dysfunction,
Dx: Minimal Brain Dysfunction

Phase progression of	Normal autistic phase	Normal symbiotic phase
a. libido (psychosexual) b. ego	a. oral needs gratification associated with irritability b. burdened by low thresholds, normo-active	a. improving gratification pattern, good progression b. auxiliary-ego improving, ego development facilitated, age adequate
a. object relation: mother b. object relation: other	a. difficulty in mother-child matching. Moderate degree irritability b. could not yield to twin's need	a. improving mother-child match, good structuring libidinal object b. good with twin, needs usually gratified first
separation-individuation	burdened by too much irritability	age-adequate, good tie to symbiotic partner
signs of strain	many rage reactions, moderately difficult to comfort	less rage, some moderate tantrums daily. comforting is good

manifestations of aggression a. unpleasure-related destructiveness		
1. painful somatic stimuli 2. traumatic object relations 3. separation & stranger responses 4. frustration of autonomous strivings	1. very prompt; many rage reactions 2. moderate-minimal 3. —.— 4. none	1. very prompt; frequent fussiness and tantrums 2. minimal mostly 3. acute stranger & separation responses 4. quick, irritable

b. nonaffective destructiveness		
1. oral nutritive activity	1. good, strong sucking	1. same; feeding well

c. nondestructive aggression		
1. exploratory activity 2. autonomous strivings 3. self-assertiveness 4. control & mastery	1. visual, alert 2. little 3. ? pressured, demanded quick gratification 4. pressured but weak	1. motoric, busy when not upset 2. active, pressured, interrupted 3. active, pressured, interrupted 4. active, pressured, interrupted

d. pleasure-related destructiveness		
1. teasing 2. taunting 3. attack	1. —— — 2. —— — 3. —— —	1. —— — 2. —— — 3. ——

NAME: CINDY

Differentiation subphase	Practicing subphase	Rapprochement subphase & Toward-object-constancy subphase
a. good b. same, age-adequate super-ego precursors	a. good; early anal b. defenses quite good, so too superego precursors, and skills	a. good; anal, early first genital b. same, neutralization de-structiveness age-adequacy-low
a. good, but some tension and irritability b. good, but some irritability	a. good practicing when not upset; numerous struggles with mother b. good with siblings and peers	a. close rapprochement, fre-quent fussing with mother b. good, some irritability
satisfactory	much pleasure, active, but episodes of irritability	good, episodic rapproche-ment crises
episodic irritability in all aspects of psychic function, daily	some anxiety when fell trying to walk, delayed new effort 4 months, irritability	toilet training fussiness with mother
1. same 2. same 3. persist, same 4. same	1. same 2. some increase, as strug-gles with mother 3. stranger & separation responses continued 4. frequent source of irri-tation	1. same 2. again increase, as strug-gles with mother 3. increase at first, then lessens 4. lessens as phase pro-gresses
1. same (some biting mother)	1. same (some biting mother persists)	1. same (biting mother and peers stops)
1. same, but 2. mounting. 3. good success, but some coordination 4. dysfunction seen	1. very busy 2. very active 3. inconstant (fussiness) 4. good, but inconstant	1. busyness levels off 2. active 3. inconstant 4. good; but inconstant
1. some grabbing things from others 2. ____ 3. ____	1. takes from peers, teases some 2. ____ 3. hits others, bit several times	1. teases mother and peers 2. taunts peers mildly 3. attacks mildly mother and peers

OUTLINE-PROFILE OF DEVELOPMENT:
Doris (age at date of tabulation: 2-1-21)

Neonatal status of drives: very good endowment, with moderate-low pressure
Neonatal status of ego apparatuses: very good

Phase progression of	Normal autistic phase	Normal symbiotic phase
a. libido (psychosexual) b. ego	a. very good, oral b. very good early function	a. very good quality b. very good functions
a. object relation: mother b. object relation: other	a. mother nicely responsive b. — — —	a. very good mother-child dialogue, very good libidinal object structuring b. — — —
separation-individuation	fine	very good quality, ample gratification
signs of strain	none	none

manifestations of aggression
a. unpleasure-related destructiveness
  1. painful somatic stimuli
  2. traumatic object relations
  3.
  4. frustration of autonomous strivings
	1. slow; no rages
	2. none
	3. — — —
	4. none
		1. same
		2. none
		3. notable stranger response, no separation response seen
		4. benign

b. nonaffective destructiveness 1. oral nutritive activity	1. good pressure; effective sucking	1. good pressure, feeding well

c. nondestructive aggression
  1. exploratory activity
  2. autonomous strivings
  3. self-assertiveness
  4. control & mastery
	1. soft, visual alert
	2.) determines feedings;
	3.} good, easy approach to
	4.) nipple
		1. visual and motoric busyness moderate
		2. moderate pressure but firm
		3. moderate pressure but firm
		4. moderate effort

d. pleasure-related destructiveness
  1. teasing
  2. taunting
  3. attack
	1. — — —
	2. — — —
	3. — — —
		1. — — —
		2. — — —
		3. — — —

NAME: DORIS

Differentiation subphase	Practicing subphase	Rapprochement subphase
a. very good b. very good; superego precursors soft	a. quite good b. good defenses, superego precursors and skills	a. good; anal b. good development
a. very good b. responsive to siblings and peers	a. very good; benign conditions in limit setting b. active, good relatedness with siblings especially	a. warm rapprochement, some rapprochement crisis tension b. good, especially within family and selected peers
fine	good quality; good, soft pleasure	good quality, good rapprochement crisis work
none	none	holds off speech, ? if strain.

1. soft reaction, moderate 2. none 3. stranger response same 4. increasing but benign	1. same 2. none 3. stranger response same 4. bursts of anger to mother	1. same 2. none 3. same, separation reaction clearer 4. same

1. same	1. same	1. same

1. increasing 2. firm, increasing 3. firm, gentle, increasing 4. success in good effort	1. busyness †, calm, contained by self 2. firm, rich 3. firm, pressured 4. very good	1. same 2. same 3. same 4. same

1. ——— 2. ——— 3. ———	1. teasing mother, playful provoking of mother 2. ——— 3. ———	1. teases mother, siblings 2. nags, occasionally pushes mother to annoyance 3. playful motoric attacks on mother; vocal attacks at times

OUTLINE-PROFILE OF DEVELOPMENT:
Harold (age at date of tabulation: 4-8-3)

Neonatal status of drives: well-endowed, with moderate-low pressure
Neonatal status of ego apparatuses: very good

Phase progression of	Normal autistic phase	Normal symbiotic phase
a. libido (psychosexual) b. ego	a. very good; oral b. very good	a. very good b. very good
a. object relation: mother b. object relation: other	a. very good mutuality b. ———	a. good evolving of smiling responses, object specificity b. ———
separation-individuation	very good	very good so far as we saw it
signs of strain	none	none

manifestations of aggression
a. unpleasure-related destructiveness
  1. painful somatic stimuli
  2. traumatic object relations
  3. separation & stranger responses
  4. frustration of autonomous strivings
	1. moderate; no rages
	2. none
	3. ———
	4. none
		1. same
		2. none
		3. saw none
		4. saw none

b. nonaffective destructiveness 1. oral nutritive activity	1. good vigor in sucking	1. same, eating well

c. nondestructive aggression
  1. exploratory activity
  2. autonomous strivings
  3. self assertiveness
  4. control & mastery
	1. alert, visual
	2.⎫ active
	3.⎬ particularly in feeding
	4.⎭ process
		1. visual and motoric, busy
		2. moderate
		3. moderate
		4. moderate

d. pleasure-related destructiveness
  1. teasing
  2. taunting
  3. attack
	1. ———
	2. ———
	3. ———
		1. ———
		2. ———
		3. ———

NAME: HAROLD

Differentiation subphase	Practicing subphase	Rapprochement subphase & Toward-object-constancy subphase
Limited as Harold was not seen between 3 to 9 months	a. very good; early anal b. good defenses, superego precursors and skills	a. very good; anal; early phallic b. same; good age-adequate level
	a. very good relation; occasional struggle over limits. Mother firm b. active with siblings and peers	a. rapprochement clear, but equally moves away. b. good, active with siblings and couple peers
	Much sensorimotor activity; pleasure; testing mother moderate	good quality rapprochement but practicing activity continues apace
	none	none
	1. moderate anger expressions 2. none 3. none 4. object-directed anger +	1. same 2. none 3. mild separation reactions, anger nicely dealt with 4. continues same
	1. same	1. same
	1. very busy † 2. very active †† 3. solid, strong 4. good efforts; struggles with mother	1. same 2. same 3. same 4. same
	1. teases mother around limits 2. ————— 3. ——————	1. teasing † mother and peers 2. taunting mother and peers 3. playful attacks of mother, more sober hitting of peers

OUTLINE-PROFILE OF DEVELOPMENT:
Jane (age at date of tabulation: 5-6-3)

Neonatal status of drives: well-endowed, with moderate-high pressure
Neonatal status of ego apparatuses: very good

Phase progression of	Normal autistic phase	Normal symbiotic phase
a. libido (psychosexual) b. ego	a. very good; oral b. very good	a. very good activity and quality b. very good
a. object relation: mother b. object relation: other	a. fine maternal responsiveness b. ————	a. very good libidinal object structuring; very good mother-child dyad b. ——·—
separation-individuation	very good	very good quality and ample gratification
signs of strain	none	none

manifestations of aggression		

a. unpleasure-related destructiveness
  1. painful somatic stimuli
  2. traumatic object relations
  3. separation & stranger responses
  4. frustration of autonomous strivings
	1. prompt; few rages
	2. none
	3. ——·—
	4. none
		1. same
		2. none
		3. few reactions, moderate
		4. emerging; prompt

b. nonaffective destructiveness 1. oral nutritive activity	1. good, moderate vigor sucking bottle and thumb	1. same, eating well, pureed solids

c. nondestructive aggression
  1. exploratory activity
  2. autonomous strivings
  3. self-assertiveness
  4. control & mastery
	1. visual, alert
	2. ⎫ tries to self-feed and
	   ⎬ thumb
	3. ⎨ sucking
	4. ⎭
		1. visual and motoric, very busy
		2. active, pressured
		3. active, pressured
		4. active, pressured

d. pleasure-related destructiveness
  1. teasing
  2. taunting
  3. attack
	1. ——·—
	2. ——·—
	3. ——·—
		1. ——·—
		2. ————
		3. ————

NAME: JANE

Differentiation subphase	Practicing subphase	Rapprochement subphase & Toward-object-constancy subphase
a. very good b. very good; superego precursors	a. very good; early anal b. good defenses, superego precursors, and skills	a. good; anal, early first genital b. good defenses, superego precursors, and skills
a. easy together and separating b. good with peers & siblings	a. good practicing; struggle with mother b. active with peers & siblings	a. notable rapprochement b. good activity with peers & siblings
clear very good	very good, much pleasure and motoric activity	excellent quality but long, stresses
none	none	fears of bedtime, few days; self-injury few days
1. same 2. none 3. same 4. mounting	1. same 2. none 3. none ($\downarrow$) 4. object-directed hostility	1. same 2. none 3. separation anxiety $\dagger$ 4. object-directed hostility $\dagger$ & $\downarrow$
1. same (biting bottle nipple)	1. same (screaming more)	1. same
1. very busy 2. in all. 3. successful in 4. efforts	1. very busy $\dagger$ 2. very active $\dagger$ 3. demanding! 4. efforts $\dagger$; struggle with mother	1. busyness levels off 2. active 3. more variable 4. cooperative with mother efforts better paced
1. ? taking toys from peers 2. — — — 3. — — — —	1. takes from peers, teases mother re: limits 2. — — — 3. sat on baby's head! pushes others	1. teasing $\dagger$ mother and peers 2. taunts mother and peers 3. attacks peers, especially vocally, attacks mother only in play

OUTLINE-PROFILE OF DEVELOPMENT:
Louise (age at date of tabulation: 1-4-14)

Neonatal status of drives: good, pressure moderate
Neonatal status of ego apparatuses: good

Phase progression of	Normal autistic phase	Normal symbiotic phase
a. libido (psychosexual) b. ego	a. good orality at first, then lessens in quality b. good early function	a. good structuring of libidinal object; but with trauma b. good defensive activity and progress
a. object relation: mother b. object relation: other	a. maternal distress, adapts satisfactorily b. — — —	a. mother had to be away for 5 days; symbiosis interrupted then resumed b. displaced from mother to other
separation-individuation	good-enough	progressing well-enough then traumatic transient separation
signs of strain	none	signs: did not recognize mother on her return home from several hours, then clinging

manifestations of aggression
a. unpleasure-related destructiveness
  1. painful somatic stimuli
  2. traumatic object relations
  3. separation & stranger responses
  4. frustration of autonomous strivings
	1. moderate reaction, few rages
	2. due to maternal stress, lag in relief from unpleasure
	3. — — —
	4. none
		1. same but unpleasure protracted
		2. traumatizing separation, aggression discharged inward
		3. intense separation response, aggression discharged inward
		4. minimal, soft

b. nonaffective destructiveness 1. oral nutritive activity	1. good pressure in feeding	1. same (gaining too much weight)

c. nondestructive aggression
  1. exploratory activity
  2. autonomous strivings
  3. self-assertiveness
  4. control & mastery
	1. moderately alert
	2.⎱ soft efforts
	3.⎰ during feeding
	4.
		1. moderate busyness, visual and motoric, inconstant
		2. moderate pressure, inconstant
		3. moderate pressure, inconstant
		4. moderate efforts, inconstant

d. pleasure-related destructiveness
  1. teasing
  2. taunting
  3. attack
	1. — — —
	2. — — —
	3. — — —
		1. — — —
		2. — — —
		3. — — —

NAME: LOUISE

Differentiation subphase	Practicing subphase	Rapprochement subphase
a. oral, symbiotic needs up- permost b. good-enough progress in ego functions	a. same, until lessens due to practicing activity b. defenses, superego precur- sors and skills emerging	
a. responsive to child, moth- er mobilizes to gratify needs b. neighbor (other) impor- tant	a. improved; practicing causes mother confusion in limit setting b. neighbor helps; cognizant of peers	
little visibility due to symbio- tic phase strain	somewhat shortened practic- ing, with good pleasure in function	
mild, protracted depression	depression lifts due to prac- ticing mood and maternal improvement	
1. same, improving 2. lessens 3. protected by mother against separation 4. emerging, moderate	1. continuing improve- ments, moderate reaction, no rage 2. improvement notable 3. same 4. little anger induced by environment, gentle handling	
1. same	1. same (too heavy)	
1. busyness increasing 2. pressure, moderate 3. pressure, moderate 4. moderate effort	1. notably increased busy- ness 2. increased to good level 3. increased to good level 4. effort greater, with suc- cess	
1. 2. 3.	1. little teasing (delayed) 2. 3.	

OUTLINE-PROFILE OF DEVELOPMENT:
Mary (age at date of tabulation: 4-3-28)

Neonatal status of drives: well-endowed, with moderate-low pressure
Neonatal status of ego apparatuses: very good

Phase progression of	Normal autistic phase	Normal symbiotic phase
a. libido (psychosexual) b. ego	a. good; oral b. very good	a. very good quality b. very good
a. object relation: mother b. object relation: other	a. fine maternal responsiveness b. — — —	a. very good structuring of libidinal object; good dyad b. — — —
separation-individuation	very comfortable, calm	very good, ample gratification
signs of strain	none	none

manifestations of aggression a. unpleasure-related destructiveness		
1. painful somatric stimuli 2. traumatic object relations 3. separation & stranger responses 4. frustration of autonomous strivings	1. moderate reaction, rare rage 2. none 3. — — — 4. none	1. same; no rages 2. none 3. moderate, few 4. minimal
b. nonaffective destructiveness 1. oral nutritive activity	1. good, moderate vigor sucking	1. same, eating well
c. nondestructive aggression 1. exploratory activity 2. autonomous strivings 3. self-assertiveness 4. control & mastery	1. moderate-low, calm 2. mild 3. effort in 4. feeding	1. visual, motoric busyness moderate low 2. effort mounting a little 3. at height of phase 4.
d. pleasure-related destructiveness 1. teasing 2. taunting 3. attack	1. — — — 2. — — — 3. — — —	1. — — — 2. — — — 3. — — —

NAME: MARY

Differentiation subphase	Practicing subphase	Rapprochement subphase & Toward-object-constancy subphase
a. very good b. very good	a. very good; early anal b. good defenses, superego precursors and skills	a. good; anal, early first genital b. good age-adequate
a. easy, warm, pleasure in dyad b. cheerful contact with peers	a. progressive sharply mounting struggle b. good with siblings and peers	a. long practicing struggle, rapprochement warm, clear b. good with siblings especially, also with peers
activity mounting, separation push clear	very active, energetic protracted subphase with sharp conflict	after delay due to long practicing subphase, clear, rapprochement
none	sharp struggle with mother	difficulty going to sleep couple weeks
1. same 2. none 3. same 4. moderate	1. same 2. † due to oppressive limits by mother 3. none 4. anger to mother ††	1. same 2. lessens 3. separation anxiety at night 4. anger ↓ to mother
1. same	1. same (vocal cursing, scolding sounds)	1. same
1. busyness moderate mounting 2. mounting 3. mounting 4. effort mounting	1. marked † busyness 2. marked † 3. pressured 4. strong	1. busyness levels off 2. strong 3. strong 4. strong
1. — — — 2. — — — 3. — — —	1. teases mother 2. — — — 3. — — —	1. teases mother, little with peers 2. taunts mother 3. attacks mother vocally and in play

OUTLINE-PROFILE OF DEVELOPMENT:
Renée (age at date of tabulation: 4-11-16)

Neonatal status of drives: good disposition, with moderate-low pressure
Neonatal staus of ego apparatuses: good

Phase progression of	Normal autistic phase	Normal symbiotic phase
a. libido (psychosexual) b. ego	a. good, early oral phase b. good functioning	a. good often; at times too frustrated b. age-adequate, good function
a. object relation: mother b. object relation: other	a. some maternal ambivalence; adapts satisfactorily to mother b. ———	a. same; good structuring of libidinal object b. ———
separation-individuation	good-enough	gratifying to a degree, weakened by maternal ambivalence
signs of strain	none	slight mood dampening

manifestations of aggression
a. unpleasure-related destructiveness
  1. painful somatic stimuli
  2. traumatic object relations
  3. separation & stranger responses
  4. frustration of autonomous strivings
	1. moderate reaction; few rages
	2. delayed quieting of unpleasure
	3. ———
	4. none
		1. same
		2. some irritability
		3. stranger response slight; separation response moderate
		4. emerging, reaction soft

b. nonaffective destructiveness 1. oral nutritive activity	1. good, moderate-soft pressure	1. same

c. nondestructive aggression
  1. exploratory activity
  2. autonomous strivings
  3. self assertiveness
  4. control & mastery
	1. moderately alert
	2. } soft efforts
	3. } during
	4. } feeding
		1. visual and motoric busyness moderate
		2. moderate pressure
		3. moderate pressure
		4. moderate effort

d. pleasure-related destructiveness
  1. teasing
  2. taunting
  3. attack
	1. ———
	2. ———
	3. ———
		1. ———
		2. ———
		3. ———

NAME: RENÉE

Differentiation subphase	Practicing subphase	Rapprochement subphase & Toward-object-constancy subphase
a. same b. good; early superego precursors	a. easier, as makes less demands on mother; early anal b. adequate defenses, superego precursors and skills	a. some tension, anal, first genital b. good-enough defenses, superego precursors, skills
a. mother cheers individuation efforts b. active amid and cognizant of peers good, welcomed by both mother and child	a. mother encourages practicing but sets limits with some sadism b. active with siblings and peers	a. tension from need for physical contact with mother b. difficulty with peers but is with, seeks, them
	good practicing, but pleasure affect dampened by reluctant refueling; brief sharp struggles	visible rapprochement, heightening of tension; further intensified with infantile genitality
none	mood dampened some	somatic complaints (were also characteristic of mother)
1. moderate, soft reaction 2. same 3. same 4. same	1. same 2. same 3. lessens 4. object-directed anger + but discharge inhibited	1. soft, angry, complaint reaction 2. soft, angry, complaint reaction 3. clinging to mother who restrainedly pushes her away 4. same
1. same	1. same	1. same (slight undue weight gain)
1. motoric busyness increasing 2. moderate pressure 3. moderate pressure 4. effort increasing	1. busyness further increases 2. pressure increased 3. pressure increased 4. increasing	1. not as constant 2. variable 3. ·variable 4. levels off
1. quickly discouraged when takes or reaches for other child's toy 2. -- -- -- 3. -- -- --	1. takes things from peers, with little manifest pleasure 2. -- -- -- 3. -- -- --	1. teases peers 2. nags mother, others 3. inhibited, masked attack on mother by mannerisms that irritate her; sadism to peers

OUTLINE-PROFILE OF DEVELOPMENT:
Temmy (age at date of tabulation: 5-6-4)

Neonatal status of drives: well-endowed; moderate pressure
Neonatal status of ego apparatuses: probably* good

Phase progression of	Normal autistic phase	Normal symbiotic phase
a. libido (psychosexual) b. ego	a. ————* b. ————*	a. good; oral b. acute separation & stranger reactions burden ego; mother facilitated progress
a. object relation: mother b. object relation: other	a. —— —— —— b. —— —— ——	a. good structuring of libidinal object; mother comforts well, responds quickly b. — —— —
separation-individuation	—— —— ——	good symbiosis, but sharp stranger and separation anxiety seem traumatizing
signs of strain	—— —— ——	excessive anxiety, at times near-panic

manifestations of aggression
a. unpleasure-related destructiveness
  1. painful somatic stimuli
  2. traumatic object relations
  3. separation & stranger responses
  4. frustration of autonomous strivings
	
	1. —— — ——
	2. —— · ——
	3. —— —— ——
	4. —— · ·
		
		1. quick, but few rages
		2. ?; mother protective
		3. actue, quickly induced
		4. little seen

b. nonaffective destructiveness 1. oral nutritive activity	 1.	 1. good, at times tense

c. nondestructive aggression
  1. exploratory activity
  2. autonomous strivings
  3. self-assertiveness
  4. control & mastery
	
	1. —— —— ——
	2. —— —— ——
	3. —— —— ——
	4. —— —— ——
		
		1. little; anxiety preempted
		2. little; anxiety preempted
		3. associate with anxiety
		4. pressured efforts

d. pleasure-related destructiveness
  1. teasing
  2. taunting
  3. attack
	
	1. —— —— ——
	2. —— · ·
	3. —— · ——
		
		1. —— —— ——
		2. —— —— ——
		3. —— —— ——

*We did not see Temmy till she was 17 weeks old.

NAME: TEMMY

Differentiation subphase	Practicing subphase	Rapprochement subphase & Toward-object-constancy subphase
a. good b. efforts to cope with anxiety some delay, age-adequacy low, superego precursors	a. good; early anal b. some delay, age-adequacy-low; superego precursors; good defenses	a. good; anal; early first genital b. good progress but neutralization destructiveness slow-weak
a. good, protective b. good; but some trouble with Jane	a. good, protective; some struggle with mother b. fair; some wariness	a. good, but some struggle continues b. same; somewhat morose
Delayed —when began used proxies** to facilitate separation	Delayed but progressed satisfactorily, actively and with pleasure	Practicing and rapprochement not clearly delineated
some lessening of acute anxiety, but tension high	some strain in peer relatedness	some unclarity in subphase activity and progression
1. no rage; quick response 2. none 3. somewhat less 4. mild, occasional	1. same 2. same with peers 3. stranger response still 4. increases (with mother)	1. same 2. same, also with mother 3. same 4. same
1. good, calmer	1. good, (some hoarding)	1. same
1. visual & motoric, busy 2. amply evident 3. increasing outside of anxiety 4. good efforts	1. busyness + 2. more active 3. more, but inconsistant 4. efforts +	1. same 2. same 3. same 4. same
1. hesitantly takes from peers 2.·　-　- 3.　　-　-	1. takes from peers, some teasing 2. —--- - 3. weakly hits peers created hit-and-chase game	1. teasing peers + 2. taunting peers + 3. attack peers frequent, mostly verbal

**We did not see Temmy till she was 17 weeks old.

OUTLINE-PROFILE OF DEVELOPMENT:
Vicki (age at date of tabulation: 5-3-18)

Neonatal status of drives: well-endowed, with moderate-high pressure
Neonatal status of ego apparatuses: very good

Phase progression of	Normal autistic phase	Normal symbiotic phase
a. libido (psychosexual) b. ego	a. very good; oral b. very good	a. undue frustration in latter months b. good, accommodates to external stress well
a. object relation: mother b. object relation: other	a. mother depressed, over-burdened, gratifies at times, frustrates at others b. — — —	a. mother gratifies sufficiently for structuring of libidinal object, turns to mother for gratification b. — — —
separation-individuation	good	symbiotic tie to mother developing well
signs of strain	none	at times flustered, jolted by mother's harsh caretaking

manifestations of aggression
a. unpleasure-related destructiveness
  1. painful somatic stimuli
  2. traumatic object relations
  3. separation & stranger responses
  4. frustration of autonomous strivings
	1. prompt, some rages
	2. painful handling, some rages
	3. — — —
	4. none
		1. slower onset
		2. same, reaction becoming more quiet
		3. some quiet separation reactions
		4. too often frustrated, pain

b. nonaffective destructiveness 1. oral nutritive activity	1. good vigor in sucking	1. uneasy, although vigorous eating

c. nondestructive aggression
  1. exploratory activity
  2. autonomous strivings
  3. self-assertiveness
  4. control & mastery
	1. active visual
	2. }
	3. } efforts to self-feed discouraged
	4. } brusquely
		1. visual and motoric, very busy
		2. } ample pressure, but
		3. } efforts disrupted by mother,
		4. } activity then halts.

d. pleasure-related destructiveness
  1. teasing
  2. taunting
  3. attack
	1. — — —
	2. — — —
	3. — — —
		1. — — —
		2. — — —
		3. — — —

NAME: VICKI

Differentiation subphase	Practicing subphase	Rapprochement subphase & Toward-object-constancy subphase
a. frustration intensifies b. depression-laden, self-protective uppermost	a. same; oral b. same; delay in conflict-free functions	a. frustration lessening; anal b. same; self-protective +, conflict-free
a. attachment strong; maternal ambivalence high; negative affect high b. very little differentiation activity	a. same b. engaging into relation with therapist; softness, warmth emerging	a. easing of tension, ministrations improving b. positive relation with therapist; siblings and peers too
	very little practicing; no clarity in phase progression	difficult to discern, dominantly symbiotic-rapprochement; some practicing
	depression deepens; psychotherapy started	slow, gradual lifting of depression
anaclitic-type depression manifest 1. slower onset, quiet reaction of pain 2. more quiet reaction 3. not visible 4. quiet pain affect reaction	1. painful affect 2. painful affect 3. not visible 4. little activty	1. sluggish reactivity, but increasing 2. decreases as mother improves and therapist helps 3. talks about therapist at home 4. decreases
1. same (gaining too much weight)	1. same, weight +, bites nipples off	1. same
1. becomes sluggish 2. pressure dampened, 3. efforts disrupted by 4. mother	1. little activity, as 2. relation to therapist engages, 3. these activities seem to 4. slowly come alive	1. these gradually gain 2. momentum especially in 3. relation with thereapist. 4. attachment to mother steadfast
1. none 2. none 3. none	1. rarely teases (?) therapist 2. none 3. none	1. teases only therapist in play. not with peers nor mother. 2. none 3. attacks only therapist in play, bossy with him.

REFERENCES

Abraham, K. 1916. The first pregenital stage of the libido. In *Selected papers of Karl Abraham,* 248–79. New York: Basic Books, 1953.
———. 1924. A short study of the development of the libido. In *Selected papers of Karl Abraham,* 418–501. New York: Basic Books, 1953.
Akhtar, S. 1996. Object constancy and adult psychopathology. In *The internal mother: Conceptual and technical aspects of object constancy,* ed. S. Akhtar, S. Kramer, and H. Parens, 127–56. Northvale, NJ: Jason Aronson.
Akhtar, S., S. Kramer, and H. Parens, eds. 1996. *The internal mother: Conceptual and technical aspects of object constancy.* Northvale, NJ: Jason Aronson.
Akhtar, S., and H. Parens, eds. 1991. *Beyond the symbiotic orbit: Advances in separation-individuation theory, essays in honor of Selma Kramer.* Hillsdale, NJ: Analytic Press.
Alexander, F., and T. French. 1946. *Psychoanalytic therapy: Principles and applications.* New York: Ronald Press.
Alpert, A., B. Neubauer, and A. Weil. 1956. Unusual variations in drive endowment. *Psychoanalytic Study of the Child* 11:125–63.
Applegarth, A. 1971. Comments on aspects of the theory of psychic energy. *Journal of the American Psychoanalytic Association* 19:379–416.
Aring, C. 1973. Aggression and social synergy. *American Journal of Psychiatry* 130:297–98.

Arlow, J. A. 1973. Perspectives on aggression in human adaptation. *Psychoanalytic Quarterly* 42:178–84.

Bachrach, H. M., R. Galatzer-Levy, A. Skolnikoff, and S. Waldron Jr. 1991. On the efficacy of psychoanalysis. *Journal of the American Psychoanalytic Association* 39:871–916.

Balint, M. 1953. *Primary love and psychoanalytic technique.* New York: Liveright.

Bandura, A., and R. Walters. 1959. *Adolescent aggression.* New York: Ronald Press.

———. 1963. Aggression. In *National Society for the Study of Education 62nd yearbook. Part I: Child Psychology.* Chicago: National Society of the Study of Education.

Basch, M. 1976. The concept of affects. *Journal of the American Psychoanalytic Association* 24:759–78.

Bell, S. M. V. 1969. *The relationship of infant-mother attachment to the development of the concept of object-permanence.* Ann Arbor, MI: University Microfilms.

Benedek, T. 1949. The psychosomatic implications of the primary unit: Mother-child. *American Journal of Orthopsychiatry* 19:642–54.

Benjamin, J. D. 1961a. The innate and the experiential in development. In *Lectures in experimental psychiatry,* ed. H. W. Brosin, 19–42. Pittsburgh, PA: University of Pittsburgh Press.

———. 1961b. Some developmental observations relating to the theory of anxiety. *Journal of the American Psychoanalytic Association* 9:652–68.

———. 1963. Further comments on some developmental aspects of anxiety. *Counterpoint, libidinal object, and subject,* ed. H. S. Gaskill, 121–53. New York: International Universities Press.

Beres, D. 1956. Ego deviation and the concept of schizophrenia. *Psychoanalytic Study of the Child* 11:164–235.

Bergman, A. 1972. Ours, mine and yours: Some developmental considerations. Paper presented to the third annual Margaret S. Mahler Symposium, Philadelphia, May.

Berkowitz, L. 1969a. The frustration-aggression hypothesis revisited. In *Roots of aggression: A Re-examination of the frustration-aggression hypothesis,* ed. L. Berkowitz, 1–28. New York: Atherton.

———. 1969b. Simple views of aggression. *American Scientist* 57:372–83.

Bibring, E. 1941. The development and problems of the theory of the instincts. *International Journal of Psychoanalysis* 22:102–31.

Bird, B. 1972. Notes on transference: Universal phenomenon and hardest part of analysis. *Journal of the American Psychoanalytic Association* 21:267–301.

Blum, H. P. 1981. Object inconstancy and paranoid conspiracy. *Journal of the American Psychoanalytic Association* 29:789–813.

———. 1996. Perspectives on internalization, consolidation, and change. In *The internal mother: Conceptual and technical aspects of object constancy*, ed. S. Akhtar, S. Kramer, and H. Parens, 173–201. Northvale, NJ: Jason Aronson.

Bornstein, B. 1949. The analysis of a phobic child: Some problems of theory and technique in child analysis. *Psychoanalytic Study of the Child* 3/4:181–226.

Bowlby, J. A. 1958. The nature of the child's tie to his mother. *International Journal of Psychoanalysis* 39:350–73.

Brenner, C. 1971. The psychoanalytic concept of aggression. *International Journal of Psychoanalysis* 52:137–44.

———. 1982. *The mind in conflict*. New York: International Universities Press.

Brown, G. 1992. Comments at the Interdisciplinary Seminar 6: Problems in the psychoanalytic theory of aggression. Co-chairs I. A. Share and R. A. Blum. Winter meetings of the American Psychoanalytic Association, New York.

Brunswick, R. M. 1940. The pre-oedipal phase of libido development. *Pscychoanalytic Quarterly* 9:293–319.

Buie, D., and G. Adler. 1973. The misuses of confrontation in the psychotherapy of borderline cases. In *Confrontation in psychotherapy*, ed. G. Adler and P. G. Myerson, 123–46. New York: Science House.

———. 1982. Definitive treatment of the borderline personality. *International Journal of Psychoanalysis*, 9:51–87.

Burlingham, D. T. 1963. A study of identical twins: Their analytic material compared with existing observation data of their early childhood. *Psychoanalytic Study of the Child* 18:367–423.

Buxbaum, E. 1970. *Troubled children in a troubled world*. New York: International Universities Press.

Carpy, D. 1989. Tolerating the countertransference: A mutative process. *International Journal of Psychoanalysis* 70:287–94.

Cobliner, W. G. 1965. The Geneva school of genetic psychology and psychoanalysis: Parallels and counterparts. In *The first year of life*, by R. Spitz. New York: International Universities Press.

Cooper, A. M. 1988. Our changing views of the therapeutic action of psychoanalysis: Comparing Strachey and Loewald. *Psychoanalytic Quarterly* 57:15–27.

————. 1989. Infant research and adult psychoanalysis. In *The significance of infant observational research for clinical work with children, adolescents, and adults*, ed. S. Dowling and A. Rothstein, 79–89. Madison, CT: International Universities Press.

De Wit, J., and W. W. Hartup, eds. 1974. *Determinants and origins of aggressive behavior*. The Hague: Mouton.

Dollard, J., L. W. Doob, N. E. Miller, D. H. Mowner, and R. R. Sears. 1939. *Frustration and Aggression*. New Haven, CT: Yale University Press.

Eissler, K. R. 1971. Death drive, ambivalence, and narcissism. *Psychoanalytic Study of the Child* 26:25–78.

Ekstein, R. 1971. *The challenge: Despair and hope in the conquest of inner space*. New York: Brunner-Mazel.

Emde, R. N. 1989. The infant's relationship experience: Developmental and affective aspects. In *Relationship disturbances in early childhood*, ed. A. J. Sameroff and R. N. Emde, 33–51. New York: Basic Books.

Emde, R. N., and J. Scorce. 1983. The rewards of infancy: Emotional availablity and maternal referencing. In *Frontiers of infant psychiatry*, ed. J. Call, E. Galenson, and R. Tyson, 1:17–30. New York: Basic Books.

Engel, G. L. 1962. Anxiety and depression-withdrawal: The primary affects of unpleasure. *International Journal of Psychoanalysis* 43:89–97.

Epstein, L. 1977. The therapeutic function of hate in the countertransference. *Contemporary Psychoanalysis* 13:442–68.

Erikson, E. H. 1959. *Identity and the life cycle*. Psychological Issues Monograph 1. New York: International Universities Press.

Escalona, S. K. 1963. Patterns of infantile experience and the developmental process. *Psychoanalytic Study of the Child* 18:197–244.

Fairbairn, W. R. D. 1954. *An object-relations theory of the personality*. New York: Basic Books.

Fenichel, O. 1945. *The psychoanalytic theory of neurosis.* New York: Norton.

Feshbach, S. 1970. Aggression. In *Carmichael's manual of child psychology,* ed. H. Mussen, 2:159–259. New York: Wiley.

Fraiberg, S. 1969. Libidinal object constancy and mental representation. *Psychoanalytic Study of the Child* 24:9–47.

Frank, A. 1969. The unrememberable and the unforgettable: Passive primal repression. *Psychoanalytic Study of the Child* 24:48–77.

Freud, A. 1936. *The ego and the mechanisms of defense.* New York: International Universities Press, 1946.

——. 1946. The psychoanalytic study of infantile feeding disturbances. *Psychoanalytic Study of the Child* 2:119–32.

——. 1951. Observations on child development. *Psychoanalytic Study of the Child* 6:18–30.

——. 1952. The mutual influences in the development of ego and id. *Psychoanalytic Study of the Child* 7:42–50.

——. 1954. Psychoanalysis and education. *Psychoanalytic Study of the Child* 9:9–15.

——. 1958. Child observation and prediction of development: A memorial lecture in honor of Ernst Kris. *Psychoanalytic Study of the Child* 13:92–124.

——. 1963. The concept of developmental lines. *Psychoanalytic Study of the Child* 18:245–65.

——. 1965. *Normality and pathology in childhood: Assessments of development.* New York: International Universities Press.

——. 1972. Comments on aggression. *International Journal of Psychoanalysis* 53:163–71.

Freud, A., and D. Burlingham. 1944. *Infants without families.* New York: International Universities Press.

Freud, A., and S. Dann. 1951. An experiment in group upbringing. *Psychoanalytic Study of the Child* 6:127–68.

Freud, S. 1895. Project for a scientific psychology. *Standard Edition* 1:281–397.

——. 1905a. Jokes and their relation to the unconscious. *Standard Edition* 8:3–236.

——. 1905b. Three essays on the theory of sexuality. *Standard Edition* 7:123–243.

——. 1909. Analysis of a phobia in a five-year-old boy. *Standard Edition* 10:3–149.

———. 1912. Recommendations to physicians practicing psycho-analysis. *Standard Edition* 12:111–20.

———. 1913a. On beginning the treatment (technique of psycho-analysis, I). *Standard Edition* 12:123–44.

———. 1913b. Totem and taboo. *Standard Edition* 13:1–162.

———. 1914. On narcissism: An introduction. *Standard Edition* 14:69–102.

———. 1915. Instincts and their vicissitudes. *Standard Edition* 14:111–40.

———. 1920. Beyond the pleasure principle. *Standard Edition* 18:1–64.

———. 1921. Group psychology and the analysis of the ego. *Standard Edition* 18:67–143.

———. 1923. The ego and the id. *Standard Edition* 19:3–66.

———. 1924. The economic problem of masochism. *Standard Edition* 19:157–70.

———. 1926. Inhibitions, symptoms and anxiety. *Standard Edition* 20:77–174.

———. 1927. Humour. *Standard Edition* 21:160–66.

———. 1930. Civilization and its discontents. *Standard Edition* 21:59–145.

———. 1933. New introductory lectures on psychoanalysis. *Standard Edition* 22:3–182.

———. 1937. Analysis terminable and interminable. *Standard Edition* 23:211–53.

———. 1940. An outline of psychoanalysis. *Standard Edition* 23:141–207.

Fries, M. E. 1946. The child's ego development and the training of adults in his environment. *Psychoanalytic Study of the Child* 2:85–112.

Fries, M. E., and J. Woolf. 1953. Some hypotheses on the role of the congenital activity type in personality development. *Psychoanalytic Study of the Child* 8:48–62.

Frosch, J. 1966. A note on reality testing. In *Psychoanalysis—a general psychology*, ed. R. M. Loewenstein, L. M. Newman, M. Schur, and A. J. Solnit, 349–76. New York: International Universities Press.

Gabbard, G. O. 1991. Technical approaches to transference hate in the analysis of borderline patients. *International Journal of Psychoanalysis* 72:625–37.

Galenson, E., and H. Roiphe. 1971. The impact of early sexual discovery on mood, defensive organization, and symbolization. *Psychoanalytic Study of the Child* 26:195–216.

Galenson, E., S. Vogel, S. Blau, and H. Roiphe. 1973. Disturbance in sexual identity beginning at 18 months of age. Paper presented at the fall meeting of the American Psychoanalytic Association, New York, December.

Gill, M. M. 1982. *Analysis of transference, Vol. 1: Theory and technique.* Psychological Issues Monograph 53. New York: International Universities Press.

Gilligan, J. 1997. *Violence: Reflections on a national epidemic.* New York: Vintage Books.

Ginsberg, B. E. 1982. Genetic factors in aggressive behavior. *Psychoanalytic Inquiry* 2:53–75.

Goodall, J. V. L. 1971. Some aspects of aggressive behavior in a group of free-living chimpanzees. *International Journal of Social Science* 23:89–97.

———. 1973. The behavior of chimpanzees in their natural habitat. *American Journal of Psychiatry* 130:1–12.

———. 1979. Life and death at Gombe. *National Geographic* 155:592–620.

Gouin-Decaric, T. 1965. *Intelligence and affectivity in early childhood.* New York: International Universities Press.

Group for the Advancement of Psychiatry. 1968. *Normal adolescence: Report of the Committee on Adolescence,* chair, C. F. Settlage. New York: Scribner.

Greenacre, 1950. Special problems of early female sexual development. *Psychoanalytic Study of the Child* 5:122–38.

———. 1960. Considerations regarding the parent-infant relationship. *International Journal of Psychoanalysis* 41:571–84.

———. 1971. Notes on the influence and contribution of ego psychology to the practice of psychoanalysis. In *Separation-individuation: Essays in honor of Margaret S. Mahler,* ed. J. B. McDevitt and C. F. Settlage, 171–200. New York: International Universities Press.

Greenspan, S. I. 1992. *Infancy and early childhood.* Madison, CT: International Universities Press.

Grotstein, J. S. 1982. The analysis of a borderline patient. In *Technical factors in the treatment of the severely disturbed patient*, ed. P. L. Giovacchini and B. Boyer. New York: Jason Aronson.

Gunther, M. 1980. Aggression, self psychology, and the concept of health. In *Advances in self psychology*, ed. A. Goldberg. New York: International Universities Press.

Guntrip. H. 1961. *Personality structure and human interaction*. New York: International Universities Press.

Hamburg, D. A. 1973. An evolutionary and developmental approach to human aggressiveness. *Psychoanalytic Quarterly* 42:185–96.

Hamburg, D. A., and M. B. Trudeau, eds. 1981. *Biobehavioral aspects of aggression*. New York: Alan R. Liss.

Hammerman, S. 1965. Conception of superego development. *Journal of the American Psychoanalytic Association* 13:320–55.

Hartmann, H. 1939. *Ego psychology and the problem of adaptation*. New York: International Universities Press, 1958.

———. 1948. Comments on the psychoanalytic theory of instinctual drives. In *Essays on ego psychology*, 69–89. New York: International Universities Press, 1964.

———. 1950a. Comments on the psychoanalytic theory of the ego. In *Essays on ego psychology*, 113–41. New York: International Universities Press, 1964.

———. 1950b. Psychoanalysis and developmental psychology. *Psychoanalytic Study of the Child* 5:7–17.

———. 1952. The mutual influences in the development of the ego and the id. In *Essays on ego psychology*, 155–81. New York: International Universities Press, 1964.

———. 1955. Notes on the theory of sublimation. In *Essays on ego psychology*, 215–40. New York: International Universities Press, 1964.

———. 1958a. Comments on the scientific aspects of psychoanalysis. *Psychoanalytic Study of the Child* 13:127–46.

———. 1958b. Discussion of Anna Freud's "Child observation and prediction of development: A memorial lecture in honor of Ernst Kris." *Psychoanalytic Study of the Child* 13:120–22.

Hartmann, H., E. Kris, and R. M. Loewenstein. 1949. Notes on the theory of aggression. *Psychoanalytic Study of the Child* 3/4:9–36.

Heimann, P., and A. F. Valenstein. 1972. The psychoanalytical concept of aggression: An integrated summary. *International Journal of Psychoanalysis* 53:31–35.

Hendrick, I. 1942. Instinct and the ego during infancy. *Psychoanalytic Quarterly* 11:33–58.

———. 1943a. The discussion of the "instinct to master." *Psychoanalytic Quarterly* 12:561–65.

———. 1943b. Work and the pleasure principle. *Psychoanalytic Quarterly* 12:311–29.

Hess, E. H. 1958. Imprinting. *Science* 130:133–41.

Hoffer, W. 1949. Mouth, hand and ego-integration. *Psychoanalytic Study of the Child* 3/4:49–56.

Jacobs, T. J. 1991. *The use of the self.* Madison, CT: International Universities Press.

Jacobson, E. 1954. The self and the object world: Vicissitudes of their infantile cathexes and their influence on ideational and affective development. *Psychoanalytic Study of the Child* 9:75–127.

———. 1964. *The self and the object world.* New York: International Universities Press.

Jones, E. 1935. Psychoanalysis and the instincts. In *Papers on psycho-analysis*, 153–69. London: Bailliere, Tindall and Cox, 1948.

Joseph, E. D. 1973. Aggression redefined—its adaptational aspects. *Psychoanalytic Quarterly* 42:197–213.

Kandel, E., J. H. Schwartz, and T. M. Jessell. 1991. *Principles of neural science.* 3rd ed. New York: Elsevier.

Kantrowitz, J. L. 1993. Uniqueness of the patient-analyst pair: Analyst's role. *International Journal of Psychoanalysis* 74:893–904.

———. 1995. The beneficial aspects of the patient-analyst match. *International Journal of Psychoanalysis* 76:299–313.

Kernberg, O. 1966. Structural derivatives of object relationships. *International Journal of Psychoanalysis* 47:236–53.

———. 1967. Borderline personality organization. *Journal of the American Psychoanalytic Association* 15:641–85.

———. 1975. *Borderline conditions and pathological narcissism.* New York: Jason Aronson.

———. 1982. Self, ego, affects and drives. *Journal of the American Psychoanalytic Association* 30:893–917.

———. 1984. *Severe personality disorders: Psychotherapeutic strategies.* New Haven, CT: Yale University Press.

————. 1991. The psychopathology of hatred. *Journal of the American Psychoanalytic Association* 39:209–38.

————. 1992. *Aggression in personality disorders and perversions.* New Haven, CT: Yale University Press.

————. 1994. Discussion of "Hatred as a core affect in aggression." Paper presented at the twenty-fifth annual Margaret S. Mahler Child Development Symposium, Philadelphia, April 30.

————. 1995. Hatred as a core affect of aggression. In *The birth of hatred,* ed S. Akhtar, S. Kramer, and H. Parens, 53–82. Northvale, NJ: Jason Aronson.

Klein, G. S. 1967. Peremptory ideation: Structure and force in motivated ideas. In *Motives and thought,* ed. R. R. Holt. Psychological Issues Monograph 18/19. New York: International Universities Press.

Klein, M. 1939. *The psychoanalysis of children.* New York: Grove Press, 1960.

Kohut, H. 1971. *The analysis of the self.* New York: International Universities Press.

————. 1972. Thoughts on narcissism and narcissistic rage. *Psychoanalytic Study of the Child* 27:360–400.

————. 1977. *The restoration of the self.* New York: International Universities Press.

Kramer, S., and S. Akhtar. 1988. The developmental context of internalize preoedipal object relations. *Psychoanalytic Quarterly* 57:547–76.

Krause, R. 1995. Book review of *Affect imagery consciousness, Vol. 3: The negative affects* by Sylvan S. Tomkins (1991). *Journal of the American Psychoanalytic Association* 43:929–38.

Kris, E. 1950. Notes on the development and on some current problems of psychoanalytic child psychology. *Psychoanalytic Study of the Child* 5:24–46.

————. 1955. Neutralization and sublimation. *Psychoanalytic Study of the Child* 10:30–46.

Lample-De Groot, J. 1960. On adolescence. *Psychoanalytic Study of the Child* 15:95–103.

Lantos, B. 1958. The two genetic derivations of aggression with reference to sublimation and neutralization. *International Journal of Psychoanalysis* 39:116–20.

Lichtenberg, J. D. 1989. *Psychoanalysis and motivation.* Hillsdale, NJ: Analytic Press.

Little, M. 1966. Transference in borderline states. *International Journal of Psychoanalysis* 47:476–85.

Loewald, H. W. 1952. The problem of defense and the neurotic interpretation of reality. *International Journal of Psychoanalysis* 33:444–49.

Loewald, H. W. 1960. On the therapeutic action of psychoanalysis. In *Papers on psychoanalysis*, 221–56. New Haven, CT: Yale University Press, 1980.

Loewenstein, R. M. 1940. The vital and somatic instincts. *International Journal of Psychoanalysis* 21:377–400.

———. 1965. Observational data and theory in psychoanalysis. In *Drives, affects, behavior*, ed. M. Schur, 2:38–59. New York: International Universities Press.

Lorenz, K. 1935. Companionship in bird life. In *Instinctive behavior*, ed. C. H. Schiller. New York: International Universities Press.

———. 1953. Comparative behaviorology. In *Discussions on child development*, ed. J. M. Tanner and B. Inhelder, 1:108–17. New York: International Universities Press.

———. 1963. *Aggression.* New York: Harcourt, Brace and World.

———. 1966. *On aggression.* New York: Harcourt, Brace and World.

Luborsky, L., P. Crits-Christoph, J. Mintz, and A. Auerbach. 1988. *Who will benefit from psychotherapy? Predicting therapeutic outcome.* New York: Basic Books.

Lussier, A. 1972. Panel on aggression (chairman, M. H. Stein). *International Journal of Psychoanalysis* 53:13–19.

Lustman, S. L. 1963. Some issues in contemporary psychoanalytic research. *Psychoanalytic Study of the Child* 18:51–74.

———. 1969. Introduction to panel on the use of the economic viewpoint of clinical psychoanalysis: the economical point of view and desence. *International Journal of Psychoanalysis* 50:95–102.

Mahler, M. S. 1952. On child psychosis and schizophrenia: Autistic and symbiotic infantile psychoses. *Psychoanalytic Study of the Child* 7:286–305.

———. 1963. Thoughts about development and individuation. *Psychoanalytic Study of the Child* 18:307–24.

———. 1965. On the significance of the normal separation-individuation phase. In *Drives, affects, behavior,* ed. M. Schur, 2:161–69. New York: International Universities Press.

———. 1966a. Notes on the development of basic moods: The depressive affect. In *Psychoanalysis: A general psychology: Essays in honor of Heinz Hartmann,* ed. R. M. Loewenstein, L. M. Newman, M. Schur, and A. J. Solnit, 152–68. New York: International Universities Press.

———. 1966b. Discussion of Greenacre's "Problems of overidealization of the analyst and the analysis." Paper presented at the meeting of the New York Psychoanalytic Society, October.

———. 1968. *On human symbiosis and the vicissitudes of individuation.* With M. Furer. New York: International Universities Press.

———. 1972a. On the first three subphases of the separation-individuation process. *International Journal of Psychoanalysis* 53:333–38.

———. 1972b. Rapprochement subphase of the separation-individuation process. *Psychoanalytic Quarterly* 41:487–506.

———. 1981. Aggression in the service of separation-individuation. *Psychoanalytic Quarterly* 50:625–38.

Mahler, M., and J. B. McDevitt. 1968. Observations on adaptation and defense in *statu nascendi*: Developmental precursors in the first two years of life. *Psychoanalytic Quarterly* 37:1–21.

———. 1975. *The psychological birth of the human infant: Symbiosis and individuation.* New York: Basic Books.

Mahler, M. S., F. Pine, and A. Bergman. 1975. *The psychological birth of the human infant.* New York: Basic Books.

Marcovitz, E. 1973. Aggression in human adaptation. *Psychoanalytic Quarterly* 42:226–33.

McCord, W., J. McCord, and I. K. Zola. 1959. *Origins of crime.* New York: Columbia University Press.

McDevitt, J. B. 1975. Separation-individuation and object constancy. *Journal of the American Psychoanalytic Association* 23:713–42.

———. 1983. The emergence of hostile aggression and its defensive and adaptive modifications during the separation-individuation process. *Journal of the American Psychoanalytic Association* 31:273–300.

———. 1996. The concept of object constancy and its clinical applications. In *The internal mother: Conceptual and technical aspects of object constancy,* ed. S. Akhtar, S. Kramer, and H. Parens, 15–46. Northvale, NJ: Jason Aronson.

McDevitt, J. B., and M. S. Mahler. 1989. Object constancy, individuality, and internalization. In *The course of life: Early childhood*, ed. S. I. Greenspan and G. H. Pollock, 2:37–60. Madison, CT: International Universities Press.

McDevitt, J. B., and C. F. Settlage, eds. 1971. *Separation-individuation: Essays in honor of Margaret S. Mahler.* New York: International Universities Press.

Mittelmann, B. 1954. Motility in infants, children, and adults. *Psychoanalytic Study of the Child* 9:142–77.

———. 1960. Intrauterine and early infantile motility. *Psychoanalytic Study of the Child* 15:105–27.

Modell, A. 1976. The holding environment and the therapeutic action of psychoanalysis. *Journal of the American Psychoanalytic Association* 24:285–308.

Moyer, K. E. 1968. Kinds of aggression and their physiological basis. *Communications in Behavioral Biology* 2:65–87.

Nagera, H. 1966. *Early childhood disturbances: The infantile neurosis, and the adult disturbances.* New York: International Universities Press.

Nason, J. 1985. The psychotherapy of rage. *Contemporary Psychoanalysis* 21:167–92.

Ostow, M. 1957. Panel on the theory of aggression (chairman, R. Waelder). *Journal American Psychoanalytic Association* 5:556–63.

Pacella, B. 1973a. Early ego development and the deja vu. Paper presented at the scientific meeting of the Philadelphia Psychoanalytic Society, October 17.

———. 1973b. The waking screen. Paper presented at the Department of Psychiatry, Medical College of Pennsylvania, Philadelphia, October 17.

Panel. 1992. Enactments in psychoanalysis, reporter M. Johan. *Journal of the American Psychoanalytic Association* 40:827–41.

Pao, H. 1965. The role of hatred in the ego. *Psychoanalytic Quarterly* 34:257–64.

Parens, H. 1971a. A contribution of separation-individuation to the development of psychic structure. In *Separation-individuation: Essays in honor of Margaret S. Mahler*, ed. J. B. McDevitt and C. F. Settlage. New York: International Universities Press.

———. 1971b. A preliminary report from the project "Correlations of the Libidinal Availability of the Mother with the Development of Psychic Structure in the Child." Unpublished manuscript.

―――. 1972a. Aggression and object relations in the first two years of life. Paper presented at the Panel on Aggression and Object Relations, Joint Meeting of the Regional Council of Child Psychiatry and the Philadelphia Society for Adolescent Psychiatry, Philadelphia, September.

―――. 1972b. Book review: Rudolph Ekstein's *The challenge: Despair and hope in the conquest of inner space. Psychoanalytic Quarterly* 41:616–23.

―――. 1973a. Aggression: A reconsideration. *Journal of the American Psychoanalytic Association* 21:34–60.

―――. 1973b. Discussion of R. J. Stoller's "Symbiosis anxiety and the development of masculinity." Paper presented at the fourth annual Margaret S. Mahler Symposium, Philadelphia, May.

―――. 1976. A psychiatric approach toward education for parenthood and the primary prevention of emotional disorders in children. Unpublished manuscript.

―――. 1979. *The development of aggression in early childhood.* New York: Jason Aronson.

―――. 1984. Toward a reformulation of the theory of aggression and its implications for primary prevention. In *Psychoanalysis: The vital issues*, ed. J. Gedo and G. Pollock, 1:87–114. New York: International Universities Press.

―――. 1989a. Toward an epigenesis of aggression in early childhood. In *The course of life: Early childhood*, ed. S. I. Greenspan and G. H. Pollock, 2:689–721. Madison, CT: International Universities Press.

―――. 1989b. Toward a reformulation of the psychoanalytic theory of aggression. In *The course of life: Early childhood*, ed. S. I. Greenspan and G. H. Pollock, 2:643–87. Madison, CT: International Universities Press.

―――. 1991a. Separation-individuation theory and psychosexual theory. In *Advances in separation-individuation theory and research: Festschrift in honor of Selma Kramer, MD,* ed. S. Akhtar and H. Parens, 3–34. Northvale, NJ: Aronson Press.

―――. 1991b. A view of the development of hostility in early life. *Journal of the American Psychoanalytic Association* 39:75–108.

————. 1992. The roots of hate, violence and prejudice. Paper presented at the symposium "Rage, Prejudice and Hatred," Philadelphia Psychoanalytic Society, Philadelphia, October 3.

————. 1993a. Does prevention in mental health make sense? An interface of psychoanalysis and neurobiology. In *Prevention in mental health*, ed. H. Parens and S. Kramer, 103–20. Northvale, NJ: Jason Aronson.

————. 1993b. Neuformulierungen der psychoanalytischen Aggressionstheorie und Folgerungen fuer die klinische Situation. *Forum der Pyschoanalyse* 9:107–21.[*Au:* If available, please provide translation of article title.]

————. 1993c. Rage toward self and others in early childhood. In *Rage, power, and aggression*, ed S. P. Roose and R. Glick, 123–47. New Haven, CT: Yale University Press.

————. 1993d. Toward preventing experience-derived emotional disorders: Education for parenting. In *Prevention in mental health*, ed. H. Parens and S. Kramer, 121–48. Northvale, NJ: Jason Aronson.

————. 1994. Comments on Kernberg's "Hatred as a core affect of aggression." Paper presented at the twenty-fifth annual Margaret S. Mahler Child Development Symposium, Philadelphia, April 30.

————. 1996a. Dealing with violence today—and for tomorrow. *AACAP News* 27 (6): 17–22.

————. 1996b. *The origins of prejudice and of healthy distinctions in identity*. South Asia Forum videotape, Philadelphia Psychoanalytic Institute and Society, S. Akhtar, moderator. Recorded for distribution October 20.

————. 1996c. *Prevention of violence via parenting education*. Furman Initiative presented at the meetings of the American Academy of Child and Adolescent Psychiatry, part of the panel Violence in School, E. Sholevar, chair.

————. 1999a. Some influences of the Holocaust on development—one man's experience. Address presented to the annual meeting of the American College of Psychoanalysts, Washington, DC, May 15.

————. 1999b. Toward the prevention of prejudice. In *En el umbral del millenio*, ed. M. R. Fort Brescia and M. Lemlij, 2:131–41. PromPeru, Peru: SIDEA.

Parens, H., L. Giacomo, and S. V. McLeer. 1982. Toward preventing the development of excessive hostility in children. Presented at the winter meetings of the American Psychoanalytic Association, New York.

Parens, H., L. Pollock, and R. C. Prall. 1974. *Film number 3: Preventionl early intervention mother-child groups.* Philadelphia: Audio-Visual Media, Eastern Pennsylvania Psychiatric Institute.

Parens, H., L. Pollock, J. Stern, and S. Kramer. 1976. On the girl's entry into the oedipus complex. *Journal of the American Psychoanalytic Association* 24:79–107.

Parens, H., and R. C. Prall. 1974. *Film number 2: Toward an epigenesis of aggression in early childhood.* Philadelphia: Audio-Visual Media, Eastern Pennsylvania Psychiatric Institute.

Parens, H., R. C. Prall, and E. Scattergood. 1970. Project protocol. Unpublished manuscript.

Parens, H., and L. J. Saul. 1971. *Dependence in man: A psychoanalytic study.* New York: International Universities Press.

Parens, H., E. Scattergood, A. Duff, and W. Singletary. 1997. *Parenting education for emotional growth: A curriculum for students in grades K thru 12.* Philadelphia: Parenting for Emotional Growth.

Parens, H., E. Scattergood, W. Singletary, and A. Duff. 1987. *Aggression in our children: Coping with it constructively.* Northvale, NJ: Jason Aronson.

Patterson, G. R., R. A. Littman, and W. Bricker. 1967. Assertive behavior in children: A step toward a theory of aggression. *Monographs of the Society for Research in Child Development* 32 (5): 1–43.

Peller, L. 1954. Libidinal phases, ego development, and play. *Psychoanalytic Study of the Child* 9:178–98.

———. 1965. Comments on libidinal organization and child development. *Journal of the American Psychoanalytic Association* 13:732–47.

Piaget, J. 1937. *La construction du reel chez l'Enfant.* Neuchatel, Switzerland: Delachaux et Niestle, 1963.

———. 1954. *Les relations entre l'affectivite et l'intelligence dans le development mental de i'enfant.* Paris: Centre de Documentation Universitaire.

Piers, G., and M. Singer. 1953. *Shame and guilt.* Springfield, IL: Charles C Thomas.

Pine, F., and M. Furer. 1963. Studies of the separation-individuation phase. *Psychoanalytic Study of the Child* 18:325–42.

Post, R. M. 1992. Transduction of psychosocial stress into the neurobiology of recurrent affect disorder. *American Journal of Psychiatry* 149:999–1010.

Provence, S., and R. Lipton. 1962. *Infants in institutions*. New York: International Universities Press.

Rangell, L. 1972. Aggression, Oedipus, and historical perspective. *International Journal of Psychoanalysis* 53:3–11.

———. 1989. The significance of infant observations for psychoanalysis in later stages of life. In *The significance of infant observational research for clinical work with children, adolescents, and adults*, ed. S. Dowling and A. Rothstein, 195–211. Madison, CT: Iternational Universities Press.

Rank, B. 1949. Aggression. *Psychoanalytic Study of the Child* 3/4:43–48.

Reis, D. J. 1973. The chemical coding of aggression in the brain. Manuscript circulated for the Colloquium on Aggression of the American Psychoanalytic Association, Leo Stone, chair, New York, December.

Reis, D. J. 1974. Central neurotransmitters in aggression. *Research Publications of the Association for Research on Nervous and Mental Disease* 52:119–48.

Ritvo, S., and A. J. Solnit. 1958. Influences of early mother-child interaction on identification processes. *Psychoanalytic Study of the Child* 13:64–91.

Rochlin, G. 1973. *Man's aggression: The defense of the self.* Boston: Gambit.

Roiphe, H. 1968. On an early genital phase. *Psychoanalytic Study of the Child* 23:348–65.

Sandler, J. 1983. Psychoanalytic concepts and psychoanalytic practice. *International Journal of Psychoanalysis* 64:35–46.

Saul, J. S. 1976. *The psychodynamics of hostility.* New York: Jason Aronson.

Scharfman, M. A. 1989. The therapeutic dyad in the light of infant observational research. In *The significance of infant observational research for clinical work with children, adolescents, and adults*, ed. S. Dowling and A. Rothstein, 53–64. Madison, CT: International Universities Press.

Schilder, 1964. *Contributions to developmental neuro-psychiatry.* New York: International Universities Press.

Schur, M. 1966. *The id and the regulatory principles of mental functioning*. New York: International Universities Press.

Settlage, C. F. 1993. On the contribution of separation-individuation theory to psychoanalysis: Developmental process, pathogenesis, therapeutic process, and technique. Paper presented at the 24th annual Margaret S. Mahler Symposium on Child Development, Philadelphia, May 1.

Shane, M., and E. Shane. 1982. The strands of aggression: A confluence of data. *Psychoanalytic Inquiry* 2:263–81.

Simmel, E. 1944. Self-preservation and the death instinct. *Psychoanalytic Quarterly* 13:160–85.

Solnit, A. J. 1966. Some adaptive functions of aggressive behavior. In *Psychoanalysis—a general psychology*, ed. R. M. Loewenstein, L. M. Newman, M. Schur, and A. J. Solnit, 169–89. New York: International Universities Press.

———. 1970. A study of object loss in infancy. *Psychoanalytic Study of the Child* 25:257–72.

———. 1972. Aggression: A view of theory building in psychoanalysis. *Journal of the American Psychoanalytic Association* 20:435–50.

Spitz, R. 1945a. Diacritic and coenesthetic organizations. *Psychoanalytic Review* 32:146–62.

———. 1945b. Hospitalism: An inquiry into the genesis of psychiatric conditions in early childhood. *Psychoanalytic Study of the Child* 1:53–74.

———. 1946a. Anaclitic depression: An inquiry into the genesis of psychiatric conditions in early childhood. *Psychoanalytic Study of the Child* 2:313–42.

———. 1946b. The smiling response: A contribution to the ontogenesis of social relations. *Genetic Psychology Monographs* 34:57–125.

———. 1950. Anxiety in infancy: A study of its manifestations in the first year of life. *International Journal of Psychoanalysis* 31:138–43.

———. 1953. Aggression. In *Drives, affects, behavior*, ed. R. M. Loewenstein, 1:126–38. New York: International Universities Press.

———. 1957. *No and yes: On the genesis of human communication*. New York: International Universities Press.

———. 1965. *The first year of life.* With W. G. Cobliner. New York: International Universities Press.

———. 1969. Aggression and adaptation. *Journal of Nervous and Mental Diseases* 149:81–90.

Spock, B. 1965. Innate inhibition of aggressiveness in infancy. *Psychoanalytic Study of the Child* 20:340–43.

Stechler, G., and A. Halton. 1983. Assertion and aggression: Emergence during infancy. Paper presented at the winter meetings of the American Psychoanalytic Association, New York.

Stern, D. N. 1985. *The interpersonal world of the infant.* New York: Basic Books.

Stone, L. 1971. Reflections on the psychoanalytic concept of aggression. *Psychoanalytic Quarterly* 40:195–244.

Storr, A. 1968. *Human aggression.* New York: Atheneum.

———. 1972. *Human destructiveness.* New York: Basic Books.

Tinbergen, N. 1968. On war and peace in animals and man. *Reflections* 4, no. 1: 24–49.

Tomkins, S. S. 1962. *Affect, imagery, consciousness: Vol. 1: The positive affects.* New York: Springer, 1992.

———. 1991. *Affect, imagery, consciousness: Vol. 3: The negative affects, anger, and fear.* New York: Springer.

Trilling, L. 1973. Aggression and utopia: A note on William Morris' "News from nowhere." *Psychoanalytic Quarterly* 42:214–25.

Waelder, R. 1956. Critical discussion of the concept of an instinct of destruction. *Bulletin of Philadelphia Association Psychoanalysts* 6:97–109.

———. 1960. *Basic theory of psychoanalysis.* New York: International Universities Press.

Wallerstein, R. 1990. The corrective emotional experience: Is reconsideration due? *Psychoanalytic Inquiry* 10:288–324.

Weil, A. 1970. The basic core. *Psychoanalytic Study of the Child* 25:442–60.

White, R. W. 1963. *Ego and reality in psychoanalytic theory.* Psychological Issues Monograph 11. New York: International Universities Press.

Winnicott, D. W. 1947. Hate in the counter-transference. *International Journal of Psychoanalysis* 30:69–74.

———. 1950. Aggression in relation to emotional development. In *Collected papers*, 204–18. New York: Basic Books, 1975.

————. 1953. Transitional objects and transitional phenomena: A study of the first not-me possession. *International Journal of Psychoanalysis* 34:89–97.

————. 1965. *The maturational processes and the facilitating environment.* New York: International Universities Press.

Wolfenstein, M. 1951. A phase in the development of children's sense of humor. *Psychoanalytic Study of the Child* 6:336–50.

Wolff, H. 1963. Observations on the early development of smiling. In *Determinants of infant behavior*, ed. B. M. Foss, 2:113–38. New York: Wiley.

————. 1966. *The causes, controls, and organization of behavior in the neonate.* Psychological Issues Monograph 17. New York: International Universities Press.

INDEX